Jesus and the Gospels

Jesus and the Gospels

AN INTRODUCTION

John T. Carroll

WESTMINSTER
JOHN KNOX PRESS
LOUISVILLE · KENTUCKY

© 2016 John T. Carroll

First edition
Published by Westminster John Knox Press
Louisville, Kentucky

16 17 18 19 20 21 22 23 24 25—10 9 8 7 6 5 4 3 2 1

Materials adapted from John Carroll's *Luke*, New Testament Library (Louisville, KY: Westminster John Knox Press, 2012) and his recent essay, "The Gospel of Luke: A Contemporary Cartography," published in *Interpretation* 68 (2014): 366–75 (http://int.sagepub.com/content/68/4.toc; doi:10.1177/0020964314540109) are reprinted by permission of the publishers.

Book design by Drew Stevens
Cover design by Mark Abrams
Cover illustration: On the Cross, *1992 (oil on wood) Parrag, Emil (contemporary artist)/Private Collection/Bridgeman Images*

Library of Congress Cataloging-in-Publication Data
Names: Carroll, John T., 1954- author.
Title: Jesus and the gospels : an introduction / John T. Carroll.
Description: First edition. | Louisville, KY : Westminster John Knox Press,
  2016. | Includes bibliographical references and index.
Identifiers: LCCN 2016009463 (print) | LCCN 2016014531 (ebook) | ISBN
  9780664239725 (alk. paper) | ISBN 9781611646894 ()
Subjects: LCSH: Bible. Gospels--Criticism, interpretation, etc. | Jesus
  Christ.
Classification: LCC BS2555.52 .C367 2016 (print) | LCC BS2555.52 (ebook) |
  DDC 226/.061--dc23
LC record available at http://lccn.loc.gov/2016009463
ISBN 0-664-23972-2

PRINTED IN THE UNITED STATES OF AMERICA

♾ The paper used in this publication meets the minimum requirements of the American National Standard for Information Sciences—Permanence of Paper for Printed Library Materials, ANSI Z39.48-1992.

Westminster John Knox Press advocates the responsible use of our natural resources. The text paper of this book is made from 30% post-consumer waste.

Most Westminster John Knox Press books are available at special quantity discounts when purchased in bulk by corporations, organizations, and special-interest groups. For more information, please e-mail SpecialSales@wjkbooks.com.

Contents

PART III. COHERENCE AND CONNECTIONS: THEMATIC PROBES FOR TWENTY-FIRST-CENTURY READERS

Acknowledgments

I am grateful to the editorial and production team at Westminster John Knox Press for their splendid support of this project and for friendship and delightful collegial collaboration over many, many years. In particular, I thank Dan Braden, Bridgett Green, Julie Tonini, and David Dobson. For the discussion of the Gospel according to Luke in chapter 5 of this book, the WJK Press generously granted permission to incorporate with adaptation materials from my New Testament Library commentary on *Luke* (2012), and I acknowledge this permission with gratitude.

Some chapters of the book have benefited from the close reading and excellent suggestions of Sam Adams, Clifton Black, Marianne Blickenstaff, Frances Taylor Gench, and Suzanne Watts Henderson. I thank each of them for helping make the book better than it would have been without their generous reading. Instrumental in the completion of this work has been the tangible support of Union Presbyterian Seminary, in the form of a sabbatical during which most of the research and writing were undertaken, as well as more routine encouragement of my work as scholar and teacher. Special thanks are owed to President Brian Blount, Academic Dean Ken McFayden, and the Board of Trustees for this generous research leave and ongoing encouragement. It is a privilege to count Brian and Ken as supportive administrative leaders and treasured friends. My other faculty colleagues offered valuable feedback on one chapter draft during a vigorous discussion at our annual faculty retreat; I deeply appreciate their friendship and collegial spirit.

Over the last two decades, several sessions of the Society of Biblical Theologians have discussed drafts of my work-in-process on the Gospels, and society colleagues have helped me sharpen my thinking and my interpretive perspective. I thank them, especially one fellow member who as my teacher and doctoral advisor did more than anyone else to set me on the path of productive scholarship and teaching that I have pursued for the last thirty years. What I have learned from David Adams's exegetical acumen, keen wit, and unsurpassed skill as seminar facilitator continues to inspire me, though he cannot be blamed for any ways in which this effort falls short.

Students in classes at Union over many years have been thoughtful conversation partners as I have worked through the issues of interpretation that this book engages. They are too numerous to mention by name, but it has been a privilege to learn with and from them. The same is true for adult classes in many congregations for which I have been a guest teacher, classes filled with persons committed to lifelong exploration of ways in which the Gospels continue to speak to matters of the heart and of life in the world.

My adult children, Andrew and Anna, did not figure directly in my writing of this book, nor did my mother, Mildred Lester Carroll—though her gentle and ever so loving weekly "progress checks" and her constant affirmation helped keep me moving forward. Each of these beloved family members, along with my late father James Rose Carroll, was constantly in my thoughts as I labored. Above all, I thank my beloved, Maria Ramos, and our beloved son Oscar James, for the delightful partnership and the deep sharing in play and work that make life, and projects like this, so much more meaningful and joyful. Their presence informs every page, and I am grateful to them, beyond words.

Abbreviations

General

AT	author's translation
BCE	before the common era
c.	century
ca.	*circa*, about
CE	common era
CEB	Common English Bible
cf.	*confer*, compare
ch(s).	chapter(s)
eadem	the same (feminine form)
ed(s).	edition; edited by, editor(s)
e.g.	*exempli gratia*, for example
enl.	enlarged
esp.	especially
ET	English translation
et al.	*et alii(ae)*, and others
etc.	*et cetera*, and so forth
ibid.	*ibidem*, in the same place
idem	*idem*, the same (author as just named)
i.e.	*id est*, that is
KJV	King James Version
lit.	literally
LXX	Septuagint
m.	Mishnah
mg.	marginal note
n(n).	note(s)
NIV	New International Version (2011)
NRSV	New Revised Standard Version
NT	New Testament
orig.	original(ly)
OT	Old Testament
par(r).	parallel(s)
p(p).	page(s)
P	papyrus manuscript
pl.	plural
Q	Qumran (Dead Sea Scrolls), or *Quelle* (Source)

repr.	reprint(ed)
rev.	revised
RSV	Revised Standard Version
sg.	singular
trans.	translation, translated by
v(v).	verse(s)
vol(s).	volume(s)
vs.	versus
x	times a form appears

Ancient Texts

Old Testament

Gen	Genesis
Exod	Exodus
Lev	Leviticus
Num	Numbers
Deut	Deuteronomy
Judg	Judges
1–2 Sam	1–2 Samuel
1–2 Kgs	1–2 Kings
Neh	Nehemiah
Ps(s)	Psalm(s)
Prov	Proverbs
Isa	Isaiah
Jer	Jeremiah
Ezek	Ezekiel
Dan	Daniel
Hos	Hosea
Mic	Micah
Zech	Zechariah

New Testament

Matt	Matthew
Rom	Romans
1 Cor	1 Corinthians
Gal	Galatians
Phil	Philippians
Col	Colossians
1–2 Tim	1–2 Timothy
Phlm	Philemon
Heb	Hebrews
1–2 Pet	1–2 Peter
Rev	Revelation

Other Ancient Sources	1 En.	1 Enoch
	1QM	War Scroll (from Qumran Cave 1)
	1QS	Rule of the Community (from Qumran Cave 1)
	1QSa	Rule of the Congregation (from Qumran Cave 1)
	2 Bar.	2 Baruch
	Ant.	Josephus, *Jewish Antiquities*
	CD	(Cairo) Damascus Document (Qumran scroll preserved in Cairo)
	Diogenes Laertius, *Lives*	*Lives of Philosophers*
	Dionysius of Halicarnassus, *Ant. rom.*	*Antiquitates romanae* (*Roman Antiquities*)
	Dionysius of Halicarnassus, *Thuc.*	*De Thucydide* (*On Thucydides*)
	Epictetus, *Diatr.*	*Diatribai* (*Dissertationes*)
	Giṭ.	Giṭṭin (Mishnah tractate)
	Gos. Thom.	Gospel of Thomas
	Haer.	Irenaeus, *Adversus Haereses* (*Against Heresies*)
	Hist. eccl.	Eusebius, *Historia ecclesiastica* (*Ecclesiastical History*)
	Ign. *Eph.*	Ignatius, *To the Ephesians*
	Ign. *Pol.*	Ignatius, *To Polycarp*
	Ign. *Smyrn.*	Ignatius, *To the Smyrnaeans*
	Jerome, *Comm. Matt.*	*Commentary on Matthew*
	Jos. Asen.	Joseph and Aseneth
	J.W.	Josephus, *Jewish War*
	Jub.	Jubilees
	Ketub.	Ketubbot (Mishnah tractate)
	Let. Aris.	Letter of Aristeas
	Lucian, *Hist.*	*How to Write History*
	Midr. Ps.	Midrash on Psalms
	Origen, *Comm. John*	*Commentary on the Gospel of John*
	Plutarch, *Mor.*	*Moralia* (Essays on morals, customs, mores)
	Sir	Sirach
	T. Levi	Testament of Levi
	Tacitus, *Hist.*	*Historiae* (*Histories*)
	Tertullian, *Marc.*	*Adversus Marcionem* (*Against Marcion*)
	Thucydides, *Hist.*	*History of the Peloponnesian War*
	Tob	Tobit

Contemporary Literature	AB	Anchor (Yale) Bible
	ABD	*Anchor Bible Dictionary*, edited by David Noel Freedman. 6 vols. New York: Doubleday, 1992.
	ABRL	Anchor (Yale) Bible Reference Library
	AcBib	Academia Biblica
	AnBib	Analecta Biblica
	ANTC	Abingdon New Testament Commentaries
	BETL	Bibliotheca Ephemeridum Theologicarum Lovaniensium
	BibIntS	Biblical Interpretation Series
	BNTC	Black's New Testament Commentary
	BZNW	Beihefte zur Zeitschrift für die neutestamentliche Wissenschaft
	CBQ	*Catholic Biblical Quarterly*
	EJL	Early Judaism and Its Literature
	ESEC	Emory Studies in Early Christianity
	EvT	*Evangelische Theologie*
	HNT	Handbuch zum Neuen Testament
	IBT	Interpreting Biblical Texts
	ICC	International Critical Commentary
	Int	*Interpretation: A Journal of Bible and Theology*
	ISBL	Indiana Studies in Biblical Literature
	JBL	*Journal of Biblical Literature*
	JR	*Journal of Religion*
	JSJ	*Journal for the Study of Judaism in the Persian, Hellenistic, and Roman Periods*
	JSNTSup	Journal for the Study of the New Testament Supplement Series
	LEC	Library of Early Christianity
	LCBI	Literary Currents in Biblical Interpretation
	LCL	Loeb Classical Library
	LNTS	Library of New Testament Studies
	NIB	*The New Interpreter's Bible*. Edited by Leander E. Keck. 12 vols. Nashville: Abingdon, 1994–2002.
	NICNT	New International Commentary on the New Testament
	NIGTC	New International Greek Testament Commentary
	NovT	*Novum Testamentum*
	NovTSup	Supplements to Novum Testamentum
	NRSV	New Revised Standard Version
	NTL	New Testament Library
	NTS	*New Testament Studies*
	NTT	New Testament Theology
	OBT	Overtures to Biblical Theology

PNTS	Studies on Personalities of the New Testament Series
PTMS	Pittsburgh Theological Monograph Series
RSV	Revised Standard Version
SBL	Society of Biblical Literature
SBLDS	Society of Biblical Literature Dissertation Series
SBLMS	Society of Biblical Literature Monograph Series
SBLRBS	Society of Biblical Literature Resources for Biblical Study
SBLSymS	Society of Biblical Literature Symposium Series
SemeiaSt	Semeia Studies
SHBC	Smyth & Helwys Bible Commentary
SNTSMS	Society for New Testament Studies Monograph Series
SP	Sacra Pagina
SUNT	Studien zur Umwelt des Neuen Testaments
TDNT	*Theological Dictionary of the New Testament*. Edited by Gerhard Kittel and Gerhard Friedrich. Translated by Geoffrey W. Bromiley. 10 vols. Grand Rapids: Eerdmans, 1964–76.
THKNT	Theologischer Handkommentar zum Neuen Testament
TI	Theological Inquiries
WBC	Word Biblical Commentary
WUNT	Wissenschaftliche untersuchungen zum neuen Testament

PART I

Jesus and the Gospels

Context and Approach

1. Contexts for Reading the Gospels

After two millennia, Jesus remains as fascinating and compelling a figure as ever, not only for Christian communities but also for countless others. We gain primary access to his life, message, and activity through the four New Testament narratives called Gospels: Matthew, Mark, Luke, and John. In this book I seek to offer clear and engaging interpretations of these narratives, highlighting the distinctive features of each story about Jesus. In a companion website, jesusandthegospels.wjkbooks.com, I provide learning tools for students and resources for teachers to facilitate their exploration of these texts.

In the field of New Testament studies within the last several decades, many new voices have joined the conversation about the meaning of these writings. Moreover, an array of new interpretive methods expand and deepen—and sometimes challenge—customary readings. Supplementing historical-critical approaches that dominated the field for two centuries, now literary and rhetorical analysis, empire studies, social-scientific criticism, and various ideologically oriented interpretations have generated new ways of viewing and understanding the Gospels. The readings of the Gospels presented in this book have been informed and energized by these new approaches, as pointers here and there indicate. Yet the primary interest in the chapters that follow is close, careful reading of each Gospel narrative, beginning with what is probably the earliest (Mark), and then proceeding to Matthew, Luke, and John. A concluding chapter selects a number of themes in the Gospels that have something important to say to the issues we face in the twenty-first century, whether as resource or challenge. First, though, it is crucial to place the Gospels in context. Chapter 1 situates Jesus and the Gospels that tell his story within the setting of first-century (CE) Judaism and the early Roman Empire. Chapter 2 then introduces two historical problems that affect how we approach the Gospels: the challenge of gaining reliable knowledge about the historical activity of Jesus; and the complexity involved in understanding the formation of the Gospels and the relationships among them.

Context Matters: The Gospels in the Setting of First-Century Judaism

Context matters—or, in reading the Gospels, multiple contexts matter.[1] Everything we encounter in the Gospels occurs within space dominated by the Roman Empire: how do these narratives and their earliest audiences both reflect and perhaps now and then articulate *against* empire? No less important, the specific setting of first-century-CE Palestine (both Galilee and Jerusalem-centered Judea), with the long history of experience (or historical memory) of Israel, is formative for each of the Gospels, whether they were composed within or outside that region. The situation of today's readers is also important in shaping their response to these stories; that needs to be a matter of explicit awareness throughout the process of interpretation and will also receive more focused attention in chapter 7 of this book.

We begin with the context of the Gospels within early Judaism. Judaism is the mother religion of Christianity.[2] Jesus was a Jew who was born and raised in Palestine; *eretz Yisrael*, the "land of Israel," was his homeland. The earliest followers of Jesus were Jews. The texts that nurtured their faith and practice were the ones that became the Jewish Bible: the sacred texts of Torah, Prophets, and Writings. The God they worshiped was the God of Israel. This cradle of the New Testament is fundamental to understanding the Gospels.

Jews within Greco-Roman Culture

How many Jews were there at the time of Jesus? Only educated guesses are possible, but a fair estimate is that between 5 and 10 percent of the population in the Roman Empire were Jews.[3] The most important cities of the empire—notably Rome and Alexandria—had large Jewish populations. In a predominantly polytheistic society, Jews often stood apart; most people acknowledged many gods and goddesses and so had trouble understanding this vigorously monotheistic faith (honoring one God). The practice of male

---

1. See Joel B. Green and Lee Martin McDonald, eds., *The World of the New Testament: Cultural, Social, and Historical Contexts* (Grand Rapids: Wm. B. Eerdmans Publishing Co., 2013); Everett Ferguson, *Backgrounds of Early Christianity*, 3rd ed. (Grand Rapids: Wm. B. Eerdmans Publishing Co., 2003).

2. Heated debate today centers on the meaning of "Judaism" and "Jewish religion" in relation to the Jewish people and their practices in the era of Jesus and the Gospels. See, e.g., Daniel Boyarin, *Border Lines: The Partition of Judaeo-Christianity* (Philadelphia: University of Pennsylvania Press, 2004); Shaye J. D. Cohen, *The Beginnings of Jewishness: Boundaries, Varieties, Uncertainties* (Berkeley: University of California Press, 1999); Martha Himmelfarb, "Judaism in Antiquity: Ethno-Religion or National Identity," *Jewish Quarterly Review* 99 (2009): 65–73. I acknowledge the importance of this debate and the complexities of Jewish identity, esp. alongside emerging distinctive identities for Jesus followers late in this period, extending well into the second century CE and beyond.

3. The 10 percent figure is the population estimate suggested, e.g., by Naomi Pasachoff and Robert J. Littman, *A Concise History of the Jewish People* (Lanham, MD: Rowman & Littlefield, 2005), 67. It may, however, be high.

circumcision was regarded as strange by many persons in Roman society,[4] as was the observance of a weekly holiday (the Sabbath—there was no such thing as a weekend in Roman culture), not to mention dietary scruples that were captured in the image of a people who would not eat pork.

Nevertheless, much about the community life and religious practices of Jews residing within Roman society was attractive. First, the antiquity of Jewish religion was often recognized; it possessed an ancient sacred text (Moses could rival Homer!). This was an advantage in a society that prized antiquity and found novelty suspect. Second, Jewish religious practice, while diverse, featured a rigorous moral code, embodied in the Torah (Law of Moses) and encapsulated in the memorable Decalogue (the Ten Commandments in Exod 20:1–17 and Deut 5:6–21). Third, Jews typically maintained a strong sense of community belonging, both within the Jewish homeland in Judea (and Galilee) and beyond, in the Jewish diaspora (the dispersion of Jews throughout the empire). Especially in the diaspora setting, where Jews faced the necessity of navigating foreign cultural space and social institutions, their shared communal life was crucial to sustaining their identity as a people.

Some non-Jews (Gentiles) became converts to Judaism, proselytes. They were usually circumcised (if male) and accepted the "yoke of Torah," observance of the Law of Moses. Far more Gentiles attracted to Jewish religious life and practice did not become full converts (if male, not undergoing the ritual of circumcision) and remained Gentile God-fearers: worshipers of the God of Israel, associated in a positive way with the life and worship of the Jewish community, but not full Jews.[5] What were the distinctive and defining features of this people and their religious practice?

Identity-Shaping Symbols

In the first century CE, the Jewish people were heirs to a shared legacy, including Israel's historical experience, much of it expressed in the narratives and prophetic writings that were in the process of becoming sacred Scripture, as well as some writings that ultimately were not. In the latter category, for example, were the books called 1–4 Maccabees, which cultivated memory and perspective on the turbulent period of Israel's history featuring the Maccabean revolt against Seleucid (Syrian) political domination (under the reign of Antiochus IV, ca. 175–164 BCE) and any accommodation to the Hellenistic (Greek-influenced) culture then being aggressively introduced in Palestine.[6] Especially the Torah, the books of

---

4. If not repugnant. In the public baths or in athletic competition, the nude adult male would be embarrassed by the absence of the foreskin.

5. God-fearers, that is, of the kind Luke introduces in the book of Acts (e.g., 13:16, 26).

6. While not ultimately included within the Jewish Scriptures (the Tanakh), the books of the Maccabees and a number of other writings from late Second Temple Judaism (e.g., Tobit, Wisdom of Solomon, and Sirach) were eventually incorporated within the canonical Scriptures of Roman Catholic and Greek Orthodox Christianity.

Moses (Genesis–Deuteronomy), provided the identity-forming symbol system for Jews navigating a world dominated by Roman political and military power and the Greek intellectual heritage.

Symbols Shaping Jewish Identity within Greco-Roman Culture

- **The Torah**: "instruction," law of Moses
- **The Shema**: "Hear: God is one"
- **The land**: remembering the promise to Abraham
- **Sabbath**: holy day for rest
- **Circumcision of males**: sign of inclusion in the covenant people

---

Torah

The Jewish people were a people of the Torah. The word means "instruction" and refers to God's instruction of the people, as embodied in the first five books of the Hebrew Bible. The Torah tells the story of the Creator God's gracious election of Israel to be a covenant people, who enjoy a special relationship with God. The human side of the covenant is obedience to the will of God, concretely in the form of obedience to the commandments recorded in the Torah. The Gospels depict Jesus, like other Jewish teachers of his day, engaged in vigorous debate about the interpretation and faithful practice of the Torah.

The Shema

At the heart of the Torah and of first-century Jewish life was the belief in one God, to the exclusion of all others (monotheism).[7] This conviction finds classic expression in Deuteronomy 6:4–9, commonly called the Shema because that is the Hebrew word with which the passage begins (*Shema Yisrael* . . .):

> Hear, O Israel: the Lord is our God, the Lord alone. You shall love the Lord your God with all your heart, and with all your soul, and with all your might. (Deut 6:4–5)

This is a core conviction for the Jewish people, one that the Gospels show Jesus fully embracing (e.g., Mark 12:28–31).

---

7. See, e.g., Let. Aris. 132–35; cf. the outsider's view in the Roman historian Tacitus, *Hist.* 5.4–5. Worship of one God and its corollary, renunciation of idolatrous worship, did not exclude acknowledgment of other emanations-expressions of the one God (e.g., Wisdom) or semidivine beings such as angels. For a radical reconceiving of the meaning of Jewish monotheism in Second Temple Judaism, see Daniel Boyarin, *The Jewish Gospels: The Story of the Jewish Christ* (New York: New Press, 2012). Boyarin argues that before the emergence of Christianity, some Jews had already come to regard the Messiah as a divine being.

The Land

The Jewish people felt a special tie to the land—to a very particular piece of land. It was the land promised to father Abraham (e.g., Gen 12:1; 13:14–17). This connection to Palestine is deep and abiding, even if in Jesus' day far more Jews lived outside the constantly shifting borders of Judea, in the diaspora.

Sabbath

Jews observed a day of rest, the Sabbath—from sunset on Friday until sunset on Saturday. They refrained from work, preparation of meals, and journeys.[8] The Torah commanded, "Remember the Sabbath day, and keep it holy" (Exod 20:8; cf. Deut 5:12), amplifying that "you shall not do any work" on this seventh day (Exod 20:10; Deut 5:14). The developing rabbinic tradition elaborated, showing one *how*, in practical terms, to keep the Sabbath holy; it eventually crystallized thirty-nine kinds of work that were forbidden (in the Mishnah tractate Shabbat, consolidating oral interpretive traditions of the early rabbis and codified perhaps mid-second century CE). The Gospels show Jesus embroiled in sometimes heated debate about faithful observance of the Sabbath commandment (e.g., Mark 2:23–3:6; Luke 13:10–17; 14:1–6), but also as a regular participant in synagogue services on the Sabbath (e.g., Mark 1:21; Luke 4:16).

Circumcision

Jewish males were ordinarily circumcised on the eighth day. This act had sociocultural and religious meaning and motivation. It was an identity marker for the Jewish male; during the Roman period, it set Jews apart from other people, and it was performed in obedience to the covenant requirement given to Abraham (Gen 17:22–27). Male Gentiles (non-Jews) who converted to Judaism (proselytes) often received circumcision. For the first groups of Jesus followers, circumcision became a matter of intense debate, at least in the apostle Paul's mission. When Gentiles became members of the Christian community, should they receive circumcision and accept the "yoke of the Torah" (e.g., Acts 15:1–21; Gal 2:1–10)? The Gospel of Luke indicates that Jesus was circumcised as an infant (2:21), as was John the baptizing prophet (1:59). The families of Jesus and John are thus portrayed as Torah-keeping Jews.

Social Institutions in Judea

Several social institutions important for first-century Jews also figure in significant ways in the Gospels. Three will receive attention here: temple, synagogue, and Sanhedrin.

---

8. Sabbath keeping thus made service in the Roman army problematic for Torah-observant Jews, who would not be able to take advantage of one of the few avenues to upward social mobility available in the Roman world.

Important Social Institutions in Judea
• **Temple in Jerusalem**: the Second Temple, destroyed in 70 CE
• **Sanhedrin**: council convened by the high priest in Jerusalem
• **Synagogue**: house of prayer

Temple

The temple at Jerusalem was a unifying symbol for most Jews throughout the empire. They paid a yearly tax of one-half shekel (Exod 30:11–16; Josephus, *J.W.* 7.6.6) to support the temple system, the worship housed there, and the priests.[9] This was the Second Temple; the first had been destroyed by the Babylonians around 587 BCE. The Second Temple was built some seventy years later. A decade or so before Jesus' birth, Herod the Great launched an ambitious and expensive temple restoration project that continued until 64 CE. Ironically, just six years later, the temple would lie in ruins (70 CE), the tragic result of the Jewish War against Rome (66–73/74 CE). The Gospels present Jesus as predicting the temple's destruction (Mark 13:1–2 and parr.).

During Jesus' day, however, the Jerusalem temple was an impressive building complex and also the center of enormous economic and political power. Here the priests carried out the worship prescribed in the Torah. Daily sacrifices, special sacrifices (such as that offered by Jesus' parents after his birth, according to Luke 2:22–24), and the annual ritual of the Day of Atonement (Yom Kippur) were observed (see Exod 30:10; Lev 16:1–34; 23:26–28)—ritual expressions of God's abiding presence and of the gracious provision of forgiveness and renewal for God's covenant people. These sacrifices were a constant reminder that the God of Israel was a holy God who called the people to be holy. Animals to be slaughtered in sacrificial rites were to be without blemish, so worshipers purchased the animals in the temple precincts. Often exchange in coinage was involved to facilitate these transactions. Needless to say, this was a zone of flourishing commerce. According to the Gospels, Jesus subjected these practices to critique (Mark 11:15–18 and parr.). His opposition to such practices within the temple system was likely a major factor contributing to his arrest and eventual execution. Considerable power and wealth came to be concentrated in the circles of the temple-based

---

9. A text from the Dead Sea Scrolls interprets the Torah's directive to pay a half-shekel temple tax not as an annual but as a once-in-a-lifetime obligation (4QOrdinances[a] = 4Q159 1 II, 6–7). Josephus gives the value (in weight) of the (silver) shekel coin as the equivalent of four Athenian *drachma* (*Ant.* 3.8.2). On the temple tax, see Fabian E. Udoh, *To Caesar What Is Caesar's: Tribute, Taxes, and Imperial Administration in Roman Palestine (63 B.C.E.–70 C.E.)*, Brown Judaic Studies 343 (Providence, RI: Brown University Press, 2006), 90. The Jerusalem temple was not the only Jewish temple in existence; one was constructed at Leontopolis in Egypt ca. 170 BCE (Josephus, *J.W.* 1.1.1; 7.10.2), and the Samaritans' cultic center was Mount Gerizim, where a sanctuary was erected in the 5th c. BCE and destroyed in the 2nd c. BCE (see Josephus, *Ant.* 11.8.1–7; 12.5.5; 13:255–56; *J.W.* 1.2.6–7).

priestly elite, though the majority of priests lived at some distance from Jerusalem and possessed limited economic resources.

Three times each year, great pilgrimage festivals were held, and many Jews from Palestine and some from the diaspora flocked to Jerusalem and to the temple. (1) *Passover*, a festival commemorating the Moses-led liberation from slavery in Egypt, opened the seven-day festival of Unleavened Bread (Exod 23:15; Lev 23:5–8; Deut 16:16). At one Passover Jesus was arrested and executed. John's Gospel differs from the other three in picturing Jesus' ministry as spanning three Passovers; Luke's Gospel adds a Passover pilgrimage to Jerusalem by Jesus' family when he was age twelve (2:41–52). (2) The Festival of Weeks (*Shavu'ot*, Shabuoth), or *Pentecost* (so-called because it comes on the fiftieth day after Passover), was linked to the offering of the first fruits of the harvest and eventually, in rabbinic tradition, also to the memory of the giving of the law to Moses on Mount Sinai. On one such Pentecost, Luke reports, Jesus' followers were first Spirit-empowered to preach, and their mission was launched (Acts 2). (3) The Festival of *Booths* or *Tabernacles* (*Sukkot*) marked the end of the harvest of grapes and other fruit, in the fall (Exod 34:22); Leviticus 23:42–43 also tied the festival to memory of the exodus.

Primary Annual Jewish Festivals	
• *Yom Kippur*: Day of Atonement	• *Shavu'ot*: Weeks (Pentecost)
• **Unleavened Bread and Passover**	• *Sukkot*: Booths or Tabernacles

Sanhedrin

The leading priests, headed by the high priest, figured prominently in the Sanhedrin, the highest council of the Jews at Jerusalem, which exercised oversight of judicial and financial concerns in Jerusalem, though subject to the Roman administrator, the prefect; other towns had their own councils, but naturally Jerusalem's was the most significant in Judea. The high priest presided over this body, which in addition to elite priests evidently also included lay scribes, who among other, more mundane tasks were trained as interpreters of the Torah.[10] In the time of Jesus, the high priest was appointed by the Roman governor, painful reminder of the fact of Roman occupation. Throughout Jesus' adult life, Caiaphas served as high priest (18–36 CE),

---

10. On the history of the high priesthood in Second Temple Judaism, see James C. Vander-Kam, *From Joshua to Caiaphas: High Priests after the Exile* (Minneapolis: Fortress Press, 2004). For discussion of the diverse roles of scribes, see Samuel L. Adams, "The Social Location of the Scribe in the Second Temple Period," in *Sybils, Scriptures, and Scrolls: John Collins at Seventy*, ed. Joel Baden, Hindy Najman, and Eibert Tigchelaar, JSJ Supplements (Leiden: Brill, forthcoming).

while Pontius Pilate filled the role of prefect (26–36 CE). The lengthy tenures of these two men, overlapping for a full decade, indicate a period of relative stability in Jerusalem and its environs, as well as alignment of the political interests of the Roman official and the Jewish high priest. Jesus, and after him many of his followers (e.g., Paul in Acts), would come face-to-face with the Sanhedrin.

Synagogue

A social institution that played an increasingly important role in shaping Jewish identity in the first and second centuries CE was the synagogue, also called a *proseuchē* ([house of] prayer).[11] The term *synagogue* referred to a gathering or assembly and also to a meeting place or building where the gathering was held (whether large private homes or separate buildings dedicated to this use; Luke 7:5 mentions the generous benefaction of a Roman army officer who funded the construction of a village's synagogue). The synagogue was especially important among Jews in diaspora, but by the late Second Temple period, Jerusalem alone may have had dozens or more synagogues. Through participation in the life and worship of the synagogue, Jewish identity was nourished; here Jewish children (mostly boys) learned the Torah, and here the community gathered each Sabbath to hear the Torah read and to pray. Luke tells us that it was Jesus' custom to participate regularly in synagogue worship on the Sabbath (4:16).

Since many first-century Jews were unable to read the Hebrew of biblical writings (particularly the Torah and Prophets), the reading from the Hebrew scroll was typically followed by a translation with interpretation in Aramaic (called a *Targum*). This was the primary language of Jesus; sayings of Jesus that we encounter in the Gospels were therefore at some point in their preservation and transmission translated from the language in which he originally spoke them into the *Koinē* (Koine, common) Greek that we encounter in the Gospels.

Thus far, the discussion has focused on some of the significant symbols and institutions that shaped Jewish identity as one people of God. But not all Jews thought, believed, and behaved alike. A number of issues divided first-century Jewish people into distinct groups. For all that they shared in common, Jews in the time of Jesus differed widely on fundamental questions. What did it mean to live as a Jew in the midst of Hellenistic (Greek) culture? What did it mean to live as a Jew under Roman rule? Jesus' own home turf is an interesting case study in cultural hybridity. Within rural Galilee, Jesus' small home village of Nazareth was just a stone's throw (5 kilometers, or 3 miles) from the city of Sepphoris, a thriving commercial center and the site of vigorous building activity after its destruction by Roman armies

---

11. For detailed discussion of the emergence, character, and activity of synagogues, see Lee I. Levine, *The Ancient Synagogue: The First Thousand Years*, 2nd ed. (New Haven, CT: Yale University Press, 2005); Eric M. Meyers, "Synagogue," *ABD* 6:251–60.

in 4 BCE, in reprisal for Jewish rebellion after the death of Herod the Great. Farther east, on the western shore of the Sea of Galilee, Tiberias was a newly established capital city built by the tetrarch Herod Antipas and named in honor of the emperor Tiberius. Greek and Roman presence and, to a degree, culture were very much in evidence in Jesus' own backyard. Jews, as well as Gentiles also living in Galilee, negotiated these realities in a variety of ways, depending on a number of variables, including socioeconomic position, social status, and access to education and to literacy (few were literate in the first century).

Diversity within Early Judaism

The first-century Jewish historian Josephus, whose extensive writings include histories of the Jewish people (*Jewish Antiquities*) and *Jewish War*, as well as an apologetic treatise defending Jewish people, culture, and religion (*Against Apion*), identified four distinct groups or social movements within the Judaism of his time: *Pharisees* (with whom Josephus most closely identified), *Sadducees*, *Essenes*, and *Zealots* (or the Fourth Philosophy). While Josephus is by no means a neutral, unbiased source, he does provide a wealth of information about Jewish political history and about the diverse perspectives and practices in the period of Jesus and the Gospels.

Important Groups in Early Judaism

- **Essenes and community at Qumran**: separatist group pursuing deep piety and rigorous fidelity to Torah
- **Pharisees**: advocates of a Torah-keeping life of holiness for everyone, even away from temple
- **Sadducees**: elite priestly circle
- **Freedom fighters (with Zealots of the Jewish War)**: practiced active resistance to Roman occupation, esp. Judean elite who collaborated with Roman rule
- **Samaritans**: remnant of the old northern kingdom, also adhered to their version of the Mosaic Torah
- **Jesus followers**, for whom he was the Messiah sent to Israel

---

Essenes

The *Essenes* protested against the temple establishment in Jerusalem and pursued a separatist agenda, regarding Judean society and its leadership as corrupt. The settlement at Qumran near the Dead Sea was probably the creation of a priestly group associated with what Josephus calls Essenes. (The Essenes are also mentioned by the eminent Jewish philosopher and statesman Philo in Alexandria, and by Pliny the Elder.) This group pursued a vision of holiness: theirs would be a holy community pleasing to God. The

Dead Sea community's voice, in particular, survives today in a set of manuscripts discovered in the mid-1940s near the Qumran settlement's ruins, in caves of the Judean desert cliffs just west of the Dead Sea: these writings are called the *Dead Sea Scrolls.*

At Qumran, in isolation, these Jews of priestly pedigree sought to live a holy life as Israel's righteous remnant, tutored in a life of deep piety and rigorous fidelity to the Torah by the Teacher of Righteousness (identity unknown). The Qumran community maintained a strict community discipline: minor lapses brought a one- or two-year probation period; weightier offenses led to expulsion from the community. This group regarded the temple system in Jerusalem as illegitimate. Problematic for them were the procedures for appointing the high priest, the calendar by which holy days were determined (not the solar calendar adopted by the Dead Sea community), and the consolidation of power and wealth in the temple.

The Qumran group was an "eschatological" community; several passages in the Dead Sea Scrolls present the belief that the group lived in the *last days,* when God was about to prevail over the forces of darkness.[12] Thus the ideology of the group was both separatist and dualistic; the people of Qumran were the children of light and would triumph with God in the final victory. The Dead Sea community was destroyed during the Jewish War, but many of its writings, most in fragmentary form, were hidden in nearby caves and preserved in the extremely arid climate of the region.[13] Probably some Essene sectarians lived in settlements elsewhere than Qumran and would have survived the Roman army's destruction of the Dead Sea settlement.

Pharisees

The *Pharisees,* unlike the priestly community at Qumran, were primarily a lay movement. Like the Essenes, however, the Pharisees had a passion for holiness. Here is the real point of difference: while the group at Qumran had largely given up on a sinful nation as beyond hope, the Pharisees became teachers of the common person, modeling the holiness that every life and the whole community should display. Holiness was not just for the temple, not just for the priests; it was for the whole community. In giving shape to that vision, Pharisees sought to make the ancient Torah alive and relevant for everyday life in the present. So the Pharisees were interpreters of the sacred texts, and they constructed a practical bridge between the Torah and first-century life, in the form of an authoritative oral tradition ("the tradition

---

12. Examples of intensified eschatological expectation appear in many of the scrolls: 1QM (War Scroll); 4Q174 (= 4QFlor: Florilegium); 4Q521 (Messianic Apocalypse); 11Q13 (= 11QMelch: Melchizedek).

13. For helpful orientation to the Dead Sea Scrolls and community, see James C. Vander-Kam, *The Dead Sea Scrolls Today,* 2nd ed. (Grand Rapids: Wm. B. Eerdmans Publishing Co., 2010). The scrolls in ET are conveniently available in Florentino García Martínez and Eibert J. C. Tigchelaar, *The Dead Sea Scrolls Study Edition,* 2 vols. (Grand Rapids: Wm. B. Eerdmans Publishing Co., 2000).

of the elders," Mark 7:5). This oral Torah and interpretive tradition eventually led to the rabbinic tradition, consolidated in the second century CE and onward, particularly in the Mishnah, the Babylonian Talmud, and the Jerusalem Talmud.

The Gospels show Jesus often in conflict with Pharisees. He criticizes their oral tradition (e.g., Mark 7:1–13). It seems likely, moreover, that his Torah interpretation and praxis viewed sin and purity or holiness differently than Pharisees did, and in social relations Jesus expressed these values concretely in a manner that drew their critique.[14] Pharisees advocated holiness through separation from sin and rigorous maintenance of ritual purity, while Jesus spoke of a holy God who embraces sinners and shows casual disregard for purity concerns in relation to meals and the like.

One last and crucial point about the Pharisees: after the Jewish War, Pharisees worked to invigorate and mold the Judaism that would survive the war. These rabbis (teachers), whose oral interpretations of the Torah eventually were compiled in the rabbinic literature (beginning with the Mishnah), played a key role in defining the future shape of Judaism. It would not be a Judaism that honored Jesus as Messiah. And that means that bitter conflict lies just ahead, conflict between the early Jewish followers of Jesus and the Pharisaic movement. The Gospels again and again reflect this struggle, sometimes portraying intense conflict.

Sadducees

Often at odds with the Pharisees were the *Sadducees*, an elite (Judean) circle of priestly descent. The Sadducees were religiously and politically conservative. They seem to have regarded only the Torah, not the Prophets, as authoritative for legal and doctrinal matters, and they rejected innovations of the Pharisees, such as the (oral) tradition of the elders and the belief in resurrection (e.g., Mark 12:18–27 and parr.). After 70 CE and the temple's destruction, the Sadducees—so heavily invested in the political and religious system revolving around the temple—soon disappeared from history.

Freedom Fighters

On the other end of the social and political spectrum were *freedom fighters or insurrectionists*. Josephus's account, which disparages Jewish revolutionaries and lays at their feet blame for the destruction of the temple and Jerusalem, brands this group *Zealots*. However, social banditry and other small-scale

---

14. Certainly the Gospels paint such a picture; see, e.g., Luke 7:36–50. Marcus Borg characterizes the core conflict as concerning the "politics of holiness" (e.g., *Jesus: A New Vision* [San Francisco: Harper & Row, 1987], 86–93). The phrase is apt, although Borg differentiates the positions of Jesus and Pharisees too neatly; Amy-Jill Levine provides important corrective to the exaggerated importance placed by Borg, among others, on matters of ritual impurity in the Gospels. See Levine, *The Misunderstood Jew: The Church and the Scandal of the Jewish Jesus* (New York: HarperOne, 2006), 144–49, 172–77.

popular resistance movements—opposing the economic exploitation as well as military-political domination of the Roman occupation of Palestine—were a factor throughout the period leading up to the Jewish rebellion.[15]

Samaritans and Followers of Jesus

Wedged between Judea and Jesus' home region of Galilee was Samaria, site of the ancient northern kingdom of Israel (in the era of the divided monarchies of Judah and Israel, until Assyria's conquest of the northern kingdom in 722 BCE).[16] The Samaritan Pentateuch offered an alternative edition of the Torah, and the community's eschatological expectations revolved around the figure of Moses. Judeans viewed Samaritans as outsiders, not faithful Israelites, and mutual distrust and disrespect, centuries in the making, continued to simmer in the first century CE (animosity reflected in Luke 9:51–55; cf. John 4:9, 20). Yet another group arose among the Jewish people in the course of the first century, a group that came to believe that Jesus from Nazareth was God's Messiah. Both John 4 and Acts 8 suggest that in at least some circles, this emerging group of Jesus followers within first-century Judaism welcomed Samaritans into its ranks.

The above sketch, simplified as it is, should suffice to demonstrate that there were diverse expressions of Jewish identity in the first century CE. Moreover, most Jewish people in the first century were not affiliated with any of the groups profiled here, but their voices are not heard in the texts that survive. In the time of Jesus, Israel was God's covenant people, to be sure, but it was far from unified. Jesus and his earliest followers experienced Jewish life and culture, however, within the larger reality of the Roman Empire and its occupation of Palestine, of which the discussion so far has taken only passing notice. We need to attend more closely to the fact of empire as the context for the life of Jesus and the emergence of the Gospel tradition that tells his story.

Context Matters: The Gospels within the Early Roman Empire

Jesus and his fellow Jews lived under Roman rule. That was nothing new: for all but about 80 of the previous 600 years, Jews residing in Palestine had lived under imperial domination by a succession of alien powers: Babylonia, Persia, Greece, the Hellenistic dynasties centered in Syria (Seleucid) and Egypt (Ptolemaic), and then Rome. Yet the Jewish sacred texts promised a land to

15. See esp. Richard A. Horsley, with John S. Hanson, *Bandits, Prophets, and Messiahs: Popular Movements in the Time of Jesus* (San Francisco: Harper & Row, 1988; orig., Minneapolis: Winston Press, 1985).

16. For helpful introduction to the Samaritans and their history, see most recently Gary N. Knoppers, *Jews and Samaritans: The Origins and History of Their Early Relations* (Oxford: Oxford University Press, 2013); and Reinhard Pummer, *The Samaritans: A Profile* (Grand Rapids: Wm. B. Eerdmans Publishing Co., 2015).

Abraham's descendants (e.g., Gen 12:1; 13:14–17) and a secure, flourishing royal dynasty descending from David (e.g., 2 Sam 7:10–17). This dissonance between the hopes of Israel and the political facts required both adjustment and explanation. Not all Jews came to terms with this conflict in the same way. Some, like the tax farmers and the local governing elite in Jerusalem, collaborated deeply with Rome. At the other extreme some, the Zealots of the Jewish War of 66–70 CE (freedom fighters or terrorists, depending on one's point of view), advocated violent resistance—to the Romans but also to the Judean elite who benefited most from the Roman occupation and who served Roman imperial interests. Most Jews fell somewhere between these two extremes.

It would be inaccurate to say that most Jews at the time of Jesus were expecting a messiah to deliver Israel from Roman rule. This was one form that Jewish hope could take,[17] but it was only one among many. Some Jews expected a prophet (an Elijah or a Moses). Some texts from the Dead Sea Scrolls corpus indicate that at least one group of Jews looked for a messiah of Aaron (a priestly messiah) *and* a messiah of Israel (a royal messiah).[18] A public figure such as Jesus, with a band of followers and considerable crowd appeal, would be perceived in relation to these kinds of hopes, and in relation to the reality of Roman rule. The fact that Jesus was executed by order of the Roman governor as a pretender to kingship has significant bearing on the historical reconstruction of his career.

Some thirty-five years after Pilate sentenced Jesus to death, Zealots (freedom fighters) gained the upper hand at Jerusalem and in Galilee, and a bloody revolt against Rome was launched (66 CE). When the decision was made to cease the daily sacrifices offered in the temple for Rome and for the emperor (not *to* his image—a Roman concession to Jewish sensibilities), this gesture amounted to a declaration of war against the empire. As the detailed account by the Jewish historian Josephus chronicles, the war resulted in catastrophic defeat for the Jewish revolutionary forces. After a lengthy siege, the city walls were breached, and the temple was destroyed in 70 CE. About sixty years later (132–135 CE), another rebellion against Roman occupation had even more devastating results. Now Jerusalem officially became a non-Jewish city, and Jews were indefinitely banned from their holiest site. The Second Temple, destroyed in 70 CE, was never rebuilt. Reading the New Testament Gospels, one discovers that the conflict with Rome and the disaster of the Jewish rebellion have left an indelible stamp on the memory of the early followers of Jesus.

There were more options for response to the bitter, dignity-depriving reality of Roman domination of Palestine than quiet acquiescence or active

---

17. E.g., note the vivid expression of such hopes in Psalms of Solomon 17–18.

18. See, e.g., 1QS IX, 11; cf. CD VII, 18–21; XX, 1; 1QSa II, 14, 20. Messianic expectations of a priest-king descended from Judah appear in T. Levi 8, and an eschatological priesthood is pictured in T. Levi 18.

collaboration, on the one hand, and violent resistance or rebellion, on the other. Drawing upon cross-cultural anthropological research, James Scott has argued that resistance to domination can take many forms, some of them quiet and hidden.[19] He offers the notion of a hidden transcript, by which an oppressed group can express its protest against the powers in ways that are concealed from public view, and that can therefore escape reprisal. From the Gospels, a good example is Jesus' reply to an attempt to trap him into public advocacy of disobedience to Rome. "Tell us, Teacher: should we pay the tribute tax to the Roman emperor?" (Mark 12:13–17 and parr., AT). Talk about a lose-lose proposition! If Jesus says "Yes," the people who chafe under Roman repression will be unhappy. But if he says "No," the Romans will charge him with sedition! But Jesus knows how to evade entrapment. His (paraphrased) response—"Show me a coin. Whose image is on it? Well then, pay to Caesar what belongs to him; and to God what belongs to God"—hints at the operation of a hidden transcript. "Pay to Caesar . . . and to God" sounds one way in public, within the temple complex, while the Roman governor is in Jerusalem for the approaching Passover Festival: the two obligations may seem to be harmonious. But out of Roman earshot, offstage, persons who know how to "read the code" will hear the words quite differently, guided by recognition of the overriding priority of allegiance and obedience to God.

Life within the Empire

In addition to Scott's anthropological research on hidden and subtle forms of resistance to domination by empire, the work of Lenski and Kautsky on agrarian empires has informed recent studies on the Roman imperial setting of Jesus and the Gospels.[20] This early Roman Empire

---

19. James C. Scott, *Domination and the Arts of Resistance: Hidden Transcripts* (New Haven, CT: Yale University Press, 1990). Among NT scholars who have drawn upon Scott's work are Warren Carter, Richard A. Horsley, Amanda C. Miller, and Neil Elliott. See, e.g., Carter, *The Roman Empire and the New Testament: An Essential Guide* (Nashville: Abingdon Press, 2006), 11–13, 16–26, 129–36; Horsley, ed., *Hidden Transcripts and the Arts of Resistance: Applying the Work of James C. Scott to Jesus and Paul*, SemeiaSt 48 (Atlanta: SBL Press, 2004); Miller, *Rumors of Resistance: Status Reversals and Hidden Transcripts in the Gospel of Luke* (Minneapolis: Fortress Press, 2014); Elliott, *The Arrogance of Nations: Reading Romans in the Shadow of Empire* (Minneapolis: Fortress Press, 2008).

20. Gerhard E. Lenski, *Power and Privilege: A Theory of Social Stratification* (Chapel Hill: University of North Carolina Press, 1984); John H. Kautsky, *The Politics of Aristocratic Empires* (Chapel Hill: University of North Carolina Press, 1982). A helpful, concise synthesis of this research for purposes of aiding analysis of NT literature is provided by Carter, *The Roman Empire and the New Testament*. The sketch in this section is indebted to Carter's summary of this enormous body of research (esp. 1–13).

- was geographically expansive and ethnically diverse, encompassing the lands, peoples, and cultures surrounding the Mediterranean Sea, and extending northwestward as far as Britain.
- was marked by wide economic disparity between the few high-status wealthy and the majority of the population, and by limited social mobility.
- concentrated power, wealth, and public leadership in the hands of very few elite persons and families, who numbered no more than 3 percent of the empire's population.
- exerted control over the majority of the population by coercion, especially through the "peacekeeping" force of the Roman army; a system of patronage and benefaction, while often reciprocal in relational structure, perpetuated disparities in wealth and status between wealthy, high-status patrons and their lower-status clients.[21]
- was agrarian: agriculture was the primary basis for the economy, and ownership of land was an important factor in economic viability, though small landholding farmers were always at risk due to unfavorable climate conditions (esp. drought) beyond their control.

Beginning with the transformation of the Roman system of governance under Octavian (Augustus), the concentration of power in the person of the emperor was enormous. Augustus's lengthy reign extended from 31 BCE to his death in 14 CE (he accumulated titles of leadership and honor, with the Roman Senate conferring the title of *imperator* [emperor] in 27 CE). Luke 2:1 and 3:1 name the two Roman emperors who reigned during Jesus' lifetime, Augustus and Tiberius (reign, 14–37 CE, after two years of transitional coregency with Augustus [12–14 CE]). Luke's narrative sequel (Acts) ends with Paul awaiting his hearing before a third emperor, Nero, though he is not named (reign, 54–68 CE). Luke's narrative acknowledges the supremacy of Rome, embodied in the person of the emperor (Caesar), but does so with considerable irony. In Luke 2, Augustus issues the decrees and calls the shots, and people fall into line. Luke knows that is how the world works. But in the process, a counter-ruler is born in the city of David: "a Savior, who is the Messiah, the Lord" (2:11). The titles and powers ordinarily given to Rome's emperor (Lord [*Kyrios*] and Savior [*Sōtēr*]) have been co-opted for another ruler, one born among the animals, his royal court a band of socially marginal shepherds.

Twenty-first-century readers (in the United States and in much of Europe, though not in many other regions) tend to think of politics and religion as separate spheres. This notion does not square with the world of Jesus and the Gospels. Politics, economics, and religion were all bound up together. Consider two examples: the political and religious roles and significance of

21. On the patronage system, see, e.g., Richard P. Saller, *Personal Patronage under the Early Empire* (Cambridge: Cambridge University Press, 1982).

the Roman emperor; and the economic, political, and religious functions of the Jerusalem temple.

In *the Roman imperial ideology*, the emperor was acclaimed as savior and a "son of god" and celebrated as such on coinage as well as in sanctuaries of the imperial cult, especially prominent in the Roman province of Asia. Many cities there competed for the rights to host an official temple for the cult of the imperial family. Even in the Jerusalem temple, prayers and sacrifices were offered for (though not to) the emperor.[22]

The Jerusalem temple was the locus of immense economic power; its high priest and his elite priestly associates wielded considerable local power in service of Roman interests: peace, stability, and security—and of course a steady flow of tax revenue. Pilate's decade-long tenure as Roman governor (prefect), from 26 to 36 CE, coincided with the even longer tenure of the high priest Caiaphas, from 18 to 36 CE. This suggests a close collaboration and convergence of interests between the Roman prefect and the temple-based local elite headed by the high priest.

The work of Lenski on agrarian empires helps us to visualize the extent of social stratification in Jesus' social world.[23] Land, wealth, and influence were concentrated in a very small number of persons and families, and the majority of the population throughout the empire, including Judea and Galilee, lived at or below subsistence level. Many landowning farmers lived one bad crop away from debt that potentially meant loss of their land. Urban dwellers—including artisans and merchants who managed through skill and industry to acquire economic resources beyond the peasant status that was the lot of most people—endured perpetual conditions of crowding, poor sanitation, and disease. Life expectancy was short: roughly half of the population did not live past age eighteen (many died in infancy). The Gospels present many scenes featuring what Lenski terms society's "expendables," persons with disability, impoverished beggars, and others who lacked means and skills to sustain economic viability and who often lived beyond the fringes of the cities. In the Gospel narratives, Jesus consistently refuses to consign such persons to a place beyond the community's margins.

Given the precariousness of ordinary living conditions and the elusiveness of good health, it is unsurprising that literary works, inscriptions, and building ruins attest the importance of charismatic healers and of social

22. On the imperial cult and the divine standing of the emperor, see, e.g., Carter, *Roman Empire and the New Testament*, 83–99; Lily Ross Taylor, *The Divinity of the Roman Emperor*, Philological Monographs (Middletown, CT: American Philological Association, 1931; repr., Philadelphia: Porcupine Press, 1975); Ittai Gradel, *Emperor Worship and the Roman Religion* (Oxford: Oxford University Press, 2002); Clifford Ando, *Imperial Ideology and Provincial Loyalty in the Roman Empire* (Berkeley: University of California Press, 2000).

23. On the economy of the early Roman Empire, see Peter Garnsey and Richard P. Saller, *The Roman Empire: Economy, Society, and Culture* (Berkeley: University of California Press, 1987); and most recently, with a focus on Judea in the Second Temple period, Samuel L. Adams, *Social and Economic Life in Second Temple Judea* (Louisville, KY: Westminster John Knox Press, 2014).

institutions that promised restoration of health. Jesus was not the only figure in the first century to whom persons turned in a quest for healing. The Gospels more than once hint at the activity of other Jewish healers and exorcists (e.g., Luke 9:49–50; 11:19). More broadly in the Roman Empire, persons seeking cures flocked to impressive sanctuaries that fostered hope of healing and promoted the cult of Asclepius in many cities. Other deities could attract interest—and followers and worship—if they appeared to provide help to persons suffering from disease and disability (e.g., one striking inscription pictures an ear and thanks the goddess Isis for having listened to a petition for healing). In such a world, one who has the reputation of being able and willing to offer the benefaction of healing will not find it difficult to attract attention and interest: so the crowds flock to Jesus in the Gospel accounts.

The period of the Gospels and the emergence of the Christian movement witnessed the publication of literary works that celebrated the magnificent achievements and benefactions of the Roman Empire and of its emperors—and Rome's divinely sponsored, universal dominion.[24] Architectural, transportation, legal, and cultural achievements of the empire were indeed remarkable, and on a scale not previously seen. The other side of the (figurative) coin stamped with these images of Rome's gift of peace and prosperity to the world was the harsh reality of military conquest and military-police-enforced stability, especially challenging on the borders of the empire—Palestine at its eastern end (buffering the Parthians further east) being a parade example.[25] Much of this imperial résumé, of course, was constructed on the backs of many poor people, including a work force composed to a large degree of slaves and extracting revenue through the imposition of a heavy burden of tribute and taxation. Viewed from the underside, the economics of empire was not attractive. Of this reality, the Gospels give many vivid glimpses. It is time, though, to narrow the focus to the Gospels and the historical figure of Jesus to whom they introduce us.

---

24. See, e.g., Virgil, *Eclogae* 4; the *Roman Antiquities* by Dionysius of Halicarnassus; and the *Library of History* by Diodorus of Sicily.

25. Cf. Tacitus, *Agricola* 30–31, recording a speech by Calgacus of Britain: "To plunder, butcher, steal, these things they misname empire: they make a desolation and they call it peace" (trans. William Peterson, LCL).

2. *Jesus and the Emergence of the Gospels*

The first part of this chapter presents a concise introduction to Jesus as a historical figure, identifying key sources for knowledge about him and problems of method in gaining access to this history. The second part discusses the genre, process of formation, and interrelationships of the Gospels.

From the Gospels to Jesus: The Problem and Quest of the Historical Jesus

Scholars speak of three (and more) "quests" for the historical figure Jesus of Nazareth, who is the central character in the canonical Gospels.[1] How did (the historical) Jesus "get lost"?

One Jesus or Many? Images of Jesus in Early Christianity

As the following chapters will show, the New Testament Gospels offer four different portraits of Jesus. Mark's Jesus shows God's power over evil—in the working of miracles, but especially in his suffering death as God's "mystery Messiah." Matthew's Jesus teaches the authentic interpretation of the Torah, the Law of Moses, against the stiff opposition of other teachers such as the Pharisees. Luke's Jesus directs his ministry primarily to the "last, lost, and least," offering forgiveness and a place in God's rule to the sick, the sinful, the outsider. John's Jesus, as God's revealer, speaks emphatically about his own relation to "the Father" (God), offering life to those who accept him. Although "the world" refuses to believe him, he overcomes that *kosmos*, using his death (his moment of glory) to bring life to the world.

To be sure, there are common themes. But the rich diversity in these four images of Jesus is impressive. Yet that is just the tip of the iceberg. Many other Gospels written by early Christians did not find a home within the canon of writings eventually deemed authoritative by Christians (mostly, though not entirely, defined by 400 CE). Among these, the most intriguing is the Gospel of Thomas.

---

1. For a helpful, compact orientation to this enormous body of scholarship, see Mark Allan Powell, *Jesus as a Figure in History: How Modern Historians View the Man from Galilee*, 2nd ed. (Louisville, KY: Westminster John Knox Press, 2013), and the bibliography provided there.

Sample of Early Christian Gospels
• Canonical Gospels
— Matthew   — Luke
— Mark   — John
• Extracanonical Gospels
— Gospel of Thomas   — Infancy Gospel of Thomas
— Gospel of Peter   — Gospel of Mary
— Gospel of Truth   — Gospel of Judas

Extracanonical Gospels

The Gospel of Thomas, probably from the early- to mid-second century CE (though likely containing earlier traditions), presents a collection of sayings of Jesus, gathered into 114 clusters of sayings (or *logia*). It claims a fictional (pseudonymous) link to the Jesus tradition via special revelation by the risen Jesus to the apostle "Didymos Judas Thomas" (both Didymos and Thomas mean "Twin"; cf. John 11:16; 20:24; 21:2). Several sayings in the Gospel of Thomas resemble variations in the canonical Gospels, while others differ greatly. Prominent in many of the sayings is an insistence that identity, wisdom, and participation in (ultimate) reality are to be sought in detachment from this world and its public, especially commercial, engagements.

A few excerpts illustrate some of the distinctive qualities of this presentation of the teaching of Jesus:

- Jesus said, "There was a rich man who had considerable wealth. He said, 'I shall invest my wealth so as to sow, reap, plant, and fill my barns with crops, lest I run short of something.' These things are what he was thinking in his heart, and that very night the man died. Whoever has ears should listen." (Gos. Thom. 63; cf. Luke 12:16–21)[2]
- Jesus said, "[What] the kingdom of the [father] resembles [is] a woman who was conveying a [jar] full of meal. When she had traveled far [along] the road, the handle of the jar broke and the meal spilled out. . . . She was not aware of the fact; she had not understood how to toil. When she reached home she put down the jar and found it empty." (Gos. Thom. 97)
- And Jesus said, "Be passersby." (ibid., 42)
- Jesus said, "Whoever has become acquainted with the world has found a corpse, and the world is not worthy of the one who has found the corpse." (ibid., 56)
- Jesus said, "What the kingdom resembles is a shepherd who had a

---

2. Translations of passages from the Gospel of Thomas come from Bentley Layton, *The Gnostic Scriptures: A New Translation with Annotations and Introduction* (Garden City, NY: Doubleday, 1987). For an online translation, presented within a five-column display alongside the canonical Gospels, see http://sites.utoronto.ca/religion/synopsis/meta-5g.htm.

hundred sheep. One of them, *the largest*, strayed away. He left the ninety-nine and sought the one until he found it. After having toiled, he said to the sheep, '*I love you* [sg.] *more than the ninety-nine.*'" (ibid., 107, distinctive features in italics; cf. Matt 18:12–14; Luke 15:3–7)

Many other accounts have been preserved, in whole or in part.[3] *The Gospel of Peter* (early- to mid-2nd c. CE) is a fragmentary narrative that (in the text that survives) joins the narrative of Jesus' trial and crucifixion midway, assigns Herod Antipas a key role alongside Pilate, and gives a visual report of the resurrection, replete with a talking cross. *The Gospel of Truth* offers a mid-second-century meditative reflection on Jesus from a Valentinian gnostic perspective. *The Infancy Gospel of Thomas* (perhaps early 2nd c.) fills in the gaps in memory in accounts of Jesus' childhood, turning him into a precocious, wonder-working child, even if not yet morally responsible. *The Gospel of Mary* (probably late 2nd c.) purports to give secret, visionary teaching (of a gnostic character) from the resurrected Jesus to Mary (Magdalene), whose credibility is contested by Andrew and Peter. *The Gospel of Judas* sets Judas apart from the other apostles as the one who truly discerned Jesus' intentions and acted to further them by the "betrayal" to the authorities. And so on.

Early Gnostic Christian Writings

- The label "gnostic" comes from the Greek word *gnōsis*, "knowledge." True insight into human identity and origins is of pivotal importance for gnostics.
- Valentinian gnostic writings come from circles influenced by Valentinus (taught in Rome, mid-2nd c. CE).
- Sample of Christian gnostic writings:
  - — Gospel of Truth
  - — Gospel of Philip
  - — Gospel of Mary
  - — Treatise on the Resurrection
  - — Secret Book of John

With most yet not all scholars, I regard these extracanonical accounts as generally unreliable profiles of the character, message, and activity of Jesus for purposes of constructing a historical account.[4] Nevertheless, as is evident both within and beyond canonical boundaries, Jesus of Nazareth was remembered by early Christians in diverse ways. Naturally, certain questions arise: What was Jesus really like? What did he really do and say? How can we

---

3. Translations of these and other extracanonical documents from early Christianity are conveniently available in Bart D. Ehrman, ed., *Lost Scriptures: Books That Did Not Make It into the New Testament* (New York: Oxford University Press, 2003). For the Gospel of Judas, see *The Gospel of Judas: From Codex Tchacos*, ed. Rodolphe Kasser, Marvin Meyer, and Gregor Wurst (Washington, DC: National Geographic, 2006).

4. John Dominic Crossan is a leading example of a scholar who does assert the historical value of materials included within such documents as the Gospel of Thomas and the Gospel

get behind these Gospel memories of Jesus—each of them colored, each of them shaped by the experiences of the Christians[5] who produced them—to the earthly career of Jesus? This is the "problem of the historical Jesus."

The Problem of the Historical Jesus

Let's illustrate the problem with a brief glance at the Gospel passion narratives. What happened at the cross between Jesus and the criminals crucified with him? Did both ridicule him (Mark 15:32; Matt 27:44)? Or did one of them defend Jesus and receive the promise of paradise (Luke 23:39–43)? Both accounts cannot be accurate. How can one decide? Or consider the final words of Jesus from the cross. Did he say, "It is finished!" (John 19:30)? Or "Father, into your hands I commit my spirit" (Luke 23:46)? Or "My God, my God, why have you forsaken me?" (Mark 15:34; Matt 27:46)? One can easily multiply the examples of these variations in the telling of the story, from the beginning of Jesus' public career and through the Easter accounts of resurrection appearances to his followers.

It is apparent that the Gospels present diverse memories of Jesus' life that do not agree in all respects. Why? Several factors should be highlighted. (1) The first Gospel was probably not written until about the year 70 CE, some thirty-five to forty years after Jesus' public activity concluded. That is a generation or more of preserving the memories of his life through oral tradition. Much can happen in a generation, as the first Christians remembered Jesus through the filter of their own experiences. (2) Moreover, each Gospel writer is telling, or retelling, the story of Jesus for his time and place, for a particular Christian community or communities.[6] Each Gospel reflects a set of convictions, a particular perception of who Jesus is and what life faithful to him looks like. Each Gospel audience lived in a setting marked by a set of important concerns, specific problems and challenges, particular needs. Therefore, operating like a field archaeologist, the historian must dig through several layers, including the setting of the first readers and the creative work of the Gospel authors, as well as a generation of oral tradition,

---

of Peter. See his major historical study, *The Historical Jesus: The Life of a Mediterranean Jewish Peasant* (San Francisco: HarperSanFrancisco, 1991); and a more compact and accessible presentation in idem, *Jesus: A Revolutionary Biography* (San Francisco: HarperSanFrancisco, 1995).

5. It is anachronistic to refer to Jesus followers as "Christians" in the earliest period of the emergence of Christianity, not least because Jesus and his first followers were not clearly distinguished from the Jewish people and the sets of practices associated with them. However, in the mid-60s, Nero was able to single out Christian believers as scapegoats in the Neronian persecution in Rome (64 CE), and the book of Acts does refer to *Christianoi* (Christians), a label perhaps first applied by opponents of the movement (Acts 11:26; 26:28; cf. 1 Pet 4:16). In this book, while acknowledging the complex questions of identity and naming bound up with the early movement's eventual differentiation from the Jewish people, I will sometimes, for convenience, use the term "Christians" as synonymous with "Jesus followers."

6. Richard Bauckham has been a leading voice for the view that, from the beginning, the Gospels were not written to and for specific communities but instead for the wider church. See, e.g., the essays collected in *The Gospels for All Christians: Rethinking the Gospel Audiences*, ed. Richard Bauckham (Grand Rapids: Wm. B. Eerdmans Publishing Co., 1998); see the critique of this argument in Joel Marcus, *Mark: A New Translation with Introduction and Commentary*, 2 vols., AB 27–27A (New Haven, CT: Yale University Press, 2000–2009), 1:25–28.

to arrive at the time of Jesus himself. (3) And there is another important consideration. The early followers of Jesus looked back on his life through the lens provided by their post-Easter experiences and beliefs. Convictions about later events (esp. Jesus' crucifixion and resurrection) lent new meaning to his earlier, public activity. As a result, any search for the "bare facts" of Jesus' life, free of any interpretation of his significance, is bound to be frustrated. Jesus was remembered by people who believed certain things about him, people for whom he was the Messiah and the crucified-but-risen Lord. The "quest for the historical Jesus" will therefore remain ever elusive. But can appropriate methods of inquiry bring us closer to the historical activity of Jesus than we might otherwise get?

Method in the Quest for the Historical Jesus

When assessing the historical reliability of elements in the Gospels (or in extracanonical documents), scholars employ several tests. Although lists of these evaluative criteria vary, the enumeration by Mark Allan Powell gives helpful orientation.[7] An affirmative answer to each question increases the likelihood that Jesus did perform the activity (saying or deed) in view.

- Multiple attestation: do multiple, independent sources attest a particular saying or event?
- Memorable content or form: would a saying or action have been easy to remember and so preserve in the process of oral transmission?
- Language and environment: does a saying credited to Jesus fit the language he spoke (Aramaic) and the cultural environment in which he lived (i.e., the culture of early Judaism within first-century Judea and Galilee)?
- Embarrassment: does a saying or action potentially cause embarrassment for the Jesus followers (e.g., his submitting to baptism by John, or his betrayal by a disciple)?
- Indifference or irrelevance: does a reported saying, action, or event bear no clear relation to the author's (or source's) interests and agenda?
- Dissimilarity or distinctiveness: does a saying or action sharply distinguish Jesus from both his own (Jewish and Galilean) cultural context and the characteristic beliefs and practices of early Christian groups?
- Plausible influence (the converse of the preceding criterion): does a saying or action reflect Jesus' Jewish cultural context *and also* help explain characteristic beliefs or practices of early Christian groups?
- Coherence: does a saying or action cohere or agree with other materials that have a high claim to historical reliability on the basis of other criteria?
- Congruity with modern views of reality: does a saying, act, or event

7. Powell, *Jesus as a Figure in History*, 59–70.

fit our perception of reality, our sense of what *can* happen in the world?[8]
- Coherence with outcome of Jesus' life: does a saying, act, or event make sense of—and make sense in the light of—Jesus' eventual arrest and crucifixion?[9]

What profile of Jesus results from careful, rigorous sifting of the materials available in early Christian writings? Recognizing that no single portrait of Jesus will win approval from all scholars, and that the nature of the evidence resists a firm, complete construction, I offer what I regard as a plausible sketch, limited to the brief period of Jesus' public ministry.

Criteria for Assessment: Did Jesus Say or Do That?

- **Multiple attestation**: more than one (independent) source includes it.
- **Memorable content or form**: not difficult to remember that!
- **Language and cultural environment**: does it fit in the cultural context?
- **Embarrassment**: no way they would have made that up!
- **Irrelevance**: does not advance the agenda of the writing that includes it.
- **Dissimilarity or distinctiveness**: it really stands out!
- **Plausible influence**: it fits the cultural context and helps explain later beliefs and practices.
- **Coherence**: it is like other things shown to (probably) come from Jesus.
- **Congruence with modern notions of reality**: Does it agree with our understanding of what *can* occur?
- **Coherence with the outcome of Jesus' life**: Does it help make sense of the end of the story (arrest and crucifixion)?

A Brief Sketch of Jesus' Public Career

Jesus (Yeshu[a])[10] began public activity teaching and healing after undergoing baptism by John the "Dipper" (Baptizer) in the river Jordan. This identification with John suggests that Jesus agreed with John's core message: John called the Jewish people to admit their sin and repent—orient their lives toward the approaching reign of God. Judgment was at hand; the ax was poised to strike the root of the tree, ready to cut down all who were unfruitful (Matt 3:10; Luke 3:9). Yet Jesus developed his own mission and message in a way that diverged from John's austerity and severity. Jesus instead won

---

8. Powell regards this as a generally *unstated*, though widely shared, assumption (ibid., 70).

9. This evaluative criterion, not included in Powell's list, is emphasized, e.g., by John P. Meier, *A Marginal Jew: Rethinking the Historical Jesus*, 5 vols., ABRL (New Haven, CT: Yale University Press, 1991–2016), 1:177; note the critique by Powell, *Jesus as a Figure in History*, 181.

10. *Yeshu(a)* is a shortened form of the Hebrew *Jehoshua* (Joshua) = Greek *Iēsous* and English "Jesus."

criticism for eating and drinking—and with the wrong crowd (e.g., Luke 7:34). He accepted the unreligious, the "sinners," those who were marginalized by their sickness or their age or their gender or their poverty.

Like John, Jesus announced the approach of the rule of God. But rather than picturing that approach with the menacing image of an ax poised at the tree root, Jesus pointed to his own cures of sick people, his acts freeing persons from oppression by demons, and his meals with saints and sinners alike—all as tangible signs of the nearness of God's rule. Indeed, God's reign was already pressing into the world, already altering the landscape of Jewish society. Jesus and his small band of followers were issuing an invitation to heaven's banquet, and the time to decide was now. "Twelve" disciples—a symbolic number, for Jesus certainly had more learners/followers than that—match the number of Israel's tribes. Thus Jesus sought to renew and restore the Jewish nation in terms of his (unconventional) vision of God and God's rule.

Much insight into Jesus' agenda, then, may be gained from observing his behavior—his meals, his cures, his gathering around himself a circle of disciples. At the center of his activity, however, was his preaching and teaching: his message. Often he packaged that message in aphorisms, short, witty sayings like these:

- Many who are first will be last, and the last will be first. (Mark 10:31)
- Do not judge, so that you may not be judged. (Matt 7:1)
- It is easier for a camel to go through the eye of a needle than for someone who is rich to enter the kingdom of God. (Mark 10:25)
- Ask, and it will be given you; search, and you will find; knock, and the door will be opened for you. (Matt 7:7)

Especially memorable, though, were his parables—brief stories drawing from the stuff of everyday life to convey something of his vision of God and of human life before God. Other Jewish teachers, too, told parables; a famous early one was that told by the prophet Nathan to David, after the death of Uriah the Hittite, Bathsheba's husband (2 Sam 12:1–4); and there are many examples in rabbinic literature, as in the Talmud.[11] Jesus' parables, however, are noteworthy for their simplicity and economy, and more often than not also for the surprises they spring on the audience. A story, for example, about a business manager who, after being fired for alleged incompetence or dishonest business practices, drastically reduces the amount owed to his master by debtors—and then is praised by his master for his cunning (Luke 16:1–8a). Or a story about two men at prayer in the temple—one seemingly

---

11. See Brad H. Young, *The Parables: Jewish Tradition and Christian Interpretation* (Peabody, MA: Hendrickson Publishers, 1998), 3–40.

a model of piety and honor, the other a contemptible tax collector—in which God listens to the humble plea for mercy from a self-acknowledged sinner rather than to a Pharisee's prayer (Luke 18:9–14). Or a tale about a justice-seeking widow whom a judge ignores until her persistence (figuratively) pummels him into submission and he finally vindicates her (Luke 18:2–5). Or a mininarrative that compares the world-transforming operation of God's realm to the hidden, fermenting activity of yeast in bread dough (Matt 13:33) or the tiniest of seeds becoming not a towering tree (e.g., a cedar of Lebanon) but a mustard bush (Mark 4:31–32).

With provocative teaching and conduct, Jesus made enemies. Apparently the Pharisees were frequent sparring partners, perhaps because they agreed on so much while clashing on some key points of Torah interpretation and practice. Did Jesus really dare to tell them, "Prostitutes and tax collectors are going into God's realm ahead of you" (Matt 21:31 AT)? "A friend of tax collectors and sinners" is what his critics labeled him (Luke 7:34). Not until Jesus took his message to Jerusalem, however, did the conflict surrounding him reach life-and-death proportions. After a dramatic, choreographed entry into the city—evoking memories of Zechariah's prophecy about the Messiah (Mark 11:1–10; cf. Zech 9:9)—Jesus caught the eye of the powerful protectors of the temple institution. In a confrontational prophetic gesture, he turned over tables of money changers in the temple courtyard (Mark 11:15–17). Whatever else he might have meant by this act of force (likely a symbolic announcement of God's impending judgment against the temple), this was a direct challenge to the authority of the priests who had custody of the temple and of its worship and commerce. The response to the challenge was swift and decisive. Aided by a disciple-turned-informant (Judas), the high priest and his advisers orchestrated Jesus' arrest and handed him over to the Roman prefect Pontius Pilate as a rebel (a messianic pretender). Pilate sentenced him to death by crucifixion, and the sentence was carried out with dispatch (Mark 14–15 and parr.).

The tragic end of Jesus' life did not, however, close the book on Yeshu(a) of Nazareth. On the third day after his crucifixion (Sunday), some women followers reported that they had seen him alive, and eventually "the Twelve," Peter, and even James the brother of Jesus all claimed to have been favored with a resurrection appearance from a crucified but now living Jesus (e.g., Luke 24:1–11; 1 Cor 15:1–11). The case of this James is especially interesting. Like the rest of Jesus' family, he seems to have distanced himself from Jesus' public activity (e.g., Mark 3:21, 31–35). Later we find him as the pillar and driving force in the Jerusalem church (e.g., Acts 15:12–29; 21:17–26; Gal 2:1–10). These earliest Jesus followers believed that God had vindicated their teacher, whose unconventional message and provocative conduct had gotten him killed. Their conviction that God had raised a crucified Messiah from the dead was the birth of the Christian movement within first-century Judaism.

The Genre of the Gospels

What is a Gospel? The Greek noun *euangelion*, commonly translated "gospel," means good news, and in the Old Greek translation of the Hebrew Bible (or OT) indicated a public, oral declaration of good news. For example, Second Isaiah, prophet of the Babylonian exile, spoke of the announcement of this happy news: the time of captivity was drawing to a close, and divine deliverance was imminent:

> Get you up to a high mountain,
> > O Zion, herald of good tidings [*euangelion*];
> lift up your voice with strength,
> > O Jerusalem, herald of good tidings [*euangelion*],
> > lift it up, do not fear;
> say to the cities of Judah,
> > "Here is your God!" (Isa 40:9; cf. 52:7; 61:1)

Paul picks up this usage in his letters, employing the word "gospel" for the oral proclamation of the good news of God's saving initiative, especially in the death and resurrection of Jesus (e.g., Rom 10:14–17; 1 Cor 15:1; Gal 1:6–9, 11; 2:2). The first lines of Mark's Gospel introduce the narrative as "the beginning of the good news [*euangelion*]" (Mark 1:1), and the term stuck, eventually becoming a genre designation for all the canonical accounts of Jesus' activity, and others besides (see the discussion above). In early manuscripts, the title "Gospel according to . . ." is often placed above or at the end of the text of each Gospel.

Although there are important variations among the four New Testament Gospels, it is now common to categorize them as *bioi*, ancient "biographies" that center on the life, virtues, and impact of the narrative's primary subject.[12] Like other such writings, the Gospels give attention to their central figure's origins and birth (Mark being an exception), nurture (clearest in Luke), accomplishments and deeds, and noble death. At the same time, the canonical narratives about Jesus employ biographical conventions with considerable freedom. Mark gives virtually no information about Jesus before his arrival on the scene as an adult about to begin his mission. Luke does not conclude with the story of Jesus but presents a narrative sequel that traces the activities and accomplishments of his followers (Acts of the Apostles). Thus many scholars prefer to classify Luke and Acts together as a history (*historia*).[13] Both Matthew and Luke begin in a manner that closely links

---

12. Especially influential has been the work of Richard A. Burridge, *What Are the Gospels? A Comparison with Graeco-Roman Biography*, SNTSMS 70 (Cambridge: Cambridge University Press, 1992); and, somewhat earlier, Charles H. Talbert, *What Are the Gospels? The Genre of the Canonical Gospels* (Philadelphia: Fortress Press, 1977). David E. Aune also classifies the canonical Gospels generally as a subtype of Greco-Roman biography (*The New Testament in Its Literary Environment*, LEC [Philadelphia: Westminster Press, 1987], 46, 64).

13. See the discussion of Luke's genre in ch. 5 below.

Jesus to the historical narratives (as well as prophetic books) of Jewish Scriptures (Matt 1–2; Luke 1:5–2:52), and John prefaces the narrative of Jesus' ministry by echoing the creation account of Genesis (John 1:1–5). Thus each of these Gospels embeds the life of Jesus in the stories of ancient Israel.

Some scholars insist that the earliest of the Gospels, Mark, does not conform to any earlier literary genre and credit the author with the creation of a distinctive new genre, the *Christian Gospel*, for use in the settings of teaching and worship in early Christian communities.[14] This view may overstate the novelty of the Gospels, but it does make the important observation that the earliest audiences of the Gospels would have encountered much that is familiar and expected of a biographical narrative in these narratives, but also much that is unexpected.[15]

The Formation of the Gospels

Matthew, Mark, and Luke have many passages in common, with much shared phrasing, and the narrative units all three share mostly follow a common sequence. Because of their largely shared view of Jesus' public ministry, it is conventional to call them Synoptic Gospels (Synoptic = viewed together). At the same time, close analysis reveals notable differences among these three Gospels. Compared to the Synoptics, John presents a generally independent account but also contains a few common or similar episodes and occasional verbal agreement with one or more of the other Gospels (see the discussion in ch. 6 below). How are these patterns of resemblance and difference best explained? What process of formation of these narratives best fits the complex data?

To illustrate these features of the Gospels, we can sample a few passages. Comparative study is facilitated through use of a synopsis that presents the Gospels in parallel columns.[16] I encourage readers to study these passages and record impressions before proceeding to the summary analyses I provide below.

14. See, e.g., Francis J. Moloney, *The Gospel of Mark: A Commentary* (Peabody, MA: Hendrickson Publishers, 2002), 16; M. Eugene Boring, *Mark: A Commentary*, NTL (Louisville, KY: Westminster John Knox Press, 2006), 8–9. For mention of other proposals regarding Mark's literary genre, see ch. 3 below.

15. I will use both "readers" and "audience" when referring to the earliest hearers of the Gospel narratives. Since the Gospels were customarily heard in oral performance within a communal or group setting, *audience* is the more accurate designation.

16. The most widely used synopsis is *Synopsis of the Four Gospels*, ed. Kurt Aland, 10th ed. (United Bible Societies, 1993), also available in Greek and Greek-English versions. A web resource presenting the texts of the four NT Gospels and the Gospel of Thomas in parallel columns is conveniently available through the University of Toronto: http://sites.utoronto.ca/religion/synopsis/meta-5g.htm.

An Ordeal of Testing (Matt 4:1–11; Mark 1:12–13; Luke 4:1–13)

In all three Gospels, Jesus undergoes testing for forty days in the wilderness. His adversary is the devil (Matthew and Luke) or Satan (Mark)—different name, but the same character. Matthew and Luke (but not Mark) exemplify the nature of the testing by presenting three specific challenges from the devil, in dialogue that shows close, though not exact, verbal agreement. Sequence varies, however: Matthew concludes with the lure of universal rule, answered by Jesus' affirmation that God alone is worthy of worship; Luke concludes with a challenge to demand miraculous divine deliverance at the Temple Mount in Jerusalem. The two accounts, then, achieve their climactic effects in different ways.[17] Moreover, Jesus is bolstered by a supporting cast of angels in Matthew and Mark, but they are absent from Luke. Finally, Luke alone closes the unit with ominous foreshadowing: "the devil . . . departed from him until an opportune time" (a time that arrives in Luke 22:3).

The Call of a Tax Collector (Matt 9:9–13; Mark 2:13–17; Luke 5:27–32)

It is immediately obvious that the three Gospels are presenting the same basic story with much the same wording. However, there are intriguing differences in detail:

- Luke clearly indicates that Levi is the host of this banquet; he also declares that Levi "left everything" to follow Jesus. (In Matthew the tax collector's name is Matthew, not Levi.)
- In Luke, Pharisees and scribes address critical remarks to the disciples concerning the behavior of the *disciples*, not Jesus himself.
- While all three Gospels have Jesus say, "I have come to call not the righteous but sinners," Luke adds "to repentance" (5:32).
- Matthew has Jesus say, "Go and learn what this means, 'I desire mercy, not sacrifice'" (9:13)—a quotation from Hosea 6:6 that reappears in Matt 12:7.

Call to Prayer (Matt 6:7–15; Luke 11:1–4; Mark 11:25)

Only Matthew and Luke have Jesus providing a compact model prayer for his disciples (Mark 11:25 resembles the petition to forgive included in the prayer by the other two). The narrative setting of the prayer differs: Matthew includes it at the very center (Matt 6:9–13) of the Sermon on the Mount (Matt 5–7), while Luke places it in the course of Jesus' long journey toward Jerusalem, as a response to the disciples' request for a model prayer (Luke 11:1–4). The two versions have common phrasing: "Hallowed be your name"; "your kingdom come"; "give us . . . our daily bread"; "forgive us"; "do not bring us to the time of trial." The most obvious difference is that Luke

---

17. And they do so in ways that make sense in each narrative. Matthew ends with Jesus' claim to have "all authority in heaven and earth"—given, however, by God rather than the devil (28:18). Luke's Gospel gives Jerusalem a central place, and with this third test (4:9–12) anticipates the final test of Jesus' fidelity to his vocation: "If you are the son of God, . . . [save yourself: come down from the cross]" (cf. 23:35, 37, 39).

abbreviates the text of the prayer, or (perhaps more likely) Matthew expands it, drawing from the prayer's liturgical use in congregations in Matthew's location. In the petition for forgiveness, Luke 11:4 mixes the images of debt and sin (or transgression), while Matthew 6:12 keeps to the debt metaphor. Matthew, however, also tacks on stern language that reinforces the mandate to show mercy to others (6:13–14), anticipating later teaching by Jesus (18:23–35, esp. v. 35).

Jesus Meets Rejection at Home (Matt 13:53–58; Mark 6:1–6a; Luke 4:16–30)

In each Gospel, when Jesus teaches in the synagogue in his hometown (specified as Nazareth in Luke), he encounters resistance to his mission and message.[18] Mark and Matthew credit this resistance to familiarity with Jesus and his family: rumors of extraordinary wisdom and acts make no sense for such an ordinary person, a carpenter (Mark) or carpenter's son (Matthew). Four brothers of Jesus are mentioned by name (James, Joses [Joseph], Judas, and Simon), and sisters are also mentioned, though no names are given. As in the Gospel of Thomas (logion 31), Jesus explains the rejection as the inevitable reception of a prophet in his own homeland and household (Mark adds among his kin). The outcome of this lack of faith in Jesus' mission is his limited capacity to heal the sick here, with Mark picturing more dramatic failure:

- He did not do many deeds of power there, because of their unbelief. (Matt 13:58)
- He could do no deed of power there, except that he laid his hands on a few sick people and cured them. (Mark 6:5)

Luke's variation on the theme actually alters the theme. In addition to repositioning the episode at the start of Jesus' mission in Galilee, Luke substantially revises the scene so that it states the Scripture-based mandate for Jesus' messianic mission and reports the synagogue audience's shift from initially favorable response to Jesus' speech to rage. The narrative even concludes with a thwarted attempt to kill him, motivated by Jesus' aligning his mission with a prophetic pattern of bringing divine succor to outsiders (invoking Elijah and Elisha). (For more detailed discussion, see ch. 5 below.)

---

18. Cf. John 1:11; 4:44; 6:42; also Gos. Thom. 31: "No prophet is accepted in his own village; no physician heals those who know him" (trans. Thomas O. Lambdin, http://www.gnosis.org/naghamm/gthlamb.html). John's modulation of the tradition of Jesus' rejection among his own people is fascinating. John 1:11 offers a general image of Jesus' "own [people]" not welcoming him. John 4:44 uses language that resembles the Synoptic Gospels' picture of a prophet's rejection in his own homeland, but appears to invert the spatial references. In the other Gospels, Jesus experiences rejection at Nazareth, but John contrasts favorable welcome in Galilee to hostility in and near Jerusalem (his own homeland?): "He went from that place to Galilee (for Jesus himself had testified that a prophet has no honor in the prophet's own country). When he came to Galilee, the Galileans welcomed him, since they had seen all that he had done in Jerusalem at the festival" (4:43–45).

An Extravagant "Waste" of Oil (Matt 26:6–13; Mark 14:3–9; Luke 7:36–50; John 12:1–8)

Unlike the passages considered so far, this one has variations in all four Gospels. Luke's version stands apart, both because it comes so early in the story, disconnected from the passion narrative for which it is an interpretive prelude in the other three Gospels, and because it reframes the scene from pre-burial honor for Jesus to his radical acceptance of sinners (a central Lukan concern). Luke and John direct the anointing to Jesus' feet rather than his head, as in Matthew and Mark. John supplies names for key actors in the episode, identifying Mary (sister of Martha and Lazarus) as the woman and Judas as the observer who objects to her waste (with the additional note that his complaint was motivated by greed). Intriguing verbatim agreements cut across the four versions, such as the "three hundred denarii" that might have been "given to the poor" (Mark 14:5 and John 12:5); "ointment of [pure] nard" (Mark 14:3 and John 12:3); and Jesus' defense of the woman, "You always have the poor with you, *and you can show kindness to them whenever you wish*; but you will [in John: "do"] not always have me" (Matt 26:11; Mark 14:7; John 12:8; italicized clause is only in Mark).

Prayer—and Sleep—in Face of Crisis (Matt 26:36–46; Mark 14:32–42; Luke 22:39–46; John 18:1; cf. John 12:27; 14:1)

Again, all four Gospels have material relating Jesus' attitude toward his impending arrest, although John's account has little contact with the others; indeed, John 12:27 reads like a direct counter to the tradition of anguished struggle prior to the arrest in the other Gospels (also cf. Heb 2:18; 5:7–8). The Synoptics present the episode with the same basic pattern: Jesus, accompanied by his disciples (in Luke) or by a small group of his closest followers (Peter, James, and John [in Matthew and Mark]), petitions God ("Father" ["Abba, Father" in Mark]) that if possible "the cup" (of suffering) might be removed; meanwhile the disciples sleep. Luke's version is the most compact, presenting the above scenario just one time (and attributing the disciples' sleep to their grief). Matthew and Mark, by contrast, narrate the rhythm of Jesus' prayer and the disciples' sleep three times, with the accent falling more sharply in Mark on the disciples' inability to be vigilant and in Matthew on the prayer of Jesus: unlike Mark, Matthew records Jesus' petition a second time, aligning the prayer with the model prayer of 6:9–13 ("Your will be done," 26:42). In each of the Synoptics, the scene in the Gethsemane garden (Matthew and Mark) on the Mount of Olives (Luke) leads immediately to the arrest of Jesus.

Explanatory Models for the Formation of the Gospels

Let us organize the data. If one expands the analysis of these few narrative units to all the passages in the Gospels, several patterns emerge. Here we focus on the interrelationships among the three Gospels of Matthew, Mark, and Luke; the problem we are working on is conventionally called "the Synoptic problem."[19] John represents a special case; while John has a few of the same episodes as the other Gospels, in general John goes its own way. The events and teaching in John are more often than not independent of the other three.

Comparing the Synoptic Gospels: Summary of Results
• Close verbal agreement in Matthew, Mark, Luke.
• Different phrasing in shared passages.
• Generally common sequence of episodes.
• Most of Mark's passages are in Matthew, and much of Mark is also in Luke.
• Matthew and Luke share material not in Mark—esp. content of Jesus' teaching.
• Material only in Matthew.
• Material only in Luke.
• Matthew's differences from Mark show some coherence.
• Luke's differences from Mark show some coherence.
• Mark's Greek is the least polished.
• Matthew and Luke are longer than Mark, but individual episodes are often briefer.

At the risk of oversimplifying the data, I offer several summary observations:

- There is often close verbal agreement in Matthew, Mark, and Luke in passages they have in common.
- Yet there are also differences in wording—sometimes insignificant, sometimes significant—and often in the very passages where the Gospels show close verbal agreement.[20]
- The same basic sequence, or order, of episodes appears in Matthew,

19. The scholarly literature on this topic is voluminous. A recent volume of essays that tackles the issues from a variety of perspectives is *New Studies in the Synoptic Problem*, ed. Paul Foster, Andrew Gregory, John S. Kloppenborg, and Joseph Verheyden, BETL 239 (Leuven: Peeters, 2011). The introductory essay by Christopher Tuckett ("The Current State of the Synoptic Problem," 9–50) gives an esp. helpful sketch and appraisal of this work. M. Eugene Boring provides a thorough synthesis of the data in *An Introduction to the New Testament: History, Literature, Theology* (Louisville, KY: Westminster John Knox Press, 2012), 473–506.

20. A special challenge is posed by the so-called "minor agreements," where Matthew and Luke agree with each other in disagreement with Mark. See the helpful discussion by M. Eugene Boring, "The Minor Agreements and Their Bearing on the Synoptic Problem," in *New Studies in the Synoptic Problem*, ed. Foster et al., 227–51.

Mark, and Luke, though with significant exceptions (e.g., Luke 4:16–30 repositions the rejection scene at Nazareth to the opening of Jesus' activity in Galilee, and Luke 7:36–50 repositions a woman's anointing of Jesus to a setting early in the story).

- Nearly all of Mark's Gospel is found also in Matthew and/or Luke (Matthew includes more than Luke, which, e.g., does not contain units parallel to Mark 6:45–8:26).

- Matthew and Luke share with each other substantial additional material not found in Mark. For the most part, this extra material consists of sayings of Jesus.

- Some material appears only in Matthew, and some only in Luke. This includes a host of memorable parables, such as ones featuring a forgiven, unforgiving slave (Matt 18:23–35); all-day and part-day vineyard workers (Matt 20:1–16); sheep and goats at the last judgment (Matt 25:31–46); an exemplary Samaritan (Luke 10:30–35); a father and his two lost sons (Luke 15:11–32); the poor beggar Lazarus and a rich man who lacks empathy for him (Luke 16:19–31); a persistent widow confronting a contemptuous judge (Luke 18:2–5); and a Pharisee and a tax collector at prayer (Luke 18:10–14).

- Matthew's differences from Mark often accumulate in patterns that cohere. For example, Matthew 9:9–13 includes a phrase not found in Mark 2:13–17: "Go and learn what this means, 'I desire mercy, not sacrifice.'" The same quotation from Hosea 6:6 appears again in Matthew 12:7.

- In the same way, Luke's differences from Mark accumulate in meaningful patterns. For example, while in Mark 2:17 Jesus says, "I have come to call not the righteous, but sinners," Luke adds "to repentance." Elsewhere Luke accents the repentance of sinners (e.g., 15:7, 10; 16:30–31).

- In syntax and word selection, Matthew and especially Luke generally write a smoother, more elevated Greek prose than Mark does.

- Matthew and Luke are much longer than Mark. Yet in individual passages, they generally use fewer words (a good example: the blended healing stories featuring a woman with a chronic bleeding ailment and a prominent man's daughter fill twenty-three verses in Mark 5:21–43 but only nine in Matt 9:18–26 and 17 in Luke 8:40–56).

How are these patterns to be explained? How are the Synoptic Gospels related to one another? Scholars today are virtually unanimous in their verdict that the data are best explained by a literary source theory: at least one of the Gospels has been used as a written source by the authors of the other Gospels. That is why they generally follow the same sequence and why they agree so extensively in wording. Although other proposals have been and continue to be advanced, three explanatory models have the widest currency today. An early approach (originally suggested by Augustine, early fifth c. CE) that has been revived more recently by a few (vocal) advocates is the *Matthean-priority* model or *two-Gospel hypothesis*.[21] According to this model, Matthew was written first, then Luke employed Matthew as a source, and finally Mark had access to both Matthew and Luke; Mark abbreviated and combined the other Gospels. The model raises serious questions, however: Is it plausible that Mark would have omitted so much of Matthew and Luke (including most of Jesus' teachings)? Is it more likely that Mark "roughed up" the more refined prose of Matthew and Luke, or that Matthew and Luke improved Mark's rougher Greek style?

The Synoptic Problem: Explanatory Models

- **Two-Gospel hypothesis**: Matthew first; Luke used Matthew as source; Mark used both Matthew and Luke.
- **Farrar-Goulder hypothesis**: Mark first; Matthew used Mark as source; Luke used both Mark and Matthew.
- **Two-document hypothesis**: Mark first; Matthew and Luke used Mark + Q as sources, and also drew from their own distinctive traditions.

A number of scholars propose that Mark came first, then Matthew used Mark as a source, and finally Luke drew from both Mark and Matthew. Often termed the Farrar-Goulder hypothesis for two prominent proponents, this view argues for *Markan priority + Luke's use of Matthew*.[22] This explanatory model accounts for the extensive material shared by Matthew and Luke but missing from Mark; however, it prompts the following question: Why does Luke clash with Matthew at many points (e.g., the birth stories and the genealogies in these Gospels agree on little), and why does Luke not include distinctively Matthean material (e.g., the parables unique to Matthew)?[23]

Certain answers can be or have been offered to such questions, but are the explanations—and the correlated picture of each Gospel author's compositional activity—convincing? These and other challenges facing the two models just discussed have led the majority of contemporary scholars to favor a third approach: the *two-document hypothesis*, which argues for *Markan priority + Q*. This explanatory model proposes that Mark was the first

---

21. This approach has often been called the "Griesbach hypothesis," after the name of an influential late-19th-c. proponent. Works arguing for this view include William R. Farmer, *The Synoptic Problem: A Critical Analysis* (New York: Macmillan, 1964); and David B. Peabody, Lamar Cope, and Allan J. McNicol, *One Gospel from Two: Mark's Use of Matthew and Luke* (Harrisburg, PA: Trinity Press International, 2002).

22. The most vigorous contemporary advocate of this position is Mark Goodacre. See, e.g., his book *The Case against Q: Studies in Markan Priority and the Synoptic Problem* (Harrisburg, PA: Trinity Press International, 2002).

23. These questions prompted by the view that Luke used Matthew as a source also pertain to the two-Gospel hypothesis.

Gospel written, and it was then used as a source by Matthew and Luke, who composed their narratives independently of each other. Matthew and Luke, however, each drew upon a common source consisting primarily of sayings of Jesus. Scholars give it the name Q, for *Quelle*, German for "source." This document is hypothetical; it has not been preserved (except in the text of Matthew and Luke), although the Gospel of Thomas (probably compiled in the second c. CE) resembles the form Q is supposed to have taken—a collection of sayings of Jesus. Moreover, to account for materials found only in Matthew and those found only in Luke, the two-document model admits oral traditions available only to Matthew and oral traditions available only to Luke (though some scholars think also of written sources: hence a four-document model).

The evidence is complex—much more so than the brief synthesis I have provided can indicate. One complicating factor is that it is impossible to be 100 percent certain regarding the exact text of any of the Gospels in the first century of their production and dissemination. Continuing influence from oral traditions that persisted for some time alongside the written Gospels, as well as textual fluidity resulting from the tendency of copyists to conform the texts of the Gospels to one another, interfere with any simple solution to the puzzle of Gospel relations. Among other things, this means that if Matthew and Luke each used Mark as a literary source, they did not have access to identical copies of Mark—nor do we have access to the precise form of Mark either of them knew. Nevertheless, my assessment of the data leads me to conclude that the most satisfactory explanatory model is the two-document, Markan-priority approach: Mark probably came first; then in composing their Gospels, Matthew and Luke, likely working independently of each other, drew upon Mark and upon a collection of Jesus' sayings (Q), along with distinctive oral traditions available to them. John or the tradition that underlies it probably had significant points of contact with the traditions that informed one or more of the Synoptics, though perhaps not the published Gospels themselves (see further ch. 6 below).

Reading the Gospels

What difference does all this make in reading the Gospels? The kind of analysis we have been doing can sharpen our reading of the Gospels: it fosters keener appreciation of the distinctiveness of each narrative, as well as the plot elements, character development, and thematic emphases that they share. For Matthew and Luke, specifically, the interpretive method of *redaction criticism* studies the ways in which Matthew and Luke have adopted, adapted, and reshaped Mark.[24] Their reworking of Mark may point to their

---

24. Assuming, of course, that Matthew and Luke used Mark as a primary source. If one adopts an alternative Gospel-formation model, one would consider Luke's revision or retelling of Matthew, or Mark's reworking of both Matthew and Luke.

own concerns and convictions and also, to some degree, the context and needs of their communities, their first audiences. Their reshaping of Mark, then, discloses something of their distinctive perspectives on Jesus and may provide valuable clues concerning the specific issues facing Matthew and Luke in the Christian communities for which they wrote.

But these are not just scissors-and-paste editors. When interpreting the Gospel narratives about Jesus, we dare not simply study the way sources are edited. The writers of the Gospels are authors; each, using available sources and traditions, tells a story. Each Gospel is a connected narrative about Jesus. So my central interest in this book will be reading each Gospel as a whole story, as a unique interpretation of Jesus of Nazareth. The focus will be the way each Gospel portrays and thus interprets Jesus by (re)telling the story of his public career. We will begin with what is probably the earliest Gospel, Mark (ch. 3), then turn to Matthew (ch. 4), Luke (ch. 5), and John (ch. 6). Before proceeding, though, it may be useful to review the array of interpretive methods that readers may encounter in literature on the Gospels, most of which will figure at some point in the analysis of the Gospel narratives in this book.

Surveying Contemporary Interpretive Methods

Most readers of this book will not be reading the New Testament Gospels in their original Greek form but a translation building on a tradition that goes back at least to the 1300s CE.[25] English (or French, German, Spanish, Korean, Chinese, etc.) was not the first language into which the Gospels were translated; there were important early versions in Latin, Syriac, and Coptic. But in whatever language, exactly what text is to be read? What is the content—what are the actual words—of each Gospel? This is the concern of the discipline of text criticism.

Textual Criticism

We have no autographs—no original manuscripts—of New Testament books. We have only later copies—several thousand, in fact, but only a few (in fragmentary form) from as early as the second century CE and a handful from the third and fourth centuries. Most manuscripts come from the medieval period. These copies were produced slowly, tediously, painstakingly by hand. It is no wonder that the manuscripts contain mistakes, countless thousands of variant readings. It is the task of textual criticism to provide as reliable a text as possible. This critically reconstructed Greek text then forms the basis for interpretation.

Among the basic rules of thumb for text-critical decisions are these:[26]

---

25. M. Eugene Boring provides a helpful sketch of Bible translation in *Introduction to the New Testament*, 37–52.

26. See Kurt Aland and Barbara Aland, *The Text of the New Testament*, 2nd ed. (Grand Rapids: Wm. B. Eerdmans Publishing Co., 1989), 280–81; Bruce M. Metzger and Bart D. Ehrman, *The Text of the New Testament: Its Transmission, Corruption, and Restoration*, 4th ed. (Oxford: Oxford University Press, 2005).

- Readings preserved in the earliest, most widely distributed, and highest-quality manuscripts are more likely original. (Manuscripts therefore should be weighed, not counted.)
- But readings that conform to the language, style, and theological views of the writing in which the passage appears are more likely to be original.
- The reading that can most easily explain the derivation of the other variant readings is most likely original. Thus more difficult readings are more likely to be original (then "corrected" in later manuscripts).
- A shorter reading is more likely to be original; the general tendency is for the texts to expand over time (e.g., with explanatory embellishments). But there are exceptions, as in the phenomenon of homoeoteleuton, when a copyist accidentally omitted a portion of text between two words with the same or similar endings.

Textual criticism is much like being a detective. Fortunately, we are able to build on the careful work of generations of text-critical scholars and have a generally reliable text to interpret, one that undergirds modern translations such as the NRSV.

Methods for Reading the Gospels

- **Diachronic methods**
  - Source criticism
  - Form criticism
  - Redaction criticism (emendation and composition)
- **Synchronic methods**
  - Narrative criticism
  - Rhetorical criticism
  - Social-scientific criticism
  - Reader-centered approaches
    - Reader-response criticism
    - Cultural studies and ideologically focused criticism (e.g., African American liberationist, womanist, feminist, postcolonial)

Diachronic Methods: Source Criticism, Form Criticism, Redaction Criticism

Now that we have been handed a text to read, what comes next? Over the last three centuries and more, a number of methods have been developed for interpreting the Gospels. Several of these approach the text by trying to reconstruct the history behind the text, the way the tradition developed until it took shape in the Gospel narrative.

Source criticism seeks to identify sources from which a Gospel author and narrative has drawn. (This interest is in evidence, e.g., in the analysis of Gospel relations in work on the Synoptic problem; redaction criticism builds on the results of this analysis.)

Form criticism notices the stereotypical forms that appear frequently in the Gospels (e.g., healing/miracle stories, pronouncement stories, conflict stories, parables). The *progymnasmata* (handbooks for training in composition and argumentation) that were instrumental in the education of youth in the Greco-Roman world cultivated skill in composing short accounts of episodes—*chreiai*, "useful" anecdotes—that reveal the character and qualities of the figure whose speech or action they highlight.[27]

Redaction criticism builds on decisions about the source(s) used by an author in composing the Gospel narrative. Redaction-critical analysis notices what happens to the source when it is taken up into the new text. How does the redactor (i.e., author as editor) work with and rework the source material? Redaction criticism has been undertaken in two distinct ways: *emendation analysis* and *composition analysis*. Emendation analysis focuses on changes to the source—the ways in which the source text is revised and transformed. Composition analysis focuses on the ways in which an author orders and arranges materials. It "counts" both changes to the source and parts of the source that are preserved intact, assuming that the author/redactor is adopting the concerns and views expressed in the material that has been included.

The aim of redaction-critical analysis is to identify the author/redactor's central concerns, convictions, commitments, and community circumstances. Although some interpreters employ redaction criticism when reading Mark and John, where no identifiable source text survives (other than what can be reconstructed from the existing narrative), this is a less common approach today.[28]

Synchronic Methods: Narrative Criticism, Rhetorical Criticism, Social-Scientific Criticism

Diachronic methods approach the meaning of a text by probing its history, especially its prehistory. Synchronic methods work with the text in its more or less "final" form.

Narrative criticism assumes that the Gospel—whatever its prior tradition history—presents a generally coherent, unified narrative. The interpreter notices the interaction of character and plot and attends to the way the story is told. Especially instructive in discerning meaning is point of view: the voice of characters, narrator, and implied author (the kind of author who

---

27. For a concise introduction to the *chreia* form, see Ronald Hock, "Chreia," *ABD* 1:912–14.

28. An example of a redaction-critical reading of Mark is Marcus, *Mark*. C. Clifton Black presents a trenchant critique of Markan redaction criticism; see *The Disciples according to Mark: Markan Redaction in Current Debate*, 2nd ed. (Grand Rapids: Wm. B. Eerdmans Publishing Co., 2012).

would tell the story this way, inscribed in or inferred from the narrative). Guided by the way in which the story is told, the narrative critic profiles the implied or ideal reader's response to the text.[29] The readings of the Gospels presented in chapters 3–6 below will primarily draw from narrative-critical analysis, though sometimes stretching or sharpening that reading through the use of other approaches discussed below.

Rhetorical criticism attends to the aesthetic dimensions of a text's design—to the *literary artistry* of the Gospels (or other writings) and how that shapes the reader's response to the text. One type of rhetorical analysis is guided by ancient canons of rhetoric, inspired by the classical work on rhetoric by Aristotle: how is the text designed to persuade readers or listeners? (Study of rhetoric, central in educating persons for public life, helped those of sufficient social status and wealth to proceed beyond what we might call "elementary education.") More recently, rhetorical study has pressed beyond aesthetics to address the practical and social role of texts, their power to direct, shape, and inspire praxis—how we live, what we do. The focus thus is on discourse as "practical exercise of power."[30]

Social-scientific criticism takes seriously the fact that when we read the Gospels, we encounter an unfamiliar social world and culture. We are guests in a world that is not our own. So insights from social history, sociology, cultural anthropology, and psychology may help us make better sense of the text. How does the cultural environment that surrounds the text shape what it says? How do features of social organization (e.g., family and kinship relations, gender roles, and economic relations) shape a story and its telling? Or cultural values and associated practices, such as patronage, honor and shame, friendship, hospitality, reciprocity? Or is social stratification—expressed in particular distributions of wealth, status, and power—in play?

Caution is appropriate when we view ancient narratives such as the Gospels through the lens of modern psychology. Narratives in the era and the culture of the Gospel authors did not show the same level of interest in the inner workings of the human mind that modern Western, therapeutically oriented culture exhibits. When we find ourselves preoccupied with the motivations and psychological processes of characters in the Gospel narratives (including Jesus), we may well be approaching the text anachronistically. To be sure, Mark will sometimes mention Jesus' raw emotions (anger included), and Luke and Matthew will sometimes report that Jesus acted to heal or nourish out of "compassion." Luke, especially, will often present interior monologues that reveal the character of the one to whose inner speech the audience is privy (see ch. 5 below). But typically we only meet narrated actions and reported words. Readers may be inclined to fill such

---

29. For a helpful introduction to narrative criticism, see Mark Allan Powell, "Narrative Criticism," ch. 12 in *Hearing the New Testament: Strategies for Interpretation*, ed. Joel B. Green, 2nd ed. (Grand Rapids: Wm. B. Eerdmans Publishing Co., 2010), 240–58.

30. C. Clifton Black offers a concise sketch of the various approaches to rhetorical study of NT writings; see "Rhetorical Criticism," in *Hearing the New Testament*, ed. Green (2nd ed.), 166–88.

gaps out of their own sense of how and why humans behave as they do. But it is important to respect the way ancient narratives both reveal and conceal information.

Reader-Centered, Cultural-Studies, and Ideological Approaches

These methods shift the center of the interpretive task to the *reader's* side of the text. Location matters: social and cultural location, to be precise. Readers read from *this* place and culture; what do readers bring with them that shapes their response to the text? Here one understands meaning to be created *in front of* the text, in the reader's engagement with the text, out of one's own social location, culture, and political commitments. It is important to acknowledge that *all* interpretation is undertaken from particular social and cultural locations, and it is shaped by ideological concerns and commitments. Although many fields within the humanities have shifted to the language of "area studies" (often geographically defined), it is perhaps still appropriate to identify certain approaches as "ideological" because of the explicitness and centrality of their engagement with these concerns.

Reader-response criticism: not all readers (ancient or contemporary) are the same, and not all readers respond to a text in the same way. Reader-response criticism accepts and embraces the notion that many readers mean many readings and therefore many meanings. There is no elusive holy grail of one normative meaning. To be sure, texts can't mean just *anything*: the interpreter must pay attention to the cues and clues that the text actually presents. But diverse understandings of, and responses to, the same text are to be expected. So readers are honest about what they are bringing to a reading of the text, and this picture will look different from one reader or reading community to the next.

Ideological criticism and cultural studies, including such approaches as feminist criticism, postcolonial criticism, African American liberationist hermeneutics, and gender analysis (e.g., masculinity studies and queer theory), wrestle seriously with social location, formation within specific cultures, and differential access to power when reading the Gospels (or other texts, both ancient and modern). Ideologically oriented analysis of texts is a type of reader-centered criticism that is explicit about the kinds of values and experiences shaping particular reading communities' responses to the Gospels (and other texts). Here I briefly profile four such approaches.

African American liberationist hermeneutics (interpretation) reads the Gospels from the context and experience of African Americans, drawing from African American tradition as a rich cultural resource.[31] So interpreters emphasize biblical themes and texts—and interpretations—that name

---

31. In addition, the experience of both racial and gender oppression by African American women informs a distinct approach: womanist interpretation. For orientation to womanist biblical interpretation, see Nyasha Junior, *An Introduction to Womanist Biblical Interpretation* (Louisville, KY: Westminster John Knox Press, 2015). A recent womanist reading of Mark's Gospel comes from Raquel A. St. Clair, *Call and Consequences: A Womanist Reading of Mark* (Minneapolis: Fortress Press, 2008).

and oppose oppression, especially as generated by racism (and related forms of subjugation—economic, political, etc.). One reads the Gospels out of and in service of a commitment to practices that move toward liberation.[32]

Feminist criticism also advocates interpretive and social practices that foster liberation. The interpreter views biblical texts as patriarchal, shaped by values, beliefs, roles, and practices of a male-centered, male-dominated social world.[33] The text is not "neutral": it expresses the (biased) views and values and serves the interests of history's "winners," thus telling not *the* story but *their* story. So the reader approaches the text with a "hermeneutic of suspicion." But if readers also regard the text as authoritative, as Scripture, they will also engage in a "hermeneutic of retrieval." Among the moves in "retrieval" are these: (1) Revise translations to be more inclusive. (2) Focus on texts with "liberating potential." (3) Bring into the open the hidden women and women's concerns in a text. (4) Expose common (antiwoman = misogynist) misinterpretations of a text (e.g., pejorative depictions of the Samaritan woman in John 4:5–42, or characterizations of the persistent, insistent widow in Luke 18:2–5 as "nagging").

Postcolonial criticism, too, views the text not as neutral but as expressing the (biased) views and values of "history's winners." Such texts—in the hands of persons and groups that enjoy power, wealth, and advantage—can be and often have been read in ways that endorse their views and sanction their position and power. Contemporary readers who come from the social, economic, and political margins will seek to expose the biases and power moves in a text and deconstruct them, so as to produce a counterreading.

Texts coming from dominated groups are particularly interesting. Some are subject, for example, to colonial domination, to occupation by a

32. See, e.g., the landmark work edited by Cain Hope Felder, *Stony the Road We Trod: African American Biblical Interpretation* (Minneapolis: Fortress Press, 1991); the one-volume commentary edited by Brian K. Blount, *True to Our Native Land: An African American New Testament Commentary* (Minneapolis: Fortress Press, 2007); idem, *Go Preach! Mark's Kingdom Message and the Black Church Today* (Maryknoll, NY: Orbis Books, 1998); idem, *Then the Whisper Put on Flesh: New Testament Ethics in an African American Context* (Nashville: Abingdon Press, 2001).

33. For concise introductions to feminist analysis of the NT, see ch. 3 on "Feminist Criticism," by Turid Karlsen Seim, in *Methods for Luke*, ed. Joel B. Green (New York: Cambridge University Press, 2010), 42–73; and ch. 14 on "Feminist Criticism," by F. Scott Spencer, in *Hearing the New Testament*, ed. Green (2nd ed.), 289–325. The scholarship of Elisabeth Schüssler Fiorenza has been particularly influential; see her now-classic work *In Memory of Her: A Feminist Theological Reconstruction of Christian Origins* (New York: Crossroad, 1983). Also see Luise Schottroff, *Lydia's Impatient Sisters: A Feminist Social History of Early Christianity*, trans. Barbara Rumscheidt and Martin Rumscheidt (Louisville, KY: Westminster John Knox Press, 1995). Accessible works on the Gospels include Frances Taylor Gench, *Back to the Well: Women's Encounters with Jesus in the Gospels* (Louisville, KY: Westminster John Knox Press, 2004); and eadem, *Encounters with Jesus: Studies in the Gospel of John* (Louisville, KY: Westminster John Knox Press, 2007); F. Scott Spencer, *Salty Wives, Spirited Mothers, and Savvy Widows: Capable Women of Purpose and Persistence in Luke's Gospel* (Grand Rapids: Wm. B. Eerdmans Publishing Co., 2012).

foreign power. What sense do we make of a demon-possessed person who claims the name "Legion" (Mark 5:9) in a society dominated by imperial Rome and its army legions? Postcolonial readings of the Gospels acknowledge that an oppressed group's resistance to domination is invariably complex and ambiguous, involving not just resistance but also forms of mimicry and ambivalence in relation to the oppressive power.[34] Since the dominant imperial group that figures in the Gospels is the Roman Empire, postcolonial studies of these narratives also draw upon the insights of empire studies.[35]

Gender analysis, including masculinity studies and queer theory, considers the representations of gender in the Gospels within their cultural environment.[36] For example, the normative role of males (or at least elite males) in the Roman world required public contests for honor in which physical and verbal aggression were expected and in which self-control and control of others were key. Females, by contrast, were expected to play compliant and receptive roles. What does the reader of the Gospels make, then, of Jesus' call to male disciples to abandon the quest for status and honor at the expense of others, or of his utter loss of dignity and control in the event of crucifixion? And what of women characters in the Gospels who assert their own initiative, independent of household relations? What, though, of Gospel passages that adopt and perpetuate conventional circumscribed roles for women? How should twenty-first-century readers navigate the path from ancient culture, with its norms of gender and sexuality, to our own space and time? Interpreters employing queer theory recognize and deconstruct or destabilize normative notions of the human and specifically of gender and human sexuality in ancient texts such as the Gospels.

One Reader's Postscript

Can readers have interests that they bring to the text and that shape their reading, their sense-making, and still be open to challenge? How can we avoid simply making the text say what we want and need, or what we always believed it to say? Can we encounter in the text a voice outside ourselves, a dialogue partner that can address us, whether in challenge or comfort?

---

34. Such observations inform my discussion of Mark (ch. 3) and, more extensively, Luke (ch. 5).

35. My analysis of Mark (ch. 3) and Luke (ch. 5) will draw, to some extent, from postcolonial and empire studies.

36. On gender analysis in NT interpretation, see Colleen M. Conway, "The Construction of Gender in the New Testament," in *The Oxford Handbook of Theology, Sexuality, and Gender*, ed. Adrian Thatcher (Oxford: Oxford University Press, 2014). For helpful bibliography on queer theory, see Stephen D. Moore, *The Bible in Theory: Critical and Postcritical Essays*, SBL Resources for Biblical Study 57 (Atlanta: SBL Press, 2010), 304–5. Judith Butler's work has been esp. influential; for her most accessible discussion, see *Undoing Gender* (London: Routledge, 2004). My discussion of Mark (ch. 3) and Luke (ch. 5) will give some attention to perspectives arising from gender analysis.

My individual reading of the Gospels may find helpful challenge and even correction when placed in dialogue with other readings offered by persons whose social location, cultural formation, and methods of analysis differ from mine. Many more voices and more diverse voices are heard at the Gospel interpreters' table in the twenty-first century, and this represents both challenge (multiple approaches and multiple readings!) and opportunity for every reader of the Gospels.

PART II

Four Portraits of Jesus

The New Testament Gospels

3. The Gospel according to Mark

Mark opens with a heading that characterizes the narrative to follow as "the beginning of the good news [gospel = *euangelion*]" (1:1), a term that eventually became a genre designation for the canonical narratives of Jesus' (life and) career, as well as numerous extracanonical texts. For many centuries, although its canonical status was not in question, Mark suffered relative neglect, no doubt in part due to the almost complete incorporation of its content into the Gospel of Matthew and to a lesser degree in Luke. Some perceived its narrative order as problematic and found it to be laced with awkward Greek expressions.[1]

In the last two centuries, however, Mark has garnered increased interest. When the view that this was the earliest Gospel gained currency (see ch. 2 above), historical interest in the life and career of Jesus (as distinct from dogmatic representations) thrust the Markan account into the center of historical investigation of the Gospel tradition. More recently, though, the appeal of this Gospel has primarily been its intriguing literary character. Sparked by the pioneering narrative-critical study by Rhoads and Michie in 1982,[2] a generation of Markan scholarship has riveted attention on literary analysis of the work as a whole. Redaction-critical probes of Mark's calibration of earlier traditions continue,[3] but interpretation has come to center on readings of the received form of the Gospel, whether narrative-critical,[4]

---

1. Early Christian writers give evidence of considerable puzzlement about Mark's arrangement. See n. 22 below. On the "clumsy" Greek constructions in Mark, see John C. Meagher, *Clumsy Construction in Mark's Gospel: A Critique of Form- and Redaktionsgeschichte*, Toronto Studies in Theology (Toronto: Edwin Mellen, 1979).

2. David Rhoads and Donald Michie, *Mark as Story: An Introduction to the Narrative of a Gospel* (Philadelphia: Fortress Press, 1982). Joined in the 2nd ed. by Joanna Dewey; the book is now in its 3rd ed. (2012).

3. Pioneered by Willi Marxsen, *Mark the Evangelist: Studies on the Redaction-History of the Gospel*, trans. James Boyce et al. (Nashville: Abingdon Press, 1969; German orig., 1956); and exemplified recently in the commentary by Joel Marcus, *Mark: A New Translation with Introduction and Commentary*, AB 27–27A (New Haven, CT: Yale University Press, 2000–2009); and the work of William R. Telford (see his sketch of redaction-critical approaches to Mark in *Writing on the Gospel of Mark*, Guides to Advanced Biblical Research 1 [Dorset, UK: Deo, 2009], 57–63). For incisive critique of the application of redaction-critical methods to Mark, see C. Clifton Black, *The Disciples according to Mark: Markan Redaction in Current Debate*, 2nd ed. (Grand Rapids: Wm. B. Eerdmans Publishing Co., 2012).

4. E.g., Robert C. Tannehill, "The Disciples in Mark: The Function of a Narrative Role," *JR* 57 (1977): 386–405; idem, "The Gospel of Mark as Narrative Christology," *Semeia* 16 (1979): 57–95; Jack D. Kingsbury, *The Christology of Mark* (Philadelphia: Fortress Press, 1983); Francis

literary-historical,[5] or reader-response.[6] In its latest turn, Markan studies have attended to the dynamics of its oral performance[7] and to its ideological dimensions and force, including explicitly sociopolitical interpretations,[8] sociolinguistic (cultural studies) interpretation from an African American perspective,[9] postcolonial readings,[10] and feminist and gender analysis.[11] These ideologically framed approaches have revived concern with the historical contexts that shaped the Markan rendition of the Gospel story, though with a focus quite different from that of older historical investigations that sought to reconstruct strata in the pre-Markan tradition.

The approach of this chapter, as indicated in chapter 2, will be primarily narrative-critical—a reading of the Markan narrative in approximately its received, canonical form, though with the significant exception that I will interpret the Gospel on the basis of the shorter ending at 16:8 (further discussion below). At the same time, as I read Mark I will draw attention to historical-contextual and ideological concerns such as gender, power, and the imperial setting of the narrative, especially as these interests will help fund chapter 7's discussion of contemporary appropriation of the Gospel presentations of Jesus' ministry.

Historical Questions

Chapter 2 has already provided general orientation to the genre of the Gospels and to the process of their formation, as well as the relationships among them. A brief sketch must suffice here.

J. Moloney, *The Gospel of Mark: A Commentary* (Peabody, MA: Hendrickson Publishers, 2002); R. Alan Culpepper, *Mark*, SHBC (Macon, GA: Smyth & Helwys, 2007); Elizabeth Struthers Malbon, *Mark's Jesus: Characterization as Narrative Christology* (Waco, TX: Baylor University Press, 2009).

5. E.g., Mary Ann Tolbert, *Sowing the Gospel: Mark's World in Literary-Historical Perspective* (Minneapolis: Fortress Press, 1989).

6. E.g., Robert M. Fowler, *Let the Reader Understand: Reader-Response Criticism and the Gospel of Mark* (Minneapolis: Fortress Press, 1991); Ira Brent Driggers, *Following God through Mark: Theological Tension in the Second Gospel* (Louisville, KY: Westminster John Knox Press, 2007).

7. E.g., Whitney Shiner, *Proclaiming the Gospel: First-Century Performance of Mark* (Harrisburg, PA: Trinity Press International, 2003).

8. E.g., Ched Myers, *Binding the Strong Man: A Political Reading of Mark's Story of Jesus*, 20th anniversary ed. (Maryknoll, NY: Orbis Books, 2008; orig., 1988); Herman C. Waetjen, *A Reordering of Power: A Socio-Political Reading of Mark's Gospel* (Minneapolis: Fortress Press, 1989).

9. E.g., Brian K. Blount, *Go Preach! Mark's Kingdom Message and the Black Church Today* (Maryknoll, NY: Orbis Books, 1998).

10. E.g., Tat-siong Benny Liew, *Politics of Parousia: Reading Mark Inter(con)textually*, BibIntS 42 (Leiden: Brill, 1999); Hans Leander, *Discourses of Empire: The Gospel of Mark from a Postcolonial Perspective*, SemeiaSt71 (Atlanta: SBL Press, 2013).

11. E.g., Amy-Jill Levine and Marianne Blickenstaff, eds., *A Feminist Companion to Mark* (Sheffield: Sheffield Academic, 2001).

Who?

By convention, this Gospel is attributed to Mark—traditionally (from the mid-second c. onward) the John Mark known to us from Acts 15:22–40, assumed to be the same person as the Mark of the Epistles (Phlm 24; Col 4:10; 2 Tim 4:11; 1 Pet 5:13). As far as we know, Mark was not a prominent early Christian leader, nor is he identified as one of the apostles, so it is plausible that the author indeed carried the name Mark. It is also possible that it was the Mark whom New Testament epistles associate with both Paul and Peter. (The association with Peter became important as this Gospel gained and maintained canonical standing.)[12] Yet none of this is certain, especially given the common use of the name Mark in the Greco-Roman world. In any event, the implied author of the narrative as we have it—the sort of author who would compose such a story—is our central interest here and the authorship question that matters for interpretation.

When and Where?

In agreement with recent and current Markan scholarship, I assign this Gospel's composition to a date shortly before or just after the fall of Jerusalem and the destruction of the temple in 70 CE, during the period of the catastrophic Jewish rebellion against Roman occupation (66–73/74 CE). The emphasis in Mark on adversity and persecution of Jesus' followers (e.g., 4:16–17; 8:34–38; 9:42–48; 10:17–31, 38–39; 13:9–13, 19) fits this setting but by no means requires it; nevertheless, details in the discourse of Mark 13 (esp. vv. 14–19) make the best sense in that context.[13]

While the traditional setting for Mark's Gospel is Rome, other locations have been suggested, among them Galilee and southern Syria.[14] Lack of precision in geographical references to Palestine (e.g., in 5:1; 6:53; 7:31; 8:22; 10:1) does not rule out composition in and for communities located near Galilee. After all, Mark and his contemporaries used neither printed maps nor GPS devices.

---

12. For a sample of patristic statements regarding Mark, including his association with (the apostolic teaching of) Peter, see, e.g., Irenaeus, *Haer.* 3.1.1; Tertullian, *Marc.* 5.3–4; Eusebius, *Hist. eccl.* 2.15.1–2 and 6.14.5–7 (on Clement of Alexandria); 3.39.14–15 (on Papias, mid-2nd c.); 6.25.3–6 (on Origen of Alexandria); Anti-Marcionite Gospel Prologue; Jerome, *Comm. Matt.*, Preface. Thorough discussion of the developing traditions regarding the authorship of Mark is provided by C. Clifton Black, *Mark: Images of an Apostolic Interpreter* (Columbia: University of South Carolina Press, 1994).

13. See the more detailed discussion in Marcus, *Mark*, 1:37–39.

14. For defense of the Roman destination of Mark, see, e.g., Ernest Best, *Following Jesus: Discipleship in the Gospel of Mark*, JSNTSup 4 (Sheffield: JSOT Press, 1981); Brian J. Incigneri, *The Gospel to the Romans: The Setting and Rhetoric of Mark's Gospel*, BibIntS 65 (Leiden: Brill, 2003). Favoring Galilee are Marxsen, *Mark the Evangelist*; Myers, *Binding the Strong Man*; and more recently, Hendrika Nicoline Roskam, *The Purpose of the Gospel of Mark in Its Historical and Social Context*, NovTSup 114 (Leiden: Brill, 2004). Arguing for (rural and small-village) southern Syria: Howard Clark Kee, *Community of the New Age: Studies in Mark's Gospel* (Philadelphia: Westminster Press, 1977), 100–105; Marcus, *Mark*, 1:30–37. See further the discussion in Boring, *Mark: A Commentary*, NTL (Louisville, KY: Westminster John Knox Press, 2006), 17–20.

Bauckham suggests that it is a mistake to imagine Mark and the other Gospels as addressed to particular early Christian communities; instead, from the beginning these were intended for a broad readership transcending specific locales.[15] Certainly the substantial incorporation of Mark into Matthew and Luke ensured that wider dissemination of Markan materials would occur beyond its first "home," and the preservation of all four canonical narratives attests to their experienced value for the wider emerging Christian movement. Nevertheless, there is no reason to discount the shaping role of the author's own setting and his community's circumstances, as evidenced by the story as told, even if there is no possibility of determining such historical details with precision.

Whether in southern Syria, not far from Jesus' Galilean turf and from the social and political turmoil there and in Judea/Jerusalem in the decade of the 60s CE, or in Rome amid the hostility overtaking Christian inhabitants there in the mid-60s—Mark's narrative is shaped by and speaks to the experience of a world dominated by the Roman Empire. Both the specific markers of hostility and potential persecution and the general issues associated with imperial control bear on the reading of this Gospel.

What kind of writing is Mark? What conventions does it employ to shape its audience's expectations for hearing it? Various attempts to specify the genre of Mark have been made. Genre designations proposed range from (tragic) drama[16] to epic;[17] and from popular novel, whether Hellenistic or Jewish,[18] to biography[19] and "eschatological historical monograph."[20] Others insist that Mark does not conform to any then-existing literary genre and that the author has instead fashioned a new genre, the *Christian gospel*, fashioned specifically for the catechetical and liturgical settings of early Christian communities.[21]

If Mark's narrative, typically heard in oral performance in public

---

15. Richard Bauckham, "For Whom Were Gospels Written?," in *The Gospels for All Christians: Rethinking the Gospel Audiences*, ed. Richard Bauckham (Grand Rapids: Wm. B. Eerdmans Publishing Co., 1998), 9–48; see critique of this argument in Marcus, *Mark*, 1:25–28.

16. Mary Ann Beavis, *Mark*, Paideia (Grand Rapids: Wm. B. Eerdmans Publishing Co., 2011), 16–17.

17. Dennis R. MacDonald, *The Homeric Epics and the Gospel of Mark* (New Haven, CT: Yale University Press, 2000).

18. Hellenistic novel: Tolbert, *Sowing the Gospel*, 48–79; Jewish novel: Michael E. Vines, *The Problem of Markan Genre: The Gospel of Mark and the Jewish Novel*, AcBib (Leiden: Brill, 2002).

19. Charles H. Talbert, *What Is a Gospel? The Genre of the Canonical Gospels* (Philadelphia: Fortress Press, 1977); Richard A. Burridge, *What Are the Gospels? A Comparison with Graeco-Roman Biography*, SNTSMS 70 (Cambridge: Cambridge University Press, 1992).

20. Adela Yarbro Collins, *Mark: A Commentary*, Hermeneia (Minneapolis: Fortress Press, 2007), 42–43

21. Among many others: Moloney, *Gospel of Mark*, 16; Boring, *Mark*, 8–9. For a compact summary of the history of research on the question of Mark's genre, see William R. Telford, ed., *The Interpretation of Mark*, 2nd ed., Studies in New Testament Interpretation (Edinburgh: T&T Clark, 1995), 15–17, 51–52 nn. 54–65.

gatherings of early Christian groups (whether for purposes of worship or instruction), bears some trademark features of biography (though without the sort of information about origins and life beginnings ordinarily supplied in *bioi*, "lives" or biographies), of tragic drama, and of popular novels, earliest audiences of the Gospel would have experienced it as not entirely strange and unfamiliar. Nevertheless, genre clearly bends in Mark's telling the story of Jesus, as the *good news* assumes shape in a narrative full of the unexpected. If this is the *beginning* of the good news (1:1), that is so in part because the work of grasping it—and enacting, embodying it—must be an ongoing project for Mark's audiences, whether in the first century or the twenty-first.

Literary Design and Techniques of Narration	Geography and spatial movement suggest a macrostructuring of the Markan narrative, with an opening prologue and closing (open-ended) epilogue providing an outer frame:

1:1	Book title or heading
1:2–13	Prologue: Introducing the Baptizer John and Jesus and placing them and Mark's audience on "the way"
1:14–8:21	Jesus' activity as authoritative teacher and healer—welcomed and resisted—in and near **Galilee**
8:22–10:52	Transitional narrative, on the way from Galilee to Jerusalem
11:1–13:37	Jesus' activity as authoritative teacher—welcomed and resisted—in **Jerusalem**
14:1–15:47	Passion narrative: Jesus prepares for death and meets arrest, interrogation, and execution
16:1–8	Epilogue: Back to Galilee, and beyond

This movement from Galilee to Jerusalem is crucial to the plot of Mark's narrative and to its interpretation.

Whatever the problems with narrative sequence that concerned some patristic writers,[22] the Markan narrative offers several additional structuring patterns that enhance audience engagement with the story.

---

22. Pointedly asserted in Eusebius's report of a (no longer extant) 2nd-c. writing in which Papias claims that "Mark became Peter's interpreter [*hermeneutēs*] and wrote accurately whatever he remembered, but not in order [*ou mentoi taxei*], of the things said or done by the Lord," and that Peter's recollections, captured by Mark, were themselves not "a systematic arrangement [*syntaxis*] of the Lord's oracles" (*Eccl. hist.* 3.19.15; ET in Black, *Mark: Images of an Apostolic Interpreter*, 83). Ben Witherington III provides a concise list of stylistic peculiarities of Mark's Gospel, including clumsy Greek expressions, in *The Gospel of Mark: A Socio-Rhetorical Commentary* (Grand Rapids: Wm. B. Eerdmans Publishing Co., 2001), 18–19.

Techniques of Narration in Mark
• Conflict scenes
• Repetition
• Interweaving episodes (intercalation)
• Rhetorical strategies of indirection: ambiguity, metaphor, irony, paradox
• Style of narration: Voice and viewpoint

Conflict Scenes

Repeating scenes of conflict between Jesus and outsider critics give shape and direction to the narrative.[23] Early in the itinerant Galilean mission, a cycle of conflict stories (2:1–3:6) presents the escalating opposition Jesus' activity provokes. With stunning swiftness, debates—over such questions as the authority to pronounce forgiveness of sins, actions permitted and forbidden on the Sabbath, and acceptable meal companions—lead to the resolve of some of Jesus' opponents (Pharisees and Herodians) to seek his death (3:6); this is an ominous foreshadowing of Jesus' ultimate destiny (anticipated already by Jesus himself in his saying about a departed bridegroom in 2:20). Conflict briefly resumes in 3:22–30, sparked by divergent assessments of Jesus' power to expel demons, an exchange framed by mutually distancing moves on the part of Jesus and members of his family (3:21, 31–35). Others close to Jesus—residents of his home village of Nazareth—rebuff his ministry, which as a result loses healing efficacy (6:1–6).

Conflict with outsiders to Jesus' band is reengaged in 7:1–13, this time centering on purity concerns (hand-washing, clean and unclean foods); here Jesus' critique of the Pharisees' oral tradition sets up broader teaching for the crowd, to the effect that concern should rest less with contamination from what one ingests than with the evil emanating from within a person (7:14–23). As the setting of Jesus' activity shifts to Jerusalem, conflict dominates the account (11:15–12:44). This last round of debates, set in the Jerusalem temple and initiated by Jesus himself with his provocative disruption of temple commerce, culminates in his arrest and execution by order of the Roman governor (chs. 14–15), but not before a stinging prophetic oracle by Jesus forecasts the continuation of hostile conflict and its ultimate resolution in the eschatological future (ch. 13).

23. These conflict stories represent *chreiai*, "concise reminiscences" of sayings or actions that exemplify character. Learning to compose such *chreiai* was a basic ingredient in one's education in rhetoric in the Greco-Roman world, as attested in the *progymnasmata* (handbooks for teaching composition and argumentation) of, e.g., Aelius Theon (late 1st c. CE) and Hermogenes (late 2nd c. CE). For a compact introduction to the topic, see Ronald Hock, "Chreia," *ABD* 1:912–14.

Repetition of scenes is not limited to conflict, nor is conflict between Jesus and other characters restricted to outsider critics—or to the menacing forces of evil (e.g., unclean spirits) whose potent opposition to God's reign lies beneath the other, more mundane forms of conflict in the story. Much of the repetition within the narrative foregrounds conflict between Jesus and his chosen disciples. They prove to be slow and resistant learners, yet time and again tutoring Mark's audience in the way of discipleship, despite themselves.

The faith of the disciples undergoes dramatic testing on a storm-tossed lake not once but twice (4:35–41; 6:45–52). On the first such occasion, one may be inclined to excuse the disciples' terror, even upon hearing Jesus' stinging questions: "Why are you afraid? Have you still no faith?" (4:40). But again the second time? The narrator rather than Jesus delivers the appraisal of their performance: "And they were utterly astounded, for they did not understand about the loaves, but their hearts were hardened" (6:51–52).

The disciples are present for two remarkable meals on the fly, when Jesus, moved by compassion for the large crowds gathered to hear his teaching and experience his healing benefaction, supervises the extraordinary feeding of five thousand, then four thousand (6:33–44; 8:1–9). Even after witnessing the first feeding miracle, the disciples are clueless about how to provide the food needed for so many people (8:4; cf. 6:35–37). Memory of the feeding miracles and the setting of a boat on the lake are fused in 8:13–21, in which Jesus focuses attention on the significance of the numbers involved (5 loaves, 5,000 people, 12 baskets of leftovers; 7 loaves, 4,000 people, 7 baskets), culminating in repeated indictment of the disciples' failure to comprehend. Given the equally emphatic and enigmatic appeal to these numbers, do readers join the disciples in cognitive puzzlement?[24]

The disciples prove to be slow, indeed resistant, learners also in two scenes in which Jesus embraces children as exemplars of the reign of God (9:35–37; 10:13–16). Intent on status maintenance, the disciples express values that collide with the values and commitments of the reign of God, as Jesus enacts it.

Repeating scenes that foreground conflict between Jesus and the disciples tutor Mark's audience in right understanding of Jesus' identity and vocation, and in the implications for the disciples' vocation. Each of three forecasts that the Human One (Son of Humanity)[25] will suffer is followed

---

24. See Robert M. Fowler, "In the Boat with Jesus: Imagining Ourselves in Mark's Story," in *Mark as Story: Retrospect and Prospect,* ed. Kelly R. Iverson and Christopher W. Skinner, SBLRBS 65 (Atlanta: SBL Press, 2011), 233–58.

25. The Greek expression *ho huios tou anthrōpou,* traditionally translated "the Son of Man" (KJV, RSV), is rendered "the Human One" in CEB. To refer to someone as the "son of the human [being]" is to assign him the distinguishing character of "human being" (hence, Human One). This prominent self-designation of Jesus in the Gospels draws from scriptural sources such as Ps 8:4; Ezek 2:1 (and many other occurrences in Ezekiel: *ben 'adam* in Hebrew); and esp. Dan 7:13–14. The usage in the apocalyptic writing Daniel informs such passages as Mark 14:62; however, Jesus esp. invokes the image of Human One to give emphasis to his vocation of suffering (8:31; 9:31; 10:33–34).

by an expression of the disciples' resistance or incomprehension (8:31–33; 9:30–34; 10:32–45). In a pivotal recognition scene in the very center of the narrative,[26] Peter applies an appropriate label to Jesus, "Messiah" (Christ) (8:29), but the reciprocal rebukes that immediately ensue, when Jesus binds his messianic role to the vocation of rejection, suffering, and death, show that clarity of christological vision will not come quickly or easily to the disciples (8:30–33)—not, indeed, until after Jesus' crucifixion and divine vindication through resurrection (see 9:9–13), though insight will struggle with fear even then (16:8).

Two accounts in which Jesus restores sight to blind men—the first healing requiring two stages of coming to sight (8:22–26), the second enacting a commitment to "follow" Jesus "on the way" that is still elusive for the disciples (10:46–52)—play metaphorically in the narrative. The physical sight and blindness of these two men illustrate the insight and incomprehension of the disciples with regard both to Jesus' mission and to their own mission as his followers. These two encounters with men whose sight Jesus restores frame the transitional "way" to Jerusalem, with its threefold passion predictions and correlated expressions of the disciples' failure to accept or understand.

Effective use of scene repetition enhances an audience's grasp and appreciation of themes that are reinforced through recapitulation. At the same time, rehearsal is sometimes accompanied by variation in detail that piques and sustains audience interest: What is different this time? What does the variation signify? For example, the two mass feeding episodes share the same basic pattern, yet the settings, the numbers involved (people, available food, quantity left over), and other details in the stories vary.[27] Mark's audience may be excused for puzzling over these variations, which assuredly spark and sustain interest, all the more since Jesus apparently expects the disciples to comprehend their meaningfulness (8:19–21).

Passion Predictions: Correlating the Path of Messiah and Disciples

- **The Human One must suffer:**
  — 8:31–32; 9:31; 10:32–34

- **Disciples fail to understand:**
  — 8:32–33; 9:32–34; 10:35–40

- **Jesus links the paths of Messiah and followers:**
  — 8:34–9:1: self-renunciation and cross bearing
  — 9:35–37: renunciation of status seeking
  — 10:41–45: renunciation of status seeking for the sake of other-service

---

26. For the view that this passage constitutes the recognition scene conventional in Greek tragedy, see Beavis, *Mark*, 25–26, 121–22, 133. It is striking, however, that the recognition scene in Mark 8 conceals as much as it discloses.

27. There are fascinating differences in narration even for a detail common to the two stories:

The threefold predictions of Jesus' passion and resurrection as the Human One (Son of Humanity) offer a second instructive example of repetition with a difference. The basic pattern of the three scenes is the same:

- Jesus prophesies the future suffering and death of the Human One, who "after three days will rise again" (8:31–32; 9:31; 10:32–34).
- The prediction leads immediately to a depiction of incomprehension on the part of the disciples (8:32–33; 9:32–34; 10:35–40).
- In monologue or dialogue, further teaching by Jesus draws correlations between the Human One's vocation of suffering and the pattern of life to which disciples are called (8:34–9:1, self-renunciation and cross bearing; 9:35–37, renunciation of status seeking; 10:41–45, renunciation of status seeking for the sake of serving others).

The core message is clear, with regard both to the identity, mission, and destiny of Jesus and to their implications for the vocation and mission of his followers. The threefold repetition concerns more than the obtuseness of the disciples. Their need for extended coaching serves to educate Mark's audience. Yet there is more: the messianic vocation of Jesus plus the manner of life and the vocation of his followers run so dramatically counter to cultural norms and expectations of their social world that this calling is scarcely easy to grasp or to embrace.

Nevertheless, variations on the theme are intriguing. A comparison of the three episodes suggests the meaningfulness of the differing details:

Scene 1 (8:27–9:1)
- *Location*: region of Caesarea Philippi
- *Characters*: disciples for private conversation (8:27–33), then the crowds (8:34–9:1)
- *Motif of silence or secrecy*: follows Jesus' prediction of his suffering and resurrection
- *Conflict between Jesus and the disciples*:
  — Question and answer prompts Peter to affirm Jesus' messianic identity.
  — This affirmation leads to Jesus' order of silence and mutual rebukes.
  — Conflict over christological understanding is thus at the heart of the passage.

---

that Jesus is motivated to act by compassion. In the first scene, the *narrator* mentions Jesus' compassion for a leaderless (shepherdless) people (flock), which prompts him to *teach* (6:34). In the second scene, Jesus' compassion arises from his awareness of the *physical hunger* of the large crowds and their lack of food, and the narrator presents this statement by Jesus *in direct speech* (8:2–3).

- *Future awaiting the Human One (Son of Humanity)*:
  — He must undergo great suffering, and be rejected
  — by the elders, the chief priests, and the scribes,
  — and be killed [passive voice],
  — and after three days rise again. (v. 30)

Scene 2 (9:30–50)

- *Location*: Galilee, then a house in Capernaum
- *Characters*: disciples throughout (in a house for vv. 33–50)
- *Motif of silence or secrecy*: begins the episode, in connection with Jesus' travels
- *Conflict between Jesus and the disciples*:
  — follows the oracle of Jesus that predicts his death;
  — centers first on the disciples' preoccupation with status seeking, which turns Jesus' message on its head (vv. 33–37), then on the concern of some disciles to draw clear boundaries between Jesus' band and others (vv. 38–41)
- *Future awaiting the Human One (Son of Humanity)*:
  — He will be betrayed into human hands [note the generic identification],
  — and they will kill him [active voice],
  — and three days after being killed, he will rise again. (v. 31)

Scene 3 (10:32–45)

- *Location*: the road (way) to Jerusalem
- *Characters*: the Twelve
- *Motif of silence or secrecy*: replaced by fear of the way to Jerusalem
- *Conflict between Jesus and the disciples*:
  — follows the oracle (as in scene 2);
  — centers again (as in scene 2) on the disciples' status and power seeking, which shows how far removed they are from grasping and accepting Jesus' message.
- *Future awaiting the Human One (Son of Humanity)*:
  — He will be handed over to the chief priests and the scribes,
  — and they will condemn him to death;
  — then they will hand him over to the Gentiles;
  — they will mock him, and spit upon him, and flog him,
  — and kill him [active voice];
  — and after three days he will rise again. (vv. 33–34)

Among the numerous differences in story details, I draw attention to only three. (1) Perhaps most obvious is the expansion of the third prediction of the Human One's suffering, with the first mention of Gentile involvement (thus, as Mark's audience later discovers, anticipating the presence of the Roman governor and soldiers in the passion narrative), the detail of mocking and physical abuse, and the twofold "handing over" image (*paradidōmi*), anticipating the repeated use of this image in the passion narrative (14:10, 11, 18, 21; 15:1, 15; cf. 13:9, 12). (2) The motif of the disciples' fear replaces the motif of Jesus' silencing of his prophetic teaching in this third scene. (3) Finally, the shift in the basis for conflict between Jesus and the disciples—from misperceiving Jesus' messianic role in relation to suffering (scene 1) to the disciples' inability to jettison conventional aspirations for power, advantage, and status (scenes 2–3)—alerts Mark's audience that acceptance of Jesus' mission and his call to discipleship is about more than having the right Christology. It also manifests itself in commitment to distinctive cultural values and social practices that align with those of God's reign.

Intercalation

A distinctive feature of Mark's narrative construction is the intercalation, or sandwiching, of scenes: the narrator introduces one scene (A) but suspends it through the insertion of a second scene (B) before the plot of the first is completed or resolved (A′). Mark's audience is thereby prompted to reflect on ways in which the two interlocking vignettes are mutually instructive.

Two accounts of the healing of female characters who do not otherwise figure in the narrative are interwoven in 5:21–43. A man of high social status, the synagogue leader Jairus, approaches Jesus and pleads for the healer's intervention before his gravely ill daughter dies. While Jesus is en route to Jairus's home, however, a woman who has for twelve years suffered from a chronic bleeding disorder interrupts the journey. The narrator observes that the treatments she has received from many doctors have left her both impoverished and physically worsened (v. 26). She approaches Jesus from behind and surreptitiously touches his cloak (v. 27). The daughter of Jairus will need to wait; suspense builds as attention shifts to this bold, anonymous woman and to Jesus' conversation first with his disciples, then with the woman (vv. 30–34). Her faith, on full display despite her attempts at stealth, has generated healing, and so Jesus dismisses her "in peace" (v. 34). His parting words address the woman as "daughter," which returns Mark's audience to the concern with which the passage began: Jairus's daughter.

The delay has proved costly, however, as messengers from the home bring news of her death (v. 35). Deterred by neither the assembled mourners' wailing nor their mocking laughter (vv. 39–40), Jesus enters, accompanied by the parents and three disciples (Peter, James, and John), addresses the child with a command spoken in Aramaic and translated for the benefit of the Markan audience (which evidently includes persons who do not speak Aramaic): *Talitha cum* ("Little girl, get up!" [v. 41]). Only now does the narrator mention that she is twelve years old, binding her story even more closely to that of the impoverished woman whose bleeding ailment has lasted the entire lifetime of the young woman. The episode concludes on two strange notes: Jesus directs that the event not be made known (scarcely imaginable) and (more reasonably) instructs that the young woman receive nourishment.

Interweaving Scenes: Help for Two Female Characters

- A plea from Jairus for his sick daughter. (5:21–24)
- But wait a minute! A woman with a bleeding disorder halts the journey to Jairus's home and finds healing. (5:25–34)
- Healing for the daughter of Jairus, too. (5:35–43)

Another parade example of the intercalation technique presents the first separate mission activity of the disciples and hints at the danger that will eventually attend it. Jesus first called disciples (illustrated in 1:16–20) and later set twelve apart for a distinctive role as his agents in both proclamation and healing (as his "apostles" = "sent ones"; 3:13–19). In 6:7–13 he dispatches the Twelve on a mission of their own, bearing the very authority to preach and heal that marks his ministry. While the narrator reports their success as healers (v. 13), their return to report the news to Jesus (vv. 30–32) is delayed until after a lengthy account of the arrest and death of John the Baptizer at the reluctant order of Herod Antipas, tetrarch of Galilee (vv. 14–29).[28] Especially in the immediate aftermath of Jesus' cold reception in Nazareth (6:1–6), the Markan audience can scarcely miss the signals of future hostility awaiting Jesus' emissaries, a motif that the eschatological discourse will accent sharply (13:9–13).

Interweaving Two Scenes: (Disciples') Mission and (Herod's) Madness

- Jesus sends the Twelve in mission. (6:7–13)
- Interlude: Herod Antipas has John the Baptizer killed. (6:14–29)
- Mission report from the returning disciples. (6:30–32)

A more complex pattern of intercalation orients readers to Jesus' teaching mission in Jerusalem and its temple. The narrator interweaves multiple scenes featuring a hungry Jesus' displeasure with a fruitless fig tree (11:12–14, 20–23) and his outrage at a temple institution that has abandoned its primary role as "a house of prayer for all the nations" and instead has become a "den of robbers" (11:17, citing Isa 56:7; Jer 7:11; temple scenes in Mark 11:11, 15–19; more expansively in 11:27–12:44). The incongruity of Jesus' harsh assault on the fig tree when "it was not the season for figs" (11:13) impels Mark's audience to ponder the interaction between fig tree and temple, each

---

28. People associated with the court of Herod Antipas (Herodians) have already figured among Jesus' menacing enemies (3:6).

the target of word and gesture expressing harsh judgment. The demise of the tree figures metaphorically—and tragically?—as a picture of the temple's approaching demise, spoken in direct prophetic speech by Jesus in 13:1–2.

Although Mark has provided several previews of Jesus' impending death as the terminus of his "way" to Jerusalem (8:31; 9:31; 10:33–34, 45; cf. 2:20; 3:6; 9:9–13), chapter 14 opens with interwoven scenes that accelerate the plot movement toward Jesus' death and specify how it will be orchestrated—in stark contrast to an act of devotion and honor on the part of an anonymous woman. The narrator makes Mark's audience privy to the deliberations within Jerusalem's halls of power: the leading priests and scribes are intent on having Jesus killed, but the prospect of rioting at the Passover festival leads them to move surreptitiously (14:1–2). Suspense builds, though, when the scene shifts to the home of "Simon the leper" (v. 3). There a woman pours a large amount of expensive spikenard oil over Jesus' head—an extravagant waste, prompting stinging criticism from observers (vv. 4–5). Jesus, the recipient of the woman's act of honor—is this intended as a royal, messianic anointing?[29]—in turn defends her honor in the face of public rebuke and assigns meaning to her act. Whatever she may have intended, in Jesus' interpretation the anointing is (re)framed as a pre-death anointing for burial (vv. 6, 8). Acts of generosity toward the poor and proclamation of the gospel message—and with it, memory of this woman's act—will continue into the future (vv. 7, 9), but this is an unrepeatable moment. What is important right now is that Jesus is on the verge of death.

The narrator then immediately follows Judas, "one of the Twelve," as he makes his way to the leading priests and strikes the deal that will ensure Jesus' arrest (vv. 10–11), picking up the plot left hanging at 14:2. The juxtaposition of the woman's anointing of Jesus and Judas's move to betray him suggests a connection between the two, but the precise connection is a narrative gap left for Mark's audience to fill.[30]

Interweaving Two Scenes: Peter and Jesus Interrogated

- Peter waits in the high priest's courtyard. (14:54)
- Jesus is questioned by the high priest. (14:55–65)
- Peter three times denies his discipleship. (14:66–72)

---

29. Like Mark, Matt 26:7 narrates an extravagant anointing of Jesus' *head* by a woman; in Luke 7:38 and John 12:3 Jesus' *feet* are anointed (the woman is given the name "Mary" in John 12).

30. John 12:4–6 identifies Judas (Iscariot) as the one who protests against the anointing woman's wasteful gesture, a detail that would (if present in Mark's account) bind the act of betrayal more closely to the anointing scene. The Johannine narrator also attributes the objection by Judas to his avaricious greed, but this character element, too, is missing from Mark's account.

In a final example of the intercalation technique, the narrator inserts Jesus' courageous witness under interrogation by the high priest (14:55–65) within a scene that first deposits Simon Peter in the courtyard of the high priest (v. 54). Suspense regarding Peter's performance thus builds as Jesus undergoes hostile examination, although Jesus' earlier prediction leaves little doubt about the outcome, given his oft-demonstrated prescience (on the forecast of Peter's failure, recall 14:27–31). Returning to Peter and the courtyard of the high priest, the narrator dramatically and with increasing intensity relates this disciple's threefold denial of any connection to Jesus (vv. 66–72)—thus putting the lie to his professed commitment to undying loyalty (14:29, 31) and fulfilling Jesus' prediction of his and his fellow disciples' desertion (14:27, 30). Jesus, not his closest followers, models the quality of witness under duress to which Mark's audience, too, is summoned (cf. 13:9–13).

Rhetorical Strategies of Indirection

The Markan narrator employs several techniques of indirect communication, each of which involves a measure of textual indeterminacy or polyvalence (i.e., multiple potential meanings) that requires the active engagement of readers to discern meaning. Fowler examines the ways in which ambiguity,[31] irony, metaphor,[32] and paradox[33] shape readers' experience of the narrative.[34] In this brief treatment, I will focus on irony, especially in the Markan passion narrative.

Irony

Irony is at play when the narrative presents two levels of meaning or significance, when there is tension or dissonance or incongruity between them, and when some (characters, the reader) recognize the tension and discern a level of meaning of which others ("victims" of the irony) are unaware. In Mark, typically, the audience is equipped to discern meaning at a level

31. E.g., God's reign pictured as having come in/with power (meaning exactly what?) within the lifetime of some of the listening disciples (9:1); Jesus' direction to pay to both Caesar and God what is due them (12:17).

32. E.g., the enigmatic parables in ch. 4; the interacting metaphors of fire and salt (9:49–50); the hyperbolic metaphor of a camel navigating a needle's eye (10:25).

33. E.g., preserving life by forfeiting it (8:35); the greatness of the least (10:43–44). Laura C. Sweat probes the presentation of God in Mark's narrative by analyzing the use of paradox (*The Theological Role of Paradox in the Gospel of Mark*, LNTS [London: T&T Clark, 2013]).

34. See Robert M. Fowler, "The Rhetoric of Direction and Indirection in the Gospel of Mark," in *The Interpretation of Mark*, ed. Telford, 207–27 (orig. published in *Semeia* 48 [1989]: 115–34); idem, *Let the Reader Understand: Reader-Response Criticism and the Gospel of Mark* (Minneapolis: Fortress Press, 1991), 155–94. On irony, see also Jerry Camery-Hoggatt, *Irony in Mark's Gospel*, SNTSMS 72 (Cambridge: Cambridge University Press, 1992). The examples listed in the notes just above are my selection. Fowler (*Let the Reader Understand*, 11–14, 156–58, 164–66) explains the distinction between verbal irony (in the speech of characters) and dramatic irony (a type of situational irony in which readers perceive incongruity between what happens in the story and their understanding of it; i.e., there is incongruity between story and discourse).

not available to or grasped by characters in the story. Nowhere is this more evident than in the passion narrative. The interweaving of Peter's threefold denial with the council's interrogation of Jesus, as we have seen, highlights the fulfillment of Jesus' prophecy that Peter would deny him before the second cockcrow. When soldiers mock Jesus, therefore, blindfolding him and ordering him to "prophesy" (14:65), the audience immediately witnesses the confirmation of Jesus' prophetic discernment (in vv. 66–72) and so gets (catches) what the soldiers fail to see: Jesus is indeed an authentic prophet.

Primarily, though, it is the peculiar character of Jesus' royal status and role that creates irony in Mark 15.[35] Repeatedly the title "king" attaches to Jesus, but no one who calls Jesus king believes it to be true, though it does appear to be the material basis for the death sentence (i.e., sedition): spoken by Pilate four times (15:2, 9, 12, 26), by soldiers mocking Jesus after Pilate's crucifixion order (vv. 17–19), and by elite priests and scribes ridiculing Jesus at the cross (v. 32). Mark's audience knows better. Jesus has questioned the association between the Messiah and Davidic descent (12:35–37), and he has repeatedly enforced silence with regard to his status as Messiah or Son of God (3:11–12; 8:29–30; 9:30–31; cf. 1:24–25; 9:9). But from 1:1 onward, readers have been tutored by the narrator (1:1), by Peter (though with only partial insight: 8:29, 32–33), by the divine voice (1:11; 9:7–8), and eventually by Jesus himself (14:61–62); therefore they know that Jesus is truly the Messiah, the Son of God, and as such the one with royal authority within the realm of God he has come both to announce and to inaugurate (see below). The incongruity remains, however, of a king who wears a crown composed of thorns (15:17), whose coronation is a crucifixion. The centurion, having witnessed the mode of Jesus' dying, calls him "God's Son" (15:39)—an ironic declaration whether taken as an affirmation or, with some scholars, as still more Roman mocking of Jesus.[36] Divinely appointed rulers and sons of God

---

35. Earlier in the narrative, conventional notions surface, tying the Messiah's royal status to descent from King David (Bartimaeus in 10:47–48; the crowd at the entry to Jerusalem in 11:10). The topic arises again at Jesus' own initiative, when he casts doubt on the scribes' notion that the Messiah should be a "son of David" (12:35–37). This passage, the only occasion on which Jesus speaks of the son of David, disputes the belief that the Messiah (David's higher-status "Lord") should be a (lower-status) son of David. This is part of Mark's radical recasting of Jesus' role as Messiah and king, not a rejection of that identity for him (on this point, disagreeing, e.g., with Norman Petersen, *Literary Criticism for New Testament Critics*, Guides to Biblical Scholarship: NT Series [Philadelphia: Fortress Press, 1978], 61–63, 67–68; also see the discussion by William R. Telford, *The Theology of Mark*, NTT [Cambridge: Cambridge University Press, 1999], 41, 52, 155). Mark's critique of the Messiah–son of David link contrasts sharply with the Matthean view, clear already from Matt 1:1–17.

36. This is the suggestion, e.g., of Donald H. Juel, *Master of Surprise: Mark Interpreted* (Minneapolis: Fortress Press, 1994), 74 n. 7; idem, "The Strange Silence of the Bible," *Int* 51 (1997): 5–19 (esp. 12–14). Elizabeth Struthers Malbon accents the irony of the centurion's affirmation in 15:39, in connection with Jesus' cry of abandonment in 15:34: "Whether the centurion is understood to be 'sincere' or 'sarcastic,' the narrator has already confirmed the truth of his statement in advance. Thus the narrator disconfirms what the Markan Jesus says (although perhaps Jesus meant more) and confirms what the centurion says (although perhaps he meant less)—an ironic situation indeed" (*Mark's Jesus*, 189).

do not end up this way. There is further irony, too, in the notice that Simon of Cyrene is compelled to carry Jesus' cross (or crossbeam)—another outsider stepping from the margins to carry out the disciples' role for them in their absence (15:21; cf. 8:34; 14:50–52, 66–72). With irony permeating the account of Jesus' passion and death, Mark's audience is given a view of Jesus' identity, vocation, and significance that no characters within the story can attain.

Not even after the resurrection and the women followers' encounter with an empty tomb—when the time of mystery is over and clarity about the identity of Jesus as Messiah and Son of God is possible—will human characters see the truth clearly and act on it with courage. Readers get it when the story's characters do not, and when the narrative ends on a note of failure and fear, the Markan audience not only will get it but must get on with it—acting as bold witnesses to the good news entrusted to them beyond the story as narrated.

Style of Narration: Voice and Point of View

The Gospel of Mark employs a distinctive style of narration. In addition to features already discussed (such as scene repetition, intercalation of episodes, and dramatic irony), several other patterns of narration affect audience experience of the story and merit brief comment. Mark's narrator often uses verbs in the historical present, cast in the present tense but describing action in the past. By one estimate, Mark contains 153 instances of the historical present,[37] many involving the verb of speaking *legei* (he says). Mark 2:1–12 presents an excellent illustration: in the Greek, historical-present verbs appear in verses 3, 4, 5, 8, and 10. The highest concentration of historical-present verbs, however, occurs in the passion narrative: 23 in Mark 14, and another 10 in Mark 15. The historical present reflects popular, oral-narrative style, and one of its effects is to create a sense of proximity, to lend immediacy to the narration, inviting the audience to experience the story up close.

Another literary technique that draws the Markan audience into intimate experience of the story is the inclusion of Aramaic phrases, usually from the mouth of Jesus, which the narrator then translates—thus indicating that some if not all of Mark's first hearers were not Aramaic speakers. Aramaic expressions appear in healing stories in 5:41 ("'Talitha cum,' which means, 'Little girl, get up!'") and 7:34 ("'Ephphatha,' that is, 'Be opened'") and form Jesus' final and only recorded words on the cross in Mark (15:34: "'Eloi, Eloi, lema sabachthani?' which means, 'My God, my God, why have you forsaken me?'"). The narrator identifies the crucifixion site as Golgotha, which, he explains, "means the place of a skull" (15:22). While perhaps initially

37. So Constantine R. Campbell, *Verbal Aspect, the Indicative Mood, and Narrative: Soundings in the Greek of the New Testament*, Studies in Biblical Greek 13 (New York: Peter Lang, 2007), 69. The figures for Mark 14 and 15 also come from Campbell's tally. Witherington counts 151 historical presents in Mark (*Gospel of Mark*, 18 n. 62).

distancing the Greek-speaking hearer from the story ("not my language!"), the Aramaic phrases sprinkled at various points in Mark's narrative enhance experience of the story up close and invite the audience to imagine being present to hear Jesus speak in his own language. Thus the narrator's authority is also reinforced.

The construction of Greek sentences in Mark is relatively simple and direct, typically linking clauses with the conjunction *kai* (usually rendered "and"), often amplified with the adverbs *euthys* or *eutheōs* ("immediately [at once]"; some 41x in Mark). The pace of narrative action is swift and conveys urgency; yet the pacing slows dramatically when Jesus reaches Jerusalem. While there, he delivers a lengthy speech about coming adversity for his followers-witnesses and hope for their deliverance, beyond the destruction of the temple (ch. 13), and the adverb "immediately" appears only four times in the Jerusalem narrative (from 11:11 to the end: 14:43, 45, 72; 15:1). This slow-motion technique of narration emphasizes the gravity of the events in Jerusalem and has the effect of immersing Mark's audience in Jesus' passion: the rejection, suffering, and death he repeatedly predicted earlier in the story.

The narrator ranges freely to describe the action and gives access even to the thoughts and motives of characters, taking Mark's audience wherever necessary to experience the story. Among the examples of the narrator's insight into the interior life of characters are internal questioning by scribes and Jesus' awareness of it (2:6, 8); the motive underlying scrutiny of Jesus' Sabbath conduct, to find basis for accusation (3:2); Jesus' compassion for the crowd (6:34); and the love Jesus is said to feel for a rich man who has kept the commandments of God and is now on a quest for eternal life (10:21).

Most readers have responded to the techniques of narration employed in Mark's Gospel by perceiving Mark's narrator as reliable, an authoritative guide to the events and characters and to their meaning and significance. The narrator's point of view is generally regarded as closely aligned with that of God, as well as with the leading character, Jesus.[38] Recently, however, Elizabeth Struthers Malbon has forcefully pressed the distinction between Mark's narrator and the implied author, and also between the points of view of the narrator and Jesus.[39] Malbon discerns not contradiction but creative tension between the perspectives of Jesus and the narrator: while Jesus' message and activity focus on God and on the reign of God, the narrator shifts the primary concern to Jesus himself, and to his identity as the Messiah and Son of God.[40] The implied author presents both voices, together with this tension between them. In my judgment, precisely because the narrative's central character deflects honor from himself to God, the narrator—for all his concern with Jesus' identity, message, and actions—finally positions

38. For a representative view, see Jack Dean Kingsbury, *The Christology of Mark's Gospel* (Philadelphia: Fortress Press, 1983), 47–50; cf. Fowler, *Let the Reader Understand*, 73.

39. See, e.g., Malbon, *Mark's Jesus*, 190–94.

40. E.g., ibid., 191, 194.

the ministry of Jesus within a theocentric landscape.[41] Whether or not one agrees with Malbon that the views of implied author and the narrator are to be so sharply distinguished, her analysis of the narrator's activity in Mark does help illumine the central concerns and strategies of the Gospel. Mark presents good news (*euangelion*), ultimately, because it is the power of the "reigning presence of God" that initiates, sustains, and completes the story.[42] A narrative of good news with significant biographical interests (whether or not formally a *bios*, a biography) necessarily centers on the activity of Jesus. Mark's Jesus, though, proclaims not himself (the "I am" of 14:62 notwithstanding) but the reign of God.

Central Motifs and Concerns

The extended discussion of techniques of narration in Mark has already surfaced several motifs that are especially prominent in this Gospel. This next section will draw focused attention to a number of the central concerns evident in Mark's narrative or in contemporary readers' engagement with it.

Central Motifs and Concerns in Mark
• The "Way": Locating the mission of Jesus within Israel's story and Scripture
• Collision of the powers: The reign of God and the empire of Rome
• Jesus' identity and mission
• Discipleship and the disciples' failure
• Orientation to Jewish tradition and praxis in the company of Gentiles
• Observations about gender
• Suffering and hope

The "Way": Locating the Mission of Jesus within Israel's Story and Scripture

The narrator begins the (beginning of) this good-news account by embedding it within a much older story, that of Israel. Thus in Mark 1:2–3 the "way of the Lord" that the baptizing prophet John will prepare out in the Judean wilderness is a metaphor—borrowed from the prophet Isaiah (esp. Isa 40:3), with help from Mal 3:1 (though without attribution)[43]—for the deliverance,

41. On Malbon's terms, the implied author who gives readers both points of view also achieves this balance.

42. I borrow this ET of the phrase *basileia tou theou* from Moloney, *Gospel of Mark*, 49. Boring gives clear articulation of the theocentric thrust of Mark: "The story is not christocentric in a way that keeps it from being finally theocentric. The story of the one who cried out to God as abandoned turns out to be God's own story" (*Mark*, 445). See also Ira Brent Driggers, *Following God through Mark: Theological Tension in the Second Gospel* (Louisville, KY: Westminster John Knox Press, 2007).

43. Matthew and Luke (as well as some of the manuscripts in the Markan textual tradition) remove the difficulty created when Mark attributes the blended Malachi-and-Isaiah citation

or liberation, that God will bring through the figure of the "more powerful" one (1:7). Mark orients his audience to the activity of Jesus, therefore, by locating it in the longer story of God's saving activity among God's people, despite the ongoing reality of exile and imperial domination, of sin and oppression. This intertextual framing of the narrative shapes readers' expectations, as the Jewish Scriptures underlie and inform much of the account; yet, at the same time, those expectations undergo reinterpretation by the impact of the Messiah's peculiar "king's highway" to Jerusalem and crucifixion (see 10:32).

Repeatedly, in the course of conflict between Jesus and other interpreters of Israel's Scriptures (usually Pharisees and scribes), Jesus counters competing readings of Scripture with his own. He depicts the reign of God, which his activity is inaugurating (1:15), as something radically new that challenges conventional interpretations and traditional practices. Yet this is a matter of interpretation, not rejection, of Israel's sacred Scripture or of the Torah lying at its heart, and the implications for the identity and social practices of the Jewish people in Mark are significant. Already in the series of conflict stories in 2:1–3:6 this pattern emerges. Two of these scenes turn on debate regarding the meaning of the Decalogue's Sabbath commandment and conduct that expresses fidelity to it (2:23–28; 3:1–6). On the heels of an episode imaging the incompatibility of old and new (2:18–22), Jesus' claim that the Sabbath is to serve human need and flourishing (2:27) appears to represent the "new thing" of God's reign. Yet to score this point, Jesus invokes Scripture—the analogy of David's "unlawfully" seizing temple bread to feed his companions (vv. 25–26, recalling 1 Sam 21:1–6). It is not a matter of unlawful conduct, as these Pharisees surmise (Mark 2:24), but of reading Scripture in light of Scripture. In a similar way, the ensuing debate over the legitimacy of healing on the Sabbath (3:1–6) does not picture Jesus discarding Torah but instead interpreting it in connection with human flourishing. The implication of verse 4 is that by refraining from performing the good or preserving life on the Sabbath, one actually performs evil or kills.

The question of fidelity to Scripture, or observance of Torah, looms especially large in 7:1–23. Here the outcome of debate between contested understandings and practical applications of Scripture has a major bearing on the shape, membership, and social practices—especially on the boundaries—of the people of God.[44] Once more, Jesus offers radical teaching—here, on matters of ritual purity and kashrut ("nothing outside a person . . . by going in can defile," v. 15; "all foods clean," v. 19)—and does so in a way that seriously engages Old Testament texts. Against the Pharisees and scribes, Jesus' appeal to passages from both the Pentateuch (Exod 20:12 // Deut 5:16 + Exod 21:17 // Lev 20:9) and the Prophets (Isa 29:13) counters their critique

---

only to Isaiah. Neither Matt 3:3 nor Luke 3:4–6 includes the line from Malachi; some manuscripts of Mark replace "the prophet Isaiah" in 1:2 with "the prophets."

44. See the discussion of this passage below in the section "Orientation to Jewish Tradition and Praxis in the Company of Gentiles."

that Jesus and his followers are not faithful to Jewish tradition. Isaiah 29:13 equips Jesus with the indictment he now levels against his detractors: "This people honors me with their lips, but their hearts are far from me; in vain do they worship me, teaching human precepts as doctrines" (Mark 7:6–7). So it is not Jesus and his band but rather his opponents who "abandon the commandment of God and hold to human tradition, . . . rejecting the commandment of God in order to keep your tradition!" (vv. 8–9).

Again in Mark 10, debate arises about Torah interpretation and application, provoked by Pharisaic examiners who approach Jesus with the hostile intent of "testing" (*peirazontes*) him, as the narrator observes (10:2). This time the issue concerns the permissibility of divorce (v. 3a). Cued by Jesus to search the Scriptures (v. 3b: "What did Moses command you?"), his examiners invoke Deuteronomy 24:1–4, which sanctions a husband's divorce of his wife for various reasons and forbids their later remarriage (Mark 10:4, "certificate of dismissal"). Yet again, Jesus offers a radical position, branding any divorce the equivalent of adultery. The Markan rendition apparently frames the question in a manner that reflects not only proto-rabbinic debates between the houses of Hillel and Shammai,[45] but also Roman legal practice and precedent, which allowed for the wife's initiation of divorce, as in Jesus' amplification for the benefit of his disciples (vv. 10–12).

Jesus again interprets Scripture by Scripture, Torah by Torah. He finds the hermeneutical key in the Genesis narrative (Gen 1:27 and 2:24, quoted in Mark 10:6–8). The creation of humankind shows the intent of the divine Creator: the couple form "one flesh" and are not to be separated. The way on which Jesus sets his followers in Mark is fresh and new, but at the same time faithful to Scripture.

In 12:28–34, Jesus and another learned interpreter of the Torah agree on the importance of keeping the central Torah commandments—Jesus highlights the Shema and the command to love neighbor as self (splicing Deut 6:4–5 with Lev 19:18), and this scribe approves (Mark 12:32–33). Such a one, who keeps these commands, Jesus responds, is "not far from the kingdom of God" (v. 34). Not far—yet not quite there, it seems. The new is both continuous and discontinuous with the old; it certainly does not nullify the old, the scriptural commandments.

Through a further cluster of Old Testament texts, Mark (through the voices of both narrator and Jesus) develops the role, identity, and vocation of Jesus. The "triumphal" entry echoes Zechariah 9:9, thus depicting a king's humble arrival in Jerusalem, and the throng gathered for the occasion acclaims him with lines borrowed from Psalms 118:26 and 148:1 (Mark 11:1–11). The allegorical parable of the tenants and the beloved son (12:1–9) echoes the biblical image of a vineyard for God's people (e.g., Isa 5:1–7), thereby interpreting Jesus' presence and experience in Jerusalem as a beloved (divine) Son's rejection by those who tend the vineyard (i.e., the

---

45. E.g., see the Mishnah tractate Giṭ. 9:10; cf. 8:4, 9 (this tractate addresses various contingencies associated with writs of divorce).

elite leaders in Jerusalem). The biblical image that Jesus then tacks onto the parable, with another appeal to Psalm 118, pictures the stone that becomes the chief cornerstone despite its rejection by builders (Ps 118:22–23, cited in Mark 12:10–11). This parable is no mystery: its auditors recognize that it takes aim directly at them, and they have one more reason to seek Jesus' arrest (v. 12).[46]

Mark 12:35–37, as we have already seen, cuts the Messiah free from the line of David, at least on Jesus' reading of Psalm 110. Verse 1 of this psalm, in tandem with Daniel 7:13, will underlie Jesus' claim to affirmation by God in response to the high priest's interrogation (in Mark 14:61–62). In Jesus' move to distance himself from the "scribal" interpretive tradition that ties the Messiah to Davidic descent, he again contests a tradition by appeal to his own reading of a scriptural text. The Messiah, acknowledged by the Psalter's "David" as "Lord," cannot be his lower-status "son."[47]

The shaping of the narrative through intertextual connections with texts from the Jewish Scriptures is especially prominent in the Markan passion narrative (chs. 14–15). Both explicit citations of Scripture texts and (more often) allusions or echoes guide readers' interpretation of the events being narrated.

- You will all become deserters; *for it is written*, "I will strike the shepherd, and the sheep will be scattered" (Mark 14:27, quoting Zech 13:7; italics added)
- "Day after day I was with you in the temple teaching, and you did not arrest me. *But let the scriptures be fulfilled.*" All of them deserted him and fled. (Mark 14:49–50, with the desertion by disciples in v. 50 forming at least part of the scriptural fulfillment being narrated; italics added)
- Jesus said, "I am; and 'you will see the Son of Man seated at the right hand of the Power,' and 'coming with the clouds of heaven.'" (14:62, splicing quotations from Ps 110:1 and Dan 7:13–14, though without explicit identification as Scripture text)
- In the crucifixion scene, several scriptural echoes (not explicitly identified as drawn from Jewish Scriptures) occur:
  — And they crucified him, and divided his clothes among them, casting lots to decide what each should take. (Mark 15:24, echoing Ps 22:18)

46. The audience within the story for this intertextual commentary by Jesus is the same group of elite priests, scribes, and elders that has been sparring with Jesus since 11:27. At 12:13 (Pharisees and Herodians) and 12:18 (Sadducees), Jesus' debate partners shift. The latter interlocutors, intent on ridiculing the notion of resurrection, provide Jesus occasion for further scriptural exploration in which he interprets Torah (levirate marriage as in Deut 25:5–10 and Gen 38:8) by way of Torah (God of the "living" Abraham, Isaac, and Jacob in Exod 3:6, 15, cited in Mark 12:26).

47. For thorough discussion of the role of OT texts in shaping Mark's Christology, see Joel Marcus, *The Way of the Lord: Christological Exegesis of the Old Testament in the Gospel of Mark* (Louisville, KY: Westminster John Knox Press, 1992).

— Those who passed by derided him, shaking their heads. (Mark 15:29, echoing Ps 22:7)
— Jesus cried out with a loud voice, "Eloi, Eloi, lema sabachthani?" which means, "My God, my God, why have you forsaken me?" (Mark 15:34, quoting Ps 22:1)
— Onlookers mistakenly suppose that Jesus is invoking Elijah. (Mark 15:35–36)

Any in Mark's audience who possess substantial knowledge of Jewish Scripture will experience the account of Jesus' death—even his cry of dereliction in 15:34—as evidence not of God's remoteness from the events, or of Jesus' disqualification from messianic status, but instead of the enactment of God's redemptive purpose, congruent with ancient scriptural testimony. Even listeners who possess limited knowledge of Jewish Scripture beyond the cues provided by Mark's narrative will hear enough to understand. Mark does not typically use fulfillment language; however, whether the narrative forges intertextual connections between narrated events and Jewish Scripture or between these events and earlier statements by Jesus (e.g., 8:31; 9:31; 10:33–34; 14:27, 30), the audience experiences even the starkest scenes in the story as moments of divine presence and faithfulness (see esp. 15:34). Suffering here does not smother hope but rather engenders hope, even for a Markan audience well acquainted with adversity. For all its enigmatic quality, the final scene at the tomb (16:1–8) will reinforce that hope-nurturing rhetorical effect of the preceding narrative (see below). This is the "way," the path from call through suffering to hope, on which Jesus has set his disciples—and Mark's audience and other readers who come after them.

Collision of the Powers: The Reign of God and the Empire of Rome

Mark's passion narrative, as we have seen, displays Jesus' ironic kingship: an improbable, counterintuitive, and counterimperial royal résumé. It draws its unusual character from its participation in the reign of God. From the outset, Jesus gives this clear focus to his activity: "The time is fulfilled, and the reign of God has come near [ēngiken]; repent, and believe in the good news" (1:15). God's reign, inaugurated in Jesus' ministry, entails reordering and reorienting life ("repent," metanoeō), a resolute turn away from other claims, commitments, and powers. As the narrative unfolds, these claims, commitments, and powers include demonic domination and oppression (1:13, 23–27, 32, 34, 39; 3:11–12, 15; 5:1–20; 6:7, 13; 7:26–30; 9:14–29, 38–39), the seduction of wealth and status seeking (4:19; 9:33–36; 10:17–31, 35–45),[48] and even long-standing religious traditions (e.g., 2:18–3:6; 7:1–23).

All of this occurs in Roman imperial space. Mark distinguishes Jesus from rebels and insurrectionists who accompany him through the passion

---

48. Jesus offers the *child* and other-regarding service, instead, as pattern of God's reign (9:35–37; 10:13–16).

narrative, notably Barabbas, the insurrectionist—still more irony!—for whom Jesus' death sentence procures release (15:6–15). Nevertheless, the set of commitments and social practices through which Jesus gives concrete definition to the reign of God are deeply counterimperial. Since the way *to* the cross, and the way *of* the cross on which Jesus sets his followers, displays the character of Jesus' messianic vocation, and therefore of the reign of God, it is power—even life itself—relinquished in self-giving vulnerability for the sake of others: "The Son of Man [Human One] came not to be served but to serve, and to give his life a ransom [to obtain liberation] for many" (10:45). Nevertheless, the empty tomb beyond crucifixion (16:1–8) provides the narrative demonstration that Roman power cannot, in the end, crush the bearer of God's reign.

The future-previewing, eschatological discourse of Mark 13 also sketches a future in which Roman power does not have the last say. For in the future that Jesus imagines—beyond the catastrophic destruction that Roman armies will inflict on an international scale, including the temple's desolation (v. 2)—lies the deliverance of God's chosen ones: "Then he will send out the angels, and gather his elect from the four winds, from the ends of the earth to the ends of heaven" (13:27). In Mark's rendition of the discourse of future horrors and deliverance, God sends angels not to judge and annihilate but, instead, to save God's people. The counterimperial character of God's ruling power continues into the future that Jesus projects. The collision of powers dramatically narrated in Mark transcends the encounter between a Galilean teacher-healer and Roman power holding court in Jerusalem, represented by the prefect Pontius Pilate, military forces at his command, and local Judean elite co-opted to serve Roman interests. Beneath and above that confrontation, this is an apocalyptic contest between God's reign and the inauthentic, distorting, oppressive realm of Satan.[49] And, as it appears, God's reign prevails without mimicking the ways of Satan *or* Rome.[50]

Mark delivers a counterimperial message that radically reconfigures imperial power, even though it also to some degree reflects the ambivalence and mimicry one would expect of discourse framed in the setting of

49. For discussion of the way in which Mark works with Jewish apocalyptic traditions, see (among many others) John K. Riches, *Conflicting Mythologies: Identity Formation in the Gospels of Mark and Matthew* (Edinburgh: T&T Clark, 2000), 69–179.

50. Even if one reads Jesus' confrontation with the unclean spirit "Legion" as a military commander's domination of an invading military force (see Warren Carter, "Cross-Gendered Romans and Mark's Jesus: Legion Enters the Pigs (Mark 5:1–20)," *JBL* 134 [2015]: 159–77), the destruction of the herd of pigs that results is apparently self-destruction, self-chosen. In Mark 9:1 Jesus does speak of the coming of God's reign "with [or, in: *en*] power," which the disciples ("you") will see, but what follows is the transfiguration's preview of Jesus' eschatological glory, and never subsequently does power wielded in the Roman way figure in Mark's representation of God's reign. Not even the image in 14:62 of the future coming (or going?) of the Human One (Son of Humanity) as coregent of God ("seated at the right hand of Power") is an exception to this pattern (though cf. 8:38–9:1). For a postcolonial reading arguing that "colonial politics has [been] so deeply inscribed on Mark that he actually reproduces it" (in mimicry of the dominant colonizers), see Liew, *Politics of Parousia*, esp. 150.

imperial (colonial) domination. Mimicry of the Roman Empire evident in Mark is consistently tinged with parody (e.g., in the expulsion of a demonic legion to its self-destruction [5:1–20]; the not-so-triumphal entry into Jerusalem [11:1–11]; and the king's cross [15:17–20, 26, 32]).[51] Mark's appropriation of Roman military and imperial imagery for Jesus and the reign of God, as ironic parody, expresses resistance to empire, yet without commending rebellion.[52]

As Mark's audience must find its way in the Roman imperial world amid or immediately after the Jewish War, how will it negotiate not only competing but also conflicting loyalties? A scene debating the legitimacy of Rome's taxation demands brings the question into sharp focus, even as it refuses to remove all ambiguity (12:13–17). Responding to attempted entrapment (on supporting or opposing the duty to pay the tribute tax [poll tax; lit., "give the census"] to Rome), Jesus answers, "Give to the emperor the things that are the emperor's, and to God the things that are God's" (v. 17). It is a matter of subtle, hidden resistance to Roman imperial control *or* of negotiation, rather than calling for overt rebellion. Mark's audience must figure out what the relative claims of those two obligations are. The rest of the narrative indicates a clear direction not accessible to, or accepted by, the group of Pharisees and Herodians who are Jesus' interlocutors in the story.

Jesus' Identity and Mission

Many readers of Mark's Gospel have perceived its central interest to be the identity and significance of Jesus, or Christology. While Malbon and Boring, among others, have (in my view, rightly) reframed the Markan emphasis on Christology in terms of a deeper concern with (the reign and activity of) God, there is no question that Mark's presentation of Jesus is both a distinctive and a crucial feature of this Gospel.[53] Ever since Wrede's provocative book *The Messianic Secret* (1901), one of the most often discussed aspects of Mark has been the motif of mystery or secrecy (*mystērion*); most though not all of it is connected with the identity of Jesus as Messiah and Son of God.[54]

A catalog of the types of secrecy and silencing in the narrative is instructive. First, Jesus orders the demons (or unclean spirits) to be silent, though they know his special status as holy one or Son of God (Mark 1:23–25; 3:11–12, in a narrator's general summary). Whatever Jesus' motive in trying to silence the demons (left as a gap in the narration), he is unsuccessful (e.g.,

---

51. For discussion of the crucifixion as parody in Mark, see Joel Marcus, "Crucifixion as Parodic Exaltation," *JBL* 125 (2006): 73–87.

52. Here agreeing with Leander, *Discourses of Empire*, 247. He writes of the ambiguity in Mark of "God's nonimperial empire" (264–65) and suggests that Mark's narrative "brings forth negotiations around what it means to be an anticipator of God's unimperial empire . . . in the midst of the empire of Rome" (293).

53. See Malbon, *Mark's Jesus*; Boring, *Mark*; pivotal on this question was the earlier essay by John Donahue, "A Neglected Factor in the Theology of Mark," *JBL* 101 (1982): 563–94.

54. William Wrede, *The Messianic Secret*, trans. J. C. G. Greig (Cambridge: Cambridge University Press, 1971; German orig., 1901).

1:28). The demons may not be reliable characters with regard to their allegiance; yet from the beginning of the Gospel, Mark's audience receives ample cues that their appraisal of Jesus is accurate, even if they desire to destroy the holy one of God whom they recognize. In addition to Jesus' expelling of demons, some other acts of healing also show his concern to keep the event private (1:44; 5:43). The signal exception in 5:19 (Legion) is perhaps explicable as an act of healing/exorcism in an area (Gerasa) to which Jesus and his disciples will not return.[55] Again, Jesus' injunctions to keep silence regarding an event of healing are frustrated (1:45; 5:20).

A second kind of silence/secrecy appears in Jesus' instruction of the disciples regarding his messianic identity and role, as well as in the transfiguration's unveiling of his eschatological glory (8:30; 9:9–10). Related to this is the recurring incomprehension by disciples. Moreover, lack of understanding is not confined to the disciples. There is a wider public lack of understanding that Jesus' teaching in parables both epitomizes and apparently engenders.[56] Parabolic teaching, Jesus tells the disciples, is *intended* to frustrate the kind of hearing and seeing that would lead to reordered life for those who are "outside" (4:11–12). Only the disciples receive private, in-depth explanation—though as we have seen, they scarcely prove able to comprehend even so. Nevertheless, concealment is not to be a permanent goal or outcome of Jesus' message. He presents the metaphor of light placed on a lampstand, not under a bushel or bed, to convey the point that what is concealed for the moment—whether in parable/riddle or, by extension, in appeals for silence—will eventually become publicly available disclosure (4:21–22).

Jesus remains a mystery Messiah, and attempted silencing of partial or demonically acquired insight into his identity prevails throughout Jesus' ministry.[57] This is a temporary state of affairs, however. The exchange in 9:9–13 between Jesus and a group of his disciples (Peter, James, and John) as they descend from the mountain of the transfiguration scene (9:2–8) indicates, in Jesus' perspective, when the veil of mystery will be lifted, or should be lifted. The depiction of fearful, silent women followers fleeing the empty tomb (16:8) scarcely corresponds to the charge Jesus gives his followers after the transfiguration: "As they were coming down the mountain, he ordered them to tell no one about what they had seen, until after the Son of Man [Human One] had risen from the dead" (9:9). On the other side of crucifixion and

---

55. The plausibility of this explanation is diminished, however, when one takes into account the narrator's earlier mention of the expansive spread of Jesus' fame (3:8). It may be that the narrative simply is not consistent on this point.

56. Observing Jesus' powerful acts of healing or hearing his authoritative teaching does lead the crowds to partial knowledge, but this typically results in their being astounded, not the deeper knowing of faith (see, e.g., 1:22; 6:2; 7:37).

57. Wrede contended that this literary pattern is a theological construction and reflects Mark's concern to explain why the Messiah Jesus was not regarded as such during his ministry (*Messianic Secret*). For further discussion and critique, see the essays collected in *The Messianic Secret*, ed. Christopher Tuckett, Issues in Religion and Theology 1 (Philadelphia: Fortress Press, 1983).

resurrection, but only then, is there the possibility of clear understanding and affirmation of Jesus' status as Messiah and Son of God. The narrative holds tightly together the messianic identity of Jesus and his vocation of suffering, rejection, and crucifixion-death. Characters in the story do not and cannot grasp the character of Jesus' messianic rule apart from, and certainly not before, the cross. (Even his repeated, explicit predictions of his suffering and death do not lead to comprehension at the time [8:31–32; 9:31; 10:33–34].)

Peter's affirmation of Jesus as the Christ (Messiah) in 8:29 documents only partial insight into Jesus' role, as the ensuing exchange of vigorous rebukes between Peter and Jesus shows. Unable to accept the notion of a suffering Messiah as Human One (Son of Humanity), outlined by Jesus in 8:31, Peter chastises Jesus and wins reciprocal harsh critique for his alignment with "human" and hence Satan's perspective (vv. 31–32). Not until the centurion's acclamation of Jesus as "truly . . . God's Son" (15:39) does a human character discern and declare the truth about Jesus' divine sonship (i.e., unaided by supernatural knowledge available to demon-possessed individuals, as in 3:11; 5:6–7; cf. 1:24). Or, depending on how one reads the Markan irony at play in 15:39, he may declare truth without discerning Jesus' true identity.[58]

Under interrogation by the high priest, Jesus has himself already lifted the veil of secrecy and publicly acknowledged his identity as Son of God ("the Blessed One," in the high priest's query), again in close connection to his role as the Human One (Son of Humanity), whose vindication and exaltation to universal authority will soon be known (14:61–62). Jesus' examiners, however, do not share the christological conviction, which indeed supplies the basis for an accusation of blasphemy and swift transfer to Pilate (14:64; 15:1).[59] It is no accident that the Markan Jesus only publicly acknowledges his identity as Son of God in this setting, when the claim will ensure his death.

Discipleship and the Disciples' Failure

Bound up with the identity and mission of Jesus is the character and mission of the disciples.[60] Early in the narrative, the disciples whom Jesus summons

---

58. Even if Mark's readers hear the affirmation of Jesus' divine sonship by the centurion as sincere, rather than sarcastic, they may appraise it as only partially correct, presuming that a Roman soldier would perceive Jesus to be one among many sons of God, including the Roman emperors. Also on this reading, the acclamation of Jesus' identity is deeply ironic: for Mark and his audience, Jesus is uniquely Son of God.

59. Before the governor, they evidently have modulated the charge from blasphemous to seditious claims, so Pilate opens the interrogation with the question "Are you the King of the Jews?" (15:2)

60. This connection is emphasized by Suzanne Watts Henderson in *Christology and Discipleship in the Gospel of Mark*, SNTSMS 135 (Cambridge: Cambridge University Press, 2006). She extends this observation to the Gospels more generally in *Christ and Community: The Gospel Witness to Jesus* (Nashville: Abingdon Press, 2015). Important earlier contributions on this topic were made by Ernest Best; see, e.g., *Following Jesus*.

into his company distinguish themselves through their willingness to leave home and livelihood to follow him (1:16–20; 2:14–15), their presence during his activity of authoritative teaching and deeds of power (e.g., 1:29–32; 3:14; 4:1–34; 5:37–42), and their privilege as specially tutored "insiders" to whom Jesus reveals the "mystery" (*mystērion*) of God's sovereign reign (4:10–11, 33–34). As the narrative unfolds, however, locations "inside" and "outside" become unstable. The disciples repeatedly fail to comprehend Jesus' teaching and significance; they show themselves unable to enact core values of his message (e.g., rejection of status seeking, exercise of power through service and suffering). As we have seen, even at the pivotal moment when, on behalf of the company of disciples, Peter articulates insight into Jesus' role as the Messiah (made clear to the reader as early as 1:1), he scarcely grasps what that messiahship entails. His resistance, stunningly voiced in his rebuke of Jesus (8:32), wins him rebuke of his own, indeed as one aligned with Satan's viewpoint (associated with "human things"), not God's (8:33).[61]

As we noticed when considering Mark's use of scene repetitions, one of the themes underscored through that literary pattern is the obtuseness of Jesus' closest followers, the disciples. Although they receive "the mystery of the reign of God," with its content and character unpacked for them privately by Jesus (e.g., 4:10–11 AT, 13–20, 33–34), understanding eludes them. Participation in one extraordinary feeding of a large crowd (6:35–44) does not keep the disciples from being at a loss when a similar situation presents itself (see 8:4; cf. v. 21). Dramatic rescue from peril in a boat on the lake (4:35–41) does not prevent their panic and befuddlement on a second such occasion (6:45–52; see esp. vv. 51–52). In another scene, the disciples are discussing among themselves which of them is "the greatest" (9:34), and Jesus urges them instead to accept the lowest station and embraces a child as his own representative, and therefore God's (vv. 35–37). Somewhat later, however, when the disciples try to obstruct access of little children to Jesus, he counters with the image of the child as paradigm of the realm of God (10:13–16). Why is such repeated, remedial instruction necessary?

The disciples find it especially difficult to grasp the nature of Jesus' leadership as one who rules by serving, who experiences desolation, defeat, and death in dishonor. The summons to follow Jesus on the way of the cross leaves the disciples fearful (10:32); they repeatedly misunderstand his descriptions of his peculiar messianic vocation as one who must suffer (8:32–33; 9:32; 10:35–41); and at his arrest they desert him, just as he said they would (14:50–52; cf. v. 27). Even Peter's insistent protest of undying loyalty cannot measure up to the challenge (14:29, 31, 66–72).

---

61. As Robyn Whitaker has argued, Mark 8 narrates a redirection of Peter's discipleship and understanding of Jesus' role, not its termination ("Rebuke or Recall? Rethinking the Role of Peter in Mark's Gospel," *CBQ* 75 [2013]: 666–82). Even Peter's threefold denial does not close the book on this apostle, for 16:7, recalling and extending Jesus' promise in 14:28, anticipates for the "disciples and Peter" future reunion with the risen Jesus in Galilee and thus, beyond the narrative, their restoration.

The place of the disciples as privileged insiders is destabilized and ulti-mately undermined as the narrative proceeds. Locations inside and out-side undergo redefinition. Not the disciples, it turns out, but a parade of seemingly minor characters embody more appropriately the character of discipleship.

Destabilizing Inside and Outside: Marginal Characters as Exemplars
• Anonymous woman with chronic bleeding (5:25–34)
• Insistent Syrophoenician woman pleading for help for her daughter (7:24–30)
• Bartimaeus: from no sight to the true insight of a follower "on the way" (10:46–52)
• A woman's radical (and foolish?) generosity (12:41–44)
• "In memory of her": An anonymous woman's extravagant act to honor Jesus secures her legacy (14:3–9)
• Cross-bearing substitute for the Twelve: Simon of Cyrene (15:21)
• "I believe; help my unbelief": a son's desperate father (9:14–29)
• Knowing the Torah and "not far from the kingdom of God": an inquiring scribe (12:28–34)

1. An anonymous woman plagued by a chronic bleeding disorder, vic-timized and impoverished by the futile efforts of countless physicians, dares to approach Jesus as he and his retinue head for the prominent synagogue leader Jairus's house. Her initiative to touch his garment calls forth healing power from Jesus. When he realizes it and stops to confront her (after she steps forward to identify herself), he affirms her faith and dismisses her in peace, her body having been restored (5:25–34). The vivid description of her suffering, affliction, and bleeding also prefigures Jesus' own suffering later in the narrative.

2. A Greek (i.e., Gentile) woman from (Syro-)Phoenicia responds with wit and persistence to Jesus' initial rebuff of her plea for her daughter to be healed, and he relents, granting the petition. In the process, Mark's audience may sense that her courageous expression of trust in Jesus' capacity as a healer presses him to expand the scope of his mission's concern (7:24–30).

3. Bartimaeus, the second blind man to seek and receive healing benefac-tion from Jesus, exemplifies a persistent, obstacle-overcoming faith (10:46–52); only at Jesus' direction to the crowd does it shift from an obstructing to a mediating role (vv. 48–49). His label for Jesus ("son of David" in 10:47, 48) may not be christologically astute (contrast Jesus' own critique of that epithet in 12:35–37). Yet Bartimaeus, though a blind beggar, does see more clearly than the disciples nearby. Indeed, after receiving his sight, he begins without delay to "follow Jesus on the way" (10:52 CEB): he assumes the

posture of a disciple-follower on the dangerous road up to Jerusalem, while the Twelve are "amazed and . . . afraid" (10:32).

4. An impoverished widow models self-sacrificing generosity (12:41–44), in tune with what Jesus has urged at least one potential follower and the overhearing disciples to do (10:17–31). Yet considerable ambiguity attends this poor woman's sacrificial gift to the temple treasury. Without wishing to rob her of agency and turning her into a passive victim, I am guided by contextual cues in the surrounding narrative that invite Mark's audience to pause and think more deeply about the episode. On either side of this passage, the narrator presents Jesus as registering vigorous critique of practices located in the temple. Lending added force to his speech with a prophetic-symbolic act of judgment (blended with another prophetic-symbolic act of judgment, the cursing of the unfruitful fig tree)—overturning the tables of money changers and dove sellers in the temple precincts (11:15)—Jesus has not minced words about a temple system that has turned away from its divinely given vocation. With a nod to Isaiah 56:7 and Jeremiah 7:11, he charges that the temple is no longer "a house of prayer for all the nations" but "a den of robbers" (Mark 11:17). And right before Jesus observes the widow's gift, he excoriates wealthy scribes who seek self-promotion and gobble up widows' homes (12:38–40). Her meager gift of two practically valueless lepta coins, though commendable in that it surpasses the value of the much more lavish gifts of the wealthy, nevertheless means that she has voluntarily relinquished her entire means of subsistence (12:42–44)—to support a corrupt system. And it is a corrupt system housed in a temple that, in spite of all its grandeur, is poised for destruction, as Jesus immediately proceeds to predict (13:1–2). Through this ambiguous character study, Mark prods the audience not only to ponder deeply the meaning of Jesus' call to renounce self and treasure and status seeking for the sake of God's reign—for women and men alike—but also to consider the stakes and the costs of practices that serve powerful, unjust systems.

5. Another anonymous woman fares better than the Twelve, if we are to judge from an emotionally charged scene in which she extravagantly honors Jesus before burial (14:3–9). Yet ambiguity relating to gender roles is again evident in the representation of this woman. In this case, the ambiguity does not center on the woman's extravagant gesture of pouring expensive oil on Jesus (despite the complaints of observers) but, instead, on Jesus' irony-laden commendation of her with which the unit concludes: "Wherever the good news is proclaimed in the whole world, what she has done will be told in remembrance of her" (v. 9). Her act will be remembered wherever Mark's narrative garners an audience. But her name, and everything else about her apart from this one act—refracted through Jesus' interpretation of it—will be forgotten.

6. Like Bartimaeus, Simon of Cyrene, another minor character who appears only once in the narrative, acts the part of a disciple, in this case

dramatically taking the place of followers who, rather than "take up their cross and follow," have deserted Jesus (15:21; cf. 8:34).[62] Simon, who hails from North Africa, is forced to carry the crossbeam to the site of Jesus' crucifixion, another not-so-subtle reminder of the coercive power of the occupying Roman military. Even so, he enacts the task of cross bearing that Jesus' own band fails to accept.

7. A somewhat more ambiguous character is the father of a demon-tormented son whom the disciples prove unable to aid while Jesus is with Peter, James, and John on the transfiguration mountain (9:14–29). When Jesus voices exasperation at a "faithless generation" (v. 19) and then seeming indignation at a renewed, desperate—but not confident—plea for help (v. 22, "if you are able"), the father presses his petition with the memorable, candid words: "I believe; help my unbelief!" (v. 24). Faith not yet fully formed proves sufficient to elicit Jesus' restorative, liberating touch.

8. The boundary between inside and outside becomes even more porous in an exchange between Jesus and a scribe in 12:28–34.[63] After observing Jesus' strong performance in a series of debates with other—and adversarial—interlocutors, this scribe, whose education and profession surely position him among the local social elite, initiates genuine theological dialogue with Jesus: "Which commandment is the first of all?" (12:28). Jesus points the scribe to the Shema (Deut 6:4–5, commanding love of God with one's whole being), in tandem with Lev 19:18 (love of neighbor as of the self). This response wins further commendation from the scribe even as he repeats, in a not quite identical paraphrase, Jesus' citation of these central Torah texts: "You are right, Teacher; you have truly said, . . . this is much more important than all whole burnt offerings and sacrifices" (Mark 12:32–34). Until this scene, scribes have been unrelenting critics of Jesus (see 2:6, 16; 3:22; 7:1, 5; 9:14; 11:18, 27–28; cf. 1:22), and beginning again in the very next pericope and continuing to the end of the story, scribes figure prominently among Jesus' adversaries, even as his mortal enemies (see 12:35–40; 14:1, 43, 53; 15:1, 31; cf. 8:31; 10:33). But for this perceptive specialist in legal interpretation, Jesus has no stinging rebuke; instead he declares, "You are not far from the kingdom of God" (12:34). Jesus unexpectedly locates this scribe in proximity to God's reign, anticipating another respected leader and member of council, Joseph from Arimathea, who, the narrator reports, has been "waiting expectantly for the kingdom of God" and who will come forward to ask Pilate for the body to provide Jesus the dignity of burial (15:43).[64]

62. Mark's narrative adds local color to the account with the detail that Simon had sons named Alexander and Rufus (15:21), perhaps meaningful information at one point in the history of this traditioning community, but not by the time the story makes its way into Matt 27:32 and Luke 23:26, neither of which includes the sons' names.

63. The boundary between inside and outside is a recurring interest in Mark's narrative: e.g., 4:11; 9:38–41.

64. These two characters, the scribe-theologian of 12:28–34 and Joseph of Arimathea, temper what appears to be for the most part a theological anthropology dominated by apocalyptic dualism. These characters—perhaps joined at the crucifixion by the Roman centurion, if his

The human landscape painted by Mark's narrative is for the most part bleak: neither his closest followers nor the people who hold the most power in Jerusalem and its environs prove to be models of virtue or of fidelity to God. But glimmers of a more hopeful future do now and then shine through the gloom. Especially from the social margins, and from outside Jesus' own circle, Mark's audience occasionally sees what a future populated by faithful seekers and witnesses might look like. The ending of the narrative will hand the baton to that audience.

Orientation to Jewish Tradition and Praxis in the Company of Gentiles

The beginning of Mark's narrative, as we have seen, places Jesus in the ongoing story of Israel, God's people. He knows, quotes from, and interprets Jewish Scripture. Indeed, he strikes many who hear him as a teacher who bears an unusual and surpassing authority, even when compared to the best educated and most knowledgeable interpreters of the Torah, the scribes (1:22, "he taught them as one having authority, and not as the scribes"; 1:27, "a new teaching—with authority" manifest in power to expel demons). The theme of innovation or novelty recurs in 2:21–22, embedded in a trio of vignettes featuring conflict over observance of specific Jewish practices, particularly fasting (2:18–22) and Sabbath (2:23–3:6). Jesus' play with the metaphors of clothing (garment and patch) and container (wine and wineskin) appears to place his own activity in the category of tradition-threatening innovation (vv. 21–22). Old and new simply do not mix. Viewed from the other side, with innovation as culturally suspect in the Greco-Roman world (and not just for traditionalist critics of Jesus), this raises a question or three about Jesus' fidelity to Jewish Scripture and tradition. It poses a significant challenge for readers seeking to locate Jesus in relation to Jewish Scripture and tradition.

Yet, in a striking reversal, it is later Jesus the seeming innovator who casts the Torah-serious Pharisees as innovators whose extension of Torah in oral tradition has resulted in violation of a commandment and its intent: honor for one's parents, concretely expressed in provision for them (7:8–13). The issue concerns purity and what renders one ritually impure. What practices and foods make clean/unclean?

Mark 7:1–23, addressing these concerns, unfolds in three steps, each having a distinctive group of auditors. In verses 1–13, Jesus responds to a question from Pharisees and Jerusalem-based scribes: "Why do your disciples not live according to the tradition of the elders, but eat with defiled hands?" (v. 5).[65] Jesus quotes both Isaiah (vv. 6–7, citing Isa 29:13) and Moses (Mark

acclamation of Jesus as "God's Son" is not mocking sarcasm (15:39)—hint that there is more to the story than rigid binary oppositions between Jesus and leaders of the Jewish local elite, between disciple insiders and outsiders, and between colonized Jews and the colonizing Roman governor and soldiers. Liew holds together apocalyptic and postcolonial-political readings of Mark (*Politics of Parousia*, 46–63).

65. In a narrator's aside, Mark 7:2b–4 explains the Pharisees' surprise that Jesus' disciples ate

7:10, citing the Decalogue's command to honor parents and the severe Torah sanction for violation of the command, as in Exod 20:12 // Deut 5:16 + Exod 21:17 // Lev 20:9) in a strident critique of what he regards as the Pharisees' departure from fidelity to the Torah and thus respect for their parents (Mark 7:11–13), justifying themselves by their oral interpretive tradition. The practice of "Corban," designating as a vow what should have been reserved for parental care, is just the tip of the Torah-dooming iceberg, in Jesus' view (v. 13).

Step 2 presents instruction of the crowds, whom Jesus specifically invites to receive his explanation of his approach to purity concerns about hand-washing and food (vv. 14–15), thus returning to the question posed by Pharisees and scribes in verse 5. What produces impurity, he avers, is not what goes into the body but what comes out of it.

In step 3, a scene set within a home, the disciples then ask Jesus the meaning of this ambiguous "parable" (Mark 7:17), and he explains (vv. 18–23). Normal bodily processes of digestion remove anything that is potentially contaminating; what truly makes one unclean is the condition of the human heart, when it produces destructive, other-harming attitudes and practices. Teaching like this, the narrator comments in another parenthetical aside, amounts to a declaration that "all foods [are made] clean" (v. 19). As in the exaggerated mention of the practices of Pharisees "and all the Jews" (v. 3), Mark's narrator and arguably also the implied author and Gospel audience here stand at considerable distance from Jewish Torah observance. Even so, it is crucial to notice that Jesus counters Pharisees' interpretive tradition by also interpreting Scripture, not by jettisoning it. Mark's community is thereby equipped to counter competing approaches to reading the Torah (and the Prophets) in favor of the approach modeled here by Jesus, which carves out a space within a Scripture-honoring community for Gentiles.[66]

Aptly, instruction that challenges boundaries between Jews and Gentiles (7:15, nothing entering the body can defile; 7:19, all foods clean) leads without delay to what may be the first encounter with a Gentile in the Markan narrative. Jesus is sought out by a Syrophoenician woman, whom the narrator also identifies as "Greek" (*hellēnis*, v. 26 CEB), for the sake of her spirit-afflicted daughter (7:24–30).[67] Jesus makes the spatial move (departing to

---

food without first undergoing a purifying washing rite. Mark's audience, evidently assumed to be unfamiliar with Jewish practices relating to ritual purity, learns that "Pharisees and all the Jews" (v. 3) observe a set of purity-conscious rules contained in the "tradition of the elders" (v. 3). Most interpreters of Mark have concluded that the author, too, shows imprecise knowledge of Jewish tradition and practice at this point. For a thorough analysis of the issues, see, e.g., Marcus, *Mark* 1:447–54, 456–61. Boring observes that a Jewish writer, when explaining customs to non-Jews, may do so inaccurately (with a nod to Let. Arist. 305); the passage, therefore, does not necessarily place the author outside Judaism (*Mark*, 199).

66. For detailed discussion of the passage, see Marcus, *Mark*, 1:439–61.

67. The common assumption that the Gerasene demoniac in 5:1–20 is a Gentile living in mostly non-Jewish territory (e.g., Marcus, *Mark*, 342; Boring, *Mark*, 149) has been questioned by, e.g., Carter, "Cross-Gendered Romans and Mark's Jesus," 143. Marcus argues that the desig-

the region around Tyre) that creates the opportunity for such an encounter, despite his frustrated attempt to conceal his presence (v. 24). Yet he unkindly rebuffs the woman: "Let the children be fed first, for it is not fair to take the children's food and throw it to the dogs" (v. 27). Has Jesus already forgotten what he said in verse 15? Was the narrator mistaken in drawing the generalization about clean and unclean foods in verse 19? The narrative creates tension between Jesus' teaching in 7:1–23, which appears to reflect openness to Gentiles, and the cold shoulder he turns to this woman.

The exchange is difficult enough without taking into account the harsh labeling Jesus uses (contrasting "children," presumably Jews, to "dogs," presumably non-Jews). How should and will Mark's audience make sense of all this? From their cultural repertoire, readers will likely be familiar with pejorative metaphorical use of "dog," including the contrast between children (people of Israel) and dogs (Gentiles).[68] They will also know from experience, more literally, the domestic scene in play, with dogs eager to devour any food scraps from the meal that fall to the ground. Rather than registering offense at Jesus' seeming insult, the woman takes the high road, intent on securing help for her daughter. She confronts excluding, boundary-setting deployment of the dog metaphor with her keen wit, making an appeal for inclusion of outsiders at a meal set for others to enjoy. Remarkably, a Greek (Gentile) woman succeeds in persuading Jesus to alter his approach to the scope of his healing mission; she tutors Jesus in a manner that anticipates later inclusion of Gentiles within the community of Jesus followers.[69]

Another Gentile character plays a critical role (though brief) that may likewise anticipate later inclusion of non-Jews within the community of Jesus followers.[70] The Roman centurion at the crucifixion site, having

nation "Greek" in 7:26 (RSV) is functionally equivalent to the label "Gentile" (NRSV) since the woman is identified as Syrophoenician, not Greek, in ethnic origin (*Mark*, 462).

68. See, e.g., Beavis, *Mark*, 124; Yarbro Collins, *Mark*, 366–68; Boring, *Mark*, 212–13; Marcus, *Mark* 1:463–64. For examples of the pejorative use of the dog image, epitomizing uncleanness or hostility to God's people or law, see 1 Sam 17:43; Ps 22:16; Prov 26:11; Isa 56:10–11; Matt 7:6; 2 Pet 2:22; Phil 3:2; Rev 22:15. Rabbinic writings use "dog" as metaphor for unlearned, ungodly, and Gentile persons (see Yarbro Collins, *Mark*, 367, who points to Midr. Ps. 4 § 11 [24a]). But as Sharon H. Ringe emphasizes, it was not in Mark's world a term of scorn that Jews used for Gentiles in general, a racial slur; see her essay "A Gentile Woman's Story, Revisited: Rereading Mark 7:24–31a," in *Feminist Companion to Mark*, ed. Levine and Blickenstaff, 79–100. On the giving of food scraps to (wild) dogs outside the house, see, e.g., Jos. Asen. 10.14; 13.8.

69. Moreover, she tutors in economics: countering an economy of scarcity that requires rivals to compete for limited goods (food), she affirms that available resources are sufficient to satisfy both metaphorical dogs and children; see Raj Nadella, "The Two Banquets: Mark's Vision of Anti-Imperial Economics," *Int* 70 (April 2016): 172–83. The ensuing second feeding of a crowd is often seen as another example of Jesus' extending his mission to include Gentiles (8:1–9). See further Marcus, *Mark*, 1:488–89, 492, 495; Boring, *Mark*, 218–21. However, the episode contains no specific markers of location or audience demographics, other than Jesus' comment that some "have come from a great distance" (v. 3).

70. Pilate deserves mention too, of course, though scarcely as an exemplary figure who might bridge between the Markan community and Roman power. He is astute enough to discern that the accusers of Jesus have spurious motives (15:10), but he orders Jesus' execution anyway, to placate the gathered assembly (15:15).

observed the manner of Jesus' dying, declares him to be "God's Son" (15:39). If the Markan audience hears the words as sincere affirmation, the centurion may be viewed as anticipating the eventual inclusion of believing Gentiles. There is irony, to be sure, as Jesus' divine sonship is recognized by an agent of coercive imperial force and precisely at the point of the crucified man's demise. Yet it is a glimmer of light and of hope in this dark and despairing scene. However, if the centurion's statement sounds to Mark's hearers like one final, crowning expression of derision (perhaps more what one would expect to hear from a Roman soldier?), then the irony runs deeper still, and they will need to look elsewhere for a model Gentile "convert." The narrative leaves this ambiguity for readers to puzzle over, though on any reading the declaration amounts to an ironic affirmation of Jesus' true identity, with or without believing comprehension on the part of the speaker. Whatever the author may have intended (finally inaccessible to us, due to the nature of the textual indeterminacy), readers who know not only Mark's centurion at the cross but also the impressive centurion exemplars of faith in Luke 7:1–10 and Acts 10:1–48 will be inclined to fill this gap in Mark's story by hearing the centurion's words as affirmation, not ridicule.

Observations regarding Gender

Gender analysis of Mark's Gospel, as with other New Testament writings, not only pays close attention to the portrayals of women in the narrative but also examines ways in which norms and expectations with regard to masculinity are refigured.[71] No women figure among the principal characters in the story, but a few (mostly anonymous) do appear in intriguing ways, not least in the Gospel's final scene (16:1–8).

Men carry most of the action in Mark's narrative: not only the Twelve specially chosen apostles, but also some minor male characters sport names (Legion, Herod, Bartimaeus, Pontius Pilate, Barabbas, Simon the father of Alexander and Rufus, Joseph from Arimathea). Nevertheless, several women outside Jesus' band do step into the story, though nameless, and typically do so in a way that invites favorable appraisal. These women all

71. For a sampling of recent work on this interpretive approach, see, e.g., Colleen Conway, *Behold the Man: Jesus and Greco-Roman Masculinity* (Oxford: Oxford University Press, 2008), 89–106 on Mark; Stephen D. Moore and Janice Capel Anderson, eds., *New Testament Masculinities*, SemeiaSt 45 (Atlanta: Society of Biblical Literature, 2003), esp. the treatments of Mark's Gospel by Tat-siong Benny Liew, "Re-Mark-able Masculinities: Jesus, the Son of Man, and the (Sad) Sum of Manhood?" (93–135), and Eric Thurman, "Looking for a Few Good Men: Mark and Masculinity" (137–62). For a nuanced approach, see Greg Carey, *Sinners: Jesus and His Earliest Followers* (Waco, TX: Baylor University Press, 2009), 55–78; also, on the image of Jesus' masculinity specifically in Mark 5, see Candida R. Moss, "The Man with the Flow of Power: Porous Bodies in Mark 5:25–34," *JBL* 129 (2010): 507–19. For a brief but helpful overview of scholarship on masculinity in NT studies and related disciplines, see Brittany E. Wilson, *Unmanly Men: Refigurations of Masculinity in Luke-Acts* (Oxford: Oxford University Press, 2015), 14–21.

are assertive initiators of action and act from a position of relative independence, not circumscribed by household relations.

As noted in the discussion of minor characters above, a woman impoverished by her attempts over twelve years to find a cure for her chronic bleeding ailment interrupts Jesus' urgent trip to Jairus's house to restore the synagogue ruler's twelve-year-old daughter. His healing power tapped by her touch, Jesus confronts her; then commends her faith, which has granted her access to healing; and dismisses her in peace (5:25–34). A Syrophoenician woman, though a Gentile, engages in challenge and spirited response (riposte) with Jesus, and her wit convinces Jesus that even an outsider to the Jewish people deserves notice and help for the sake of her demon-afflicted daughter (7:24–30). In the process, it appears that Jesus' own sense of the scope of God's saving concern broadens in a threshold-crossing enactment of the impulse evident in 7:1–23.

Another unnamed woman's extravagant anointing of Jesus may scandalize some observers but wins his favorable comment. He interprets her gesture, whatever she may have intended (prophetic anointing of the Messiah?), as a burial rite in advance of Jesus' death (14:3–9). Her act, one of the last in the narrative to accord dignity to Jesus, will be told in her memory wherever the gospel is proclaimed (v. 9), as indeed hearers of Mark's Gospel can well attest. It is a shame that her name was forgotten (likely already in the tradition Mark has inherited; contrast John 12:1–8!), thus indicating ambivalence regarding women in the story and reflecting the deep ambivalence in Greco-Roman culture about the place and activity of women. The sacrificial gift of the poor widow in 12:41–44 enacts the radical, self-forsaking commitment that a rich man proved unable to undertake (10:17–22). At the same time, the destitute widow's offering amounts to a dramatic exposé of the exploitative abuses of the wealthy elite and the institutions they control. More ambiguity.

Ambiguity also extends to the portrayal of women followers of Jesus who, in the absence of the disciple deserters, observe the crucifixion from a distance and then visit the tomb (15:40–41, 47; 16:1–8). In each of the three mentions of these women, they bear names: the trio of "Mary Magdalene, Mary the mother of James the younger and of Joses, and Salome" in 15:40; the duo of "Mary Magdalene and Mary the mother of Joses" in 15:47; and again the trio of "Mary Magdalene, Mary the mother of James, and Salome" in 16:1. Their presence in these culminating scenes of the account, reflected also with variations in the other canonical Gospels, was beyond doubt one of the signal features of the crucifixion-and-resurrection tradition from the very beginning. Their presence in Mark's rendition registers the ambiguity we have discovered elsewhere in Mark's depiction of women. In some ways they embody a faithfulness that surpasses that of the male disciples: they are, after all, still present for these events! Nevertheless, it is striking that only now, after the report of Jesus' death, does the narrator mention that these women "used to follow him and provided for him when he was in

Galilee; and there were many other women who had come up with him to Jerusalem" (15:41). There has been a silent presence—or absence from the narration—until this retrospective aside.

Moreover, in the concluding participation by women in Mark's story, they fare no better than the male disciples do, at least within the limits of the narrative. Although the time to end secrecy has arrived, and although faith should prevail over fear in the light of the life-bearing announcement by the young man at the tomb, the women's final moment sees them fleeing in silent fear (16:8). Thus the hope that Mark's good-news account bears into the future rests no more in Jesus' women followers, or any other of the "minor" characters, than it does in the male disciples whose failure has received more prominent display. Regarding the activity and engagements of women in twenty-first-century faith communities, contemporary readers will find some suggestive cues in Mark's narrative, but they will need to press further.

Naturally, in a story for which the activity of men forms the central interest, the representations of masculinity are important in any gender analysis. Here I focus on the depiction of Jesus in Mark. According to Warren Carter and Colleen Conway, throughout the first part of Jesus' ministry, he displays the qualities of masculinity emphasized in Greco-Roman culture.[72] For example, Jesus demonstrates impressive capability in public speech and dialogue, and considerable power as the "stronger one" (1:7; cf. 3:27) who is able to heal sick people and expel demons. Ironically, his encounter with the Gerasene man tormented by an army of demons, Legion, when read symbolically as a confrontation with the invading Roman legion, exposes that army as out of control and also as subordinate (to Jesus), as unmanly and effeminate—and indeed not only as unmanly but also as demonic. Yet by the end of the story, Rome reasserts its domination, and the manly Jesus loses masculinity in his crucifixion: stripped naked, his body pierced, giving voice not to control of passion but to desolation, and utterly powerless.[73] Moreover, the prescription Jesus supplies male followers and potential disciples for their social engagements runs counter to conventional notions of masculinity: eschew both wealth and honor seeking (e.g., 9:34–35; 10:21–22, 23–25, 42–44); affirm the young child as community model (9:36–37; 10:13–16); forsake family and household (e.g., 10:28–30); bear a cross (8:34–37). This is not what real men look like in Mark's world. But it is the kind of life to which Jesus summons the members of the band for whom his divine "Father" is the sole household head.[74]

72. Carter, "Cross-Gendered Romans and Mark's Jesus," 142–43; Conway, *Behold the Man*, 95; cf. Carey, *Sinners*, 55–78.

73. For more detailed analysis of the story of Legion along these lines, see Carter, "Cross-Gendered Romans and Mark's Jesus."

74. It is revealing that when 10:30 lists the household members to be restored to disciples who have left all to follow Jesus, there is no mention of a father to head the household: no paterfamilias!

Gender Bending: Jesus Recruits Men of a Peculiar Kind

- No quest for wealth and honor
- The young child as community model
- Forsake family and household
- Self-surrender, too: carry a cross
- Position of household head is taken: no paterfamilias but the divine Father

---

As we have seen, several women in Mark's Gospel step from the narrative and social margins; in their encounters with Jesus, they improve on the disciples' performance of the distinctive values of God's reign. The Syrophoenician woman may even tutor Jesus on the scope of his vocation to heal and nourish. If one extends the analysis of gender to incorporate concern for low-status children, one sees even more clearly the refiguring of power and reversals of status in Mark's narrative. And men are given an unusual status-renouncing, wealth-renouncing, and power-renouncing ideal for their conduct. How might such a narrative, which reflects shaping by its culture but in significant ways challenges those mores and norms, contribute to the formation of an alternative community that enacts a distinctive set of values and relational commitments—whether in the first century or the twenty-first century?

Suffering and Hope: Jesus' Re-Mark-able Teaching

Discussion of Jesus' identity and vocation, as well as the role and mission of the disciples, has already highlighted the motif of suffering. In the selective analysis of Jesus' teaching in this section, I focus on two major teaching blocks in Mark that highlight the nexus of suffering and hope: the parable set of 4:1–34 and an extended discourse about the future in 13:1–37.[75]

Even though Mark presents much less of the content of Jesus' teaching than Matthew and Luke, the teaching authority of Jesus is a central feature of the Markan characterization (signaled at the outset in 1:22, as well as in the programmatic core-message summary of 1:15). The power of this teaching is evident both in bold and convincing speech and in mighty acts (esp. healing the sick and expelling demons [e.g., 1:27], at least when there is some faith present to welcome it [see 5:34; 10:52; cf. 6:1–6 and 9:14–29]).

75. Mark contains other substantial blocks of Jesus' teaching, mostly in the context of dialogue and debate. Especially important is a vineyard parable that centers on conflict between an absentee landlord and his tenants (within the narrative unit 11:27–12:12), followed by the image borrowed from Ps 118:22–23 of a chief cornerstone that brings ruin to those who reject it. This vineyard parable and scriptural stone metaphor orient Mark's audience to the meaning and course of Jesus' rejection at the hands of the local elite, about to culminate in the passion narrative. The temple-based custodians of power are represented as willfully rejecting the divine Son sent to the vineyard Israel (cf. 12:12: they recognize that Jesus has directed the parable and stone metaphor against them).

As a programmatic, interpretive commentary on the entire course of Jesus' ministry, Mark offers a parable about a sower and the various soil conditions and resulting diverse outcomes for the seeds he sows (4:3–8, with allegorical explication in vv. 14–20 for the disciples, and of course readers, in a private audience with Jesus).[76] The narrator frames the parable with clear signals that it epitomizes Jesus' message as a whole: (1) a "very large crowd" hears Jesus teach "many things in parables, and in his teaching he said" this parable (vv. 1–2); and (2) when the disciples register puzzlement about the meaning of the parable, Jesus responds with exasperation, "Do you not understand this parable? Then how will you understand all the parables?" (v. 13).

Without trying to pinpoint just which character groups correspond to each of the seed-soil-outcome figures in the parable (as, e.g., Tolbert does), Mark's audience will nevertheless be on alert as the narrative unfolds to observe whether believing response to the seed/word broadcast by Jesus will endure and prove fruitful. The seeming pessimism of the parable's structure—three-fourths of the seed groups fail in the end—anticipates the sober realism, if not outright despair, about the possibilities for positive human engagement with Jesus' proclamation and enactment of God's reign. Yet the climax of the parable casts the spotlight on the enormous yield that results from the one-fourth of the seed groups that do bear fruit (in escalating numbers: thirty-, sixty-, and a hundredfold; vv. 8, 20; cf. the hundredfold blessing of Isaac's planting in Gen 26:12). Beyond manifold and intense resistance and opposition from others (esp. scribes and Pharisees), repeated disciple failure, and the crucifixion of a desolate Jesus, there will be an abundant harvest, of which Jesus' promise of future reunion in Galilee and the discovery of an empty tomb are the only positive indicators (14:28; 16:7).

Two parables about the reign of God with which Jesus further explicates the message of the sower-seeds parable hint at the source of the abundant harvest, and therefore the basis for hope in the face of repeated discouragement. Even if a farmer has no idea how the growth occurs and indeed does not cause it to happen, seeds he has planted do issue in crops that he can harvest (4:26–29). And even the tiniest of seeds (the mustard) eventually yields, if not a towering tree, at least "the greatest of all shrubs" and a nesting place for birds (vv. 30–32). Hope, not discouragement, has the last word because the final outcome—the reality of God's reign—is a divine accomplishment.

One other detail of the parable of the sower and seeds is worth pausing for comment. Jesus injects the sobering image of persecution into the parable's explanation. From within the community's life, acquisitive greed is a serious threat to faithful discipleship (symbolized in the parabolic thorns, vv. 18–19). But so too, from the outside, is the prospect of adversity and opposition: despite initial reception of the message "with joy" (v. 18), "trouble or persecution arises on account of the word," and "they fall away" (v.

---

76. On the narrative function of this parable as "plot synopsis" for the Gospel, see Tolbert, *Sowing the Gospel*, 127–75.

17).[77] This theme sounds again in 10:30, where the phrase "with persecutions" unexpectedly intrudes in a series of good fortunes awaiting disciples who have "left everything" to follow Jesus (vv. 28–29).

Much of the eschatological discourse of Mark 13 is given over to this theme, especially verses 9–13 (the time of witness bearing to all nations will also bring hatred from all, even from within one's own household) and verse 19 (unprecedented suffering in the time before the end; cf. 8:34–38). Strife and hardship will not be limited to the community of Jesus' followers: international conflict will be intense (13:7–8), and even the heavens will be shaken (vv. 24–25).[78] It will be a protracted time of suffering during which perpetual vigilance will be crucial (the image of "watchfulness," using the imperatives *blepete* and *grēgoreite* in 13:5, 9, 23, 33, 35, 37). Yet the hard-pressed community of Jesus followers will not be left to their own devices: the Holy Spirit will guide their testimony (v. 11); they have assurance that they, God's chosen ones, will not be forgotten but will ultimately be rescued from peril (vv. 13, 20, 27). And this will happen soon, within a generation, though only after the period of deep and wide suffering that the discourse previews (vv. 28–30), notwithstanding the deceptive claims and activities of messianic pretenders (vv. 6, 21–22).

Through this longest discourse of Jesus in the Gospel, Mark's audience is equipped to navigate perilous times with confidence and courage, not being misled by the times or the prophets who misread them to their own and others' destruction. Suffering for God's people is therefore not ultimate and is only temporary. In the meantime, however, it is potent and menacing. Jesus walked the "way" of and to the cross. That same path awaits his followers, and to the degree that Mark's audience has firsthand experience of it, they will be empowered to face it well.

Ending the Story: The Rhetorical Impact of an Open-Ended Narrative

With an ending that resists narrative closure, Mark springs one final surprise on readers. In agreement with most recent scholarship, I regard 16:1–8 as the earliest conclusion of the (complete) Gospel and count the variety of

77. Although Satan is mentioned as the threat only in 4:15 (for the seeds sown along the path or "way"), mention of this archetypical enemy of God's reign (and word) hints that his enmity is a factor in other forms of unfruitful response to the message. Jesus' proclamation and praxis of the reign of God constitute an invasion of a world in which potent forces arrayed against God's reign must be rendered powerless. Jesus develops the meaning of his assault on demons in these terms in the tense conflict scene of 3:22–30.

78. Sacred space, too, will be violated: Jesus invokes the image of a "desolating sacrilege" positioned where it should not be (presumably the temple, though this is left implicit) from Daniel (8:13; 9:27; 11:31; 12:11) as the cue to listeners located in Judea to "flee to the mountains" (Mark 13:14) to escape what will be sudden, inescapable destruction (vv. 15–18). The historical referent of the desolating sacrilege remains undefined within Mark's text, but when "it" happens, it will be difficult to miss, though Mark's readers may need an interpretive aid (the narrator's parenthetical insertion "let the reader understand" in v. 14).

longer endings attested in the textual tradition (vv. 9–20 and other, shorter expansions) as secondary, resulting from many early Christians being dissatisfied with Mark's seemingly incomplete ending.[79] (One may judge the amplified endings in Matt 28, Luke 24, and John 20–21 as more effective responses to Mark's conclusion, with its lack of resurrection appearances and parting shot of disciple failure and silence.)

What is the rhetorical impact of this open-ended account on Mark's audience?[80] Is there hope for the future, beyond the present circumstance of Roman imperial domination, disciple confusion and failure, and a divine realm imagined—and experienced as effective in Jesus' activity—yet not fully established? The ending of the narrative intimates that assurance for the future, for hard-pressed Jesus followers, rests in and can only derive from the reliability of Jesus' promise and God's faithfulness to complete the work begun in Jesus' inauguration of God's reign. That is what the call back—and ahead—to Galilee must mean. The future for Mark's audience does not depend on human success or noble efforts at reform any more than does its present or its recent past as narrated in the Gospel.[81]

Nevertheless, right through to the close of the narrative, the juxtaposition of divine promise and activity, on the one hand, and comprehensive human failure, on the other, leaves a twofold task to the Markan audience. Even as they will be impelled to revisit the full story to seek deeper understanding, that understanding will also direct and energize their ongoing response to the narrative's "beginning of the good news." They will take their cue not from the failure of Jesus' followers but, instead, from his own model of bold proclamation and enactment of the good news of God's reign and from the imperative for divinely nurtured, courageous witness that he has left with them. Perhaps they will also find encouragement in the example of several "marginal" characters who, more consistently than Jesus' inner circle of followers, express trust (sometimes born of desperate need) in the benefaction—the salvation—that flows from participation in the realm of

79. On the ending of Mark, including the text-critical issues, see the detailed analysis—with commentary on the various later, longer endings—in Collins, *Mark*, 797–818; Black, *Mark*, 345–62. Telford (ed.) gives a brief summary in *The Interpretation of Mark*, 37–39 and accompanying notes on 60–61.

80. According to Camery-Hoggatt, the rhetoric of the Markan ending forces readers back into the story again with questions about what this all means and what is an apt response (*Irony in Mark's Gospel*, 177). Andrew T. Lincoln emphasizes the juxtaposition of human failure (16:8) and fulfillment of divine promise (16:7) and suggests that "the story and its ending were meant to give reassurance to its readers, who in all probability were facing persecution" ("The Promise and the Failure: Mark 16:7, 8," in Telford, ed., *The Interpretation of Mark*, 229–51, esp. 238, quote from 242; orig. published in *JBL* 108 [1989]: 283–300).

81. Henderson says it well: "The paradox of Mark's gospel is this: for disciples of Jesus, and thus for 'disciples' in Mark's hearing, hope lies finally not in anything they are able to do or not do, to believe or not believe, but rather in the immensely vulnerable act of Jesus' self-sacrifice, which fully exposes the firm hold of God's rule upon the earth" (*Christology and Discipleship*, 260). While not wishing in any way to temper that strong reading of Mark's message, I add that the crucifixion—which defines the content and character of God's reign—does need the resurrection, for all the mystery attending it, if the final note of Mark's story is not to be one of defeat and despair.

God.[82] As Tannehill reads the Gospel's ending, "The story is not over. It continues into the time of the reader, and the author anticipates that each reader will decide how it comes out for himself [or herself]."[83] Or, better still, given the communal character of the Markan audience and its experience of the narrative, the communities of Jesus followers, of participants in the present-and-still-future divine reign, will decide together what all this must mean for their life together and their witness in the world.

Concluding Reflection: The Aims and Impact of Mark's Narrative

How does such a story shape audience response? Much depends on the ways in which readers are prompted by rhetorical signals in the narrative, especially as their identification with the leading characters in the story (particularly the disciples) is facilitated—and thwarted—and as they are tutored on their own vocation and mission, above all by the example and word of Jesus. Much also depends, of course, on the composition and circumstance of the audience, though we have little certainty about either. Nevertheless, with Mark's foregrounding of the elements of witness, danger, and potential persecution, what would this Gospel's earliest audience make of such a rendition of Jesus and his first followers?[84]

Vigorous argument has pressed the view that a primary aim of Mark's Gospel is to correct a "false Christology," one that highlighted Jesus' powers as a miracle worker.[85] It does seem clear that Mark is (re-?) educating its audience to embrace a peculiar understanding of the messianic role, one that eschews conventional notions of power, status, and kingship (whether inspired by Rome's emperor or King David) and makes room on the Messiah's résumé for vulnerability, the experience of desolation, and even the

---

82. As Malbon points out, Mark *generally* portrays the disciples as "fallible followers," while "the minor characters are *most often* presented as exemplars"; although they appear only briefly, "they serve as models for attitudes and behaviors" for both major characters and "especially for the implied audience" (*Mark's Jesus*, 221, emphasis orig.).

83. Robert C. Tannehill, "The Disciples in Mark: The Function of a Narrative Role," in Telford, ed., *The Interpretation of Mark*, 169–95, esp. 190; orig. published in *JR* 57 (1977): 386–405.

84. I prefer this angle of approach to the more conventional discussion of the author's aims and purposes, which are of course accessible indirectly through the kind of story Mark has told—though only by way of readers' construction of it (for perceptive analysis of the reader's experience of Mark's narrative, see esp. Fowler, *Let the Reader Understand*).

85. Norman Perrin, "The Christology of Mark: A Study in Methodology," in Telford, ed., *The Interpretation of Mark*, 129; cf. 132; orig. published in *JR* 51 (1971): 173–87. An influential early study proposing this interpretive approach was Theodore J. Weeden, *Mark: Traditions in Conflict* (Philadelphia: Fortress Press, 1971). Weeden correlates the negative portrait of the disciples in Mark and the accent on Jesus' messianic suffering and concludes that Mark is countering a misguided Christology that emphasizes Jesus' powers as a miracle-working divine man. Clifton Black captures the provocative force of Weeden's view of Mark's Gospel, which he brands "a polemical attack against miracle-mongering heretics" (*Mark: Images of an Apostolic Interpreter*, 13).

deep dishonor of crucifixion. Yet the claim that Mark, in the last half of the narrative, opposes Jesus the suffering Messiah to the first half's depiction of Jesus the mighty wonder worker—that claim is not finally convincing.[86] Mark offers more than a remedial course in ideas about Jesus as the Messiah and Son of God. The Gospel binds tightly together the peculiar vocation of Jesus the Messiah and the equally strange vocation of those who follow him, from the Twelve onward to Mark's earliest audience, and across the centuries until the present.

Recognition of this bond between Jesus and his disciples has led many readers to emphasize the paraenetic force of Mark's narrative.[87] Even as readers take the baton of mission and witness in the face of strenuous opposition, they are both challenged and encouraged to persevere, emboldened by the promise of the risen Lord's return (sooner rather than later) and, in the meantime, empowered by God's Spirit presence. Moreover, that witness and the communal practices that nourish it reflect cultural hybridity: identity for these early Christians is still a matter of some negotiation and even experimentation. Mark's Jesus carries out his mission mostly among Jews—even voicing a distinct preference for that demographic (7:24–30)—and engages in animated debates with other Jewish teachers about wise interpretation and faithful practice of the Torah (and Scripture more generally). Yet there are enough signals in what he says and does (esp. in 7:1–30) of porous or expanding communal boundaries that the presence of non-Jews in Mark's audience surely is not disconcerting but a matter of course. Such renegotiated, culturally blended, and heterogeneous communal identity and correlated practices were probably situated amid or immediately after the fall of Jerusalem and the demise of its institutions centered on the temple. That also means that, to the degree that the formation of the Markan audience occurred in Roman imperial space, the Gospel is fostering imagination of the possibilities of a counterimperial presence in an alternative community that engages in a distinctive set of practices, though not insurrection (like Barabbas). Mark charts a course that Luke especially (in both Gospel and Acts) will amplify. Sovereign rule with a difference: the *basileia theou* (reign of God)!

---

86. For sharp critique of the view that divides Mark's Christology into two narrative halves, and splits the miracle working of Jesus from his cross, see Henderson, *Christology and Discipleship*, 9–13.

87. For vigorous presentation of this approach, see, e.g., Best, *Following Jesus*; Tannehill, "Disciples in Mark"; cf. Boring, *Mark*, 21–22; Henderson, *Christology and Discipleship*, 5–9, 257–58; Telford, *Theology of Mark*, 151–63.

4. The Gospel according to Matthew

Although Mark's Gospel suffered from relative neglect in the early centuries of Christian history, many treasured Matthew as the favored Gospel. Especially useful as a teaching document, Matthew builds on Mark's narrative pattern but greatly expands the presentation of Jesus' teaching, provides opening and ending frames (ancestry and birth-infancy narrative in chs. 1–2 and resurrection appearances in ch. 28), and arranges the materials into a more systematically structured whole.

Historical Questions
Who?

As with the other canonical Gospels, the author of Matthew is unknown to us; the earliest attribution to the apostle Matthew comes from the second century CE. In his fourth-century history of Christianity, Eusebius attributes to the mid-second-century bishop of Hierapolis, Papias, the view that "Matthew made an ordered arrangement of the oracles in the Hebrew [Aramaic?] language, and each one translated [or, interpreted] as he was able" (*Hist. eccl.* 3.39.16).[1] However, appeal to Papias in the quest to identify the author of Matthew is problematic. To mention only two issues, this statement refers to oracles (sayings), not a complete Gospel narrative, and although it identifies Hebrew as the original language of composition, the consensus position is that Matthew was first composed in Greek, even if the author lived in a cultural-linguistic environment that was bilingual or trilingual.[2] Perhaps one might read Papias as opining that "Matthew arranged the traditions in a Jewish manner" (rather than in the Hebrew language).[3] That position, while

1. The ET is from W. D. Davies and Dale C. Allison, *Matthew*, ICC, 3 vols. (Edinburgh: T&T Clark, 1988–97), 1:8; cf. Irenaeus, *Haer.* 3.1.1). On the testimony of Papias, see Robert H. Gundry, *Matthew: A Commentary on His Handbook for a Mixed Church under Persecution*, 2nd ed. (Grand Rapids: Wm. B. Eerdmans Publishing Co., 1994), 609–20.

2. For detailed discussion of the authorship of Matthew, see Davies and Allison, *Matthew*, 1:7–58. Davies and Allison carefully analyze the view that the author of this Gospel was a Gentile (e.g., K. W. Clark, "The Gentile Bias in Matthew," *JBL* 66 [1947]: 165–72; cf. John P. Meier, *The Vision of Matthew: Christ, Church, and Morality in the First Gospel*, TI [New York: Paulist Press, 1979], 17–25). They conclude, with most Matthean commentators, that the author of Matthew was a Jew; cf. Daniel J. Harrington, SJ: an "anonymous" author of "Jewish background" (*The Gospel of Matthew*, SP 1 [Collegeville, MN: Liturgical Press, 1991], 8). For convenience, I refer to the author as Matthew but without advancing any claims regarding personal identity.

3. Ulrich Luz, *Matthew*, trans. James E. Crouch, ed. Helmut Koester, Hermeneia, 3 vols.

certainly true to the character of this Gospel, still does not purchase much when it comes to naming an author.

One of the intriguing details in Matthew's Gospel is its renaming of the tax collector Levi as Matthew, in the call story of Matthew 9:9–13 (cf. Mark 2:13–17; Luke 5:27–32; and Matt 10:3, unlike Mark 3:18 and Luke 6:15, also specifies the occupation of this member of the Twelve). Has early inference given rise to the tradition of Matthew's authorship? Or was the teaching authority of this apostle an important factor at some stage as the Gospel tradition was developed in this community, yet not in the eventual composition of the narrative?

Whatever the precise personal information about this author, now elusive, it is difficult to emerge from immersion in this narrative world without sensing the good fit between the image of the scribe Jesus provides at the close of the parables discourse (Matt 13:52) and the Gospel's author. If this is indeed a self-portrait of sorts, we encounter an author who is well-trained as a scribe, being both literate and knowledgeable in the Jewish Scriptures, but who has now been (re)educated for the "kingdom of heaven," who is able to draw out of his treasure chest both what is new and what is old. That is to say, this rendition of the story of Jesus will forge positive connections between the "new thing" of heaven's reign, as commended and enacted by Jesus, and the Jewish Scriptures and traditions. It will be a story marked by both continuity and discontinuity.

Matthew writes from and for a Christian-Jewish community that has been engaged in serious dialogue and sometimes heated debate with synagogues for which the narrative's coalition of "scribes and Pharisees" represents the emerging leadership and ideology—"formative Judaism," on the path toward rabbinic Judaism—in the aftermath of the Jewish War's catastrophic conclusion (66–74 CE).[4] Among the competing proposals for Judaism's future identity and practice in the last third of the first century, Matthew's narrative makes a case (for the sake of its first hearers, the Christian-Jewish community in which it arose, and for others reading after them) for a construction of Jewish identity, conviction, and practice centering on the claim that, in Jesus, God's Messiah has come to restore Israel. Evidently the diminishing power of this claim late in the first century, in the face of ascendant proto-rabbinic teaching, required of this author a concerted endeavor of both legitimation, in support of the formation of a Jewish community for which the Messiah Jesus is focal, and delegitimation, countering the views and practices associated with Pharisees/rabbis. But where?

(Minneapolis: Fortress Press, 1992–2005), 1:46. Here Luz follows Josef Kürzinger's interpretation of the Papias testimony: *Papias von Hierapolis und die Evangelien des Neuen Testaments* (Regensburg: Pustet, 1983), 20–23.

4. Especially helpful sketches of Matthew's location within this milieu are provided by J. Andrew Overman, *Matthew's Gospel and Formative Judaism: The Social World of the Matthean Community* (Minneapolis: Augsburg Fortress, 1990); and Anthony J. Saldarini, *Matthew's Christian-Jewish Community*, Chicago Studies in the History of Judaism (Chicago: University of Chicago Press, 1994).

When and Where?   Galilee is prominent in Matthew's account of Jesus' ministry, and Capernaum, a Galilean city on the north shore of the Sea of Galilee, even figures as Jesus' home city when he begins his ministry (4:13). Moreover, the proximity of Matthew's narrative (and the first audience its concerns appear to imply) to the life, debates, and concerns of Judaism in Palestine after Jerusalem's fall to Roman armies in 70 CE points toward an origin there. At the same time, for all its absorption in the affairs and debates of Jewish communities (note, too, the limited mission focus in 10:5–6 and 15:24), the Gospel also creates an opening for Gentiles, especially in the concluding scene (28:16–20), but with earlier anticipations, such as the magi's acclamation of King Jesus (2:1–12) and the exemplary centurion of 8:5–13.

When seeking a home for Matthew, one finds significant clues in its preoccupation with Jewish identity and practice in contest with formative (proto-rabbinic) Judaism, and in a setting that also holds in prospect some interaction with Gentiles. If that setting likely, though not certainly, was urban,[5] a plausible case can be made that the initial home of Matthew was one of the cities in Syria or northern (upper) Galilee. Antioch is the most common suggestion, a locale supported by the early attestation of Matthew's Gospel in the letters of Ignatius, bishop in that city early in the second century (ca. 110–115 CE).[6] Several scholars situate Matthew's earliest audience in or near Syria, but are hesitant to specify Antioch, though also without ruling out that city.[7] Overman is inclined to locate Matthew's community in a Galilean city such as Sepphoris or Tiberias, leaning toward Sepphoris because of its importance in nascent rabbinic Judaism.[8] Whatever the precise location, the Gospel reflects the intense struggle of Matthew's author and its first readers for a legitimate place on the landscape of emerging Judaism, in (or near) northern Palestine after Jerusalem's fall in 70 CE.

The time of the Gospel's composition can be estimated with some confidence within a fairly narrow range, approximately 80–90 CE. If one assumes Matthew's dependence on Mark as a primary source and places Mark's composition and dissemination around the year 70, the earliest possible date for Matthew would be the decade of the 70s. Even without those assumptions, the presence in Matthew of explicit indications of the catastrophic destruction of the temple and Jerusalem in 70 CE points to the period after 70 (see 22:7; 24:1–2). Possible allusions to portions of Matthew in the letters

---

5. On Matthew's preference for the Greek word *polis* (city), see, e.g., Jack Dean Kingsbury, *Matthew as Story*, 2nd ed. (Philadelphia: Fortress Press, 1988), 152. While Mark employs the nouns for city (*polis*) and village (*kōmē*) in about equal proportion (8 vs. 7 occurrences), Matthew shows decided preference for "city" (27 vs. 4).

6. E.g., ibid., 148, "a good conjecture"; Gundry, *Matthew*, 609, "best guess"; Davies and Allison, *Matthew*, 1:147, "best educated guess."

7. E.g., R. T. France, *The Gospel of Matthew*, NICNT (Grand Rapids: Wm. B. Eerdmans Publishing Co., 2007), 15–18; Luz, *Matthew*, 1:56–58; Harrington (*Matthew*, 9–10) deems a Syrian city plausible (Antioch, Damascus, or Edessa) but thinks "a good case can also be made for Palestine" (perhaps Caesarea Maritima or a Galilean city).

8. Overman, *Matthew's Gospel and Formative Judaism*, 159 n. 20.

of Ignatius, bishop of Antioch in the first decade of the second century, set the close of the first century as the latest date for the Gospel's composition.[9]

What?

Matthew's expansions of Mark, especially its attention to the family origins and remarkable birth and early childhood of Jesus, fit the Gospel even more securely within the Greco-Roman biographical tradition.[10] Drawing on the work of Aune, Stanton observes that the genre of Graeco-Roman *bios* (life or biography) enables Matthew to legitimate the social belief or value system that is personified in the subject of his biography.[11] Thus, as Aune points out, "Greco-Roman biographies often have a teaching or didactic function, presenting the subject as a paradigm of virtue," and therefore have an encomiastic quality (i.e., praise for the central figure of the *bios* and defense against attack).[12] Neyrey makes this feature of the genre definitive for Matthew, classifying the Gospel as "encomiastic biography."[13] Encomium praises its hero for (1) origins and birth; (2) nurture and training; (3) accomplishments and deeds (soul, body, and fortune); and (4) noble death—all of which Neyrey finds in ample supply in Matthew.

As a biographical narrative, Matthew not only extols its central figure but also commends his manner of life as model for readers. Particularly in a Jewish document like Matthew, which emphasizes integrity of life that puts teaching into practice, this is a primary interest (notable, e.g., in the conclusion to the Sermon on the Mount: 7:15–27; cf. 23:2–3). But Matthew's

9. At a number of points in his letters, Ignatius invokes Matthew, or traditions attested in Matthew: e.g., Ign. *Eph.* 5.2 and Matt 18:19–20; Ign. *Eph.* 14.2 and Matt 7:15–20; Ign. *Eph.* 15.1 and Matt 23:8; Ign. *Eph.* 19.2–3 and Matt 2:1–12; Ign. *Smyrn.* 1.1 and Matt 3:15; Ign. *Smyrn.* 8.2 and Matt 18:20; Ign. *Pol.* 2.2 and Matt 10:16. William R. Schoedel is uncertain whether Ignatius draws from Matthew as a written source or from "materials of a Matthean type" that were available to Matthew apart from the Gospel ("Ignatius and the Reception of the Gospel of Matthew in Antioch," in *Social History of the Matthean Community: Cross-Disciplinary Approaches*, ed. David L. Balch [Minneapolis: Fortress Press, 1991], 129–77, esp. 129, 158, 175–77). Schoedel nevertheless concludes that "Matthew or materials close to Matthew form the backbone of the gospel materials in Ignatius" (ibid., 154). Regarding the relation of Matthew to the *Didache* (ca. 100 CE), Alan J. P. Garrow argues that Matthew has made use of the *Didache*, rather than the reverse (*The Gospel of Matthew's Dependence on the* Didache [London: T&T Clark, 2004]). This view, if correct, would require a later date for Matthew's composition.

10. David E. Aune classifies the canonical Gospels generally as a subtype of Greco-Roman biography (*The New Testament in Its Literary Environment*, LEC [Philadelphia: Westminster Press, 1987], 46, 64).

11. Graham Stanton, *Studies in Matthew and Early Christianity*, ed. Markus Bockmuehl and David Kincicum, WUNT 2/309 (Tübingen: Mohr Siebeck, 2013), 97–103, esp. 102.

12. Aune, *New Testament in Its Literary Environment*, 36. He observes that there is some tension between the historical interests of the biography genre and its concern to present its subject as exemplary for readers.

13. Jerome H. Neyrey, *Honor and Shame in the Gospel of Matthew* (Louisville, KY: Westminster John Knox Press, 1998). Neyrey is followed by Charles H. Talbert, *Matthew*, Paideia (Grand Rapids: Baker Academic, 2010), 6. Philip L. Shuler was an earlier proponent of this view, in *A Genre for the Gospels: The Biographical Character of Matthew* (Philadelphia: Fortress Press, 1982).

horizon of concern extends beyond the individual Jesus and his disciple followers. Matthew inserts the life of Jesus (and the lives of his followers) into the ongoing history of a people, with a view to situating his Christian-Jewish group securely within Israel's story. So it comes as no surprise that Jewish Scripture (primarily through the vehicle of the Old Greek or LXX) also exerts great influence on Matthew's account of Jesus. If claims that the narrative presses on behalf of Jesus are to convince readers (hearers), it is crucial to demonstrate that his life and messianic activity fulfill Old Testament prophetic promise and pattern and, moreover, that his teaching and example constitute a legitimate interpretation of the Torah. Matthew leaves no doubt that, for this author and audience, Jesus is not merely a credible exponent of Torah, of Scripture, but is the definitive Teacher (the claim is explicit in 23:8, 10). Matthew appropriates Greco-Roman biography in service of a claim to the Jewish heritage.

Literary Design

Matthew provides readers a clear road map for navigating his story. The opening lines make the identity and significance of the central character crystal clear: "Jesus the Messiah, the son of David, the son of Abraham" (1:1). The genealogy of the next sixteen verses then situates him within Israel's history and structures that history in fourteen-generation spans that arc from Father Abraham to King David, from David to the Babylonian exile, and from exile to the arrival of the Messiah (v. 17). So Matthew orients readers from the beginning to Jesus' import as the *telos*—the goal and fulfillment—of Israel's story. The account of Jesus' birth and relocation from Bethlehem to Nazareth, by way of Egypt (1:18–2:23), reinforces this fundamental affirmation of 1:1–17: five prophecy-fulfillment quotations occur within this section (see 1:22–23; 2:5–6, 15, 17–18, 23).[14] Matthew's narrative opens with repeated claims that God is guiding Israel's history toward its long-awaited completion, as announced by the ancient prophets. The dual names the narrative assigns the newly born Messiah/King—Jesus and Emmanuel—reveal the deep meaning of his arrival: "He will save his people from their sins" (Jesus, 1:21) and, by way of fresh appropriation of Isaiah 7:14, he will embody divine presence "with us" (Emmanuel, 1:23).

Beginning at 3:1, Matthew joins Mark's narrative.[15] The section 3:1–4:11 prepares for the ministry of the adult Jesus by situating hearers in the Judean

---

14. Indeed, the whole narrative of preparation for the Messiah's coming to Israel (through Matt 4:16) is laced with scriptural quotations and allusions; see also 3:3, 17; 4:4, 6 (quoted by the devil), 7, 10, 14–16.

15. Gundry observes that early in the Gospel, Matthew "freely rearranged his Markan materials" and inserted other material, much of it shared with Luke (*Matthew*, 10). After 14:1, however, Matthew's narrative "faithfully follows Mark" (Davies and Allison, *Matthew*, 1:72). What Gundry explains as the result of "editorial fatigue" (*Matthew*, 10) makes sense to Davies

wilderness. There they first encounter the baptizing prophet John (3:1–12) and then, following Jesus' submission to John's repentance washing in the Jordan River (vv. 13–17)—not in confession of sins but "to fulfill all righteousness" (v. 15)[16]—they overhear Jesus' struggle to discern the meaning of his vocation (4:1–11). Though seemingly driven by the devil, the ordeal of testing is actually depicted as divinely purposed: the Holy Spirit leads Jesus into the desert *for the purpose* of undergoing the devil's testing (4:1). Publicly revealed by heaven to be the beloved Son of God (3:17—"this is" differs from "you are" in Mark 1:11), Jesus must embrace a particular understanding of that status: "If [indeed] you are the Son of God . . ." (Matt 4:3, 6). Not exploiting special powers to benefit himself, not expecting divine intervention to rescue him from mortal danger at the Temple Mount, not coveting glorious rule over the nations at the expense of loyalty to God, but—as 3:15 anticipates and the course of Jesus' ensuing ministry will confirm—a life of integrity, obedient to God's purpose, so as "to fulfill all righteousness." The wilderness testing presents Jesus' "no" to a wrongly conceived messianic vocation. The rest of the story will display the content of his "yes" to God.

Matthew 4:12–25 is a transitional narrative in two parts. First, verses 12–16 mark shifts in spatial location, from the Judean wilderness to Galilee and then from hometown Nazareth to a new home at Capernaum, and spell out the scripturally informed significance of that spatial movement. Jesus takes up residence in "Galilee of the Gentiles [nations]," who will now receive light in the midst of darkness and death (by way of a quotation from Isa 9:1–2 [8:23–9:1 LXX]). Second, Matthew 4:17–25 presents the launch of Jesus' public activity: "From that time [*apo tote*] Jesus began to proclaim, 'Repent, for the kingdom of heaven has come near'" (v. 17).[17] Heaven places its signature on Jesus' ministry, with its focal message that God's reign is now pressing into Israel's story. At the Sea of Galilee, Jesus immediately recruits followers in the tandem fisher-brother duos of Peter and Andrew, James and John (vv. 18–22), who without delay answer a summons to turn from (dead) fish to catching people (alive). Concluding this transitional narrative, verses 23–25 then provide a general narrator's summary of Jesus' initial activity of teaching and healing, emphasizing its effectiveness ("curing every disease and every sickness among the people," v. 23; "They brought to him all the

---

and Allison as a compositional strategy, since Matthew by this point has incorporated all his Q material, except for what he has reserved for the discourses of chs. 18, 24–25. So he must "change his procedure" in following his sources after ch. 13 (*Matthew*, 1:71).

16. So Matthew's account diminishes the potential embarrassment of this event, too deeply embedded in the tradition to omit.

17. Kingsbury takes the tag *apo tote ērxato ho Iēsous*, "from that time on Jesus began," in 4:17 and 16:21 as the key to the literary structure of Matthew, which therefore has three large sections (*Matthew: Structure, Christology, Kingdom* [Philadelphia: Fortress Press, 1975], 1–39); note the brief critique in Donald Senior, *The Gospel of Matthew*, IBT (Nashville: Abingdon Press, 1997), 28–31. For summary and appraisal of diverse analyses of Matthew's structure, see David Bauer, *The Structure of Matthew's Gospel: A Study in Literary Design* (London: Bloomsbury Academic, 2015; orig., Sheffield Academic, 1988).

sick, . . . and he cured them," v. 24) and its extensive impact ("His fame spread throughout all Syria," v. 24; "Great crowds followed him from Galilee, the Decapolis, Jerusalem, Judea, and from beyond the Jordan," v. 25).[18] With the notice of "great crowds," Matthew sets the stage for the first major statement of Jesus' teaching, his unpacking of the message that God's reign is (re)claiming God's people.

After this narrative prelude, Matthew presents Jesus' public career in five segments, alternating between extensive discourses of Jesus and accounts of his activity (healings, controversies, etc.). Although Jesus teaches throughout the narrative (e.g., in collections of episodic anecdotes, or *chreiai*, that pivot on conflictual encounters of challenge and riposte),[19] Matthew focuses the presentation of Jesus' teaching in five major discourses, each concluding with a narrator's summary that marks the transition to episodes of healing, conflict, and dialogue (7:28; 11:1; 13:53; 19:1; 26:1: "Now when Jesus had finished [these sayings, etc.]").

Discourses of Jesus in Matthew

- Sermon on the Mount (Matt 5–7)
- Instruction for the disciples' mission (Matt 10)
- Parables about the reign of God (Matt 13)
- Practical wisdom shaping the community of disciples (Matt 18)
- Indictment of scribes and Pharisees (Matt 23)
- Pictures of end-time judgment and deliverance (Matt 24–25)

The discourses (actually, compilations or anthologies of sayings of Jesus) have considerable thematic coherence:

- Matthew 5–7: Sermon on the Mount, a challenging articulation of the pattern of discipleship and its radical "righteousness" (*dikaiosynē*, 5:6, 10, 20; 6:33) in the world God rules (lit., "the kingdom of the heavens," 5:3, 10, 19–20)

18. By my count, Matt 4:23–24 presents the first two of nine statements by the narrator that highlight the extraordinary effectiveness of Jesus' healing ministry, aiding all the sick and demon-possessed persons in the crowds that flock to him: 4:23, 24; 8:16; 9:35; 12:15; 14:35–36; 15:30–31; 19:2; 21:14 (only Matthew narrates healing activity by Jesus within the temple precincts). This is one of the striking features of Matthew's narrative, as is the explicit claim that Jesus' healing activity fulfills the prophetic paradigm for God's Servant-Messiah (see 8:17; 12:17–21; cf. 4:16). In 10:1 Jesus conveys this healing capability to the Twelve.

19. On the *chreia* form, see ch. 3 above. In sociorhetorical analysis, public exchanges between social peers like Jesus and Pharisees in Matthew's Gospel are viewed as agonistic contests for honor, in which a verbal (or physical) challenge from another requires an effective response (riposte); the analysis draws upon maneuvers in the sport of fencing as metaphor for social interactions. For description of challenge and riposte in honor-focused social exchanges and their prominence in Matthew, see Neyrey, *Honor and Shame*, 44–52.

- Matthew 10: Instructions for mission to be undertaken by followers of Jesus, in this first phase only among the "lost sheep of the house of Israel," throughout "the towns of Israel" (vv. 5–6, 23)
- Matthew 13: Parables revealing the character of God's reign
- Matthew 18: Practical wisdom to shape the disciple community's relations and interactions, featuring images of humility, mercy, and accountability
- Matthew 24–25: Beyond adversity and suffering that will soon greet the Messiah in Jerusalem, and later his followers in mission, images of the consummation of God's reign and purposes in a set of scenarios of eschatological judgment and deliverance

One might think that the fifth discourse actually begins in chapter 23 (a harsh indictment of the scribes and Pharisees, addressed to the crowds and disciples), which proceeds with brief transition (24:1) into the eschatological discourse of Matthew 24–25. However, 24:1 signals a shift in location (away from the temple) and audience (now restricted to the disciples in private session), so differing topic, setting, and audience indicate that these are distinct discourses. Indeed, Matthew presents substantial teaching by Jesus throughout the narrative, beyond the five major discourses that conclude with the formula "when Jesus had finished [these things, instructing, parables]." These five discourse-closing formulas from the narrator do reinforce hearers' impression of the thematic coherence of each preceding sayings cluster.[20]

Although the incorporation of substantial materials not present in Mark results in a less obvious geographically oriented structuring in Matthew (Galilee → journey to Jerusalem → Jerusalem), this basic spatial movement does continue to shape the narrative design to some degree.[21] Matthew's Gospel appears, then, to present a mixed structure, a combination of multiple techniques for ordering material tapped from Matthew's several source traditions, both oral and written.[22] Nevertheless, recognizing the importance of the major blocks of teaching material and the character of the narrated activity that surrounds them, one might sketch the structure of 5:1–25:46 as follows:

---

20. Recognition of the presence of teaching material throughout the narrative of Jesus' activity renders less convincing the argument that the five major discourses hold the key to Matthew's narrative design—even less so the once-influential view of Benjamin Bacon that the five discourses contribute to the Matthean portrayal of Jesus as the new Moses, who delivers five "books" of a new Torah corresponding to the books of Moses (e.g., *Studies in Matthew* [New York: Henry Holt, 1930]); notice the refinement of Bacon's structural analysis in Christopher R. Smith, "Literary Evidence of a Fivefold Structure in the Gospel of Matthew," *NTS* 43 (1997): 540–51.

21. France emphasizes this structuring principle in Matthew (*Gospel of Matthew*, 4); cf. Harrington, *Matthew*, 5.

22. Gundry (*Matthew*, 10–11) and Davies and Allison (*Matthew*, 1:72) also observe that Matthew's Gospel is "structurally mixed."

5:1–7:27	*Discourse:* Jesus summons disciples and overhearing crowds to a life of radical righteousness, responding to the gracious benefaction of God and befitting participation in heaven's reign
7:28–29	*Transitional notice:* Teaching concluded; Jesus impresses as a teacher with unparalleled authority
8:1–9:35	*Cycle of stories* about healing and discipleship, eliciting divergent responses from recipients of healing, observing crowds, and critical scribes and Pharisees
9:36–10:4	*Transitional narrative,* highlighting Jesus' teaching activity and effective healing ministry, the presence of shepherdless crowds, and the need for more workers for an abundant harvest (9:36–38), then Jesus' call and grant of authority to the Twelve
10:5–42	*Discourse:* Directions for mission (phase 1: restricted to "the towns of Israel," v. 23)
11:1	*Transitional notice:* Teaching concluded, but Jesus continues his itinerant proclamation
11:2–12:50	*Cycle of conflict stories*—even acts of healing spark opposition
13:1–2	*Transitional notice:* Burgeoning crowds force Jesus into a boat lakeside to teach
13:3–52	*Discourse:* Parables about God's reign, in two parts • Public teaching in parables addressed to the crowd (vv. 3–35) • Private explanation and further parables addressed to disciples (vv. 36–52)
13:53	Transitional notice: teaching in parables concluded
13:54–17:27	Diverse responses to the activity of Jesus
18:1–35	*Discourse:* Forming a community with values and practices that mirror the character and commitments of God
19:1–2	*Transitional narrative:* Teaching concluded, change in spatial location to Judea/Jerusalem, and another notice of crowds and expansive healing activity
19:3–23:39	Actions, debates, and teaching centering on the character of authentic leadership
[23:1–39	*Discourse:* How *not* to lead—critique of scribes and Pharisees addressed to the crowd and disciples]
24:1–2	*Transitional notice:* Leaving the temple behind—in spatial movement and prophetic oracle

24:3–25:46   *Discourse*: Jesus' final public teaching, offering images of culminating judgment and liberation

26:1–2   *Transitional notice*: Teaching concluded, and Jesus gives a poignant reminder of the location in the story's plot

The final section of the narrative relates culminating events in and near Jerusalem, with the exception that the concluding scene returns to a mountain in Galilee, where Jesus issues parting directions for the (remaining) eleven leaders of the disciple group (28:16–20).

26:3–27:66   Narrative of the passion
28:1–15   Easter narrative: Resurrection appearance (vv. 1–10) and conspiracy to deceive regarding the empty tomb (vv. 11–15)
28:16–20   Return to Galilee and parting mountaintop instructions for the Eleven

Other Narrative Strategies (with an Eye to Mark)

Matthew's Gospel presents evidence of considerable care in narrative construction. If Mark and Q stand behind the Gospel as basic sources (each in a form no longer accessible), along with other traditions only preserved in Matthew, (re)arrangement of materials yields a more coherent narration with identifiable topical or thematic concentrations.[23]

Narrative Techniques in Matthew with an Eye to Mark
• *Inclusio* (bookends) framing a unit or section
• "Two is better": doubling of scenes, sayings, and characters
• Three's company: triads
• Compact narration of healing stories
• Revisionist sketch of the disciples
• Multiplication of the narrator's summary notices: Healing and Scripture fulfillment

23. On Q and the question of Matthew's literary sources, see ch. 2 above. Luz offers a concise summary of structuring methods (*Matthew*, 1:5–8). Matthew gathers materials similar in form or content; composes sections that show symmetry in length; employs numerical schemes (esp. 3, but also 2, 4, and 7); suggests themes through repetition of key words and title-like or summarizing verses; favors repetitions, doublets, inclusions, and chiastic ring compositions; and uses predictions and signals that prepare readers for what comes later. In a detailed analysis of Matthew's literary style, Davies and Allison (*Matthew*, 1:72–96) identify a similar set of compositional techniques: Semitisms (80–85); triads (86–87); "twos" (87); repetitions, including doublets (88–92); inclusion (92–93); and parallelism (94). Davies and Allison regard the prominence of inclusio (inclusion), chiasm (ring composition = inverted parallelism, as with A B B′ A′), numbers, repetition, and both Septuagintisms and Semitisms as "evidence of a mind steeped in the OT and Jewish tradition" (96).

Inclusio Bookends

At several points, Matthew frames a portion of the narrative through the device of inclusio, in which similar expressions or ideas both begin and end the section. Virtually the entire life of Jesus is placed within one encompassing frame:

- They shall name him Emmanuel, which means, "God is with us." (1:23)
- And remember, I am with you always, to the end of the age. (28:20)

The Gospel thereby presents the full course of Jesus' life and mission as mediating divine presence among God's people and then, after his death and resurrection, continuing that presence through the mission of his followers to all nations. One discovers additional examples of less sweeping inclusios.

Enclosing the first phase of Jesus' activity of teaching and healing in Galilee:

- Jesus went throughout Galilee, teaching in their synagogues and proclaiming the good news of the kingdom and curing every disease and every sickness among the people. (4:23)
- Then Jesus went about all the cities and villages, teaching in their synagogues, and proclaiming the good news of the kingdom, and curing every disease and every sickness. (9:35)

Framing a set of eight beatitudes formulated as third-person declarations:

- Blessed are the poor in spirit, for theirs is the kingdom of heaven. (5:3)
- Blessed are those who are persecuted for righteousness' sake, for theirs is the kingdom of heaven. (5:10)

Introducing and concluding a set of dialogues focused on eating and ritual practices:

- Why do your disciples break the tradition of the elders? For they do not wash their hands before they eat. (15:2)
- These are what defile a person, but to eat with unwashed hands does not defile. (15:20)

Use of the technique of inclusio provides a structuring framework and also effectively reinforces audience discernment of the central concerns and affirmations in a section of the narrative.

Doubling of Scenes, Sayings, and Characters

Matthew's narrative often presents patterns of two. Sometimes these are received from the Matthean source or tradition, and sometimes they result from combination of sources that both contain variants of the same material.

But they can also stem from creative compositional activity by the author. The narrative repeats sayings of Jesus, as in these examples:

- On receiving Jesus:
  — Whoever welcomes you welcomes me, and whoever welcomes me welcomes the one who sent me. (Matt 10:40; cf. Luke 10:16)
  — Whoever welcomes one such child in my name welcomes me. (Matt 18:5; cf. Mark 9:37; Luke 9:48)
- On following Jesus and denying self:
  — Whoever does not take up the cross and follow me is not worthy of me. Those who find their life will lose it, and those who lose their life for my sake will find it. (Matt 10:38–39; cf. Luke 14:27; 17:33)
  — If any want to become my followers, let them deny themselves and take up their cross and follow me. For those who want to save their life will lose it, and those who lose their life for my sake will find it. (Matt 16:24–25; cf. Mark 8:34–35)
- Jonah as a sign for a generation:
  — Then some of the scribes and Pharisees said to him, "Teacher, we wish to see a sign from you." But he answered them, "An evil and adulterous generation asks for a sign, but no sign will be given to it except the sign of the prophet Jonah." (Matt 12:38–39 [vv. 40–42 elaborate]; cf. Luke 11:16, 29–30)
  — The Pharisees and Sadducees came, and to test Jesus they asked him to show them a sign from heaven. . . . An evil and adulterous generation asks for a sign, but no sign will be given to it except the sign of Jonah. (Matt 16:1–4; cf. Mark 8:11–12)
- Appeals for repentance in the face of the arrival of heaven's reign:
  — Repent, for the kingdom of heaven has come near. (Matt 3:2, spoken by John)
  — Repent, for the kingdom of heaven has come near. (4:17, spoken by Jesus)
- Mercy is more important than ritual sacrifice (Jesus quoting Hos 6:6 to his detractors among the Pharisees):
  — Go and learn what this means, "I desire mercy, not sacrifice." For I have come to call not the righteous but sinners. (Matt 9:13)
  — But if you had known what this means, "I desire mercy and not sacrifice," you would not have condemned the guiltless. (12:7)
- Mission focus restricted to Israel's lost:
  — Go rather to the lost sheep of the house of Israel. (10:6)
  — I was sent only to the lost sheep of the house of Israel. (15:24)
- Status reversal (also an example of inclusio, enfolding the parable of one-hour and full-day field workers):
  — But many who are first will be last, and the last will be first. (19:30)
  — So the last will be first, and the first will be last. (20:16; cf. the order of payment in 20:8, at the parable's center)

- Community entrusted with judicial authority to "bind and loose":
  — Whatever you bind on earth will be bound in heaven, and whatever you loose on earth will be loosed in heaven. (16:19)
  — Whatever you bind on earth will be bound in heaven, and whatever you loose on earth will be loosed in heaven. (18:18)

Matthew also repeats narration of miracles, as in these examples:

- Lake rescues (also in Mark): Matthew 8:23–27 → 14:22–33 (with considerable amplification!)
- Restoration of sight to a duo of men who are blind: 9:27–31 → 20:29–34
- Liberation from speech disability caused by a demon, prompting criticism from Pharisees: 9:32–34 → 12:22–24
- Feeding for a large crowd (also in Mark): Matthew 14:13–21 → 15:32–38

One effect of the repetition of scenes is reinforcing for hearers the impression left by the activity narrated, whether vivid sayings of Jesus or powerful acts such as healings: *this* is the sort of thing Jesus said and did. These narrative patterns exemplify Matthew's effectiveness as a teaching document, especially considering the typical mode of its earliest reception—hearing oral performance of the story.

Also, characters are sometimes doubled in scenes. For example, the man tormented by a demon in Mark 5:2 becomes two in Matthew 8:28. Bartimaeus (Mark 10:46–52) becomes two anonymous men who are blind (Matt 20:29–34)—a scene that also doubles an earlier restoring of sight for two men (9:27–30). In the Jerusalem council's final interrogation of Jesus, "some" speak as false witnesses against Jesus in Mark 14:57, but in Matthew 26:60–61 two witnesses in particular lodge an accusation that Jesus spoke against the temple. There is irony in the story here, for Matthew seems to know the judicial import of testimony by "two or three" (note "two or three" in 18:16, 20; and see Deut 19:15). And not only human characters are "cloned." The Matthean account of Jesus' entry into Jerusalem has Jesus ride on a donkey and its foal (21:7), not a single animal as in Mark 11:7. In keeping with Matthew's accent on fulfillment of prophecy, the narration is conformed more closely to the prophecy of Zechariah just quoted in Matthew 21:5 (Zech 9:9).

Three's Company: Triads

Matthew's Gospel also makes regular use of patterns of three, much of it, again, inherited from source or tradition but with ample expansion by the author.[24] As in Mark, for example, Matthew presents three observing disciples and the suggestion of three booths at the transfiguration (Matt 17:1, 4;

24. Davies and Allison document the extensive use of triads in Matthew (*Matthew*, partial listing, e.g., on 1:86–87), though they perhaps exaggerate its role as a structuring principle in the narrative.

Mark 9:2, 5), three prayers by Jesus before his arrest (Matt 26:36–46; Mark 14:32–42), and three denials by Peter (Matt 26:69–75; Mark 14:53–72). Moreover, as in Luke 4:1–13 (hence, Q?), three specific challenges illustrate Jesus' ordeal of testing (Matt 4:1–11). In uniquely Matthean materials, magi bring three gifts to the child Jesus (2:11); Jesus prioritizes three expressions of fidelity to the Torah (23:23: justice, mercy, faith; contrast justice and the love of God in Luke 11:42); and Roman soldiers appear in three scenes in the immediate aftermath of Jesus' death (Matt 27:62–66; 28:4, 11–15). Often the pattern of three is not borrowed from sources but is the product of Matthew's own composition. To mention two such instances: in a passion prediction of Jesus, Matthew 20:19 converts the fourfold enumeration of abuse awaiting Jesus in Mark 10:34 to a more compact triad (mocked, flogged, crucified); and Matthew 15:21–28 gives the non-Jewish woman who seeks healing for her daughter three pleas for help (only two in Mark 7:24–30). The examples of such triads could be multiplied.

Compression of Healing Stories

Like Mark, Matthew presents extensive, robust healing activity by Jesus. Nearly all Mark's stories of healing and of the expelling of demons also appear in Matthew (there are thirteen in Mark, fourteen in Matthew).[25] As I will point out below, Matthew also greatly expands the use of general summary notices from the narrator that feature Jesus' healing activity and explicitly cast this ministry as the fulfillment of the prophetic paradigm "the servant of the LORD." Although Matthew's Gospel focuses attention on Jesus' royal identity as the Messiah descended from David and on his legitimate authority to offer definitive interpretation of the Torah, these christological emphases do not result in any diminution of Jesus' healing activity. The Messiah both teaches and heals, and does so out of compassion for God's people (Matt 9:36; 14:14; 15:32; 20:34). Matthew's presentation of individual healing stories, when compared with Mark, is compact and stereotypical. Unnecessary descriptive details (including personal names) fall away from the narration, and the narrator favors direct-speech dialogue between Jesus and the suppliant seeking healing, in a manner that often rivets attention on the faith of the seeker.[26]

25. The expelling of an unclean spirit in Mark 1:23–28 does not appear in Matthew, nor does the two-stage restoring of sight to a man in Mark 8:22–26 (though its place is taken in Matthew by the first of two accounts of Jesus' giving of sight to *two* men who are blind, in 9:27–31; cf. 20:29–34). Matthew converts one healing of an individual (with hearing and speech disability) into a general narrator's summary (Matt 15:29–31; cf. Mark 7:31–37). Matthew's narrative contains a doublet of the healing of a demon-possessed man who cannot speak (9:32–33; 12:22 [he is also blind]), neither of which Mark includes.

26. For these and other observations on Matthew's style of narration, see the classic form- and redaction-critical analysis of the miracle stories by Heinz Joachim Held, "Matthew as Interpreter of the Miracle Stories," in *Tradition and Interpretation in Matthew*, by Günther Bornkamm, Gerhard Barth, and Heinz Joachim Held, trans. Percy Scott, NTL (Philadelphia: Westminster Press, 1963), 165–299 (esp. the summary on 225–26).

Three examples suffice to illustrate Matthew's typical narration of Jesus' healing acts. First, Matthew 8:28–34 drastically abbreviates Jesus' encounter with the demon-possessed man Legion (Mark 5:1–20), who has become two anonymous demon-possessed men in Matthew. The detailed sketch of the man's condition in Mark 5:3–5 (fifty-seven words in Greek) is reduced to eleven words in Matthew 8:28. Matthew does preserve a lengthy and vivid report of the demons' self-destructive migration into a herd of pigs (vv. 30–32), as well as the element of dialogue between Jesus and the men he releases from demonic torment—though the intriguing exchange between Jesus and Legion at the end of the episode in Mark 5:18–20 is missing in Matthew, which shows no interest in the event's impact on the men themselves.

A second example: Matthew 9:18–26 preserves the Markan interweaving of two healing interventions by Jesus but again omits much descriptive detail (cf. Mark 5:21–43).[27] Matthew's rendition of these two intersecting healings—one giving relief to a woman plagued for twelve years with a bleeding condition, the other restoring life to a ruler's daughter—places direct speech-in-dialogue in the foreground, highlights the bleeding woman's bold faith (Matt 9:22, also in Mark 5:34; Luke 8:48), and removes puzzling elements of the Markan scene that render ambiguous the source of Jesus' healing power and his command and knowledge concerning it (Mark 5:29–33). Accompanying a seeker's faith in Jesus' power to heal is thus a sharpening of the christological profile of the Healer.[28]

A third example: Matthew 15:21–28 (cf. Mark 7:24–30) illustrates the expanded use of dialogue in Matthew's telling of the story (Matt 15:22, 23, 25), and also the explicit praise of the woman's faith (v. 28), a story element missing from Mark's account. Unlike the first two examples considered, this episode is about the same length in the two Gospels; indeed, Matthew inserts two elements: the disciples' request that Jesus dismiss the troublesome woman (15:23) and his response, seemingly siding with the disciples' oppositional stance toward her but framed as an articulation of Jesus' restricted mission field among "the lost sheep of the house of Israel" (15:24; cf. 10:5–6).[29] He will eventually commend mission among Gentiles but not until the end of the narrative (28:19). For now, the focus of his concern is

---

27. What Mark tells with some 373 words, Matthew retells with only 138. While all three panels of this A-B-A´ intercalation are much more concise in Matthew, the last two panels (B-A´) are esp. brief, about one-third the length of the corresponding components in Mark 5.

28. Among details missing in Matthew's version of the story: the ruler's name (Jairus) and his link to the synagogue (Mark 5:22; cf. Matt 9:18), the bleeding woman's long history with ineffectual physicians (Mark 5:26), the age (twelve) of the ruler's daughter (Mark 5:42), the Aramaic words spoken by Jesus (Mark 5:41), and his instructions to the parents afterward, including the direction to keep silence (Mark 5:42–43).

29. The omission of the passage in Luke (if it was included in the version of Mark available to Luke's author) is not difficult to explain, both because of its depiction of Jesus' harshness toward the woman and because of its restricted scope of mission, relegating Gentiles to the beyond-marginal status of unfed dogs.

resolutely fixed among Jewish people, despite the exceptional case of the centurion in 8:5–13.

Revisionist Sketch of the Disciples

In passages that Matthew shares with Mark, Jesus' disciples appear in a much more favorable light in Matthew's narrative. To be sure, they are far from perfect—they bear little resemblance to the *teleioi*, the "mature or whole" persons Jesus challenges followers to be, with character modeled after the divine character (Matt 5:48). Repeatedly they demonstrate "little faith" (8:26; 14:31; 16:8; 17:20; cf. 6:30), and some even doubt when face-to-face with the risen Jesus on a Galilean mountain (28:17). As in Mark, they sleep in Gethsemane (Matt 26:40, 43, 45) and flee in panic from the arrest scene, as Jesus predicted (26:31, 56); Peter denies Jesus three times in the courtyard of the high priest, again as predicted (26:34, 58, 69–75); and Judas betrays him with a traitor's kiss (26:47–49; his eventual remorse cannot undo the damage, and he ends his life [27:3–5]). Jesus, not his closest followers, models the radical trust, obedience, and integrity that participants in the divine realm are to exhibit.

Nevertheless, the twelve Matthean disciples prove to be far better students of their Teacher than the uncomprehending Markan disciples (see the discussion in ch. 3 above). Since their central role beyond the narrative is as teachers—conveying the teaching of Jesus (28:20)—it is crucial to the plausibility of their characterization that they improve on the cluelessness of Mark's portrayal of the disciples.[30] A few examples document the character transformation that follows readers who move from Mark to Matthew:

- The Matthean disciples understand Jesus' parables about the sovereign rule of God. (Matt 13:18, 51; contrast Mark 4:13)
- After experiencing a second rescue on the lake, the Matthean disciples confess Jesus' identity as Son of God (Matt 14:22–33; contrast Mark 6:45–52). Matthew inserts a dramatic scene featuring Peter, who shows himself to be a disciple with bold faith, though in the end it contends with fear and turns out to be "little faith" (Matt 14:28–31). Here he represents the larger band of disciples in Matthew: they possess real faith in Jesus, but it needs to grow, to become deeper and more tenacious.

---

30. Emphasized by Overman, *Matthew's Gospel and Formative Judaism*, 128. The disciples come to understand only because it is Jesus who tutors them, not because of any intrinsic perceptiveness (e.g., Matt 15:12–20; 16:5–12; 17:9–13); cf. Luz, *Matthew*, 1:17. According to Luz, Matthew also sharply distinguishes between the understanding of the disciples and Jesus' "ignorant and malevolent opponents" (Ulrich Luz, *Studies in Matthew*, trans. Rosemary Selle [Grand Rapids: Wm. B. Eerdmans Publishing Co., 2005], 90, emphasis removed).

- Matthew's account of Peter's confession at Caesarea Philippi is also quite different from Mark's (Matt 16:13–23 // Mark 8:27–33). Again, Matthew expands Mark with material focusing on Peter, which casts the disciples in a somewhat more favorable light.
  — Peter's declaration enhances "Messiah" (Mark 8:29) with "the Son of the living God." (Matt 16:16)
  — Jesus commends Peter for an answer that shows he has been receptive to special divine revelation. (16:17)
  — On this foundation, Jesus will construct a church with powers of authoritative interpretation and binding judicial decision and discipline. (16:18–19)

Multiplication of the Narrator's Summary Notices of Jesus' Healing Activity and Scripture Fulfillment

In addition to no fewer than fourteen episodes in which Jesus grants the benefaction of healing or demon expulsion to one or two individuals,[31] Matthew's narrator frequently draws readers' attention to the effective healing ministry of Jesus, as well as to its expansive reach, through general summaries: 4:23, 24; 8:16; 9:35; 12:15; 14:35–36; 15:30–31; 19:2; 21:14 (cf. Jesus' own summary for the benefit of John the Baptizer and his followers in 11:4–5).[32] Even in his final days of public activity, when he is about to be immersed in vigorous debates in the temple precincts, he performs acts of healing, a distinctive feature of Matthew's narrative (21:14). The exception that proves the rule is the relative ineffectiveness of Jesus' healing ministry in Nazareth. Healing's obstruction here is the absence of faith among the prophet's hometown people (13:58), the flip side of Matthew's accent elsewhere on the intimate connection between healing and faith (see 8:10, 13; 9:22, 28–29; 15:28). The narrator also forges explicit links between Jesus' healing activity and prophetic descriptions of the "servant of the LORD" (Matt 8:17, quoting Isa 53:4; Matt 12:17–21, quoting Isa 42:1–4).[33] Matthew's audience will easily discern that this is characteristic activity of Jesus' mission, expressing his deep compassion (Matt 9:36; 14:14; 15:32; 20:34) and exemplifying his fulfillment of scriptural promise for God's people.

31. Twice, Mark's single healing recipient becomes two anonymous persons in Matthew (cf. Mark 5:2 and Matt 8:28; Mark 10:46 and Matt 20:30; also note the doublet of the two men who are blind in Matt 9:27). Matthew knows the power of the testimony or agreement of two persons (18:15–20).

32. Only three of these healing-summary notices are shared with Mark (Matt 8:16 and Mark 1:32–34; Matt 4:24–25 and Mark 3:7–12; Matt 14:35–36 and Mark 6:53–56). Twice Matthew adds mention of healing to general summaries of Jesus' teaching activity (Matt 9:35; 19:2); once Matthew converts a healing of an individual (with hearing and speech disability) into a general narrator's summary (Matt 15:29–31; cf. Mark 7:31–37).

33. In 12:15–21, one of the few Matthean passages that preserve a residual element of Mark's messianic mystery theme (see ch. 3 above), Matthew reframes Jesus' injunction to silence about healing as an instance of his fulfillment of the prophetic pattern of Isaiah's Servant (Isa 42:1–4).

Central Motifs and Concerns

Christological Soundings: Jesus the Messiah— Son of Abraham, Son of David, Son of God, Son of Humanity

From its opening line, the Gospel of Matthew signals its interest in the identity and significance of Jesus. Senior indeed holds that "the most fundamental characteristic of Matthew's Gospel is its robust Christology."[34] As son of Abraham, Jesus belongs to the covenant people Israel (1:2, 17; 3:9; 8:11; 22:32), through whom blessing is to come also to all peoples of the earth (anticipating 28:19; cf. Gen 12:3; 22:18). As son of David, he can stake a claim to royal status as the Messiah, or king.[35] Jesus makes clear in 22:41–45, however, that the Messiah as Lord has status that surpasses David's.[36] As Son of God, he not only exercises legitimate authority as Messiah and wields power to heal, forgive, nourish, and restore people but also embodies the very presence of God as Emmanuel, "God with us" (1:23; cf. 18:20; 28:20).[37] Together, these markers of identity, established already in 1:1, uniquely qualify Jesus as Israel's Messiah and as such the one who fulfills and brings to resolution the exile-disrupted history of the nation (1:17).

Although the Matthean Jesus can voice his unique relation as Son to God his Father (esp. vivid in 11:28–30), much more often he identifies himself as (or with) the Human One, the Son of Humanity.[38] As Luz has shown, Matthew does not employ this epithet to identify Jesus but does fill it with content by telling the story of Jesus: with this self-designation, Jesus sketches the full course of his life and mission.[39] Future participation in the glorious rule and righteous judgment of God will come to the same man whose present life entails homelessness, vulnerability, and suffering—yet also divinely granted authority to pronounce forgiveness and the prerogative as Lord of the Sabbath to determine acceptable conduct during that sacred time. Developing

34. Donald Senior, *Matthew*, ANTC (Nashville: Abingdon Press, 1998), 27. But he rightly also observes Matthew's emphasis on ethics in its presentation of Jesus as teacher and interpreter of Jewish law (28).

35. On Jesus as son of David, see 9:27; 12:23; 15:22; 20:30–31; 21:9, 15; cf. 1:20 (of Joseph). For Jesus as king, see 2:2; 21:5; 25:34, 40 (= Human One of 25:31); and with dramatic irony in 27:11, 29, 37, 42.

36. Luz argues that the label "son of David" in Matthew "is associated exclusively with miracles, especially with healing of the blind" (*Studies in Matthew*, 86–87); cf. Kingsbury, *Matthew as Story*, 47–48. This is one aspect of Matthew's use of the expression, but not the whole story.

37. Matthew identifies Jesus as Son of God in 8:29; 11:27; 14:33; 16:16; 26:63; 27:54; and, with dramatic irony, in 4:3, 6; 27:40, 43. The phrasing "my Son" appears in 3:17 and 17:5 (cf. 2:15 and, in parable metaphor, 21:37–39).

38. The title "Human One" (Son of Humanity [AT]) appears in Matt 8:20; 9:6; 10:23; 11:19; 12:8, 32, 40; 13:37, 41; 16:13, 27–28; 17:9, 12, 22; 19:28; 20:18, 28; 24:27, 30, 37, 39, 44; 25:31; 26:2, 24, 45, 64.

39. See Luz, *Studies in Matthew*, 91: the title Son of Man (Human One) has "a horizontal dimension, encompassing the entire story of Jesus"; it connects "the various stages of Jesus' story" (emphasis removed) and aids readers in placing "the individual sayings of Jesus in the perspective of his whole history" (108); e.g., the homeless Human One is also the coming judge of the world. The Matthean Jesus, then, uses this self-identification "to comment on and pretell his whole history from his humility until his final exaltation and vindication" (110). "It is not the title 'Son of the Man' which makes clear who Jesus is; rather, the history of Jesus makes clear who Jesus the Son of the Man is" (111). On the Matthean Jesus' use of this epithet, see also Kingsbury, *Matthew as Story*, 95–103.

those glimpses of sovereign authority evident in Jesus' public career, he links his own role as the Human One to his royal status and authority in several passages (13:41; 16:28; 19:28; 25:31; 26:64).

Jesus' role as king (of Israel), however, cannot be separated from the full story of the reign or realm of God—of *heaven*, as Matthew ordinarily puts it. This is the note on which Jesus' ministry begins (4:17, echoing the message of John before him [3:2]), and his teaching and proclamation return to this image of divine governance again and again. The "robust Christology" of this Gospel is thus framed from beginning to end as God's story, the saving activity of the reigning God in Israel and among the nations.

Assertion of the imminent approach and present, powerful activity of "the reign of heaven" is the core message of Jesus in Matthew, beginning with his opening statement (4:17). Typically, he speaks of the *basileia tōn ouranōn* (lit., the "kingdom [or empire] of the heavens"),[40] but occasionally (as in Mark) more directly of the "reign of *God*."[41] In either formulation, the claim is about the present and future reigning activity of the sovereign God.[42] Jesus' public activity announces, displays, enacts, and represents this reigning activity of God, which amounts to "gospel"—good news—because the divine presence brings salvation in its various senses: healing of sickness, forgiveness of sins (mercy), liberation (from demon domination), restoration to community (symbolically expressed in meals), rescue from danger, and the fostering of justice in human relations. The narrative opens and closes with images celebrating divine presence both within the story of Emmanuel ("God with us," 1:23) and beyond the story line to the close of history (28:20; cf. 18:20). Moreover, in a world apparently dominated by a different empire (Rome's), Matthew's focus on the operation of God's powerful, sovereign rule has counterimperial implications, even if Matthew's audience must wait for Rome's ultimate demise (e.g., 24:27–31).[43]

---

40. "Reign of [the] heaven[s]" in 5:3, 10, 19–20; 7:21; 8:11; 10:7; 11:11–12; 13:11, 24, 31, 33, 44, 45, 47, 52; 16:19; 18:1, 3–4, 23; 19:12, 14, 23; 20:1; 22:2; 23:13; 25:1. "The kingdom [reign/ realm]," with "God's" or "heaven's" implied, occurs in 4:23; 8:12; 9:35; 13:19, 38; 24:14; 25:34. Once, Jesus uses "kingdom [reign]" with the subjective-genitive pronoun "your" referring to God (6:10), and once a petitioner (the mother of James and John) speaks of "your kingdom [reign/realm]" referring to Jesus (20:21).

41. *God's* reign in 6:33 (textually uncertain); 12:28; 21:31, 43; cf. 13:43 ("of their Father"); 26:29 ("my Father's").

42. See Kingsbury, *Matthew as Story*, 61. Notice that "reign of [the] heaven[s]" and "reign of God" are synonymous in the parallel lines of 19:23–24 (though with some textual variation in v. 24).

43. For thorough analysis of Matthew's treatment of the Roman Empire, see Warren Carter, *Matthew and Empire: Initial Explorations* (Harrisburg, PA: Trinity Press International, 2001). Carter holds that "Matthew presents God's empire as though it is Rome's empire writ large," esp. in relation to the future; Matthew's strategy is to make God's empire "bigger, more menacing, more powerful, and more extensive . . . than Rome's" (idem, *John and Empire: Initial Explorations* [New York: T&T Clark, 2008], 341; cf. idem, *Matthew and Empire*, 169–79).

Jesus, the Messiah—son of Abraham, son of David, Son of God, and Son of Humanity—calls Israel to its true vocation and destiny as God's people. But he cannot do so simply by bearing particular names of honor. As Messiah, Jesus is also the one true Teacher (23:8, 10). Much of his instruction of disciples and crowds alike (adversaries, too, if they are attending and teachable) centers on interpretation of Scripture, especially of Torah but also its elaboration in the Prophets. Therefore, to take Matthew's Christology seriously also calls for paying close attention to ethics, to moral formation of a people obedient to the will and purposes of God. In this Gospel, Jesus declares that whoever calls him "Lord, Lord" (even rightly) but fails to put his teaching into practice and thus does not live in a way congruent with Torah and Prophets, wisely interpreted (i.e., as interpreted by Jesus), courts disaster (see 7:21–23). (See below, the discussion of Jesus' teaching in Matthew.)

Central Motifs and Concerns in Matthew

- Christological soundings: Jesus the Messiah—Son of Abraham, Son of David, Son of God, Son of Humanity
- Fulfillment of Scripture and prophecy
- Jesus: **THE** authentic teacher
  — Reading the Sermon on the Mount (Matt 5–7)
  — Reading the discourse on community formation (Matt 18)
- Conflict with other teachers
- The composition of the people of God
- Apocalyptic chords: eschatological judgment
  — Reading the discourse of parables on heaven's dominion (Matt 13)
  — Reading the discourse on future judgment and deliverance (Matt 24–25)
  — Jesus' death and resurrection as apocalyptic events

Fulfillment of Scripture and Prophecy

Undergirding Matthew's claim that Jesus is the Messiah, the narrator repeatedly invokes the Jewish Scriptures to show that they find fulfillment in the circumstances of his birth, in his place of residence and spatial movements, in his healing activity, and in his vocation as one rejected as well as specific details of his passion. The narrative of Jesus' birth and early years repeatedly quotes from Matthew's Bible and, with the preceding genealogy, presents "a 'concentrated manifesto' setting out how Jesus the Messiah fulfills the hopes of . . . Israel."[44] Mary's pregnancy without Joseph's paternity but by

---

44. France, *Gospel of Matthew*, 13–14.

the agency of the Holy Spirit (Matt 1:18–23) realizes the promise of Isaiah 7:14. Jesus' birth in Bethlehem, home of ruler-shepherds for Israel, receives meaning from what a prophet has "written" (Matt 2:5, citing Mic 5:1–3). The ensuing flight of the child's family to Egypt to escape a king's violent rage and the recall of God's Son from Egypt when the danger had passed (Matt 2:14–21) recapitulate Israel's story and actualize Hosea 11:1 (and Jer 31:15: Rachel's lament for her children, cited in Matt 2:17–18). Relocation to Nazareth then follows the script for a "Nazorean" (Matt 2:22–23, evoking an unspecified prophetic text).

After encounter with the baptizing prophet John in the Judean wilderness, a Capernaum-based ministry in Galilee (Matt 4:12–16) fulfills the promise of Isaiah 9:1. Then Jesus' healing ministry gives substance to that life-bearing hope, in tune with expectations for the Servant of the Lord (Matt 8:16–17 and 12:15–21, quoting Isa 53:5 and 42:1–4). The sometimes puzzling Markan motif of secrecy extended to acts of healing and liberation from oppression by demons (e.g., Mark 1:23–25, 45; 3:11–12; 5:43) is thus reframed in Matthew as fulfillment of a prophetic scriptural pattern: this is how God's Servant behaves. Also in the message of Jesus, with its centerpiece parabolic form, scriptural patterns spring to renewed life. Scripture fulfillment marks both the act of speaking in parables and the mode of their reception by auditors, two sides of the same rhetorical coin (Matt 13:13–14, quoting Isa 6:9–10; and Matt 13:34–35, invoking Ps 78:2 as prophetic declaration). At his approach to Jerusalem, Jesus choreographs a royal entry into the city that enacts prophetic vision (Matt 21:1–5, inspired by Zech 9:9); the selective excerpt from Zechariah 9 casts Jesus' entry to public acclaim as an act of humility rather than triumphant conquest (Matthew uses Zech 9:9a and 9c but omits v. 9b).

At the scene of Jesus' arrest, he twice asserts that the events must unfold according to scriptural script, and he therefore refuses to petition for a spectacular rescue by angelic armies (Matt 26:53–54, 56). He mentions no specific biblical texts; the point is that everything is occurring as God has long purposed that it would (thus reinforcing the similar claims Jesus has made in predictions of his disciples' acts of betrayal and desertion as had been "written" [26:24, 31]).[45]

Under interrogation by the high priest, who is pressuring Jesus to admit his messianic pretensions as divine son (26:63), Jesus audaciously splices together quotations from Daniel 7:13 and Psalm 110:1 to stake a claim—present and future—to God's public vindication and to a share in divine power and rule (Matt 26:64). This is an interpretation of Scripture that is

---

45. Jesus refers to what has been "written" to introduce biblical quotations also in Matt 11:10, where Mal 3:1 and Exod 23:20 supply language for Jesus' portrait of John the baptizing prophet; and in Matt 21:13, where appeal to the dual prophetic texts of Isa 56:7 and Jer 7:11 provides the warrant for Jesus' action of disrupting temple commerce. What prophets "wrote" also lends deep meaning to John the Baptizer's ministry of preparation for the Messiah in the Judean wilderness (Matt 3:3, drawing from Isa 40:3).

guaranteed to provoke, and it indeed leads to the charge of blasphemy and a death sentence (vv. 65–66). When a remorseful Judas attempts to return his betrayer's compensation of thirty pieces of silver, the Jerusalem council diverts the blood money toward purchase of a field—ironically, for burial of foreigners (27:3–10). This too Matthew portrays as a series of events unfolding according to prophetic pattern (Matthew credits Jeremiah, but the passage presents a creative blend of Zech 11:13; Jer 18:2; and 32:6–9).

The narrative includes other biblical quotations and a host of echoes and allusions that readers steeped in Jewish Scripture and tradition would recognize.[46] Moreover, early in Jesus' formal teaching, he presents a global claim that his activity fulfills the Law and the Prophets (5:17). He backs up that claim when he repeatedly guides listeners toward wise discernment of and faithful response to the divine will expressed in the Torah and the Prophets (e.g., 7:12; 22:40; 23:23; cf. 11:12). Matthew's case for Jesus' messianic role by way of sustained reading and reinterpretation of the Jewish Scriptures is likely not intended primarily to convince Jews in Matthew's city who do not already participate in the group of Jesus followers there. Certainly, in terms of rhetorical effectiveness, given the history of polemics and mutual antagonism, it would probably not have convinced them. This aspect of the narrative would, however, confirm and reinforce the convictions and commitments of Christ-following Jews (and any Gentiles now affiliated with them), assuring them that they have chosen well, despite their present estrangement from the other synagogue(s) within that social world.

Jesus, the Definitive and Authentic Teacher

As we have seen, central to Matthew's portrayal of the Messiah Jesus is his vocation to teach. At the heart of this teaching activity is a practical wisdom fashioned out of interpretation and appropriation-for-life of the Torah (and the Prophets). This generates a narrative that merges christological conviction and preoccupation with moral formation, or disciple formation. As a narrative governed by an interest in praxis, Matthew exhibits its deeply Jewish character. In the selective discussion that follows, I focus attention on significant themes developed in two of the major discourses (chs. 5–7 and 18).[47]

46. Noting that a recent critical edition of the Greek NT lists 54 direct OT citations and 262 allusions and verbal parallels, France appraises this as a "conservative figure" (*Gospel of Matthew*, 10–11). For France, the "textual freedom" in Matthew's biblical quotations suggests that this Gospel author "was sometimes willing to modify the wording of the text in order to draw out more clearly for his readers the sense in which he perceived it to have been fulfilled in Jesus"; these represent "editorial comments, arising from Matthew's own creative biblical interpretation" (13). See the detailed analysis of Matthew's quotations from and allusions to the OT in Davies and Allison, *Matthew*, 1:34–57. Davies and Allison hold that Matthew was able to read his Bible in both Greek and Hebrew, a bilingual capacity evident in the numerous quotations that are closer to the Masoretic (Hebrew) Text than the Old Greek (LXX).

47. I will discuss the discourses in Matt 13 and 24–25 below, under the heading "Apocalyptic Chords: Eschatological Judgment."

The Sermon on the Mount (5:1–7:27)

The Matthean Teacher's "inaugural lecture" is the Sermon on the Mount.[48] Speaking to newly recruited disciples (5:1–2) about what life governed by the claims and commitments of God's reign looks like, he impresses large crowds who are also listening with teaching that bears unmatched authority (7:28–29; cf. 5:1). The movement of the sermon is from transformative grace, in the performative speech of the beatitudes that already begins to create the joyful blessedness it promises (5:3–12),[49] to radical demand that summons disciples to a surpassing righteousness (5:21–7:27)—a way of life that is fundamentally Torah affirming (5:17–20).

Recipients of God's Favor	*Images of God's Favor*
the poor in spirit	theirs is the kingdom of heaven (5:3)
those who mourn	they will be comforted (5:4)
the meek	they will inherit the earth (5:5)
those who hunger and thirst for righteousness [or, justice]	they will be filled (5:6)
the merciful	they will receive mercy (5:7)
the pure in heart	they will see God (5:8)
the peacemakers	they will be called children of God (5:9)
those who are persecuted for righteousness' sake	theirs is the kingdom of heaven (5:10)
when people revile you and persecute you and utter all kinds of evil against you falsely on my account	rejoice and be glad, for your reward is great in heaven, for in the same way they persecuted the prophets who were before you (5:11–12)

Nine declarations of blessing open the sermon, all except the last cast in the third person: "Blessed are those who. . . ." (5:3–10). "Blessed are you [pl.] . . ." (5:11–12). Jesus affirms God's special favor for persons who appear to most observers to be suffering life's "slings and arrows":

48. For analysis of the discourse of Matt 5–7, in addition to commentaries on Matthew, see W. D. Davies, *The Setting of the Sermon on the Mount* (Cambridge: Cambridge University Press, 1964); Hans Dieter Betz, *The Sermon on the Mount: A Commentary on the Sermon on the Mount, Including the Sermon on the Plain (Matthew 5:3–7:27 and Luke 6:20–49)*, ed. Adela Yarbro Collins, Hermeneia (Minneapolis: Fortress Press, 1995); Warren Carter, *What Are They Saying about Matthew's Sermon on the Mount?* (New York: Paulist Press, 1994).

49. Cf. John T. Carroll, *Luke: A Commentary*, NTL (Louisville, KY: Westminster John Knox Press, 2012), 150: "Jesus' words begin to *create* the reality of which they speak (i.e., they are performative speech acts)," drawing from John L. Austin, *How to Do Things with Words*, ed. J. O. Urmson and Marina Sbisà, 2nd ed. (Cambridge, MA: Harvard University Press, 1975).

The ninth beatitude not only differs in form (second-person address) but also duplicates the assurance for the persecuted given in the preceding beatitude. The first and eighth affirmations of divine favor thus frame the rest (as an inclusio) with present-tense assertions that listeners—who are among the "poor in spirit" or who are "persecuted" as a result of their commitment to just practices ("righteousness")—already in the present belong to heaven's dominion ("theirs is," vv. 3, 10). Beatitudes 2–7 all depict reversals of circumstance in the *future* (vv. 3–9). Despite the experience of low status, deprivation, loss, and abusive treatment, disciples enjoy special status as persons favored by God.[50]

Matthew 5:13–16 begins to construct a bridge from grace to demand. Jesus challenges his auditors to live in a way that effectively expresses the qualities granted to them as "salt of the earth" and "light of the world." In this discourse Jesus seeks to foster an obedience that acts faithfully in the world, a concern that the closing lines emphasize (7:21–27). The obedience to which Jesus summons auditors turns out to be a radical commitment indeed. In 5:17–20 Jesus asserts that his teaching fully upholds the exacting claim of both Torah and Prophets and alerts his audience that his vision of the righteousness (or justice) that God expects is even more stringent than what the Torah-knowledgeable scribes and Torah-earnest Pharisees embody. The antitheses in 5:21–48 proceed to show what this greater righteousness entails.

The Greater Righteousness: Six Antitheses (Matt 5:21–48)
• No murder → actively seek reconciliation
• No adultery → refrain from inappropriate desires
• Procedures for divorce → divorce amounts to adultery
• Perform vows → no oaths
• Limits on retaliation → no retaliation (strategy of nonviolent resistance)
• Love near ones → love enemies

The Law of Moses and its elaboration in Jewish tradition hold the covenant people to a high standard of conduct. But the antitheses press for even deeper, more radical praxis. "You have heard" it said, or "it was said," Jesus says six times (5:21, 27, 31, 33, 38, 43), and then counters each time with a searching "but I say to you." What does the life he commends look like? (1) Attuned to the Decalogue, it refrains from murder, to be sure (Exod

---

50. As Neyrey emphasizes, in the beatitudes "honor from Jesus reverses the social shame which disciples have suffered" (*Honor and Shame*, 188). Neyrey argues that the adversity pictured in 5:3–12 results from the family's shunning and disinheriting the disciple (168–73).

20:13; Deut 5:17); however, it also eschews rage and insult and is intent on seeking reconciliation (Matt 5:21–26). (2) Again aligned with the Decalogue, it avoids adultery (Exod 20:14; Deut 5:18), yet beyond that it even turns away from the lustful gaze (Matt 5:27–30). (3) Torah provides a procedure for a man to divorce his wife (Deut 24:1–4), but Jesus brands divorce, which the Law permits, the equivalent of adultery (Matt 5:31–32). (4) Pressing beyond the faithful performance of vows made, a practice commended by many biblical texts (e.g., Lev 19:12; Num 30:2; Deut 23:21–23), the path on which Jesus sets followers is so governed by integrity of word and action that oaths simply vanish (Matt 5:33–37). (5) The Law of Moses set limits on retaliation, insisting on a principle of retributive equivalence ("eye for eye" and "tooth for tooth," as in Exod 21:23–25; Lev 24:20; Deut 19:21). However, Jesus directs followers to forego retaliation entirely and instead counter harm with generosity (Matt 5:38–42). This does not mean capitulation to evil; rather, it is a form of nonviolent resistance, a posture validated by Jesus' own approach to his death at the close of the Gospel. (6) Love for those who are near (neighbors, including one's own kin), then, does not go far enough (Lev 19:18), especially when yoked to hatred for one's enemies. Instead, Jesus urges disciples to love even their enemies, and in prayer to seek the well-being even of those who harm them. The true model for this radical, countercultural praxis is none other than God (Matt 5:43–47). Surpassing righteousness this certainly is, for if one emulates God, one is aspiring to perfection—not a mistake-free existence as persons obsessively insisting on moral perfectionism (no doubt for others, if not for themselves!) might imagine, but a life of complete, mature integrity (5:48).[51]

The first chapter of the Sermon on the Mount (Matt 5) presents both grace and demand, both gift and obligation, both indicative and imperative.[52] This dual accent continues throughout the discourse. Matthew 6:1–18

---

51. According to Neyrey, the antitheses repudiate the conventional "honor game" in Jesus' (or Matthew's) social world (*Honor and Shame*, 190–211). In 5:38–41, Jesus "requires males to play the role of the victim, the submissive one, the person imposed upon, but *not* the honorable man who defends his worth" (207). This "strike[s] at the heart of ancient notions of manliness, and thus honor" (ibid.). In 5:45, even God risks honor by failing to retaliate (209). Verses 39–41 and vv. 43–45 "prohibit the disciple from any defense of his honor" (210). The world of the antitheses was an "agonistic world in pursuit of honor, where males strove for a reputation through physical, verbal, and sexual aggression" (ibid.). Jesus, however, rules out honor claims (vv. 34–37) and honor challenges (vv. 21, 27–32, 33); he calls for honor challenges already issued to be abandoned (vv. 23–26) and for no retaliation if one is challenged (vv. 22, 39–45).

52. This is true as well of Jesus' teaching elsewhere in the Gospel. Talbert vigorously argues that "Matthean soteriology is grace-oriented from start to finish" (*Matthew*, 27), though one has to discern Matthew's conceptual repertoire in order to appreciate this. Matthew's "indicative controls his imperative" (ibid., 24). Similarly, Luz maintains that salvation's indicative and imperative "are connected in the person of Jesus because he himself is both giver and author of the demand" (*Studies in Matthew*, 137). For Matthew, "grace is given in the form of commandment, and the commandments in turn are the epitome of grace. This enables him in exemplary manner to see practice as the essence of the Christian faith, and the effect of grace evidenced in Christians being sustained in action and called on to act" (ibid., 217–18). As "Lord and helper of the community," Jesus sustains it with his power until the end of the age (216); again,

sketches ritual practice that expresses authentic piety. Verse 1 supplies the key: genuine piety does not seek notice and approval from others, for only honor from God counts.[53] (1) *Almsgiving*—generous gifts to aid the poor—is a good thing (as Matthew's Bible has made clear),[54] but let this generosity be known only to God! (6:2–4). Benefaction should not be motivated by concern with reciprocal benefit. (2) *Prayer*, too, should be between oneself and God, not an occasion for conspicuous display of one's faith and verbal virtuosity calculated to impress others (6:5–6). The one praying certainly does not need to impress God either, for the benevolent divine parent already knows well precisely what is needed (vv. 7–8). Jesus then supplies a model prayer exemplifying these values (vv. 9–13) and pauses to reinforce one of the petitions, stressing that petitioners should not expect to benefit from God's mercy (v. 12a) if they refuse to extend mercy to others (vv. 14–15, building on v. 12b; Matt 18:23–35 returns to this theme with a vengeance [no pun intended!]). (3) Finally, like almsgiving and prayer, the discipline of *fasting* is of value only when disguised so that God alone is aware (6:16–18).

Re-forming Practices of Piety
• **Almsgiving for the poor**: give in secret!
• **Prayer**: simple and direct, not to make an impression
• **Fasting**: not to gain honor

How is such an unusual, indeed countercultural, way of life conceivable? The next section of the discourse suggests an answer (6:19–34). Here, Jesus offers a set of images that highlight the radical trust from which springs authentic religious practice that is unconcerned with one's own status in the view of others. In particular, generosity toward others is possible because even disciples of "little faith" (6:30) come to trust in their gracious God's sure provision of all that is needed. So why not commit oneself entirely to pursuit of the realm of God and its surpassing righteousness, which is the very faithfulness and justice of God (6:33)?

---

via grace. Luz maintains that Matthew, by adopting Mark's narrative as the basis for his own, "joined Jesus' ethical proclamation of the kingdom of God to the story of God's activity with Jesus, making it the proclamation of grace" (*Matthew*, 1:13, emphasis removed).

53. Neyrey proposes that Matt 6:1–18 urges male disciples to withdraw from public (i.e., predominantly male) space and perform their deeds of piety within the household (*Honor and Shame*, 212–28). Jesus "issues an honor challenge to the prevailing practice of males performing acts of piety in public" (227) and upholds "the household as the locus of piety" (220).

54. See, e.g., Deut 15:7–11; Prov 19:17; 22:9; 28:27; Job 31:16–22; Isa 58:7, 10; cf. Tob 4:7–11; Sir 3:30; 29:12–13.

In 7:1–6 Jesus returns to concern with other-regard, so prominent in the antitheses of 5:21–48. Now, though, he challenges his audience to refrain from judging others (7:1–5). Discernment, yes, so as not to squander the rich resources of the tradition one has inherited (v. 6), but not the too-common bent to build up the self by condemning others. Jesus exposes that illusion—or hypocrisy—for what it is. Honest self-examination is better by far than turning a critical eye toward others. Matthew 7:7–11 loops back to the theme of God's generous provision, offering additional images that evoke trust of the kind needed to fund the countercultural praxis envisaged within the Sermon on the Mount. Disciples may expect generous benefaction when they ask or seek something (vv. 7–8), and a lesser-to-greater argument finds in even flawed parents' care of their children pointers toward the kindness of God (vv. 9–11). Returning again to other-regard, the Golden Rule of verse 12 connects the dots: one who trusts deeply in God's benevolent care is free simply to act toward others as one would wish to be treated oneself. This, the Matthean Jesus avers, "*is* the law and the prophets," the heart and soul of Scripture. Much later in the narrative, responding to a challenge laid down by a specialist in Torah interpretation, Jesus makes a similar point about the centrality of other-regard in Scripture. There he offers the double love commandment (love for God and for neighbor as for self) as the focus of Scripture, around which everything else coheres (22:34–40).

Next in this sermon, the discourse shifts into a more somber key: employing the metaphor of life as a journey-with-a-destination, Jesus cautions that few are able to follow the arduous path, through a narrow gate, that opens up access to genuine, enduring life (7:13–14). Even within the believing community, he goes on to warn, false prophets will emerge and will cause great harm (7:15); the eschatological discourse will reinforce this warning, perhaps hinting that the communities first hearing this Gospel have firsthand experience of conflict over contested prophetic speech (see 24:11, 24–25). The key to wise discernment is scrutiny of self-proclaimed prophets' actions: What do they do? How do they live? What fruit do they produce? (7:16–20). This concern with faithful performance continues to the end of the Sermon on the Mount: Jesus' audience has now heard extensive teaching, but what really matters is putting it into practice (7:21–27). Correct Christology and power to effect miracles (vv. 21–23)—not to mention amazement at the impressive authority of Jesus' speechmaking (vv. 28–29)—are of no avail if one does not conform conduct and attitude to the pattern of life Jesus has taught.[55]

---

55. In a word, "righteousness" (*dikaiosynē*), which appears 5x in the discourse (5:6, 10, 20; 6:1, 33 [translated "piety" in 6:1 NRSV]). While this word occurs only 2x elsewhere in Matt (3:15; 21:32; the related adjective *dikaios* another 17x), Overman regards it "as an all-embracing notion for the actions, behavior, and disposition of the disciples and followers of Jesus" (*Matthew's Gospel and Formative Judaism*, 92).

Discourse on Community Formation (18:1–35)

The fourth major discourse in Matthew is prompted by the misguided query of one of the disciples: Who enjoys status as "the greatest" in heaven's realm? (18:1). Honor seeking may be customary in the social world of speaker, listeners, and earliest authorial audience, but high status and public reputation are not to be prized in the community of disciples. Rather, the low status of the child is the pattern for God's dominion (18:2–5)—not self-aggrandizement but humility. This means other-regarding humility, to judge from the rest of this discourse. All such "little ones," community members ("who believe in me") with meager social capital, are of great value to the "Father in heaven" (v. 10), and one would be smart to avoid inflicting any harm on the least among them (vv. 6–10). A picture of an alternative community of radically different character is emerging.

In view of the stringent demands placed on Jesus' followers earlier in the Gospel (esp. in the Sermon on the Mount), it is perhaps unsurprising that some members among these "little ones" will not successfully navigate the arduous path and enter by the narrow gate with which Jesus imaged the disciple's life in 7:13–14. In the community of disciples that Jesus is forming, other-regard is so important that not a single community member who strays is to be left behind. First, a brief parable makes the point in metaphor: If a single sheep has gone missing from the flock, forget the ninety-nine! The shepherd—here meaning the community—must keep searching until the one that wandered off is restored (18:11–14).

This sharp accent on mercy in response to failure or misconduct by a community member will be resumed in verses 21–35. But the interlude of verses 15–20 develops the other side of the coin. Not just mercy, but also justice and accountability are to prevail in this community in which heaven's reign is to be determinative. It is inevitable in a close-knit group that harm will be inflicted by one member of the group on another. Matthew mixes language of kinship/household (*adelphos*, "sibling") and public political life (*ekklēsia*, assembly), though this is obscured in the NRSV translation (church "member" for sibling and "church" for assembly throughout the passage).[56] For such an occasion, Jesus prescribes an intentional process of community discipline that holds the wrongdoer accountable and gives opportunity for admitting the harm done and making restitution for it; this is the flip side of Jesus' call to seek reconciliation so as to preserve the integrity of ritual observance in 5:23–26.

Whenever the one who has inflicted harm refuses to acknowledge it, the community is empowered to discern, to discipline, and even, if necessary, to exclude. In seeking justice, the group aligns itself with the divine will (18:18–19; cf. 16:19)—and not remotely, either, for even as small a group as two or three will experience wise guidance from Jesus' presence (18:20). When

---

56. In the canonical Gospels, only Matt 16:18 and 18:17 employ the Greek word *ekklēsia*, which is routinely rendered as "church" in its frequent usage in Acts and the NT Letters.

community members are harmed and when social cohesion is damaged, communal restoration does not mean looking the other way, pretending that nothing happened and nothing needs to be made right: such a response neither aids the one harmed nor restores the one who harmed. In the extreme case of exclusion from the assembly—"Let such a one be to you as a Gentile and a tax collector" (18:17)—there appears to be no hope for restoration to and of the community. However, in a narrative that numbers tax collectors among those who are receptive to John's call to repentance and Jesus' invitation to discipleship (9:9–13; 10:3; 11:19; 21:31–32) and Gentiles among those who model genuine faith (8:10–13), the former (fictive) sibling[57] now excluded may yet be the object of earnest attempts to restore the lost.

The tensive interplay of mercy and justice or accountability, evident to this point in the discourse, receives further probing in a brief dialogue between Simon Peter and Jesus on the question of limits to mercy (18:21–22). This exchange prompts Jesus to tell a provocative parable centering on the actions of a king's forgiven but unforgiving servant (vv. 23–35). First, picking up the strands of mercy (vv. 11–14) and justice accountability (vv. 15–20) in Jesus' teaching, Peter asks whether he should grant forgiveness as many as seven times to a sibling/community member who sins against him (v. 21). Jesus replies with hyperbole: not a generous seven times but seventy-seven times (or seventy times seven, v. 22 mg.)! That is to say, keep forgiving, without limit (there is no mention of the forgiven one's repentance, as in the parallel saying, Luke 17:3–4). Standing alone, the exaggerated counsel to forgive without limitation is potentially problematic—especially when the one who "needs" to forgive possesses less power in the situation (such as a woman or child suffering from domestic violence).[58] The limitations the Matthean discourse imposes here concern not the number of times mercy is needful but, instead, the tensive relation between the demand for mercy and the insistence on accountability in the passages preceding (Matt 18:15–20) and following (vv. 23–35) Jesus' exchange with Peter.

The parable in 18:23–35 is high drama, with enormous stakes. Jesus introduces it (like the parables of ch. 13) as a parable/metaphor for the realm of heaven. But how so? Jesus' (and Matthew's) audience need to work hard to discern. A king's (obviously highly placed) slave has managed to accrue a debt of ten thousand talents owed to his master, scarcely a calculable amount and certainly unpayable (v. 24). This king is a powerful despot and far from

---

57. The phrase "fictive sibling" (or "fictive family") seeks to capture the emphasis in Matthew (and often throughout the NT) on the group of Jesus followers as an alternative (metaphorical) family, where "family" belonging is defined not by biological relation or location within a conventional kin-based household but by shared commitment to the beliefs and practices of the group for which Jesus is Lord.

58. See the helpful discussion of this issue by Sharon Ringe, "Solidarity and Contextuality: Readings of Matthew 18:21–35," in *Reading from This Place: Social Location and Biblical Interpretation*, ed. Fernando F. Segovia and Mary Ann Tolbert (Minneapolis: Fortress Press, 1995), 1:199–212. Ringe offers an interpretation of the passage from a place of solidarity with battered women.

benevolent: for debt repayment, he orders that the debtor-slave, his wife, and children be sold, along with all his possessions (v. 25). The parable springs its first surprise on hearers when the king, moved to compassion by his slave's desperate plea for more time to pay the debt, does not simply grant an extension but releases him and simply cancels ("forgives") the debt (vv. 26–27). The second surprise comes when this slave, his life spared by mercy, callously refuses even to allow a fellow slave more time for repayment of a much smaller debt (100 denarii) and has him jailed (vv. 28–30). The same appeal for mercy elicits dramatically different responses from these two creditors. (The parable's narrator, Jesus, gives no explanation for the forgiven slave's motivation or reasoning. Does he suppose that in the patronage system and its webs of reciprocal exchange and obligation, he owes allegiance, gratitude, and faithful service only to the one who forgave him, not to someone else?) The parable springs one final surprise on listeners: other slaves have observed the transactions, and when they inform the king, his compassion yields to rage, and he reinstates the full amount of the formerly cancelled debt. The king sends the "wicked slave" off to jail, with no prospect of an end to the torture to be suffered there (vv. 31–34).

Verse 35 drives home the point: God's punishment will be just as severe "if you do not forgive your brother or sister from your heart" (v. 35). Show mercy, or else . . . ! So that is how the parable illumines the character of the realm of heaven! Or is it? What is the reader to do with the tension between this discourse's emphasis on mercy in human-to-human social interaction, confronting an obligation seemingly without limit, and the harsh concluding image of a punitive king (representing God?) who forgives just once? This is one of the Matthean passages that forces the question: Is Matthew's narrative coherent? Later in the chapter I will take up that interpretive challenge. For the time being, at least readers seeking to hold together the various strands of Matthew 18 will appreciate that the community Jesus is forming here will prize humility rather than enhancement of social status and public honor. They will take seriously the wrongful actions that harm individuals and damage the group's cohesion; hence they will vigorously seek to repair the damage. And they will think long and hard about the mandate to forgive, fully aware that it matters greatly how they respond to the generous gift of mercy in the way they deal with others within the group. But not everyone is within the Matthean group, and that brings us to another prominent thematic interest of this Gospel.

Conflict with Other Teachers

Matthew does not invent the plot element of conflict between Jesus and various other leaders and groups among his contemporaries in Judaism: it figures prominently in Mark as well (see Mark 2:1–3:6; 7:1–13; 11:27–12:27; 14:2, 10–11, 43, 53–65; 15:1, 3). In Matthew's narrative, however, the magnitude and stakes of the conflict intensify dramatically. Repeatedly, Jesus' teaching and healing activities, his provocative associations (symbolically expressed in shared meals), and his approach to Sabbath keeping spark debate, objection, and antagonism:

- Teaching and interpretation of the Torah: 15:1–9; 19:3–9 (cf. 16:1–12); 22:34–40[59]
- Healing and the expelling of demons: 9:1–8, 32–34; 12:22–45; 21:14–16
- Meals and other social interactions/associations: 9:9–13
- Sabbath keeping: 12:1–8, 9–14

Conflict escalates after Jesus reaches Jerusalem. As in Mark, the temple provides the setting for a series of sharp exchanges between Jesus and various other teachers and leaders, who contest his authority in the tense aftermath of his disruption of temple commerce (Matt 21:12–13). However, the narrative gives Jesus the final word (i.e., before his arrest). His unsparing critique of failed leadership on the part of the scribes and Pharisees, in a speech addressed to a blended audience of disciples and crowds, brings the volleys of reciprocal confrontation and criticism to a climax (23:1–39). In a surprising statement, yet one with biting verbal irony, Jesus acknowledges the teaching authority of the scribes and Pharisees (vv. 2–3). But his ensuing, blistering attack undermines their legitimacy: among other failings, they do not practice what they teach, a severe violation of the norms of Jesus' teaching in this Gospel (v. 3; cf. 5:29; 7:21–27; 12:49–50). They also are preoccupied with trivial matters of legal observance while neglecting the Torah's heart and soul (justice, mercy, faith, 23:23), and they violently persecute agents sent by God (vv. 29–37). What immediately follows this speech is Jesus' oracle forecasting the temple's future destruction (24:1–2): within the logic of Matthew's narrative rhetoric, both are symptom and effect of failed leadership and repudiation of the Messiah (expressed metaphorically in 21:33–45; cf. 22:1–10). On occasion, Jesus levels harsh critique at his entire generation (11:16–24; 12:39–45; 16:4; 17:17), and by story's end the local Judean elite has recruited many more in the crowd to join the chorus calling for Jesus' death (27:15–25). Still, the primary conflict is with the scribes and Pharisees, and then with the powerful ruling group in Jerusalem.

Composition of God's People

At stake in Matthew's conflict-laced narrative is not only the identity of the Messiah, and not only the character of leadership among God's people, but also the composition and membership of the people. (For discussion of the sociohistorical correlate of this narrative feature, the setting and community in which the Gospel first appeared, see the first section of this chapter above.

---

59. In Matt 22:34–40, unlike Mark 12:28–34, the exchange with a lawyer (in Mark, a scribe) centering on the central commandments in Torah is adversarial, a test/challenge to Jesus' teaching authority as interpreter of Scripture.

On the related rhetorical, theological, and ethical issues, see the final section of this chapter, as well as ch. 7 below.)

Although Jesus' disparaging words for his contemporaries primarily concern the failure in perception, faith, and practice of specific leader groups (scribes, Pharisees, Sadducees, and the cohort of elite priests), there are moments when his sharp critique has wider scope. God's righteous judgment will eventually overtake any and all: the Jewish people, crowds, and the community of disciples. Unsure what to do with John the Baptizer and Jesus, the two very different agents sent by God, the people are like children who cannot agree what game to play (11:16–20). Jesus then reproaches unreceptive towns just north of the Sea of Galilee—Chorazin, Bethsaida, and even his adopted hometown of Capernaum—which will fare worse in the end-time judgment than the pagan cities of Tyre and Sidon (11:21–24).

In 12:39–45, taking his cue from the sign seeking of scribes and Pharisees (v. 38), Jesus castigates an entire "wicked . . . generation" (v. 39 NIV), his contemporaries, who are hunting for special signs but fail to perceive and welcome the extraordinary sign of divine activity already present among them in the ministry of the Human One (Son of Humanity). The only sign that will be granted is the figure of Jonah (v. 39), already available in Scripture and tradition, with his summons to repentance and warning of divine judgment.[60] Although Nineveh averted a catastrophic fate by repenting in response to Jonah's message, Jesus holds out less hope for his own generation (vv. 40–41). And another outsider to Israel, the queen of Sheba, will also fare better than Jesus' peers, for in contrast to their lack of discernment, she at least recognized the remarkable wisdom of Solomon (v. 42). In both 11:16–24 and 12:39–45, Jesus pictures outsiders to Israel as recipients of greater favor or mercy (or less condemnation) than peers among his own people, unless they repent in response to his message of God's reign (a warning that recalls the similar message of the baptizing prophet in 3:7–10).

The Matthean rendition of Jesus' explanation of his teaching in parables to the people, outside the disciple group (13:10–15), differs from Mark's version, in which the parables are *intended* to provoke imperceptive and therefore unrepentant response (Mark 4:10–12, though even in Mark the concealment is not pictured as permanent; see ch. 3 above). By contrast, Matthew pictures a failure to perceive that "this people" has chosen for itself, thus fulfilling the prophetic vision of Isaiah (Isa 6:9–10, cited in Matt 13:14–15). Jesus uses the parable genre in teaching them precisely because they look without seeing, hear without listening, and so do not understand (13:13). The people, not the message, have produced dull hearts, ears hard of hearing, and closed eyes (v. 15). Here Matthew offers a creative rereading (misreading) of Isaiah 6:9–10, which (as in both Markan and Lukan

---

60. Matthew again invokes Jonah in a more concise reprise of this scene in 16:1–4, generalizing the sign seeking of Pharisees and (this time) Sadducees to lambaste an evil, sign-seeking generation. Jesus also gives a sweeping indictment of a faithless generation when his disciples struggle to best an esp. tenacious demon (17:17).

intertextual play with this passage in Isaiah) does conceive nonresponse to the prophetic message as *intended* by God in sending the prophet (see Mark 4:10–12; Luke 8:9–10).[61]

The mission discourse forecasts that Jesus' followers will encounter the same mixed reception that he has among the people. He holds before disciples the prospect of hostility and persecution (Matt 10:11–23, 24–26). The eschatological discourse in Matthew 24–25 reinforces this cautionary warning (24:9). Jesus' own mission, and that of his disciples, addresses Israel's "lost sheep," which means that they have presently strayed from covenantal faithfulness, though it also means that they are the potential beneficiaries of the message that can bring mercy and hope.

Accompanying images of cautionary warning for members of Israel are occasional notes of hope for outsiders. Reading from the end of the story ("teaching . . . all nations [*panta ta ethnē*]," 28:19–20) backward, one more distinctly hears early hints that Matthew's narrative centering on the fulfillment of Israel's history and hopes presses outward, beyond the boundaries of the *ethnos* (nation or people): the presence of Gentile women in Jesus' genealogy (1:3, 5–6: Tamar, Rahab, Ruth, and the Hittite soldier Uriah's wife [Bathsheba]);[62] the juxtaposition of the malevolent ruler at Jerusalem and Messiah-seeking, Messiah-honoring magi from the East (2:1–16); and the image of Jesus' ministry terrain as "Galilee of the Gentiles [nations, *ethnōn*]" (4:15, citing Isa 9:1–2 [8:23–9:1 LXX]). Boundaries begin to stretch, and Jesus' healing of the servant of a Roman centurion offers a programmatic preview of future directions in mission (Matt 8:10–13). The closing scene of the Gospel leaves the Matthean audience with this final impression: Jesus dispatches the eleven (remaining) disciples as tutors of all nations (28:19–20), certainly encompassing Gentiles (even if not excluding Jews).[63]

Still, for the period of Jesus' ministry, as well as the initial mission of his followers, Gentiles fall outside the field of vision. Jesus is clear on this:

- [Jesus sent twelve followers] with the following instructions: "Go nowhere among the Gentiles, and enter no town of the Samaritans, but go rather to the lost sheep of the house of Israel." (10:5–6)

61. Acts 28:25–27 stands closer to Matthew's reading of Isa 6: "Go to this people and say, 'You will indeed listen, but never understand, and you will indeed look, but never perceive. *For this people's heart has grown dull. . . .*'" (emphasis added).

62. The inclusion of these four women anticipates the unusual circumstances surrounding Jesus' birth. In a narrative that shows great concern with righteousness (within the birth story, it is Joseph who is said to be righteous [or just, 1:19]), the backstory of Tamar in particular invites reflection. Perhaps father-in-law Judah's appraisal of Tamar's character rubs off on Mary, too: "She is more righteous than I" (Gen 38:26 RSV).

63. Douglas R. A. Hare and Daniel J. Harrington contend that *panta ta ethnē* in 28:19 means "all the Gentiles" ("Make Disciples of All the Gentiles," *CBQ* 37 [1975]: 359–69). John P. Meier, however, counters with an argument for "all nations" (see also 24:14) and regards Matt 21:43 as an indicator that the *ethnos* (nation) to which the kingdom will be given includes both Jews and Gentiles ("Nations or Gentiles in Matthew 28:19?," *CBQ* 39 [1977]: 94–102). See Stanton, *Studies in Matthew and Early Christianity*, 42.

- [After his initial rebuff to a Canaanite woman, Jesus told the disciples], "I was sent only to the lost sheep of the house of Israel." (15:24)

During this phase of the activity of heaven's reign, Gentiles represent outsiders to the community and typically carry negative valence, alongside tax collectors (e.g., 5:46–47, practices not to be emulated; 18:17, outsiders to the community). Yet even here there is ambiguity. Though protesting that his mission does not encompass such persons as the Canaanite woman and her daughter, Jesus heals the daughter instantaneously with a word from a distance (15:28). And if the tandem of the socially marginalized Gentiles and (Jewish) tax collectors represent outsiders, Jesus can later point to tax collectors and prostitutes as exemplars of positive reception of the message of John and Jesus (God's realm) alike (Matt 21:31–32). In view of 8:5–13, he might just as well have paired tax collectors once more with Gentiles in this passage.

Boundaries of the people (*ethnos*) are being opened up, at least partially and provisionally; the composition of God's people is undergoing redefinition. And part of the story is Jesus' sometimes harsh critique of his contemporary Galilean and Judean Jews. Yet his words of sobering realism extend even to the company of his followers. Indeed, he warns about future judgment that will befall those whose lives do not conform to the divine will, whether inside or outside the boundaries of Matthew's (or Jesus') group.[64] The disciple group, no less than the world beyond its boundaries, is a mixed company that includes both good and bad, righteous and evil (e.g., 7:15–23; 13:24–30, 36–43, 47–50). The criterion that determines one's status is not aptness of christological confession but performance: conduct that expresses and mirrors the divine commitments and commands. Judgment that separates the two is not the prerogative of the community member (7:1–5; 13:27–30), though accountability and community discipline are appropriate and necessary (16:19; 18:15–20), as well as wise discernment (7:6). Decisive judgment belongs to the future—God's future (see 7:2; 13:27–30, 36–43, 47–50; 18:35; 24:45–51; 25:1–46; cf. 6:14–15). It is God's prerogative, with the agency of Jesus as the Human One (Son of Humanity), as the climactic metaphorical judgment scene of 25:31–46 makes clear (cf. 9:6; 13:41–42; 16:24–28).

Apocalyptic Chords: Eschatological Judgment

The robust Matthean interest in the motif of judgment has already surfaced. I will amplify my earlier discussion now with particular attention to two of the major discourses, one centering on parables of heaven's reign (ch. 13) and the other on images of eschatological judgment and hope (chs. 24–25).

---

64. With reference to 7:19, 23; 13:36–43; and 24:51, Stanton writes, "Matthew was as ferocious in his denunciation of his fellow Christians as he was of the Jewish religious leaders" (*Studies in Matthew and Early Christianity*, 114).

Judgment imagery is not confined to these chapters; consider, for example, the refrain "the outer darkness [or furnace of fire], where there will be weeping and gnashing of teeth" (8:12; 22:13; in addition to 13:42, 50; 24:51; 25:30). And in strongly allegorical parables commenting on the Jerusalem leaders' failure to welcome Jesus or his mission, the violent rejections of a vineyard owner's agents (servants and son) and of a king and his marrying son lead to catastrophic outcomes (21:33–41; 22:1–14)—including a city's destruction, mirroring the fall of Jerusalem to Roman armies (22:7). Jesus' proclamation of "the good news of the kingdom" (4:23; 9:35; cf. 24:14) does not clash with the baptizing prophet's sharp warning of coming judgment (3:7, 10, 12). Their agreement in core message—a summons to reorder life for the sake of participation in the realm of heaven (3:2; 4:17)—extends to the theme of eschatological judgment.

Parables about Heaven's Dominion (13:3–52)

Chapter 13 offers seven parables as metaphors for the divine reign. A formula comparing heaven's dominion to an aspect of farming, household labor, or commercial activity introduces six parables (13:24, 31, 33, 44, 45, 47), and the first, concerning a sower and his seeds (vv. 3–8), is explained as a parable about diverse responses to the message of God's reign (vv. 18–23). The parables present positive images celebrating joyful embrace of the message and reality of God's dominion: an abundant, fruitful harvest (vv. 8, 23); tiny mustard seeds turned into bird-sheltering trees (vv. 31–32); the transformative effect of yeast (v. 33); and buried treasure and precious pearl worth so much that one would sell everything to possess them (vv. 44–46).

In each parable, to be sure, there is an element of ambiguity or irony, perhaps even subversion. The majority of the seeds broadcast by the farmer fail and do not contribute to the splendid harvest (vv. 4–7). A farmer was not likely to plant mustard seed in his field, and who promoted the mustard plant to become a tree, anyway?—some towering tree, this! (vv. 31–32; cf, Mark 4:32). Yeast leavens a whole loaf (v. 33), but this is conventionally an image of corruption (see, e.g., 1 Cor 5:6–8; Gal 5:7–9). And as for the treasure, is there something amiss with the double mention of a treasure *hidden* in a field, which the finder *hides* once more till he can buy the field (v. 44)? Still, the accumulation of parabolic images leaves hearers in no doubt that, for Jesus at least, something extraordinary is happening, beyond expectation, and having a piece of the action, participating in the world transformation, is worth more than anything else one now possesses.

However, what of the one who declines the invitation? What about the three-fourths of the sown seeds that do not spring to life? The motif of judgment-as-separation in this chapter suggests an answer, and not a cheery one. Alongside wheat, weeds unexpectedly grow, due to the unwelcome and malicious intrusion of an "enemy" (13:25, 28). The farmer does not permit his field workers to remove the weeds, for fear the good wheat would be pulled up with them (vv. 28–29). At the harvest, the separation can be handled efficiently—and with the secondary gain of weeds routed to the furnace as fuel (v. 30). The allegorical unpacking of this parable in verses 36–43 connects the dots for readers. Evil coexists with good in the world (in the domain of the Human One, v. 41), and the two will be separated, for gloom or glory, but not until the "end of the age" (vv. 39–40). In due course, God will judge, and it is not the prerogative of the faithful to usurp that divine authority (here, aligned with 7:1–5 and also qualifying the grant of authority to "bind and loose" in 16:19 and 18:18). A final parable in Matthew 13 paints much the same picture: God's empire, like a fishing net that catches all sorts of fish, both good and bad, includes righteous and wicked alike, and not until the "end of the age" will God (through an army of angels) separate them (13:47–50). In Matthew's Gospel, judgment is primarily an eschatological (end-time) matter. The apocalyptic character of the narrative's development of the theme becomes even clearer in Jesus' climactic discourse orienting disciples (and Matthew's audience) to the future.

Discourse on Future Judgment and Deliverance (24:3–25:46)

Again a question posed by Jesus' followers elicits from him a major discourse, this time orienting listeners to the future: "Tell us, when will this be [i.e., the temple's destruction, predicted by Jesus in 24:1–2], and what will be the sign of your coming and of the end of the age?" (v. 3). Beyond the destruction from the Jewish War against Rome, which now lies in the past for Matthew and his first audience, Jesus forecasts a period of international and cosmic turmoil, conflict both within and outside the community of Jesus' followers, and persecution. The discourse prepares hearers for the coming crisis and assures them that God's righteous judgment will prevail.

The cumulative effect of the kaleidoscopic images in the discourse is impressive, all the more so because of its climactic position in Jesus' public activity.[65] Imagery both conveying warning and fostering hope draws together major threads from Jesus' teaching earlier in the Gospel. Notably, the discourse extends previous intimations of end-time judgment (e.g., 13:24–30, 36–43, 47–50; here in 25:1–46) and also amplifies the sobering message of the earlier mission discourse that intense persecution awaits Jesus' followers as they engage in mission (10:17–22; here in 24:9–14; cf. 24:15–22). Now the domain of witness and attendant suffering is not a local setting within "the towns of Israel" (10:5–6, 23) but the whole world, "all nations" (24:9, 14).

Compared to Mark's shorter version of the discourse (Mark 13:5–37)

---

65. Added to the discourse of Matt 23, addressed to a different audience and on a different topic, the apocalyptic discourse of chs. 24–25 gives Jesus an emphatic final voice in the narrative, leading up to his arrest. Luke presents parallel eschatological teaching in multiple distinct discourses (12:35–53; 17:22–37; 21:5–36; also 19:12–27), but Matthew combines all these sayings from Mark and Q, along with substantial additional uniquely Matthean material (notably the allegorical parables in 25:1–13, 31–46), in one large teaching block addressed privately to the disciples.

and Luke's parallel discourses (Luke 12:35–53; 17:22–37; 21:5–36), several distinctive features of Matthew's rendition are noteworthy and interesting variations.

The disciples' prompting question has much larger scope than in Mark, not only asking about the timing of the temple's ruin but also probing for a signal (*sēmeion*, "sign") of Jesus' future coming (*parousia*) and the completion of the age (Matt 24:3). The discourse responds to these questions specifically and emphatically. Jesus predicts that in a protracted period of strife and suffering, there will be delay (24:48; 25:5); during a first phase of intense distress the *telos* (end) "is not yet" (24:6), and "all this" will be but the "beginning of the birth pangs" (24:8). "The end" will not come until after a period of witness "to all the nations" (24:14). And to the question concerning a warning sign, Jesus offers a series of vivid images, though not without considerable ambiguity. As in Mark, Matthew has Jesus give a clear signal of coming conflict in Jerusalem, conflict that should provoke an immediate, emergency response: flee Judea urgently and without delay! (24:16–20).[66] The triggering event is one prophesied in Daniel, the erection of a desolating sacrilege (Dan 9:27; 11:31)—Matt 24:15 adds to Mark 13:14 the specific location within the temple ("the holy place").[67]

Specific "sign" language in the query of Matthew 24:3 recurs in verses 24 and 30 (only Matthew mentions the sign of the Son of Humanity [v. 30]).[68] Jesus also presents other images that respond to the desire for a warning sign. One must be ever vigilant and ready for a sudden, unpredictable event (24:37–44, 50; 25:13), and Jesus insists that no one knows or can know the timing of the end (24:36, 42, 50). Yet he also uses the image of a fig tree in leaf, signaling the approach of summer (24:32–33), to reinforce expectancy that the Human One will return soon after the occurrence of "all these things"—including a set of extraordinary cosmic portents and the dramatic return of the Human One from the sky, accompanied by angels who will gather all the chosen people from the whole earth (24:27–31). Jesus also

66. Verse 20 expands Mark's admonition to pray that this not happen in winter (Mark 13:18); let it not happen on the Sabbath either—one of the indicators in Matthew that the audience to which the Gospel is first addressed still keeps Sabbath as a Torah-observant group.

67. Matthew offers this mysterious sign (v. 15 does not use the word *sēmeion*), interestingly, not of the parousia (as in the disciples' question in v. 3) but of the fall of Jerusalem. Unlike Luke, though, Matthew depicts the strife in and around Jerusalem in general terms, without explicit description of the siege of Jerusalem and catastrophic destruction there (see Luke 19:41–44; 21:20–24). Compared to Matthew, Luke more sharply distinguishes the Jewish rebellion against Rome and the destruction of the temple from the end-time events. Like Luke, however, Matthew applies the eschatological brakes when describing events that late-first-century readers would associate with the Jewish War and fall of Jerusalem, now past (motif of delay, "the end is not yet," etc.).

68. In addition to the redactional insertion of the sign of the Human One, (only) Matt 24:30 also incorporates an allusion to Zech 12:10–14, imaging the global distress that will attend his parousia: "then all the tribes of the earth will mourn" (Rev 1:7 offers a similar, creative rereading of that oracle from Zechariah).

warns his disciples against being misled by deceptive signs such as the claims of some to be the Messiah (24:5, 23–24) or prophetic misinterpretations of international strife as the end time (24:6–8).

Matthew 24–25 paints an especially grim picture of turmoil within the communities of Jesus' followers during the period of global conflict and intense persecution. Twice Jesus forecasts the appearance of (false) Messiah claimants who, along with false prophets, will try with some success to mislead the disciples (24:5, 23–24; deception that has the potential to lead astray figures in vv. 5, 11, 23–26). Internal dissension will result from external pressure facing the community: hated by all nations (or Gentiles) because of their attachment to Jesus (v. 9), the disciples will also experience betrayal and hatred within their number, and some will "fall away" (v. 10). Prophets will arise among them, and many will be misled (v. 11). And while *anomia* (lawlessness) multiplies, love will grow cold (v. 12). These internal troubles represent a serious departure from norms of the Matthean Jesus' teaching, for which faithful living of *nomos* (the Law = Torah), with the twofold love commandment at the center, is crucial (e.g., 5:17–20; 22:34–40).

Despite the protracted social and political turbulence and the ordeal of persecution that Jesus predicts will overtake the community, as well as deterioration in relations within the disciple group, all is not lost. Deliverance of God's faithful, of "the chosen" ("elect," *eklektoi* in 24:22, 24, 31), will come, and those who persevere to the end will experience it (v. 13). But when? One cannot know. However, Matthew 24:36–25:30 gives Jesus' followers the guidance they will need. Dual admonitions structure the presentation: (1) be ever vigilant and ready, and (2) serve faithfully in the meantime. These twin counsels are developed narratively in two lengthy parables in 25:1–30:

- Parable of wise and foolish wedding bridesmaids: Be vigilant and prepared! (25:1–13)
- Parable of talents for investment: Serve productively in the time before the master's return. (25:14–30)

Jesus urges listeners: Be vigilant and prepared, and until the unpredictable moment arrives, be faithful! Or else. . . . In each parabolic vignette, including the generic mini-parable of 24:45–51, the consequences of unpreparedness or failure to perform assigned duties are dire. The stakes mount as auditors follow Jesus' rhetorical appeals through the last section of the discourse, culminating in severe, unending punishment (24:51; 25:30, 46; cf. the shut door of 25:10–12) or bliss in the company of the Holy One, as those who share in heaven's reign (25:34, 46; cf. vv. 21, 23). The Matthean Jesus' public teaching concludes on this note of decisive and final judgment, deferred for the moment in a world in which Rome dominates in military, political, and economic terms, a world in which evil and good coexist (even within the community of God's people)—as anticipated in the parables of chapter 13 (see 13:24–30, 36–43, 47–50).

As with apocalyptic literature generally, the paraenetic rhetoric of Matthew 24–25 appeals for persevering fidelity to God under duress and supports that appeal both by warning what the stakes of failure will be and by providing assurance that deliverance from God will certainly come.[69] Many twenty-first-century readers will squirm uncomfortably when they encounter this blend of encouragement and dire warning, of comfort and seeming threat—all the more since Jesus' own word and God's own justice are the source. For Matthew's late-first-century audience, however, such an apocalyptic message would have been heard in concert with similar teaching attested in other late Second Temple Jewish apocalyptic writings (e.g., 1 Enoch, 4 Ezra, 2 Baruch), especially texts that like Matthew are responding to the catastrophic destruction of the Jewish rebellion against Rome.[70] In this culminating discourse in the Gospel, Matthew's earliest audience would have found reason to endure in the commitment they have made as (mostly) Jewish followers of Jesus, despite its costs and perils, and basis for hope grounded ultimately in the character of a faithful God.

Excursus: Contested Readings of Matthew 25:31–46

While all interpreters of Matthew can agree on the importance of the parabolic judgment scene that concludes Matthew 24–25, and Jesus' public teaching as a whole, they offer divergent readings of the passage. The picture that Jesus sketches is one of universal, final judgment of "all the nations" (25:32), which the King (aka Human One or Son of Humanity) will pronounce. In the fashion of a shepherd separating sheep and goats, he will separate the nations into the doomed and the blessed. The sole criterion for the destiny of the nations is whether they have performed deeds of effective, compassionate care for those of lowest status who are in deepest need: "one of the least of these, my siblings" (vv. 40, 45 AT). A fourfold refrain dominates the passage: "For I was hungry and you gave me food, I was thirsty and you gave me something to drink, I was a stranger and you welcomed me, I was naked and you gave me clothing, I was sick and you took care of me, I was in prison and you visited

---

69. On these dual expressive-pragmatic functions of apocalyptic writings, to console and exhort, see John J. Collins, *the Apocalyptic Imagination: An Introduction to Jewish Apocalyptic Literature*, 2nd ed. (Grand Rapids: Wm. B. Eerdmans Publishing Co., 1998), 282–83 and passim. Warren Carter emphasizes that promised deliverance from oppressive Roman domination is a central concern of Matthew's apocalyptic theological vision. Matthew "builds an alternative worldview which shows the imperial claims of Rome to be limited. Rome is not ultimate. Rome, agent of Satan (4:8), will succumb to God's purposes" (*Matthew and the Margins: A Sociopolitical Reading* [Maryknoll, NY: Orbis Books, 2000], 8). David C. Sim situates Matthew's adoption of the symbolic universe of Jewish apocalyptic eschatology within the Matthean community's social setting (*Apocalyptic Eschatology in the Gospel of Matthew*, SNTSMS 88 [Cambridge: Cambridge University Press, 1996]). Sim identifies several functions of this apocalyptic view in the Gospel: identification and legitimation, explanation of circumstances experienced; encouragement; consolation and vengeance; group solidarity and social control (ibid., 222–42).

70. See Harrington, *Matthew*, 13–14.

me" (vv. 35–36; repeated in vv. 37–39; then negatively, in compressed form, in vv. 42–43, 44). Effective compassionate care extended to, or withheld from, "the least of these," determines destiny; the motif of surprise in the parable—"When was it that we saw you . . . ?" (vv. 37, 44)—indicates that the actions of the blessed were not undertaken for the purpose of seeking reward, even if eternal reward is the outcome.

This analysis of the rhetorical effect of the Matthean parable would be difficult to contest. However, who are the nations being judged here, and who are the "least of these" whom Jesus portrays as the recipients of care? Are the nations of the earth (i.e., outside the people of God) being judged on the basis of their treatment of the Christian group(s) or, more specifically, its itinerant missionaries?[71] If so, the prag-matic-rhetorical function of the passage would be primarily to engender confident hope in a beleaguered community of Matthew's readers (or to reassure its traveling missionaries): not only will God preserve and deliver them, but also the treatment they have endured will be the primary criterion for judgment of the whole world!

Or is the message of the parable directed primarily to the reading community, exhorting them one last time (within the narrative) to embody, in concrete and prac-tical acts of compassionate love, the core teaching of Jesus, which he reads right out of the pages of Matthew's Bible—the twofold love command (22:34–40)?[72] In the logic of this parabolic judgment scene, they will in fact love God with all their being, energies, and resources (the first and greatest commandment, 22:38) when they love other persons in the depths of their need (the second commandment, 22:39). For the King's solidarity-of-identity with low-status, high-need persons means that actions toward them are performed in relation to *him*. If one hears the passage along this line, its pragmatic-rhetorical function is primarily hortatory.

Like other parables and other stories, this one possesses an ambiguity or textual indeterminacy that requires readers to make a choice. My own preference is to opt for the second reading. In my view, the way Matthew's narrative as a whole shapes its reading communities works against the notion that they themselves stand at the center of the universe and its calculus of accountability. Moreover, the preceding parables urging vigilance and faithfulness have centered on the character of the dis-ciples' activity (24:45–25:30), and Matthew's audience may well expect concern with the disciples' performance to continue in this concluding, comprehensive judgment scene. If so, this culminating judgment scene has more to do with ethics than hope; better put, it integrates the two. It reinforces Jesus' earlier appeals for followers who, in practical actions of commitment and care, display the other-regard, the mercy,

71. This is the interpretive approach, e.g., of Senior, *Matthew*, 280–86; Graham N. Stan-ton, *Gospel for a New People: Studies in Matthew* (Edinburgh: T&T Clark, 1992), 207–31; Har-rington, *Matthew*, 357–60; cf. Douglas R. A. Hare, *Matthew*, IBC (Louisville, KY: Westminster John Knox Press, 1993), 288–91. Harrington reads *panta ta ethnē* as "all the Gentiles," not "all the nations," and argues that Matthew conceives of separate judgments of Jews and Gentiles (*Matthew*, 358–59); similarly Hare, *Matthew*, 288–89, esp. 288, "judgment of the pagans."

72. This is the interpretive approach, e.g., of Arland J. Hultgren, *The Parables of Jesus: A Commentary* (Grand Rapids: Wm. B. Eerdmans Publishing Co., 2000), 309–27; Francis W. Beare, *The Gospel according to Matthew* (Peabody, MA: Hendrickson Publishers, 1981), 491–97; Eduard Schweizer, *The Good News according to Matthew*, trans. David E. Green (Atlanta: John Knox Press, 1975), 475–80. For the history of interpretation of this passage to the 1980s, see S. W. Gray, *The Least of My Brothers: Matthew 25:31–46: A History of Interpretation*, SBLDS 114 (Atlanta: Scholars Press, 1989).

the love that mark the very character of God (e.g., 5:43–48; 7:12; 22:34–40).[73] But let the (my) reader beware, lest I impose my own preferences on a text that others read differently! Still, I have little doubt which interpretive approach is more constructive for the daunting ethical challenges people of faith and goodwill face in the conflicted world of the twenty-first century.

Before leaving this section on apocalyptic judgment in Matthew, it is fitting to attend briefly to the Matthean rendition of the death of Jesus. Matthew paints the crucifixion scene in the bold hues of apocalyptic judgment and life-giving liberation, fitting transposition of passion-narrative chords in tune with the preceding elaboration of the motifs of eschatological judgment and hope.

Shaking Ground, Shifting Aeons: The Death (and Resurrection) of Jesus as Apocalyptic Event

Matthew's narrative of the death of Jesus, and the events in Jerusalem that led to it, largely adheres to the account in Mark 14–15. Matthean embellishments, when they appear, are especially meaningful. Among the most interesting are the following:

1. Judas's betrayal earns him thirty pieces of silver, not an unspecified sum of money as in Mark 14:11 and Luke 22:5 (Matt 26:15; 27:3–10). In Matthew 27:9–10 the narrator points to the specific sum's fulfillment of prophecy (Zech 11:12–13, though the narrator credits a blended quotation to Jeremiah).
2. At the last meal shared by Jesus and his disciples, a brief dialogue initiated by Judas affords Jesus the opportunity to display precise prophetic awareness of the identity of his betrayer (Matt 26:25; this is ambiguous in Mark 14:18–21 and Luke 22:21–23; John 13:21–30 presents a more extensive dialogue, including the beloved disciple, that reveals the betrayer's identity). In the scene of Jesus' arrest, Matthew also has Jesus address Judas with a distancing address, "Friend," right after the betrayal kiss (26:49–50).
3. As a narrative interlude between the council's decision regarding Jesus and Pilate's interrogation, only Matthew provides an account of Judas's

73. Carter offers an interpretation of Matthew's "apocalyptic eschatology" that holds these two perspectives (admonishing righteous conduct and engendering hope) in balance. The dualism of righteous and wicked, and of punishment and vindication, is part of a worldview that legitimates Jesus' followers "as the group that is faithful to God's purposes. . . . The constant emphasis on future accountability in the judgment functions to strengthen group solidarity and to control group behavior and practices. This apocalyptic mind-set reinforces their identity as recipients of God's favor, fashions a lifestyle according to God's will, warns of dire consequences for failing to live accordingly, but promises reward and salvation for continued faithfulness" (*Matthew and the Margins*, 10–11).

regret, failed effort to undo his betrayal, and ultimate demise (27:3–10). (Acts 1:16–20 also narrates the death of Judas, with most of the details differing from Matt 27.)

4. Immediately after the final meal scene, Jesus makes a more precise prediction than in Mark 14:27 of imminent desertion by his followers, adding "this night" (Matt 26:31), as well as the link between desertion and attachment to Jesus ("because of me").

5. In the Gethsemane scene, even though (like Mark 14:32–42) Matthew 26:36–46 narrates the disciples' sleeping (hence failing to pray) three times, the account in Matthew shifts the accent more sharply to the triad of prayers by Jesus, in part by including direct speech by Jesus in the second petition (26:42, only in Matthew).

6. Under interrogation by the high priest, Jesus (true to his own counsel in 5:33–37) refuses to take an oath as challenged: "I put you under oath before the living God, tell us if you are the Messiah, the Son of God" (26:63). The spoken reply is ambiguous in 26:64, apparently reading verbal irony into the high priest's words. Jesus answers, "You have said so." This replaces the affirmative "I am" in Mark 14:62. In Matthew 26:64–65, as in Mark 14:62–63, Jesus proceeds to draw imagery from Daniel 7:13 and Psalm 110:1, asserting before his accuser his divine vindication as the Human One. Matthew 26:64 and Luke 22:69 alike add the phrase "from now on," intimating more clearly than Mark's future reference that Jesus' vindication and honor from God do not wait until the future parousia.

7. Unlike Jesus, Peter is willing—twice—to take an oath, swearing to deny his attachment as disciple to Jesus and so save his own neck (Matt 26:72–74). The contrast Matthew draws between the responses of Jesus and Peter to high-pressure interrogation is thus even sharper in Matthew than in Mark 14:66–72, where Peter swears and curses just once (v. 71).

8. Matthew enriches Pilate's interrogation of Jesus with the unusual mention of an intervention by the governor's wife (Matt 27:19). In a Gospel that has employed dreams as vehicle of divine revelation (1:20–21; 2:12–13, 19, 22) and emphasized the virtue of righteousness (e.g., 3:15; 5:6, 10, 20; 6:33), it is striking that Pilate's wife has a dream and (unsuccessfully) seeks to dissuade Pilate from having anything to do with "that righteous man" (NRSV: "innocent man"; the word is an inflected form of *dikaios*).

9. Not heeding his wife's recommendation, Pilate proceeds with the judicial case, but even as he prepares to release (Jesus) Barabbas and order a capital sentence for Jesus the so-called Messiah, he tries to deflect from himself any blame for the act by symbolically washing Jesus' blood from his hands (27:24). "All the people" assembled, by contrast, do take "his blood" upon themselves (and their "children," v. 25), accepting responsibility and—ironically—also the merciful forgiveness stemming from the new-covenant blood (26:28).[74] This is part of an important, distinctive

74. See Timothy B. Cargal, "'His Blood Be upon Us and upon Our Children': A Matthean

Matthean narrative strand that traces the blood of Jesus in connection with responsibility for his death (27:4, 6, 8, 24–25; cf. 23:30, 35).

Particularly suggestive are several details Matthew sketches into the crucifixion scene and its immediate aftermath (27:33–54). As Jesus hangs on the cross, 27:40 embellishes the derision by passersby to include the challenge "If you are the Son of God, come down from the cross." Since the centurion and others with him[75] name Jesus to be Son of God after they have witnessed his death and the events accompanying it (v. 54), ironic affirmation of Jesus as divine Son (perhaps only ridiculed in v. 40 but acknowledged in v. 54?) brackets the account of Jesus' dying. As mockery continues from the Judean elite (chief priests, scribes, and elders), the irony is biting, and the speakers' unwitting self-critique is transparent for Matthew's audience, who have been tutored by the preceding narrative: "He saved others; he cannot save himself. *He is* the King of Israel; let him come down from the cross now, and *we will believe in him. He trusts in God; let God deliver him now, if he wants to; for he said, 'I am God's Son'*" (Matt 27:42–43; italicized phrasing, including the concluding quotation from Ps 22:8 [21:9 LXX], appears only in Matthew). The narrative throws a bright spotlight on the oppositional stance of the local elite in Jerusalem, with the negative consequences it portends—and much more to come (27:62–66; 28:1–15)!

The apocalyptic stamp on the scene comes to the fore at the moment of Jesus' death. As in Mark, the temple curtain is torn from top to bottom (Matt 27:51 // Mark 15:38), the direction of the rending suggesting divine agency—proleptic (anticipatory) fulfillment of Jesus' prediction of the temple's ruin (Matt 24:2). Matthew, however, adds apocalyptic fireworks to the scene. Resurrection potency jumps ahead of the story line,[76] as ground tremors split rocks in the Jerusalem area, and tombs open, emptying their dead (another tremor opens Jesus' tomb in 28:2). These saints among the dead are raised and walk the streets of the holy city—though not, the narrator clarifies, until

Double Entendre?" *NTS* 37 (1991): 101–12. With many others, Luz finds it unlikely that the self-curse of 27:25 pictures the blood of Jesus as benefiting humankind (*Studies in Matthew*, 258 and n. 49). Rather, Matthew interprets the destruction of Jerusalem as "God's punishment for the rejection of Jesus. There is no hint at a positive future for Israel beyond this" (ibid.). I am inclined, however, to acknowledge ambiguity or ambivalence in the narrative, which readers need to resolve in ways that not only answer to the historical circumstances that generated Matthew's text but also foster constructive religious, theological, and ethical readings for today. See further ch. 7 below.

75. Only the centurion speaks this line in Mark 15:39, but Matt 27:54 lends added credibility to the testimony by multiplying the number of witnesses. In Luke 23:47 only the centurion speaks, but he attests Jesus *dikaios* (just or righteous) rather than calling him Son of God.

76. On Matthew's reworking of this scene and its theological nuances, see John T. Carroll and Joel B. Green, *The Death of Jesus in Early Christianity* (Peabody, MA: Hendrickson Publishers, 1995), 48–49; Donald Senior, *The Passion of Jesus in the Gospel of Matthew* (Collegeville, MN: Liturgical Press, 1985), 143–47; Raymond E. Brown, *The Death of the Messiah: From Gethsemane to the Grave. A Commentary on the Passion Narratives in the Four Gospels*, 2 vols., ABRL (New York: Doubleday, 1994; New Haven, CT: Yale University Press, 1998), 2:1118–33, 1137–40.

after Jesus has been raised from the dead (27:51–53; these verses contain echoes of several prophetic texts, including Ezek 37:12–13; Isa 26:19; Dan 12:2). Thus the theological priority of Jesus' resurrection is preserved while, at the same time, the narrative pictures the crucifixion/death of Jesus as the decisive, epoch-shifting, liberative, life-bestowing event.

The last two chapters of the Gospel also assign a much expanded role to Roman soldiers. There is no ambiguity in Matthew 27:27–31 that it is Roman soldiers who mock and abuse Jesus, then proceed to crucify him: they are "soldiers *of the governor*" (emphasis added), and a whole cohort assembles! Twice the narrator mentions that they guard Jesus at the crucifixion site (a detail mentioned only in Matthew; 27:36, 54); verse 54 specifies that the centurion and others with him are the ones "keeping watch." After Joseph from Arimathea has placed Jesus' body in his own tomb (vv. 57–60),[77] soldiers reappear to participate in unsuccessful plots to guard the tomb and, when that fails, to spread false rumors about the empty tomb and the disciples' theft of the body (27:62–66; 28:4, 11–15).[78] When it comes to the Son of God, and God's power over oppressive evil in the world, Roman military might is impotent.[79] So too is the fierce enmity of the local Jerusalem elite, who have been co-opted by imperial power to promote Roman interests in Judea, who conspire to have Jesus executed, and who then attempt damage control in the wake of discovering an empty tomb, yet who are powerless to prevent God's triumph. In a (Jewish) apocalyptic narrative like this, power is not what it seems, and despite present appearances to the contrary, the polarity of good and evil in history will ultimately yield to the holy justice of God.

77. Matthew enhances the portrayal of Joseph: he is wealthy and places the dead body "in *his own new* tomb" (27:60, emphasis added; cf. Luke 23:53: "a rock-hewn tomb where no one had ever been laid"; Mark 15:46: "a tomb that had been hewn out of the rock"). Especially striking is his promotion to *disciple* in Matt 27:57.

78. While Matt 27:27 refers to soldiers "of the governor," the account in vv. 62–66 is ambiguous. Is Pilate attempting (cf. vv. 24–25) to distance himself and his military force from the plot to secure the tomb? He tells the apprehensive Pharisees and leading priests, "You have a guard of soldiers; go, make it as secure as you can" (27:65). There is ambiguity here. Pilate might be heard as saying, "*You* have soldiers; don't ask for mine!" Or rather: "Of course, you have [use of my] soldiers; make the tomb secure." Either way, the initiative and agency appear to rest more clearly with the local Judean elite, whose character profile continues to deteriorate to the end of the story—and beyond, as the false rumors continue to circulate among Jews to Matthew's own time, according to 28:15. This troubling conclusion to the Jerusalem narrative reflects the bitter conflict and polemic between Matthew's Christian-Jewish group and other Jews in their location.

79. Indeed, the centurion and his troops even affirm Jesus' status as Son of God. If the parallel acclamation by Mark's centurion (Mark 15:39) may be heard as sarcasm, an instance of verbal irony (see the discussion in ch. 3 above), the detail in Matt 27:54 that the centurion's declaration is prompted in part by his observation of the earthquake suggests that he means what he says, even if he does not comprehend what *kind* of divine son Jesus is.

Is Matthew a Coherent Narrative? Exploring Thematic Tensions

We have discovered that Matthew's Gospel presents evidence of care in narrative design, particularly the fashioning of thematically cohesive narrative units and blocks of teaching (discourses). At the same time, at several points in the literary analysis, tensions have surfaced.

Thematic Tensions in Matthew's Narrative

- Mercy or judgment?
- Ethical dualism?
- "Love your enemies": Pharisees, too?
- "Like Gentiles and tax collectors"? Insiders and outsiders
- "Not one letter": Does Jesus affirm or negate the law?

Mercy and Judgment

On the one hand, the Matthean Jesus highlights the importance of *mercy*, in both the divine character and the practice of the disciple community (e.g., 5:7; 6:12; 18:12–14, 21–22). Yet equal if not greater weight is given to severity of *judgment*, which in the working out of divine justice may even entail the nullification of mercy (e.g., 6:14–15; 18:34–35). Matthew contains harsh rhetoric of judgment and exclusion (e.g., 5:26; 7:21–23), including the haunting images of abandonment to the "outer darkness," where divine retribution brings "weeping and gnashing of teeth" (8:12; 13:42, 50; 22:13; 24:51; 25:30). Yet Jesus challenges followers to forgive and show mercy, love enemies (5:43), and seek reconciliation as a priority concern (5:21–25). The path to life is treacherous, and few are able to gain entrance through a narrow gate (7:13–14). Yet Jesus promises listeners a light burden and rest (11:28–30), and the opening lines of the Sermon on the Mount offer unexpected blessing to persons who are experiencing anything but good fortune (5:1–12). What is a reader to do with this set of images-in-contest?[80]

Ethical Dualism?

Polarity appears to be basic to this Gospel and Jesus' message within it. The world, and even the company of Jesus' followers, comprises both good and bad (*agathoi* and *ponēroi*), righteous and unrighteous (*dikaioi* and *adikoi*), as in 7:15–23; 13:24–30, 36–43, 47–50. Future (eschatological) judgment will disentangle what present experience throws together in this untidy mix (7:2; 13:27–30, 36–43, 47–50; 18:35; 24:45–51). There will be abundant blessing and reward for some, but at the same time condemnation for others (e.g.,

---

80. Barbara E. Reid, OP, offers helpful reflections on some of these tensions in "Matthew's Nonviolent Jesus and Violent Parables," in an issue of *Christian Reflection: A Series in Faith and Ethics* (Waco, TX: Baylor University Press, 2006), 27–36, http://www.baylor.edu/ifl/christianreflection/ParablesArticleReid.pdf.

25:1–46). Yet Jesus also says, "Love your enemies and pray for those who persecute you, so that you may be children of your Father in heaven; for he makes his sun rise on the evil and on the good, and sends rain on the righteous and on the unrighteous" (5:44–45). Does this depiction of the divine character—and precisely as model for the followers of Jesus—not undermine the polarity that is so dominant throughout the narrative?

"Love Your Enemies" (Unless They Are Pharisees!)

A practical aspect of the tension observed in the preceding section concerns the narrative's preoccupation with Pharisees and scribes as Jesus' primary antagonists. The vigorous and sometimes heated debates in which these rival teachers engage culminate in a volley of stinging rebukes from Jesus in Matthew 23, spoken to the crowd and disciples (and "out the window," so to speak, to Matthew's audience).[81] What are readers to do with such vitriol, especially when the same speaker (Jesus) has commended radical love of enemies, plus principled and transformative nonretaliation toward those who (would) harm one (5:38–47)? In a narrative that by biographical convention offers its central character as moral exemplar for readers, surely Jesus (not to mention the God whose dominion he represents) would not be allowed to meet a lower standard of righteousness than he expects of his followers (esp. in the light of 23:2–3). Mulling over these matters, an audience would scarcely emerge from a hearing of Matthew's Gospel with the notion that the demanding moral vision it inculcates, above all in the Sermon on the Mount, is easily attained. The love of the near one and the enemy alike remains as command—and aspiration.

"Let Such a One Be to You as a Gentile and a Tax Collector": Insiders and Outsiders

Perspectives on community boundaries, on status as insiders and outsiders, also seem complicated in Matthew's Gospel. Tax collectors and Gentiles, in particular, can typify marginalized outsiders (e.g., 5:46–47; 18:17) who are of no concern to the mission of Jesus and his followers (10:5–6; 15:24). On the other hand, pagan magi from a distant land acclaim the child-king Jesus (2:1–16), a Roman soldier expresses exemplary faith (8:10–13), and tax collectors join prostitutes in the ranks of those who model acceptance of God's agents (21:31–32). And of course Jesus' parting directions for his followers

81. Verses 1–12, addressing the crowd and disciples, criticize the scribes and Pharisees indirectly, employing third-person forms. Without indication of a change in audience, vv. 13–36 shift to the second plural (e.g., the refrain "Woe to you, scribes and Pharisees, hypocrites!" in vv. 13, 15, 23, 25, 27, 29). Ulrich Luz views all the major discourses of Matthew (though excluding ch. 23) as addressed not to the auditors within the story but "out the window" to Matthew's reading community (e.g., *Matthew*, 1:12; idem, *Studies in Matthew*, 147). This is an aspect of Matthew's character as an "inclusive story" that "reflects the experiences and the history of the post-Easter church" (Luz, *Studies in Matthew*, 104). Luz observes an inconsistency between Jesus' acknowledgment of the Pharisees' teaching authority in 23:2–3 and his earlier warning in 16:12, a clash in views that he attributes to tension between Matthew and the tradition he has inherited (ibid., 187).

cancel his earlier mission restrictions: at the end of the story he dispatches the disciples to teach (and through baptism incorporate) all nations/Gentiles (28:19–20). Taken together, these images-in-tension begin to poke at firm, rigid boundaries between the community and those outside. As with Tamar of genealogy fame (1:3), seen in a new light by her father-in-law Judah (Gen 38:26); as with Mary and Joseph (Matt 1:19–23); as with John and baptism-seeking Jesus (3:15); and as with Pharisees and disciples (5:20)—there is more to "righteousness" and good standing in the community and honor before God than one might have imagined.

"Not One Letter":
Does Jesus Affirm or
Negate the Torah?

One other area of tension within the Gospel requires attention. When compared to Mark (yet even apart from a redaction-critical analysis), Matthew presents Jesus as a radical exponent of the Law of Moses (Torah).[82] Far from advocating any lessening in its authority, he insists on impeccable observance of the least commandment (5:18–19; 23:23)—not to mention the greatest commandments (22:34–40)—and positions himself as one who fulfills the Law and the Prophets (5:17). Yet the Matthean Jesus also sets his authoritative "I say to you" against both Scripture and its interpretive tradition among his Jewish contemporaries. At points his teaching manifests what appears to be remarkable freedom, perhaps even subversion, in relation to Mosaic Law and its interpretation (e.g., the antitheses of 5:21–48). Reading between the lines of the apocalyptic discourse in Matthew 24–25, one sees footprints of a community that still observes the Sabbath (24:20). But earlier in the narrative, controversy provoked by the disciples' conduct on the Sabbath prompts Jesus to claim sovereign authority over the Sabbath, as one who is greater than the temple and who is Sabbath Lord (12:6, 8). To defend his position on Sabbath observance, he appeals to Scripture, to be sure (David's actions in 1 Sam 21:3–6), but in doing so he highlights a passage that appears to sanction conduct forbidden by the Torah (bread unlawful for any to eat except priests, echoing Lev 24:5–9), and then claims even higher status for himself. Moreover, he grants his followers a share in the authority to bind and loose, under his supervising presence (Matt 16:19; 18:18–20), which may be taken to mean prerogative to determine which commandments should be relaxed and which should continue to be enforced.[83]

Luz locates Matthew at the intersection of two traditions, one of which (Q) views Jesus as upholding the Law, while the other (Mark) accents

82. Luz speaks for many when he calls Matthew "the clearest exponent of a Law-affirming Jewish Christianity" (*Studies in Matthew*, 185).

83. See David L. Balch, "The Greek Political Topos *peri nomōn* and Matthew 5:17, 19, and 16:19," in *Social History of the Matthean Community*, ed. Balch, 68–84). In Balch's view, Matthew affirms that the law (as a whole) is not abolished, even as Jesus authorizes Peter (and the disciples) to relax (i.e., annul) particular laws or imperatives (84). Balch situates this approach in relation to Greek philosophical tradition and the writings of Josephus. Respect for law does not preclude creative appropriation of its precepts to meet changing circumstances.

criticism of the Law. He argues that Matthew "saw it as his theological task to integrate these traditions."[84] Surely this is part of the story and an element of any satisfactory explanation of the tensions within the Matthean narrative. This complex narrative weaves together strands from several sources and traditions, and they in turn were fashioned from and for diverse settings and groups, with varying challenges and specific practices. As a more fruitful metaphor, we may consider the Matthean narrative as a mosaic that contains tiles of varying hues, shapes, and sizes, all of which retain their distinctive character even as they contribute to a new gestalt.

With such a complex narrative, coherence will finally be the concern and achievement of readers or reading communities. Nevertheless, they will follow the cues the author has provided. Among those cues will be the portrait of Jesus not as one who discards the Torah or sanctions neglect of the claim of Torah and Prophets but as one who instead (in Matthew's view) shows the best and most faithful path to obedience. The small things in the Torah still claim a serious hearing, but what matters most of all is the triad of "justice and mercy and faith" (23:23), the other-regard that acts toward others as one would be treated (7:12), the deep and broad love of God and neighbor-as-self, even enemy, that is at the heart of the whole of Scripture (22:34–40; 5:43–44). This is what fidelity to Law and Scripture looks like, Matthew-style, with Jesus as the definitive Teacher. For all the vitriol in Matthew toward other Jewish teachers among Jesus'—and Matthew's—contemporaries, this approach places Matthew, and Matthew's Jesus, squarely within Jewish tradition and practice.

| Concluding Reflection: The Aims and Impact of Matthew's Narrative | Throughout the history of Christianity, from the late first century onward, the Gospel according to Matthew has played an especially important role in shaping faith, teaching, practice, and organizational patterns in congregations. The very same document that has proved to be so useful for forming and nurturing Christian communities, however, has too often been toxic in relation to the Jewish religion and people.[85] As we have discovered, this most Jewish of Gospels is at the same time punctuated with bitter invective toward Jewish leaders and sometimes also the entire people. |

84. Luz, *Studies in Matthew*, 186.

85. Saldarini puts it sharply: "Even though the Gospel of Matthew was written for Jews within the first-century Jewish community, it has had its effect and its home among gentiles for the last nineteen hundred years. . . . The gospel's polemics have been used again and again by gentile Christians as a club to beat the whole Jewish tradition, marginalizing the Jewish community and threatening its existence. The actual history of the gospel thus ironically includes a large measure of anti-Semitism [I would say, "anti-Judaism"] along with its honorable role in promoting a healthy communal life within the Christian churches" (*Matthew's Christian-Jewish Community*, 205).

Matthew's narrative builds a case for the legitimacy of a particular reading of Jewish Scripture and tradition, a Christian-Jewish interpretation of the Torah and the Prophets for which the Messiah Jesus is the primary authority. In Matthew's late-first-century setting within the Jewish communities in upper Galilee and Syria, this is becoming an increasingly marginal view.[86] The Matthean Jesus' vigorous, contentious exchanges with scribes and Pharisees over the understanding and faithful enactment of the Torah reflect the mutual antagonism, often intense, between Matthew's community and the (proto-rabbinic) leader groups among the Pharisees' successors with whom they must now reckon.[87]

The language of the Gospel distances Jesus' followers from "your" or "their" synagogues (Matt 4:23; 9:35; 10:17; 12:9; 13:54; 23:34), where indeed harsh discipline may await them (e.g., 10:17; 23:34). But this does not mean that Matthew's group has somehow left Judaism behind. Contested interpretations of Torah praxis and sustained polemic regarding authentic leadership suggest, rather, that this is still a struggle within Jewish communities in Matthew's location. It is a wrenching conflict over the identity, composition, boundaries, and future of the Jewish people—and in a world in which *all* Jews must also make sense of and come to terms with the continuing reality of Roman imperial governance and military domination in the aftermath of Jerusalem's fall and the temple's destruction. In this setting, as its position becomes that of a deviant, marginal group, Matthew's *ekklēsia* (assembly, church), while alienated from the larger Jewish community, still hopes to reform it.[88] No wonder this intrafamilial conflict is so intense! On nearly every page, it has left its stamp on Matthew's telling of the "good news of the kingdom."

Once Matthew's Gospel left the arena of Judaism and became the possession of Gentile Christians, sharp debates and vigorous polemics internal to Jewish communities were converted into material that has the potential to

---

86. In my sketch of Matthew's social setting and rhetorical impact, I am drawing heavily upon the work of Overman, *Matthew's Gospel and Formative Judaism*; and Saldarini, *Matthew's Christian-Jewish Community*.

87. As Overman points out, the harshness of the polemic in Matthew suggests "a current and hotly contested struggle which the Matthean community seems to be losing" (*Matthew's Gospel and Formative Judaism*, 147); it is in the position of minority "underdog" in this crisis (cf. ibid., 19). Overman also observes that rejection of Jewish leadership on the part of sectarian communities was common during this period and by no means unique to Matthew (ibid., 23). For Luz, Matthew's narrative reflects an intense "family conflict" between two "siblings" (*Studies in Matthew*, 250–52, 255), a conflict in which Jewish Christians, as a minority, "needed 'anti-Judaism' as part of their self-definition" (ibid., 256). By contrast, the majority, rabbinic tradition did not need to identify itself in reaction to this minority group.

88. Saldarini, *Matthew's Christian-Jewish Community*, 197. Responding to Saldarini's analysis, Stanton argues that Matthew represents a "foundation document" for Christian communities, including both Jews and Gentiles, who regarded themselves "as a 'new people,' over against both local synagogues and the Gentile world at large" (*Studies in Matthew and Early Christianity*, 123–29, esp. 129). For Stanton, the separation of the Matthean community from Judaism lies in the past (ibid., 115); so also Luz, *Studies in Matthew*, 250; idem, *Matthew*, 1:54.

arm wounding missiles lobbed from the outside. Far too often, struggle for identity and mutual critique within Jewish life have become all too useful to those located outside it who foment hatred that seeks to destroy Jewish religion and people.[89] That script has played out again and again across the centuries. It draws from (a portion of) Matthew's script, to be sure. But let the voice of Matthew's Jesus—in his appeal for the deepest fidelity to Israel's Scriptures and God, exhibited through a life driven by love of the near one and the enemy alike—have the last say.

89. I offer further reflections in ch. 7 below. For a brief survey of early Christian texts that follow this trajectory, see the discussion of "the cross and anti-Judaism" in Carroll and Green, *Death of Jesus in Early Christianity*, 182–204, esp. 182–89. Among many other works addressing the problem of Matthew and anti-Judaism, see Ulrich Luz, "Anti-Judaism in the Gospel of Matthew as a Historical and Theological Problem: An Outline," in *Studies in Matthew*, 243–61 (orig. published in *EvT* 53 [1993]: 310–28); Harrington, *Matthew*, 20–22; Terence L. Donaldson, *Jews and Anti-Judaism in the New Testament: Decision Points and Divergent Interpretations* (Waco, TX: Baylor University Press, 2010), 30–54; Overman, *Matthew's Gospel and Formative Judaism*; Saldarini, *Matthew's Christian-Jewish Community*; idem, "Reading Matthew without Anti-Semitism," in *The Gospel of Matthew in Current Study: Studies in Memory of William G. Thompson, S.J.*, ed. David E. Aune (Grand Rapids: Wm. B. Eerdmans Publishing Co., 2001), 166–83; Amy-Jill Levine, *The Social and Ethnic Dimensions of Matthean Social History: "Go Nowhere among the Gentiles" (Matt. 10:5b)*, Studies in the Bible and Early Christianity 14 (Lewiston, NY: Mellen, 1988); Scot McKnight, "A Loyal Critic: Matthew's Polemic with Judaism in Theological Perspective," in *Anti-Semitism and Early Christianity: Issues of Polemic and Faith*, ed. Craig A. Evans and Donald A. Hagner (Minneapolis: Fortress Press, 1993), 55–79.

5. The Gospel according to Luke

Like Matthew, Luke builds on Mark's narrative pattern, greatly expanding the content of Jesus' teaching, providing opening and ending frames (a birth-childhood narrative in chs. 1–2 and resurrection appearances in ch. 24), and rearranging the materials into a carefully ordered narrative, including a long central journey to Jerusalem (9:51–19:27). Into this journey narrative, Luke incorporates most of the materials (both discourse and action stories) shared with Matthew but not in Mark (Q materials; on the two-document hypothesis, see ch. 2 above) as well as materials found only in Luke. Like Matthew, Luke begins the story in a way that embeds the life and ministry of Jesus in Israel's ongoing history, though not in the fulfillment-formula style so prominent in Matthew. Another distinctive feature of Luke's rendition of the "good news" is that the closing chapter not only brings closure to the account of Jesus' life and activity but also—indeed, even more—anticipates the mission of Jesus' followers in the narrative sequel for which the Gospel prepares: the Acts of the Apostles. Formal literary prefaces, both addressed to Theophilus, link Luke's two books (Luke 1:1–4; Acts 1:1–2). This sketch will focus on the interpretation of Luke's Gospel, but at many points the reading of Luke will be enhanced through pointers to the further development of Lukan concerns in the narrative sequel.[1]

Historical Questions
Who?

Like the other canonical Gospels, Luke does not identify its author by name. The earliest mention of Luke as the author comes from the late second century CE.[2] In a manner that appears to draw inferences from references in letters of the New Testament (Phlm 24; Col 4:14; 2 Tim 4:11), together with the anonymous "we" sections in Acts (16:10–17; 20:5–15; 21:1–18; 27:1–28:16), these early documents paint a portrait of the author, Luke, as a physician,

---

1. For this chapter, I incorporate with adaptation some materials from my volume *Luke: A Commentary*, NTL (Louisville, KY: Westminster John Knox Press, 2012). I am grateful to the publisher for permission to draw from that work here.

2. This attribution appears in the Bodmer papyrus P[75]; Irenaeus, *Adversus Haereses* (e.g., 3.1.1; 3.14.1); the Muratorian Fragment; and the Greek preface of the Anti-Marcionite Prologue. See Andrew F. Gregory, *The Reception of Luke and Acts in the Period before Irenaeus: Looking for Luke in the Second Century*, WUNT 2/169 (Tübingen: Mohr Siebeck, 2003), 43.

Paul's "inseparable companion" (Irenaeus, *Haer.* 3.1.1; 3.14.1). The Greek preface to the Anti-Marcionite Prologue places Luke in Syrian Antioch and blesses him with a long life (death at the age of eighty-four).

This tradition of authorship by a Doctor Luke who had a hand in the Pauline mission originates a half century or more after the composition of Luke and Acts, as far as we can tell, and cannot be reliably established. More helpful in any event is the author profile that close reading of the narrative surfaces. In the preface with which the Gospel opens, this anonymous author (I will use the traditional name Luke) self-identifies as a second- or third-generation participant in the Christian movement (1:1–3). He claims to be offering a carefully designed narrative—on close examination, one that adopts Greco-Roman literary conventions from both biographical (*bios*) and historical (*historia*) narratives.[3] And he does so in a fashion that presents the events narrated as purposeful ("events that have been fulfilled among us," 1:1)—realizing, it will soon become clear, divine aims and promises. It is therefore unsurprising that from the very start, Luke's narrative immerses readers deeply in the Jewish Scriptures. For Luke, those Scriptures bear authority for faith and living—fidelity to Torah and Prophets alike is important (see 2:22–24; 10:25–28; 11:42; 16:17, 27–31; 18:18–20)—and convey a message of hope that ancient promises for the covenant people now find fulfillment. Hence the note of exuberant joy on which the Gospel opens (chs. 1–2).

The Prefaces of Luke and Acts

Luke 1:1–4
Since many have undertaken to set down an orderly account of the events that have been fulfilled among us, just as they were handed on to us by those who from the beginning were eyewitnesses and servants of the word, I too decided, after investigating everything carefully from the very first, to write an orderly account for you, most excellent Theophilus, so that you may know the truth concerning the things about which you have been instructed.

Acts 1:1–2
In the first book, Theophilus, I wrote about all that Jesus did and taught from the beginning until the day when he was taken up to heaven, after giving instructions through the Holy Spirit to the apostles whom he had chosen.

---

3. Among those associating Luke with the biographical genre (*bios*) are Richard A. Burridge, *What Are the Gospels? A Comparison with Graeco-Roman Biography*, SNTSMS 70 (Cambridge: Cambridge University Press, 1992); Charles H. Talbert, *Literary Patterns, Theological Themes, and the Genre of Luke-Acts*, SBLMS 20 (Missoula, MT: Scholars Press, 1974), 125–40; and most recently Mikeal C. Parsons, *Luke*, Paideia (Grand Rapids: Baker Academic, 2015), 13–15. Proponents of Luke as history (*historia*) have specified the genre variously: general history (e.g., David E. Aune, *The New Testament in Its Literary Environment*, LEC 8 [Philadelphia: Westminster Press, 1987], 138–41), historical monograph (Eckhard Plümacher, *Lukas als hellenistischer Schriftsteller: Studien zur Apostelgeschichte*, SUNT 9 [Göttingen: Vandenhoeck & Ruprecht,

Was the author, then, a Jew? Possibly.[4] Certainly, he shows himself to be well informed about and deeply committed to the God, Scriptures, and community of the Jewish people. However, he may come to that stance as a "God-fearer" not unlike the Gentiles whom his second book portrays as models of piety (Acts 10:35; 13:16, 26).[5] Compared to the other Gospels (esp. Mark), Luke has composed Greek prose of relatively high quality and sophistication. Moreover, he can vary the style of expression to suit speaker and occasion; already the shift in diction from the polished, solemn Greek of the preface (Luke 1:1–4) to the LXX-steeped language of 1:5–2:52 alerts readers to this linguistic flexibility.[6] Like many other histories written before and during Luke's era, his two-volume work includes a formal preface, speeches by characters, a plotted sequence of dramatic episodes, and narrative summaries that connect those episodes. To craft and then disseminate such a work, the author would likely have possessed considerable social status, education, and access to resources.[7]

For whom did Luke (first) write? Luke's deep engagement with the Jewish Scriptures signals that the concerns with community definition, identity formation, and legitimation evident throughout these two volumes[8] have to do, at least in part, with linking the audience to the history of God's people Israel. At the same time, encounter with the reality of empire is prominent, intensifying in the passion narrative (Luke 22–23) and again in the book of Acts. This engagement indicates that the place of Christian groups within the world dominated by Rome is a major concern as well.

A man of high status (*kratistos*, "most excellent," Luke 1:3), Theophilus, finds mention in the prefaces of both Luke (1:3) and Acts (1:1) as the recipient of these twin narratives. But other God-lovers, too (living up to the meaning of the name Theophilus), would have heard Luke's story along with him. These first readers probably already belonged to groups that, like Theophilus, had been taught the tradition and would now benefit from an artful and rhetorically effective work that confirmed and nourished their identity

---

1972]), and apologetic historiography with concern for a new group's identity formation (Gregory E. Sterling, *Historiography and Self-Definition: Josephos, Luke-Acts and Apologetic Historiography*, NovTSup 64 [Leiden: Brill, 1992]). For Marianne Palmer Bonz, Luke has written an epic that aims to construct a foundational myth-and-history for a new people (*The Past as Legacy: Luke-Acts and Ancient Epic* [Minneapolis: Fortress Press, 2000]).

4. Argued most recently by Karl Allen Kuhn, *The Kingdom according to Luke and Acts: A Social, Literary, and Theological Introduction* (Grand Rapids: Baker Academic, 2015), 59–64: "of the house of Israel" (62), and of elite social status so as to be capable of producing a work of the literary quality of Luke-Acts (63–64).

5. Joseph B. Tyson offers a suggestive profile of the implied reader as God-fearer, in *Images of Judaism in Luke-Acts* (Columbia: University of South Carolina Press, 1992), 19–41.

6. Other historians also valued the practice of tailoring diction to the speaker and occasion; see Dionysius of Halicarnassus, *Thuc.* 41; Lucian, *Hist.* 58; Thucydides, *Hist.* 1.22.

7. Kuhn, *Kingdom according to Luke and Acts*, 59–64—though his placement of Luke among the "elite" is probably exaggerated.

8. See Aune, *Literary Environment*, 137; Sterling, *Historiography and Self-Definition*, 386–89; Philip Francis Esler, *Community and Gospel in Luke-Acts: The Social and Political Motivations of Lucan Theology*, SNTSMS 57 (Cambridge: Cambridge University Press, 1987), 205–19.

as members of this new movement, despite its marginal status with regard to both the Jewish heritage and Greco-Roman culture and social systems. As conflict within synagogues persisted and Gentiles assumed an increasingly prominent place in the Christian groups,[9] pressing questions confronted Luke and his audience. Among them were these: Who are we as a people? What legitimate right do we have to stake a claim to Israel's story—its Scriptures, its hopes, its future? And because the one we call Savior and Lord (Jesus) and important leaders in our history (notably, Paul) were executed in the Roman judicial system, do (and should) we have a secure place in Roman society? The story Luke tells addresses this need of early Christian audiences in urban centers of the Roman Empire to answer such questions, while also binding them to the ancient story of Israel.

If, as seems likely, Luke first wrote for a community that included members of diverse social status, occupation, and religious-cultural background,[10] it would have been no easy task to compose a persuasive account of the origins of the emerging Christian movement, engendering confidence in the "sure reliability" (*asphaleia*) of the presentation (1:4 AT) and also fostering social cohesion.

When and Where?   It is customary to date the composition of Luke's Gospel, like Matthew's, around 75–95 CE. While possible, such a time frame is not certain. The earliest date for Luke would be some years after 70 CE if Luke used Mark as a primary source and if Mark was written near the close of the Jewish rebellion against Rome. Confirming a date after 70 are several narrative details (all in speech by Jesus) that betray knowledge of the siege of Jerusalem by Roman armies and the Second Temple's destruction (Luke 13:34–35; 19:43–44; 21:20–24). As to the latest possible date of composition, passages from Luke were cited by the apologist Justin Martyr (writing ca. 150–160 CE), and Marcion relied on a version of Luke as "his" Gospel (writing ca. 130–140 CE).[11] Therefore, Luke must have found wide acceptance by about 125.

The specific location of the Gospel's composition and first reception is uncertain, although it was likely an urban center in the eastern Mediterranean; Antioch, Caesarea, Ephesus, Corinth, and Rome have all received nominations.[12] Whatever the specific provenance, the narrative's setting

---

9. A scenario suggested by the trajectory in the Acts narrative, culminating in the Roman prisoner Paul's image of the message of salvation extending to receptive Gentiles (28:28).

10. So, e.g., Robert C. Tannehill, *Luke*, ANTC (Nashville: Abingdon Press, 1996), 24–26; Esler, *Community and Gospel*, 187–97.

11. Andrew Gregory finds probable references to Luke in Marcion, Justin, 2 Clement, Gospel of the Ebionites, Gospel of Thomas, and Protevangelium of James (*Reception of Luke and Acts*, 293–98).

12. In the words of one eminent commentator, this Gospel's provenance is "anyone's guess" (Joseph A. Fitzmyer, *The Gospel according to Luke: Introduction, Translation, and Notes*, 2 vols., AB 28–28A [Garden City, NY: Doubleday, 1981–85], 1:57). For the range of locations proposed, see Michael Wolter, *Das Lukasevangelium*, HNT 5 (Tübingen: Mohr Siebeck, 2008), 10.

within the Roman Empire is crucial to its rhetorical working and thus its interpretation. It may be that Luke imagined an audience for his narrative broader than the household-based churches of a single city; after all, his two volumes conclude by drawing readers into the very heart of the Roman Empire and project sustained witness in that domain (Acts 28:14–31).[13]

What?

Like Matthew, the Gospel of Luke may be read as a *bios*, a biographical narrative centering on the life of Jesus (see n. 3 above). Yet in tandem with its narrative sequel, Acts, it better fits one of the genres of history writing in Luke's world.[14] The panoramic vision of Luke-Acts envisages the whole world as an arena for mission, a world for which Jesus (not the emperor) is the divine Son, Savior, and Lord (*kyrios*). This feature of Luke's narrative may suggest comparison with the universal histories by Polybius and Diodorus of Sicily.[15]

At the same time, Luke's two books show special concern for the emergence of Christian groups within the history of Israel. So Luke-Acts may be described as an apologetic history, which tells the story of a specific group to establish its identity within the larger world.[16] This multinational, multicultural community may live in a world dominated by Rome, but its primary allegiance is to the God of Israel. A narrative that shapes their identity and provides legitimation for them as an emergent group must therefore connect their story to the history of the Jewish people. Luke thus builds upon the models of history writing represented by such works as 1–2 Samuel and 1–2 Kings (= 1–4 Kingdoms LXX). Luke's two-volume literary project chronicles the next and indeed decisive phase in Israel's history. Luke interprets that history, then, in a manner comparable to the compact, programmatic claim of Matthew's genealogy (Matt 1:2–17; see ch. 4 above). Aptly, the story that Luke narrates begins not with Jesus, or with his precursor John the Baptizer, but with a faithful God's ancient promises to Israel (esp. apparent in Luke 1–2). Luke's Gospel invites readers to enter a story in which they may imagine, and now and again even begin to perceive, a world in which the God of Israel and of all peoples actually reigns.

Like other narratives of both *bios* (biography) and *historia* (history) genres, Luke's two books have a rhetorical interest to edify and guide, to form readers' character. As the Gospel's opening lines indicate (1:1–4), Luke offers a well-ordered narrative to cultivate readers' confidence in the reliability of

13. See, e.g., Sterling, *Historiography and Self-Definition*, 374–78. Richard Bauckham goes even further, arguing that Luke and the other Gospel authors wrote for "any church . . . to which [their] work might find its way" (*The Gospels for All Christians: Rethinking the Gospel Audiences* [Grand Rapids: Wm. B. Eerdmans Publishing Co., 1998], 9–48, esp. 11).

14. See n. 3 above; for detailed discussion, see Aune, *Literary Environment*, 77–111; Sterling, *Historiography and Self-Definition*, 1–19.

15. Aune, *Literary Environment*, 138–41.

16. Agreeing with Sterling, *Historiography and Self-Definition*, 16–19, 386–89.

its teaching (v. 4). The following story delivers on audience expectations that the work's preface and genre engender: readers engage "adventure in travel, persuasive and memorable discourse, scenes of intense life-and-death conflict, and tales of peril and dramatic rescue, . . . populated by diverse characters whose actions readers will do well to emulate or avoid."[17] Belonging to a newly emergent religious group whose beliefs and practices brought them into frequent conflict both with Jewish groups and with the wider Roman culture, Luke's first audience surely benefited from an artful narrative of their origins that nourished group identity and secured their place in the Roman world. The product of this confluence of circumstance and communal exigency is the two-book history that we now call Luke-Acts.

Literary Design and Techniques of Narration

On cue from the Gospel preface's statement of the author's aims and credentials, it is helpful to observe the ways in which the narrative weaves together the discrete episodes that together build its plot. Like Matthew, Luke expands the Markan narrative at both ends and also incorporates an extensive body of Jesus' public teaching, especially in parables (of approximately thirty parables in Luke, roughly half appear only in this Gospel).[18] Luke introduces the leading character Jesus through a birth-and-childhood narrative, though also drawing the prophet John's birth into the sketch (1:5–2:52). Like Matthew, Luke embellishes Mark's compact report of the baptizing ministry of John (Luke 3:1–20; cf. Mark 1:2–8) and provides a pedigree-establishing, status-confirming roster of Jesus' ancestors (3:23–38, though not to open the Gospel, as in Matt 1:2–17). The genealogy traces Jesus' roots all the way back to Adam, the "[son] of God" (Luke 3:38 AT), from the outset reinforcing the narrative's interest in Jesus' identity as Son of God (1:32, 35; 2:48–49; 3:22) as well as early narrative signals that Jesus' life and mission bear significance for the whole human family (e.g., 2:32; 3:6).

The close of the Gospel amplifies Mark's mysterious, open-ended closure with multiple stories of the risen Jesus' encounters with his followers, and does so in a way that sets the stage for the story's continuation, or resumption, in Luke's book 2, Acts (see Luke 24, esp. vv. 44–49). In the center of the narrative, Luke builds upon Mark's transitional journey section (Mark 8:22–10:52; see ch. 3 above), retaining the spatial orientation—the journey ushers Jesus from Galilee to Jerusalem[19]—but also inserting substantial dialogue and discourse material (some shared with Matthew [Q], some drawn

---

17. Carroll, *Luke*, 6.

18. See Matthew S. Rindge, "Luke's Artistic Parables: Narratives of Subversion, Imagination, and Transformation," *Int* 68 (2014): 403–15, esp. 403.

19. Indeed, Luke accents the intentionality of Jesus' directional shift: the deliberate orientation toward Jerusalem in 9:51 opens the journey narrative, which continues until 19:28.

from special Lukan traditions). The result is a character-defining, character-building section of the Gospel that extends through 19:27. On this journey toward Jerusalem, Jesus seeks to form the disciples into a group that emulates and enacts the pattern of God's reign and also challenges his critics (with only limited success) to embrace his vision and practice of God's ways. Luke's audience, then, finds guidance from both positive and negative character models in this central portion of the Gospel.

Since Luke has apparently drawn from Mark as a primary source, of special interest are several places in which the narrative reorders the sequence of events in Mark's plot.[20] Among the most interesting shifts in sequence are these: (1) Jesus' unfriendly reception in his hometown Nazareth becomes a dramatic, ministry-inaugurating and mission-defining episode, rather than an event in the middle of the Galilean ministry (Luke 4:16–30; cf. Mark 6:1–6). (2) The narrator (tersely) mentions the arrest of John the baptizing prophet before reporting Jesus' baptism (Luke 3:19–20; cf. Mark 1:14; 6:14–29). (3) Simon Peter is first introduced after the healing of his mother-in-law rather than before, and Jesus recruits him after a dramatic fishing catch (Luke 5:1–11; cf. Mark 1:16–20).[21] (4) An unnamed woman anoints Jesus at the home of Simon (a Pharisee in Luke, a man identified as "Simon the leper" in Mark), not as preface to the passion narrative but well before Jesus even begins the journey toward Jerusalem (Luke 7:36–50 // Mark 14:3–9). And (5) disrupting a Markan interweaving of (intercalated) episodes, Luke relates Peter's threefold denial *before*, not after, Jesus' interrogation by the high priest (Luke 22:54–71; cf. Mark 14:53–72).

---

20. Luke also omits nearly all the materials in Mark 6:45–8:26, which perhaps not coincidentally presents a concentrated dose of redundant and troublesome texts. Mark 6:45–52 and 8:1–10 present repeat performances of a lake rescue and a feeding miracle, in a fashion that highlights the disciples' failure and incomprehension. Also missing from Luke are a unit centering on purity concerns that seems to jettison stipulations of Mosaic law (Mark 7:1–23); a healing story in which Jesus speaks harshly to a Gentile woman (7:24–30); and two healing stories that depict Jesus using physical contact (7:31–37; 8:22–26), perhaps leaving the impression that Jesus is a magician. (Susan R. Garrett discerns in Luke's writings an "anti-magic apology": *The Demise of the Devil: Magic and the Demonic in Luke's Writings* [Minneapolis: Augsburg Fortress, 1989], 103.) Was Luke familiar with this part of Mark and chose not to include these passages? Luke Timothy Johnson thinks so and terms this a "daring excision": *The Gospel of Luke*, SP 3 (Collegeville, MN: Liturgical Press, 1991), 154. The parallel between Mark 8:15 and Luke 12:1 ("beware of the yeast of the Pharisees") does suggest that the copy of Mark familiar to Luke included (at least part) of this larger section of Mark's Gospel.

21. Luke's episode shares some elements with a postresurrection occurrence in John 21:1–19.

**Luke's "Orderly Account" and Changes
to the Episode Sequence of Mark**

- Rejection at Nazareth *opens* Jesus' mission. (Luke 4:16–30)
- John's arrest is mentioned before the narration of the baptism of Jesus. (3:21–22)
- Jesus recruits Simon Peter *after* healing Peter's mother-in-law. (4:38–39; 5:1–11)
- An anonymous woman anoints Jesus long *before* the Jerusalem narrative. (7:36–50)
- The narrator reports Peter's denials *before* the interrogation of Jesus by the high priest. (22:54–71)

In keeping with this Gospel's emphasis on journeys (prominent also in Acts, with Paul's several mission journeys and his eventual travel to Rome), Luke's narrative configures space and time in meaningful ways. Scenes set in the Jerusalem temple begin and end the story (Luke 1:8–23 and 2:22–38, 41–50; 24:50–53). After Jesus' mission activity in Galilee (4:14–9:50), he makes the long trek back to the temple (9:51–19:27). Then book 2 proceeds from Jerusalem (Acts 1–7) to Rome, and outward from there to "the nations [*ethnē*]" (28:16–31), charting a global mission that extends into the present activity and future of Luke's audience. The figuring of time is thus also significant. Repeating patterns of prophecy (or promise) and fulfillment bind narrated events to the Jewish Scriptures and history. The story moves toward the crucified Messiah's vindication by God "on the third day" (Luke 24), then through an era of contested witness (anticipated in Luke 21:12–19, enacted in Acts) and the geopolitical crisis that will result in the temple's destruction (Luke 19:41–44; 21:5–6, 20–24). In the future of Luke's audience, the narrative anticipates the return of the crucified-but-risen Lord to both judge and deliver (Luke 21:25–36; cf. Acts 3:19–21; 10:42–43; 17:30–31).

After a compact outline of the narrative design of Luke's Gospel, I will identify and briefly discuss several prominent narrative techniques: prophecy and fulfillment, banquet scenes, parallel scenes and characters, interrupted speeches, interior monologues (esp. in parables), and open-ended stories.

Macro-Outline of Luke's Gospel	1:1–4	Formal literary preface orienting Luke's audience to the aims and content of the book
	1:5–2:52	Narrative of preparation, part 1: The birth and childhood of John and Jesus
	3:1–4:13	Narrative of preparation, part 2: The vocation of a people and their Messiah

- The prophetic ministry of John the Baptizer (3:1–20)
- The baptism and ancestry of Jesus, Son of God (3:21–38)
- The testing of Jesus' fidelity to his identity and vocation as Son of God (4:1–13)

4:14–9:50	Public ministry of Jesus in and around Galilee, beginning in his hometown
9:51–19:27	Continuation of Jesus' ministry during a circuitous journey toward Jerusalem, signaled by a decisive shift in direction (toward Jerusalem) at 9:51
19:28–21:38	Culminating public ministry by Jesus in Jerusalem: the "son of Joseph"/"Son of God," who at age twelve sat among the teachers in the temple and now teaches in the same sacred space, but with a dramatically different outcome
22:1–23:56	The death of the Messiah

- Betrayal and a final meal with the Twelve and in that setting a farewell speech (22:1–38)
- Prayerful preparation for the ordeal (22:39–46)
- Jesus' arrest (22:47–53)
- Peter's failure and interrogation of Jesus by the council at Jerusalem (22:54–71)
- Interrogation by the Roman governor Pilate and the tetrarch of Galilee Herod (Antipas) (23:1–25)
- The crucifixion and burial of Jesus (23:26–56)

24:1–53	The resurrection of the Messiah: closing the book on Jesus' ministry and anticipating the narrative sequel (Acts)
Then:	Book 2! Acts 1 overlaps with Luke 24, marking the transition from the pre-Easter ministry of Jesus to the ongoing, Spirit-guided, Spirit-empowered mission of his followers.

As we have seen, arrangement matters in Luke's narrative. Some techniques of narrative design have already surfaced; in what follows, I will identify and illustrate several of the most important techniques employed by the Lukan narrator.

Techniques of Narration in Luke

- Prophecy and fulfillment
  - — OT prophecies
  - — Predictions by Jesus
- Banquet scenes
- Parallel scenes and characters
- Interrupted speeches
- Interior monologues
- Open-ended stories

*Prophecy and
Fulfillment*

Rich use of the device of prophecy (or anticipation, foreshadowing) and fulfillment (realization, occurrence) lends both temporal direction and cohesion to the plot of Luke's narrative. Readers progressively discover meaning as anticipated events occur, and (esp. on multiple experiences of hearing the narrative) retrospectively deepen understanding as their recognition of a moment of fulfillment prompts them to recall or revisit the earlier prediction/foreshadowing. The preface characterizes the events to be narrated as a (divine purpose) coming-to-fulfillment (1:1), and the prophets of Israel's Scriptures are often invoked in the Gospel. Jesus, too, assumes the mantle of prophet (e.g., Luke 4:24; 7:16; 13:33; Acts 3:22–24; 7:37; cf. Luke 4:18–19). Accordingly, I will use the categories of prophecy and fulfillment to unpack this facet of the narrative.[22]

A few examples of this pattern will document its importance in a narrative preoccupied with the enactment of the divine purpose in this account of Christian origins:[23]

1. Old Testament prophecies are said to be fulfilled:
   • Zechariah paints images of deliverance and divine visitation, as spoken by prophets and keeping vows to Abraham (Luke 1:68–75). These are partially fulfilled in the ensuing narrative, but with some redefinition of key terms like *deliverance* (salvation), in terms of forgiveness rather than defeat of enemies (prefigured already in the elaboration of 1:71, "saved from our enemies," in v. 77, "knowledge of salvation to [God's] people by the forgiveness of their sins").
   • The message and activity of John the baptizing prophet actualize the oracle of Isaiah 40:3–5 (Luke 3:4–6, extending the quotation from Isaiah to encompass all humans in v. 6; Mark 1:3 stops at Isa 40:3).
   • Jesus invokes words of the prophet Isaiah (61:1–2a; 58:6) to claim Spirit anointing and divine impulse for his now-inaugurated mission to persons on the underside of history and society (Luke 4:17–19, 21). From the beginning, Luke places the stamp of Spirit fulfillment on Jesus' activity.

22. Luke Timothy Johnson gives particular emphasis to prophecy and fulfillment as a primary narrative pattern in Luke-Acts (e.g., *Luke*, 15–21). My summary is limited to a few passages that explicitly invoke prophetic oracles; attention to the ways in which (implicit) biblical echoes and allusions give deep texture to the whole narrative would expand the account considerably. In fact, much of Luke's Christology is conveyed precisely through such echoes and implicit quotations (not identified as such): see, e.g., 3:22; 7:22; 8:10; 9:35; 23:46. Sometimes the appeal to Scripture is explicit while the way in which it illumines Jesus' activity is implicit, though the connection is scarcely to be missed (e.g., 4:25–27; 20:17–18). Scripture citations do more than construct webs of prophecy and fulfillment. For example, appeal to what is "written in the law of the Lord" underscores the fidelity to the Torah of Jesus' parents (2:23–24 RSV). Later Jesus frames his act of prophetic-symbolic judgment disrupting temple commerce as prophetically sanctioned (19:45–46, tapping imagery from Isa 56:7; Jer 7:11).

23. See esp. John T. Squires, *The Plan of God in Luke-Acts*, SNTSMS 76 (Cambridge: Cambridge University Press, 1993).

2. Predictions by Jesus are realized in the ensuing story (including Acts):

- Jesus predicts his Nazareth co-villagers' rejection (Luke 4:23–24), immediately realized in verses 28–30. In the process, Luke has Jesus explain that rejection as prompted by their concern for border maintenance (i.e., objecting to divine aid for outsiders).
- Jesus forecasts his approaching, though not immediate, demise: it will happen to him as to all prophets, in Jerusalem (Luke 13:32–33), and thus it happens (chs. 22–23).
- Jesus predicts his betrayal by an intimate follower, Peter's threefold denial, and his association with the lawless (Luke 22:21–22, 31–34, 37 [also fulfilling Isa 53:12]), and it all happens right on script.
- Jesus outlines a future period of witness that will also entail hostility and persecution for his followers (Luke 12:11–12; 21:12–19), a prediction repeatedly fulfilled in the narrative of Acts (e.g., 4:3; 5:18, 27–41; 6:12–8:1; 8:3; 12:1–4; 16:19–40; 22:30–23:11; 24:1–21, 24–26; 25:6–12; 25:23–26:32; cf. 9:15–16).
- Jesus speaks of a future empowerment from above, "what my Father promised" (Luke 24:49), which is dramatically realized in the Pentecost story of Acts 2. It is this Spirit empowerment that enables the apostles to become the witnesses (*martyres*) that Jesus has declared them to be (Luke 24:48). Because Luke does not (like Mark) narrate the disciples' flight from the scene of Jesus' arrest (Luke 22:47–53) and because the narrator implies that they were among the persons known to Jesus who observed his crucifixion from a distance (23:49), they can legitimately play the role of witness for which the book of Acts casts them (see esp. Acts 1:21–22). The central post-Easter role of the disciples in Matthew (teaching what Jesus has commanded) requires a revision to Mark's uncomprehending disciples (see ch. 3 above). In Luke's narrative, it is the apostles' primary role as witnesses that necessitates revision of the Markan portrait of fearful, fleeing disciples who abandon Jesus at the end. In Luke's account, the Twelve, though flawed, truly persevere as companions of Jesus throughout his ministry, right through to Easter (cf. Luke 22:28).

3. Prophetic oracles by Jesus are fulfilled beyond the story in the past of the Lukan audience:

- Jesus predicts the destruction of Jerusalem and the temple in Luke 13:34–35 (v. 35 is perhaps partially fulfilled in the acclamation of 19:38); 19:43–44; 21:5–6, 20–24 (the end point—"Jerusalem will be trampled on by the Gentiles, until the times of the Gentiles are fulfilled" [v. 24]—lies still in the future of Luke's first readers); compare 23:28–31.
- Jesus anticipates the leadership role to be played by the apostles (22:28–30), partially fulfilled in Acts (Acts 3–5 narrates, from

Luke's vantage, a leader swap in Jerusalem), but consummation in the fellowship of God's realm still awaits.

4. Prophetic oracles by Jesus await fulfillment in the future of the Lukan audience:

- Jesus assures listeners that the future will bring full realization of the reign of God, the triumphant return of the Human One, and deliverance for the faithful (Luke 17:22–37; 21:25–33). These promises remain outstanding in the time of Luke's audience.
- Jesus speaks of future resumption of his meal fellowship with disciples in the dominion of God, but not before then (22:16, 18; post-Easter meals celebrated with the risen Jesus, as at Emmaus [24:28–32], anticipate but do not complete the fulfillment of this declaration).

Beyond injecting temporal movement, dynamism, and cohesion to the narrative, what is the effect of this web of prophecies and their fulfillments? Among other things, this narrative pattern reinforces readers' impression of the reliability of the account (cf. 1:4). It also specifically confirms Jesus' status and role as prophet (indeed, as the prophet-Messiah, who speaks authoritatively on behalf of God). Moreover, it deeply roots the story of Jesus and his followers in the story of Israel. Whatever the apparent discontinuities in the unfolding events—notably the repudiation and execution of the Messiah, the rejection of the apostolic witness by many Jewish auditors in Acts, and the inclusion of many Gentiles in the apostolic community—more impressive still is the continuity in the divine activity in Israel. In all the events connected with Jesus and his followers, the divine purpose is still at work, taking them and their witness from Galilee to Jerusalem, and outward to all nations of the earth, until history's curtain falls.

Banquet Scenes

Meals are prominent in Luke's Gospel (as well as Acts) and, as in the wider Greco-Roman culture, express basic social values. Especially intriguing, and unique in Luke's rendition of Jesus' activity, are three meals set at the home of Pharisees, with Jesus as invited guest (Luke 7:36–50; 11:37–52; 14:1–24). Each time the conflicting values and practices of host and guest clash. Since Greco-Roman banquets were contests for honor and provided the occasion for status display, maintenance, and enhancement, much is at stake in these episodes. By the time the narrator allows Luke's audience to follow Jesus into the home of Pharisees, however, Jesus has already earned a reputation for his meal practice: indeed, Jesus' meal associations have become a serious provocation for Pharisees and specialists in legal interpretation, as well as others (e.g., 5:27–32; 7:34; cf. 19:5–7). Jesus, it turns out, routinely welcomes at table—or in the countryside (9:12–17)!—just about anyone, even persons who would be perceived as diminishing rather than enhancing his honor: "tax collectors and sinners," to use the labels Pharisee detractors provide

(5:30). In defense of his meal practice, Jesus adopts the metaphor of doctor for his activity in restoring sinners—centerpiece of a mission that embraces such religious outsiders, or the "lost" (5:31–32; 19:10). Jesus even borrows the tag his critics have supplied: "the [Human One] has come eating and drinking, and you say, 'Look, a glutton and a drunkard, a friend of tax collectors and sinners!'" (7:34). He later offers a memorable parable trio in explanation and defense of his hospitality at banquets (15:1–32).

Hospitality, Table Talk—and Conflict: Jesus Dines with Pharisees

- Jesus defends a sinful woman and confronts his banquet host (7:36–50)
- Critique of the status seekers; instead, prize justice and the love of God (11:37–52)
- Revising the honor code—and social maps—at banquets (14:1–24)

In the third banquet hosted by a Pharisee, Jesus goes on the offensive, advocating a radical departure from conventional banquet practice (14:7–24). Rather than use meals to increase status and enhance public reputation, one should extend generous hospitality toward others who cannot be expected to reciprocate and whose presence at table certainly cannot promote the host's honor. With vivid meal scenes such as these, Luke is not educating Jesus' peers among the Pharisees but is instead nurturing an alternative, convention-transgressing community among his own readers.

Throughout Luke's narrative, conflict sparked by meals displays competing understandings of God and of the communal boundaries of God's people. Hospitality at table thus becomes a matter of social solidarity, to be sure, but even more an expression of the generous, welcoming divine hospitality toward all.[24]

Parallel Scenes and Characters

Luke's two books often present parallel scenes, characters, and occurrences; this is another technique of narration that lends cohesiveness and continuity to the story and reinforces the audience's impression that a (divine) purpose drives it.[25]

---

24. Brendan Byrne offers an interpretation of Luke's Gospel that centers on the image of divine hospitality: *The Hospitality of God: A Reading of Luke's Gospel* (Collegeville, MN: Liturgical Press, 2000). For concise, recent discussion of the symposium in Luke, see Kuhn, *Kingdom according to Luke and Acts*, 88–89. For full discussion of banquets in NT texts and their sociocultural environment, see Dennis E. Smith, *From Symposium to Eucharist: The Banquet in the Early Christian World* (Minneapolis: Fortress Press, 2003).

25. Because Luke does not include material from Mark 6:45–8:26, some parallel episodes in Mark's narrative—two feeding stories, two lake rescues, two encounters with men who are blind—become only one episode in Luke.

Parallel Scenes and Characters in Luke's Gospel
• John and Jesus
• Mary and Zechariah
• Simeon and Anna
• Jesus with teachers in the temple
• Mission for the Twelve and for seventy-two more
• Sabbath healing of a man and a woman

- A set of parallels juxtaposes John and Jesus in birth and childhood, with Jesus the divine Son always surpassing John the prophet in stature (Luke 1–2).[26]
- Mary and Zechariah, recipients of parallel angelic annunciations (1:8–20, 26–38), eventually form a two-voice chorus praising God for the fulfillment of ancient promises of salvation, with the arrival of John and, in prospect, Jesus (1:46–55, 68–79).
- Simeon and Anna form another two-voice chorus celebrating the coming of deliverance in the person of the child Jesus (2:25–35, 36–38), though the narrator records only Simeon's spoken words.
- Jesus positions himself among the teachers in the temple, as a youth listening and impressing favorably but as an adult teaching actively to fierce opposition (2:46–47; 19:47–20:44).
- Twice Jesus dispatches followers to declare the message of God's reign and heal (the Twelve in 9:1–6; seventy-two others in 10:1–12), with sharper accent on opposition accompanying the more expansive second sending.
- In close succession, Jesus twice heals on the Sabbath: a woman bent double, a disability that Jesus interprets as imposed by Satan (13:10–17); and a man afflicted with dropsy, a disorder associated in Luke's social world with avarice (14:1–6).[27]
- Parallels in the activity of Jesus, Peter, and Paul:
  1. Each delivers a substantial inaugural speech that cites Jewish Scriptures (Luke 4:16–27; Acts 2:14–36; 13:14–41).
  2. Each performs healing acts:
     — restoring a man who is unable to walk (Luke 5:17–26; Acts 3:1–10; 14:8–10; he "leaps" for both Peter and Paul)
     — restoring life to a dead person (Luke 7:11–17; 8:49–56; Acts 9:36–41; 20:9–12)

---

26. See Carroll, *Luke*, 31; Joel B. Green, *The Gospel of Luke*, NICNT (Grand Rapids: Wm. B. Eerdmans Publishing Co., 1997), 50–51.

27. On this appraisal, common in Luke's culture, of the dropsy victim's moral failing, see Carroll, *Luke*, 297; Willi Braun, *Feasting and Social Rhetoric in Luke 14*, SNTSMS 85 (Cambridge: Cambridge University Press, 1995), 22–42.

— narrator's summary of extraordinary healing activity (Luke 4:40; 5:15; 6:18–19; Acts 5:15–16; 19:11–12).[28]

3. And each is arrested—though unlike Jesus, both Peter and Paul experience dramatic rescues with divine aid (Acts 12:6–19; 16:19–40).

The use of parallel scenes narrating comparable activities by key characters underscores the continuity in God's saving, healing, restoring activity in Israel. More than the remarkable achievements of individuals (whether Peter, Paul, or even Jesus), Luke tells the story of God.

Interrupted Speeches

From the beginning of book 1 (Luke 1:13–17, 46–55, 68–79) to the end of book 2 (Acts 28:23–31), speech by both major and minor characters is a prominent feature of Luke's narrative.[29] Occasionally a speech is interrupted, and the intrusion draws attention to both the content of the speaker's message and the character of the audience's response.[30] A parade example occurs when Jesus opens his public ministry in his hometown. Provocatively, he anticipates Nazareth residents' rejection of one of their own, then recites selective excerpts from the accounts of two earlier prophets, Elijah and Elisha, excerpts biased in favor of outsiders and against insiders (Luke 4:24–27, recalling 1 Kgs 17:8–16; 2 Kgs 5:1–14). Enraged reaction by the Nazareth synagogue listeners stops the speech (Luke 4:28), but not before Jesus and the Lukan narrator have boldly outlined Jesus' mission program. It remains only for the assembled crowd to confirm the prophet's foresight, seeking—for the time being unsuccessfully—to put him to death.

In 11:27 Jesus' talk about tenacious demonic spirits (vv. 24–26) is interrupted by a voice from the crowd; an anonymous woman declares blessing for the woman who gave birth to him and nursed him (in tune with 1:48!). Taking advantage of the sudden redirection in topic, Jesus reroutes blessing to whoever hears and performs (keeps) the word of God (11:28). Again talking of blessing, this time as enjoyed by persons who dine in God's realm,

28. Unlike Jesus, however, both Peter and Paul have a hand in punitive miracles (Acts 5:1–11; 13:9–12).

29. For an esp. perceptive study of the rhetorical power of speech and also of silence in Luke's narrative, see Michal Beth Dinkler, *Silent Statements: Narrative Representations of Speech and Silence in the Gospel of Luke*, BZNW 191 (Berlin: de Gruyter, 2013). Silence, too, communicates and requires the listener's active engagement in making sense of the narrative. Luke's penchant for open-ended stories that do not narrate a character's response is a good example (see the discussion of open-ended stories below). So also is Luke's frequent use of interior monologues, which are "silent" to other characters in the story but not to readers (see the discussion in the next section).

30. For thorough analysis of this narrative pattern in Luke's writings, see Daniel Lynwood Smith, *The Rhetoric of Interruption: Speech-Making, Turn-Taking, and Rule-Breaking in Luke-Acts and Ancient Greek Narrative*, BZNW 193 (Berlin: de Gruyter, 2012), 186–210 (Luke), 211–43 (Acts).

an unnamed speaker in 14:15 responds to Jesus' countercultural advice
about honor seeking through banquet seating and guest lists. More on topic,
perhaps, but Jesus sharply corrects any false assumptions about assured
spots at the banquet, offering a vivid parable that resumes his unconventional advice regarding honor seeking at banquets. What happens when
guests invited to a banquet (metaphor for God's realm) decline to come?
The insulted would-be host will fill the hall anyway, with anyone who can
be persuaded to come (vv. 16–24). Some say yes and some say no—both in
the banquet parable and in Luke's account of Jesus' ministry. In any case the
realm of God will be filled by celebration: it's party time! (cf. the image of
feasting as hallmark of Jesus' activity in 7:34 and the emphasis on celebration of the restoration of the lost in 15:6–7, 9–10, 22–24, 32).[31]

In Luke's second volume, enraged listeners bring Stephen's stinging
criticism dressed as a history recital to a full stop (Acts 7:2–54). The Holy
Spirit brings premature closure to Peter's speech at the home of Cornelius,
unambiguously signaling divine endorsement of Peter's affirmation of God's
impartiality and the embrace of Gentiles (Acts 10:34–44). Later, Paul, taken
into custody when his presence in the temple incites rioting, defends his
fidelity as a Jew, but when he recalls his recruitment as emissary to Gentiles,
his auditors erupt in rage (Acts 22:1–22), reminiscent of the Nazareth synagogue reaction to Jesus' inaugural mission statement (Luke 4:28–30).

Interior Monologues

Like many other writings in both Jewish and Hellenistic cultures, Luke
makes rich use of characters' self-talk, presenting interior monologue that
reveals the (otherwise unspoken) thoughts and attitudes of the character.[32]

31. In a reversal of the usual pattern, in 21:5 Jesus is the one who interrupts others' speech. Some are enamored by the temple complex's splendor, but he brings their speech to an abrupt end by countering with the image of the temple's complete devastation (v. 6). Similarly, in two parables a God figure with word or action interrupts the interior speech of a character (12:20, 46)—an interruption that both accents the folly of the character who has been speaking and shows its sure outcome.

32. See the excellent discussion of the function of Luke's interior monologues in Michal Beth Dinkler, "'The Thoughts of Many Hearts Shall Be Revealed': Listening in on Lukan Interior Monologues," *JBL* 133 (2015): 373–99. Dinkler shows that moments of interiority in Luke merge "Hellenistic literature's structural uses of inner speech and Hebrew tropes about the danger of foolish self-talk" (398). Like ancient Hellenistic narratives, interior monologues in Luke's Gospel "depict the inner turmoil his characters experience in moments of crisis," but "Luke's thinking characters are far from heroic; they demonstrate foolish perspectives" (ibid.). In this respect, Luke's interior monologues are more similar to characters' speech in ancient Jewish literature than Hellenistic narratives. In several Lukan parables (e.g., those featuring a rich farmer, a fired manager, and a younger son who has fallen on hard times), interior monologues foster readers' "identification with the thinking character. If the reader accepts this invitation, she also will experience the corrections implied by the narrative rhetoric." In other parables (the unjust judge and the owner of the vineyard), guidance from the narrator prompts the audience to identify not with the characters who are given interior monologues (the judge, the vineyard owner) but with other characters (the widow, the tenants). In the parables of Luke 18:2–5 and 20:9–16, then, "inner speech introduces dramatic irony, privileging the reader over the thinking characters in the story. In each case, internal monologue functions rhetorically to invite readerly transformation" (ibid.).

Sometimes this self-disclosure to the audience will draw listeners to identify with the characters and their plight and decisions they face. But not always: auditors will find themselves distanced from other characters to whose interior speech they are privy. Often Luke focuses the interior monologue on a question about a choice to be made: "What will [or should] I do [*ti poiēsō*]?"[33] Even when this is not the case, the rhetorical function of this technique of narration is to pose this question to readers.

Revealing Character: Interior Speech

- "If this man were a prophet": angry Simon (Luke 7:39)
- Larger barns to "store all my grain and my goods"—eat, drink, enjoy! (12:17–19)
- An unreliable servant exploits delay—to his ruin (12:45)
- A lost son far from home decides to return (15:17–19)
- Fired but still scheming (16:3–4)
- A judge's resolve: No fear of God, no respect for persons, but "I will give her justice" (18:4–5)
- "I will send my beloved son": a vineyard owner's miscalculation (20:13)

Seven times in all, Luke's Gospel employs the device of interior monologue, six within parables (also the indignant Pharisee-host in 7:39). The parable speakers whose thoughts Luke's audience can read are a rich but foolish farmer (Luke 12:16–20 [vv. 17–19]); an unreliable servant (12:42–46 [v. 45]); the lost son of a generous father (15:11–32 [vv. 17–19]); a fired manager who proves himself a cunning survivor (16:1–8 [vv. 3–4]); an unjust judge facing a persistent, justice-demanding widow (18:2–5 [vv. 4–5]); and a vineyard owner (20:9–16 [v. 13]).[34] In the process of assessing the responses of the narrative's characters to the choices they confront, Luke's audience is placed in the position of choosing well for themselves: adopting practices and engaging others in a way that reflects the values and commitments of God's reign. As they form the character of figures in the story, members of the Lukan audience at the same time form their own character.[35] Or so the narrative would bid them to do.

---

33. As Rindge points out ("Luke's Artistic Parables," 413), some version of this deliberative question ("What will [should] I do?"), spoken or silent, occurs 10x in Luke-Acts: Luke 3:10, 12, 14; 10:25; 12:17; 16:3; 18:18; 20:13; Acts 2:37; 22:10 (cf. Luke 18:41); three of these are in parables (12:17; 16:3; 20:13). Rindge also observes that the question "is almost always associated with the use of wealth or possessions (3:10, 12, 14; 10:25; 12:17; 16:3; 18:18)" (ibid.).

34. Here I am drawing on the work of Dinkler, "Thoughts of Many Hearts," 383–93.

35. Especially helpful is John A. Darr's study *On Character Building: The Reader and the Rhetoric of Characterization in Luke-Acts*, LCBI (Louisville, KY: Westminster John Knox Press, 1992).

Open-Ended Stories   Often Luke tells a story, or has Jesus tell a parable, that ends with a suspended outcome, as the response of a key character is left open.[36] As with the narrative technique of interior monologues (as well as broader use of the question "What shall I/we do?"), open-ended stories reroute a character's decision, left hanging at the end of a scene or parable, to the Lukan audience. What now shall *we* do? A few examples will show how this aspect of Luke's Gospel engages its audience.

The first occasion on which a Pharisee invites Jesus into his home is complicated by the intrusion of an uninvited, unwanted guest; by Pharisee Simon's label, she is a "sinful" woman whose touch Jesus should avoid (7:39). By scene's end Jesus has turned the tables on host and guest, rebuking the named host and commending the unnamed woman. His parable in explanation pictures the cancellation of a large debt and a small debt. Queried which debtor will show greater gratitude (love), Simon astutely points to the one forgiven a larger debt (7:43). So we have observed a profuse display of grateful affection (the woman's), implying that she has received mercy. But what about the host? Will Jesus' attempt at persuasion move him to a different view of Jesus, and of this woman who has burst onto the scene from the social margins, and also of his own status as one with a debt to pay? The story ending leaves these questions with Luke's audience; they must supply the answer.

A lawyer's public challenge to Jesus' acumen as Scripture interpreter opens up a vigorous exchange that accents the path to enduring life for those who keep two love commandments in the Torah (10:27, in the lawyer's voice, quoting Deut 6:5 and Lev 19:18) and then presses the question of the scope of the command to love neighbor (Luke 10:29). Jesus answers the question with a parable in which not a priest or a Levite but a quintessential outsider, a despised, distrusted Samaritan, models neighbor-love (vv. 30–35). Following the parable with a question of his own, one that inverts the lawyer's question, Jesus asks the lawyer which of the trio performed as a neighbor toward the man who had been assaulted by robbers (v. 36). "The one who acted in mercy, of course" (v. 37, paraphrased), the savvy lawyer responds, prompting Jesus to dismiss him with the charge "Go and do likewise." Will he conform his future actions to the boundary-transgressing other-love modeled by the Samaritan in the parable? Luke's audience can only ponder—and face the full force of the charge to "Go and do" themselves.

In a parable centering on a father's response to two very different sons, the older son reacts with outrage to his father's extravagantly generous welcome

---

36. Rindge provides helpful analysis of this feature of Luke's narrative ("Luke's Artistic Parables," 408–11). What effect do such undetermined endings have on readers? As Rindge puts it, "By refusing to impose closure on characters, Luke invites his readers/hearers to make such choices themselves. The generative rhetoric of the parables seeks animation and embodiment in the lives of actual readers and hearers. . . . Responsibility for action is transferred from literary characters to Luke's audience. The parable's ending is determined not within the literary contours of the parable or Gospel, but in the lives of its readers and hearers" (411).

of the returning wasteful younger son (15:28–30). Seeking still to reconcile these estranged brothers, the father pleads with the offended older son to accept his brother and join the celebration of his return (vv. 31–32). Here the story ends. Jesus' (and Luke's) audience can only imagine what the older brother decides. Within the narrative setting, this means that the response of Jesus' critics among Pharisees and lawyers—for whom the older son is a parabolic representation—to his embrace of the lost (cf. 15:1–2) remains undetermined, at least for the time being. Readers eventually discover that their critical reserve toward Jesus persists through their final appearance in the Gospel (19:39–40).

Luke's Open-Ended Stories

- Indignant Simon and the unwelcome guest: will the host understand—and accept? (7:36–50)
- A model Samaritan and a lawyer: will he "go and do likewise"? (10:25–37)
- Furious older son: will he join the feast for his brother? (15:11–32)
- A rich man challenged to sell all and give to the poor: will he? (18:18–25)
- What comes next for such disciples as Judas and Peter? (chs. 22–24)
- Ending of Acts: Paul's unhindered teaching, while he waits for his hearing before the emperor (Acts 28:14–31)

A final example: Jesus encounters a wealthy (Torah-keeping) man on a quest for "eternal life" (18:18–25). He summons the man to go a step beyond his past faithful observance of the commandments—a very big step, it turns out. Jesus challenges the rich man to renounce all his possessions for the sake of the poor, and to follow Jesus (i.e., as disciple). While both Mark 10:22 and Matthew 19:22 bring closure to their renditions of the episode by having the rich man depart "grieving" due to the impediment of his wealth, Luke leaves the outcome in doubt. There is no mention of the man's departure, so readers have reason to think he is still listening to Jesus' more hopeful remark (Luke 18:27) about the capacity of God to do what is humanly impossible (as in saving the wealthy). Is there still hope for this rich man in his quest for eternal life? Maybe so, if Luke's audience takes its cue from Jesus' affirmation of salvation for the household of the wealthy tax-collector Zacchaeus in the very next chapter (19:1–10). But the future choice and action of the rich man in response to Jesus' challenge remain undetermined. Response to that challenge, then, transfers to Luke's readers. What will they decide?[37]

---

37. In a similar way, the fate of another parabolic rich man's five brothers (16:27–31), as yet undetermined despite Abraham's skepticism regarding their willingness to heed what "Moses and the prophets" teach about faithful use of possessions (v. 31), reroutes to Luke's audience the question of faithful (compassionate and generous) response to the claim of Torah and Prophets.

It is not just individual episodes or parables that remain open in Luke's writings. The Easter narrative of Luke 24 concludes the story of Jesus' life and work, to be sure, but it also leaves important questions unresolved. What of disciples such as Judas and Peter, who failed Jesus at the end? What about people from Jerusalem who left the site of his crucifixion while beating their chests in remorse (23:48)? And what of the mandate, grounded in Scripture, to take the message of forgiveness "to all nations" (24:47)? What form will "power from on high" take (24:49), and how will Jesus' followers fare? Luke's readers are primed to discover the answers to these questions in the Gospel's narrative sequel (Acts). The ending of Acts, likewise, leaves important questions unanswered. What will come of Paul's hearing before the emperor? How effective will his "unhindered" teaching be under house arrest (Acts 28:30–31), and who exactly will be coming to hear him—Jewish people, still, after Paul's final word about salvation going out to receptive Gentiles (28:28)? And so on. Those undetermined—or, perhaps better, underdetermined—narrative outcomes arc from story time to the time of Luke's audience. If, despite sometimes intense opposition, more witness bearing and proclamation of the good news of God's reign remain to be completed as the narrative ends, readers will have their mission orders, too.

Central Motifs and Concerns

The literary artistry of Luke's narrative, evident in the sample probes in the previous section of the chapter, conveys a set of theological and ethical concerns that claim the attention of Theophilus, as they have for many generations of God-lovers since.[38] Here I select the following topics for discussion; all of them are important in Luke's Gospel: Christology (Jesus as prophet, Messiah, Savior, and Lord); the narrative as God's story; salvation as a matter of both vertical and horizontal reversals, including poverty and wealth, gender analysis, the depiction of children, and inclusion of sinners, Samaritans, and Gentiles; and the encounter between the reign of God and the empire of Rome. Throughout, we will notice the stout challenges to social-cultural conventions raised by Luke's rendition of the good news of God's reign.

Central Motifs and Concerns in Luke's Gospel
• Jesus: Prophet, Messiah, Savior, Lord
• This is *God's* story
• Salvation by reversal: Upside-down transpositions
• Salvation by reversal: Inside-out transpositions
• Luke and empire: Capitulation, cooperation, subversion, or ambivalence?

38. For the sketch of central themes in this section, I have adapted materials from my

Jesus: Prophet-
Messiah-Savior-Lord

Luke tells the story of God's work of salvation in Israel, encompassing the nations as well. Jesus—in concert with the Holy Spirit, especially in Acts—is the one through whom God's rule exerts itself and God's saving initiative is carried out. Jesus thus shares with God the titles of Savior (God, Luke 1:47; Jesus, 2:11) and *kyrios,* or Lord (God, 1:17, 25, 46, 68; 4:18; Jesus, 1:43; 2:11; 10:1). In message, meal, and acts of mercy (healing, forgiveness), Jesus enacts God's reign and brings liberation from oppressive powers that thwart human flourishing.

As primary agent of God's reign, Jesus is Israel's Messiah and Son of God, realizing ancient promise (Luke 1:32–35, 68–75; 2:11, 49; 3:22, 38; 9:35). God's Spirit anoints him for a dual role as both Messiah and prophet (4:18–19, 24–27; cf. 7:16, 39; 13:33–34; 24:19). He heals after the pattern of the prophets Elijah and Elisha (7:1–17), whose activity his Nazareth speech highlights (4:25–27). Like prophets of old he announces God's word (e.g., 5:1; 8:21) and rails against leaders whose conduct opposes God's purposes (11:29–32, 37–52; 12:1; 19:45–20:18) and who exploit and oppress the poor (20:45–21:4). True to form for a prophet, he also can discern others' thoughts (5:22; 6:8; 7:39–40; 9:47) and predict future occurrences (9:22; 13:32–35; 17:25; 18:31–33; 19:43–44; 21:5–24; 22:10–12, 21–22, 34; 23:28–31). And he also experiences opposition as prophets invariably do (4:24; 13:33–34; cf. 11:47–51).

Jesus is also the Human One (Son of Humanity), who has authority (5:24; 6:5), suffers (9:22, 44, 58; 17:25; 18:31–33; 22:22), and then is vindicated by God (17:30; 21:27; 22:69, citing Dan 7:13–14). In each role, then—prophet, Messiah, and Human One—Jesus faces suffering and death (prophet: 13:33; Messiah: 24:26, 46). Though righteous, he suffers injustice and violence. Yet to the end and without wavering, he trusts in God for vindication: in his last words from the cross, he invokes Psalm 31:5 (30:6 LXX), speaking as a righteous sufferer (Luke 23:46). Jesus is Lord with a difference, therefore; he wields authority not in the fashion of Rome's emperors but in servant mode, befitting his message about the reign of God, with its radical challenge to prevailing notions of status and honor. This is leadership very different from Roman domination, and Jesus would have his followers emulate the paradigm he has provided (22:24–30).

God's Story

Luke's narrative, centering on the activity of Jesus, is more than a *bios,* a biography of Jesus. From beginning to end, Jesus' story is part of a larger narrative, the story of God, of God's saving activity in Israel, and through Israel for all peoples. God's sovereign reign is reordering the world, and people are

commentary on *Luke,* New Testament Library (Louisville, KY: Westminster John Knox Press, 2012) and a recent essay, "The Gospel of Luke: A Contemporary Cartography," published in *Interpretation* 68 (2014): 366–75 (http://int.sagepub.com/content/68/4.toc; doi:10.1177/0020964314540109).

being liberated from potent forces that harm and constrain. Attuned to the prophetic message of Isaiah 58 and 61, Jesus makes *aphesis*, "release," the centerpiece of his enactment of God's powerful deliverance (Luke 4:18–19). As the story unfolds, this *aphesis* assumes various forms: forgiveness of sins, liberation from domination by demonic spirits, cancellation of debts, and "rescue from social systems and cultural values that—by valorizing status, wealth, and power—effectively oppress most people."[39]

God's voice is seldom heard directly in the narrative, but it speaks distinctly in affirmation of Jesus' singular status (3:22; 9:35). Less directly but no less distinctly, God's aims and activity find authoritative expression in the speech of heavenly messengers (1:13–17, 30–33, 35; 2:10–14), in speech and action directed and empowered by the Holy Spirit (1:35, 67; 2:25–27; 3:22; 4:1, 14, 18), in Scripture (4:18–19; 18:31; 24:25–27, 45–47), and in passive-voice verbs implying God's agency (8:17–18; 9:22; 11:9–10; 13:13, 16; 18:34; 24:16, 31). Thus the God of the Jewish Scriptures, who is also the God of all peoples, directs and interprets the saving events being narrated. Driving Luke's story, therefore, is the purpose of God (*boulē theou*; cf. 7:30). Overcoming formidable obstacles, this purpose guides the "events that have been brought to fulfillment among us" (1:1 AT). Salvation for Israel, and for all nations, becomes present reality and sure hope for the future.

Salvation by Reversal: Status Transpositions

Vertical Status Transpositions

Luke's narrative features role reversals that turn society upside down and inside out; Jesus' ministry thus fulfills the promise—and provocation—of his opening, programmatic statement of his mission in the Nazareth synagogue (4:16–27).[40] Led and empowered by God's Spirit (3:22; 4:1, 14, 18 [quoting Isa 61:1]), Jesus sets about speaking and embodying "good news to the poor" (Luke 4:18): "release" (*aphesis*) for all whose lives are diminished by poverty, sin, sickness, or oppression. What is good news for persons at the bottom or on the margins of society, however, can be bad news for the elite, for those who command privilege, wealth, and high social status (see 4:18–19; 6:20–26; 9:46–48; 14:12–14; 16:19–31; 18:15–17, 18–30).

Salvation by Reversal: Upside-Down Transpositions

- "Good news for the poor" (and bad news for the rich): Wealth and poverty
- Gender analysis: Women (and men) in Luke's narrative
- Children, model citizens in God's dominion

---

39. Carroll, *Luke*, 10.
40. And that, in turn, begins to meet readers' expectations prompted by the radical reversals celebrated in Mary's Song (1:46–55, esp. vv. 51–53).

Readers do not have to wait long to see Jesus put this vision of God's aims and work into practice. He launches a major address, the Sermon on the Plain (6:20–49), by declaring blessings and woes that reverse present conditions for the advantaged and disadvantaged, the suffering and the comfortable (vv. 20–26). He then provides for disciples of John the Baptizer a snapshot of his ministry that follows this same script (7:18–23). And in a haunting parable about the impoverished Lazarus and a rich man who ignores him (16:19–31), Jesus emphatically hammers home the point: in God's domain, the places of rich and poor, powerful and vulnerable, privileged and oppressed undergo dramatic reversal. What society prizes, God despises (16:15; 18:14). In his farewell meal with his closest followers, Jesus offers his own willingness to relinquish status and privilege as model for their leadership (22:27).

The salvation that God is effecting thus runs counter to social convention and patterns of governance and control. Jesus' ministry of "release" privileges persons on the underside and outside, rather than persons of high social status. Jesus invites everyone to a banquet table where a welcoming, generous God confers honor without regard to reputation, resources, and power. Again and again, Luke presents scenes in which community insiders (labeled "righteous") and persons on the social margins (branded "sinners") trade places (5:27–32; 7:36–50; 15:1–32; 18:9–14). Jesus stretches social borders even further when he tells a story in which a Samaritan models faithful living-out of the Torah's call to other-love (10:30–35) and when he commends a healed Samaritan as model of grateful response to benefaction (17:11–19). He even praises a Gentile, a Roman centurion at that, for his exemplary trust (7:1–10).

Horizontal and vertical reversals meet in the person of a "very rich" man who happens also to be a socially marginal tax collector, Zacchaeus (19:1–10 AT). Jesus affirms that salvation has come even to a household with such mixed status indicators, and the outcome is a tax collector with a difference: generous compensation for any victims of excessive taxation and wealth sharing for the poor.

Wealth and Poverty

Repeatedly, vertical status reversal in this Gospel centers on poverty and wealth, and this concern reappears in Acts (see Acts 2:44–45; 4:32–5:11; 8:18–24). But the presentation of the theme is complex.[41] On the one hand, Jesus summons disciples to place their confidence in God's sure provision and so to renounce wealth, releasing it to address the needs of others (e.g., Luke 12:22–34; 14:33; 18:18–23). Wealth entangles a person in preoccupations that oppose the values and commitments of God's rule (8:14; 12:22–34;

---

41. In the oft-cited appraisal of Luke Timothy Johnson, "The problem we face is that although Luke consistently talks about possessions, he does not talk about possessions consistently" (*The Literary Function of Possessions in Luke-Acts*, SBLDS 39 [Missoula, MT: Scholars Press, 1977], 130).

14:18–20; 16:13; 17:26–30), which effects reversals in status for rich and poor (1:51–53; 6:20–21, 24–25; 16:19–31).

On the other hand, there are portraits of faithful use of possessions that fall short of total renunciation. The tax agent Levi "left everything" (5:28), to be sure, but he still has a home and resources sufficient to host a banquet (5:29). Several women command enough wealth to fund the itinerant ministry of Jesus and his followers (8:2–3). In parables, a compassionate Samaritan and a banquet host use their resources to help persons in need (10:34–35; 14:21–23). Generosity like this would not be possible if disciples relinquish everything they possess (cf. the apostolic community's sharing of goods to meet every member's need in Acts 2:44–45; 4:32–37). Wealthy tax collector Zacchaeus pledges to compensate anyone he has cheated and to share his wealth with the poor (Luke 19:8), but if this falls short of total divestment, it earns no rebuke from Jesus.[42]

It may be that the complexity of Luke's presentation on this theme reflects a degree of socioeconomic diversity in Luke's earliest audience. Still, the basic message is clear and challenging. Jesus is forming a community of disciples who will share their wealth with persons who lack status, privilege, and economic resources. This redistribution of resources entails a sustained practice of generosity like that of Zacchaeus or Jesus' women benefactors, not necessarily sudden divestment (as 14:33, e.g., appears to command). Yet accumulating and hoarding possessions for oneself, oblivious to the needs of others, betrays lack of trust in God's provision and is not acceptable (12:13–34). The parabolic rich farmer (vv. 13–21) and Lazarus's rich neighbor and his brothers (16:19–31) are thus negative models. Making wealth an ultimate concern means one is no longer serving God (16:13). But one *can* use economic resources wisely and faithfully—not to improve one's social position or provide illusory economic security, but to share generously with persons who lack what is needed to sustain life. This was a serious matter for Luke's audience: the majority population in the Roman Empire was always vulnerable to climate-related food shortages and famine.[43] Possessions, then, potentially thwart the values and practices of God's realm, but they may serve God's purposes in the world.[44]

---

42. Nor does the narrator of Acts hint at any moral deficit in the well-resourced, high-status members of the movement (see Acts 17:4, 12; 18:8; cf. 16:14–15).

43. See Kyoung-Jin Kim, *Stewardship and Almsgiving in Luke's Theology*, JSNTSup 155 (Sheffield: Sheffield Academic, 1998), 52, 253–83.

44. Luke's interest in the topic of wealth and poverty and the complexity of its development in the narrative may suggest that the first Lukan audience included both rich and poor persons (so, e.g., Esler, *Community and Gospel*, 171–79, 187–97; Amanda C. Miller, *Rumors of Resistance: Status Reversals and Hidden Transcripts in the Gospel of Luke* [Minneapolis: Fortress Press, 2014], 78–86). If so, members of Luke's communities who lacked economic resources would benefit from belonging to a group that shared resources with its poorest members. Wealthier members, however, would experience considerable pressure to make their resources available for the sake of the poor in the group, without expecting anything in return (e.g., 6:27–36; 14:12–14)—including any gain in honor as community patrons and benefactors. If basic needs of impoverished members in the group were not being met, moreover, the poor would have grounds for protest against wealthier members.

Luke does not stand alone in this concern for wise, responsible use of wealth. Jewish Scripture and tradition commend generous sharing of resources with the poor, as the parable of Lazarus and the rich man acknowledges (esp. 16:27–31; see, e.g., Exod 23:11; Deut 15:7–11; 24:14–15; Prov 19:17; Job 31:16–22; Isa 58:7, 10). And when the wealthy and powerful disregard the needs of the poor, they become the target of blistering prophetic critique (e.g., Isa 3:14–15; Jer 2:34; Ezek 18:12–13; 22:29; Amos 2:6–7; 4:1; 5:11–12; 8:4–6). The practice of almsgiving is commended (e.g., Tob 4:7–11; Sir 29:12–13). A work like 1 Enoch 92–105 paints a radical picture of vertical role reversal that resembles Luke's; this text associates the poor with the oppressed righteous and the rich with their evil oppressors.

Hellenistic moralists such as Plutarch, too, attack avarice (e.g., "On Love of Wealth," in *Moralia*), and the life of simplicity and poverty advocated by Cynic philosophers entails vigorous critique of wealth (e.g., Epictetus, *Diatr.* 3.22; Diogenes Laertius, *Lives* 6.87–88). Euergetism, expending one's wealth in benefaction for the wider social good, is an honored practice in Luke's world. And a historical writing such as the *Roman Antiquities* composed by Dionysius of Halicarnassus relates stories that manifest attentiveness of the powerful rich to the concerns of the poor (esp. books 6–7). In the case of the promotion of the poor plebeian man Brutus to tribune (6.89) and the humiliation of the arrogant and wealthy Coriolanus owing to his hostility toward the impoverished (7.21; 46.2, 6; 63.1; 65.2–3), one even finds a concrete instance of vertical status reversal.[45] So while Luke's treatment of wealth and poverty is radical and countercultural, it has important points of contact with other texts, traditions, and social practices known to author and audience alike.

That the rhetoric of Luke's narrative does not aim simply to condemn persons with wealth is suggested by the mutually interpreting episodes of a rich, Torah-keeping ruler on a quest for authentic life (Luke 18:18–23) and (just a few verses later) the rich "chief tax collector" Zacchaeus (19:1–10). Jesus challenges a member of the social elite to disperse his wealth for the sake of those who lack resources (18:22–23). But as we noticed earlier in this chapter, Luke, unlike Mark 10:22, does not report the final decision of the rich ruler. Such a story without resolution reroutes Jesus' radical challenge to any well-resourced members of the Gospel audience. After hearing also about Zacchaeus and his generous response to Jesus' gift (or recognition?) of salvation, and perhaps also reflecting on the parable of Lazarus and the poor man, they will understand what they must do. There may yet be hope for them, and through them God's blessing and the community's blessing may reach those in desperate need.

---

45. See the discussion by David L. Balch, *Contested Ethnicities and Images: Studies in Acts and Art*, WUNT 2/345 (Tübingen: Mohr Siebeck, 2015), 82–101, ch. 4, "Rich and Poor, Proud and Humble in Luke-Acts," summarized on 100–1. Balch argues that Luke's teaching about poverty and wealth does not introduce new values to Gentile Christian members of the congregations addressed but instead "is reinforcing these Gentiles' pre-Christian values" (ibid., 100).

Gender Analysis: Women (and Men) in Luke's Narrative

This Gospel has many women characters, but while some interpreters discover strong affirmation of women, others conclude that Luke restricts them to conventional roles. Luke, it seems, presents a double message: gender roles in the story involve ambivalence and ambiguity.[46] No women are numbered among the apostles, and their spoken lines are few, apart from the lengthy conversation between Mary and Elizabeth (1:39–56); Martha does speak, but to express indignant protest, which Jesus promptly corrects (10:40–42). Still, women exemplify piety and prophetic discernment (Elizabeth and Mary in 1:39–56; Anna in 2:36–38), generous sharing of resources (Susanna, Joanna, and Mary Magdalene in 8:1–3), hospitality and attentiveness to Jesus' word (Martha and Mary in 10:38–42), and courageous insistence on justice (the widow in the parable of 18:2–5). Disciples of any gender would do well to follow such models of faithfulness.

Jesus' mother may lack the pedigree of the priest Zechariah, but she exhibits trust in God's promise (conveyed by the angel Gabriel) that surpasses his (1:18–20, 26–38). Near the end of the Gospel, women observe the events at Jesus' tomb (from burial to empty tomb), then hear the announcement of resurrection and report their experience to the (male) apostles (23:55–24:11). The skepticism with which their news is greeted (24:11) serves as reminder of dominant constructions of gender in Luke's social world.

Women recede in importance in the book of Acts, although readers do encounter prominent women such as Lydia and Priscilla (Acts 16:14–15; 18:26). Still, the mixed signals continue. Widows are passive recipients of assistance, or should be (6:1), but their plight only sets the stage for the important action: the selection of seven (male) Hellenistic Jewish believers like Philip and Stephen, who expand the witness of the twelve apostles. Sapphira is given a measure of initiative, but neither her failed attempt (with her husband) at deception nor its outcome presents a positive model like that of Barnabas (5:1–11; cf. 4:32–37). The narrator praises Tabitha (Dorcas) as a woman known for her virtue displayed in acts of charity, but her role in the story is passive: she dies, and Peter restores her to life (9:36–41). The spirit world grants a slave girl insight into the salvation that Paul and his companions bear with them, but they abruptly silence her, and she then vanishes from the narrative (16:16–18). Philip's four daughters wear a prophetic

---

46. For the view that Luke's Gospel presents affirmation of women, see, e.g., Robert J. Karris, "Women and Discipleship in Luke," *CBQ* 56 (1994): 1–20; Warren Carter, "Getting Martha out of the Kitchen: Luke 10:38–42 Again," *CBQ* 58 (1996): 264–80. For Luke's restriction of women to conventional roles, see, e.g., Mary Rose D'Angelo, "Women in Luke-Acts: A Redactional View," *JBL* 109 (1990): 441–61; Barbara E. Reid, *Choosing the Better Part? Women in the Gospel of Luke* (Collegeville, MN: Liturgical Press, 1996). For Luke's ambivalence about women, see, e.g., Turid Karlsen Seim, *The Double Message: Patterns of Gender in Luke-Acts* (Nashville: Abingdon Press, 1994). Acknowledging ambivalence in Luke's portrayal of women, F. Scott Spencer nevertheless argues for a more positive overall view, in *Salty Wives, Spirited Mothers, and Savvy Widows: Capable Women of Purpose and Persistence in Luke's Gospel* (Grand Rapids: Wm. B. Eerdmans Publishing Co., 2012).

label, but the narrator records Agabus's prophetic oracles, not theirs (Acts 21:8–11; cf. 11:28).

Both of Luke's books, then, present mixed signals about women: women's voices as prophets and preachers take a backseat to men's voices (as one expects in the first-century Greco-Roman world), but they are not mute. Still more can be said, though, if one considers the varying social status of women characters. In keeping with the Lukan pattern of vertical status reversal, lower-status women gain in dignity while higher-status men enjoy diminished honor (e.g., Mary vs. Zechariah in Luke 1:5–56 and the uninvited woman guest vs. the Pharisee Simon in 7:36–50). When higher-status women join the Christian group, on the other hand, they receive neither gain nor loss of position in relation to lower-status persons regardless of gender.[47]

Luke's narrative reflects the constraints of his own culture and social location; the public leadership of women does not match that of the apostles and other prominent men (Philip, Stephen, Barnabas, Paul) in Acts. Yet Luke's two books do clearly indicate their importance in the early Christian groups and include them—beginning with the prophetic speech of Elizabeth and Mary in Luke 1 and continuing with Mary Magdalene's resurrection report on Easter, and beyond—among the "eyewitnesses and ministers of the word" on whose teaching Luke depends in composing his narrative of Christian origins (Luke 1:2 RSV).

It may be that Luke's depiction of unmanly men has a sharper and more distinctly countercultural profile than that of women. To be sure, Jesus demonstrates prowess and boldness in speech, and his strength overpowers demons; nevertheless, the ideal of masculinity for Jesus and his followers otherwise bears little resemblance to the (elite) status-driven male who especially prizes self-control (certainly not the shame and weakness of a cross), winning contests for honor in public exchanges, and power over others.[48]

Children, Model Citizens in God's Dominion

Children also figure in the vertical status transpositions in Luke's narrative.[49] Although they enjoy low social status in Luke's world, Jesus elevates children—including the very youngest and most vulnerable, infants (*brephē*)—as model members of the reign of God (Luke 9:46–48; 18:15–17).[50] True,

47. A point emphasized by James Malcolm Arlandson, *Women, Class, and Society in Early Christianity: Models from Luke-Acts* (Peabody, MA: Hendrickson Publishers, 1997), 188, 192.

48. See Brittany Wilson, *Unmanly Men: Refigurations of Masculinity in Luke-Acts* (Oxford: Oxford University Press, 2015).

49. For more detailed analysis of how Luke's Gospel presents children, see John T. Carroll, "'What Then Will This Child Become?': Perspectives on Children in the Gospel of Luke," in *The Child in the Bible*, ed. Marcia Bunge, Terence E. Fretheim, and Beverly Roberts Gaventa (Grand Rapids: Wm. B. Eerdmans Publishing Co., 2008), 177–94.

50. While Luke's Jesus presents the child as symbol of God's reign, in one passage he also uses children's play in the town market as symbol of his contemporaries' refusal to "play the game" that either John the Baptizer (wailing) or Jesus (dancing) invites them to join (7:31–35, ironic reversal of Zech 8:5, in which children's play in the streets of Zion signals the restoration of the city).

the (adult male) disciples have some trouble understanding or accepting this revised estimation of children's worth (evident, e.g., in 18:15). But Jesus embraces the child with honor, a welcome all the more striking in 18:15–17 because this scene immediately precedes one in which an elite man on a quest for eternal life hears with difficulty Jesus' summons to relinquish wealth and become a disciple—emblematic of the challenge that accompanies the inviting, welcoming grace of God's realm (18:18–27). A last meal shared by Jesus and the apostles before his death provides the occasion for a final status-refiguring statement. Their culturally formed notions of leadership and authority require adjustment as they jockey for position even after hearing somber words about betrayal (22:21–24). Jesus acknowledges that by convention, the ruling elite dominate, exercise power-over, and exploit the practice of benefaction to extract honor and acclamation (v. 25). The Twelve, however, must be leaders of a radically different kind, eschewing preoccupation with power and status. They should seek the place of the low-status young and offer themselves in service of others. Jesus presents his own leadership style as the defining model (22:24–27).

In the Roman world, perhaps only one-half of children survived beyond age ten.[51] Jesus' choice of the vulnerable young as exemplars of God's dominion is therefore particularly striking. This Gospel also presents images of parental devotion to and care for children, as parents on several occasions bring a child to Jesus seeking his help as healer (8:41–42; 9:37–43; 18:15–17). Indeed, Jesus points to parents' (typical) attentiveness to the needs of their children as image of the (even more trustworthy) gracious provision of God for those who call God Father (11:9–13).

Horizontal Status Transpositions

Alongside and sometimes overlapping vertical status reversals in Luke's Gospel are inside-out transpositions.[52] Indeed, this is one of the most prominent features of the narrative, clearly signaled by Jesus' inaugural statement of mission in Nazareth. Jesus knows that prophets are not welcomed at home and cites a familiar proverb about physicians to the effect that they should take care of their own health, then invokes the activity of Elijah and Elisha as benefiting outsiders rather than people within Israel (4:22–27). The implication, that Jesus will be *this kind of* prophet, does not play well with Jesus' fellow synagogue attenders (vv. 28–30). Horizontal reversals in

---

51. See Thomas Wiedemann, *Adults and Children in the Roman Empire* (New Haven, CT: Yale University Press, 1989), 11–17. Precise data, of course, are elusive. As Marianne Meye Thompson puts it, "In the ancient world, all children were children at risk" ("Children in the Gospel of John," in *Child in the Bible*, ed. Bunge et al., 195–214, esp. 202).

52. Horizontal and vertical status transpositions merge in Jesus' comment on his parable about two men at prayer who exchange roles as sinner and righteous (18:9–14): "This man went down to his home justified rather than the other; for all who exalt themselves will be humbled, but all who humble themselves will be exalted" (v. 14). They also meet in the person of Zacchaeus, a socially marginalized tax collector who is also wealthy (19:1–10).

the Gospel narrative focus on Jesus' relationships with persons labeled "sinners" and with those identified as "righteous," especially Pharisees, although Samaritans too play a role (9:52–55; 10:30–35; 17:11–19). In book 2, the theme extends to encompass God-fearing Gentiles like Cornelius (Acts 10:1–48) and eventually pagan Gentiles as well. Paul captures the horizontal reversal theme in recurring programmatic statements (Acts 13:46–47; 18:6; 28:25–28; cf. 19:8–10). The two-part narrative's development of the horizontal reversal theme foregrounds concern with community boundaries. Both Jesus and his followers after him press against humanly constructed borders, expanding participation in the people of God, all in fulfillment of scriptural vision (e.g., Acts 13:47; 15:13–21; 28:25–28; cf. Luke 2:30–32; 3:6; 24:47; Acts 2:39; 3:25) and the divine purpose (e.g., Acts 9:15; 10:1–11:18).

Salvation by Reversal: Inside-Out Transpositions	
• Sinners and righteous • Samaritans	• Gentiles and the Jewish people

Inside-Out Reversals: Sinners and Righteous

After an initial, programmatic mission statement in his synagogue message at Nazareth (Luke 4:16–27), Jesus later reinforces this preview of his primary aims with concise, explicit declarations of purpose:

> Those who are well have no need of a physician, but those who are sick; I have come to call not the righteous but sinners to repentance. (5:31–32)

> Today salvation has come to this house, because [Zacchaeus] too is a son of Abraham. For the Son of Man [Human One] came to seek out and to save the lost. (19:9–10)

Again and again, Jesus enacts just such a mission to the sick, the religious outsider, those who have lost their way or lost a place within the community. The movement is not in one direction, however, simply expanding access to God's domain. Jesus' initiative to extend favor to persons on the social margins elicits a negative reaction from those who enjoy position at the community's center. Typically, Pharisees are the characters who resist Jesus' moves to embrace "lost sinners." In Acts, Torah-serious Jewish believers in Jesus take their place, as in 11:1–3; 15:1–2, 5 (identified as Pharisees); 21:18–24.

Often scenes featuring hospitality and banquet conviviality bring into focus the inside-out reversal pattern. On such occasions Jesus' primary concern for the restoration of socially marginal "tax collectors and sinners" clashes with the moral rigor of some observing Pharisees (Luke 5:27–32; 7:36–50; 15:1–32; 19:5–7; cf. 14:1–24). At the banquet hosted by a new disciple recruit, the tax collector Levi, Jesus responds to detractors among the Pharisees ("and their scribes") by imaging his ministry as a doctor's care for sick patients, not the healthy who "have no need of a physician" (5:31)—metaphor for his extension of mercy to "sinners," "not the righteous" (v. 32). Is Jesus implying that there are righteous people (e.g., the Pharisees whom Jesus is addressing) who do not have need of mercy or repentance (see 15:7)? By the end of his ministry, the repeating horizontal-reversal pattern surely prompts Luke's audience to probe deeply the question of just who enjoys right relation with God and who needs forgiveness (e.g., 7:36–50; 15:1–32; 18:9–14). It turns out that Jesus' mission, centering on restoration of persons labeled as sinners, exposes the need of all for repentance, the need of all to reorder life, to be aligned with the values and commitments of God's reign.[53] No less a star of Luke's narrative production than Simon Peter is first introduced to the audience as just such a sinner whose transformation commences when he recoils from the holy, only to experience gracious acceptance (5:8–11).

Jesus quickly earns a reputation as a man who enjoys a good feast with questionable company: "Look, a glutton and a drunkard, a friend of tax collectors and sinners!" (7:34). Immediately after he acknowledges this public image, Jesus finds himself invited to dine with the Pharisee Simon. This episode (7:36–50) perfectly exemplifies the inside-out status reversal theme: Jesus accepts a sinner, while a man who appears to be righteous expresses indignation and as a result puts his own position in jeopardy. When an uninvited woman joins the banquet party and showers Jesus with affection (the imagery in v. 38 is lavish and suggests intimacy and unashamed physical touch), Simon the host, who is identified four times as a Pharisee by the narrator before Jesus mentions his name (v. 40), is offended. In a private soliloquy (see the discussion of interior monologues earlier in this chapter), Simon questions Jesus' prophetic credentials because he should have known the woman is a sinner (v. 39, repeating the narrator's label for her in v. 37). He assumes, of course, that a virtuous prophet would avoid a sinful woman's physical touch.

Jesus comments on the situation with a parable about two canceled debts of differing quantity, which Simon astutely interprets at Jesus' prompting: the person forgiven a larger debt will love the merciful creditor more (v. 43). Only now does the narrator disclose—or have Jesus disclose—that the banquet host has deprived a supposedly honored guest of basic elements of hospitality (vv. 44–46). Corresponding to the woman's extravagantly physical actions is their complete absence in the host's welcome of Jesus, as he recalls it. In Jesus' reframing of the scene, she has assumed the role of host

---

53. For thorough discussion of the category of sinners in Luke's narrative, see David A. Neale, *None but the Sinners: Religious Categories in the Gospel of Luke*, JSNTSup 58 (Sheffield: JSOT Press, 1991). On the topic of repentance, see Guy D. Nave, Jr., *The Role and Function of Repentance in Luke-Acts*, AcBib 4 (Atlanta: SBL Press, 2002).

that the Pharisee neglected. Jesus defends the honor of a "shameless" woman and deprives the righteous Simon of his own honor. Although the narrator has related no prior contact between Jesus and the woman, Luke's audience will probably infer, from the logic of the story, that she previously encountered Jesus, received his merciful acceptance, and therefore has sought him out to express her gratitude (her love). But that detail is unimportant to the story as narrated. A sinner is forgiven, dismissed in peace (v. 50), and her profuse gratitude paints a stark contrast to Simon's indignation and his lack of empathy or of capacity for warm hospitality. So which of the two is morally upright? Who has need for repentance?

At Jesus' declaration of the woman's forgiveness (v. 47: "her sins, which were many, have been forgiven"; v. 48: "Your sins are forgiven"), puzzled dinner guests, silent until now, debate among themselves: "Who is this who even forgives sins?" (v. 49, reprise of 5:21). Jesus' acceptance of a sinner who, he says, has received God's forgiveness (a "divine passive," implying that God is the one who has forgiven her) raises the question of Jesus' identity. Despite the Pharisee Simon's incredulity, Jesus enacts his role as God's prophet-Messiah precisely through a mission that seeks and restores the lost, the outsider, the sinner. Tearful touch and glad celebration express grateful human response to the gift of mercy that the bearer of God's welcoming, gracious reign mediates.

The narrator leaves in suspense the Pharisee host's response to Jesus' comments of explanation (of his conduct) and critique (of Simon's). Many chapters later, the narrative picks up this thread (though for generic Pharisees and scribes, not Simon) in a chapter-long elaboration of the theme (Luke 15:1–32). The episode presents an ideal-type scenario of horizontal status reversal. Jesus' bent for sharing meals with "tax collectors and sinners" elicits once more the complaint that he "welcomes sinners and eats with them" (v. 2). Jesus replies with a parable triad; each parable pivots on the restoration of the lost—sheep, coin, son—and highlights joyful celebration of its recovery (sheep, vv. 3–7; coin, vv. 8–10; son, vv. 11–32). Jesus' commentary on the sheep parable explicitly links its plot to the plot of the wider Lukan narrative: "Just so, I tell you, there will be more joy in heaven over one sinner who repents than over ninety-nine righteous persons who need no repentance" (v. 7). Commentary on the parable of the woman and her lost coin also forges this connection, though leaving out any mention of the righteous: "Just so, I tell you, there is joy in the presence of the angels of God over one sinner who repents" (v. 10). No such comment, linking parable to the wider narrative, amplifies the third parable, which is by far the longest (indeed, the longest of the preserved parables of Jesus). This parable as metaphor for Jesus' ministry stands alone, without need for explicit linkage. And that is because this more complex parable adds a character and a plot element that allow both sides of the inside-out status reversals of Luke's account of the mission of Jesus to have full play—through the character of the older son, even giving voice to the viewpoint of Jesus' critics among the Pharisees.

The prodigal returns home with his shame and his empty belly and finds undeserved, welcoming mercy—vividly imaged in a father's exuberant sprint and intimate embrace of his returning son (v. 20), investiture with the tokens of sonship (v. 22: robe, sandals, ring),[54] and a feast to which the whole village has been invited (vv. 23–24). Everyone is celebrating, it seems, but the older son (vv. 25–28). His understandable anger at his father (v. 28) merges with still-simmering contempt for "this son of yours" (v. 30). The father of these two estranged brothers, having embraced a lost-but-found, dead-but-alive son in undeserved love, now pleads with the not-lost-but-enraged son to join the party too, to be reconciled to his brother (vv. 31–32). Right there the parable's plot is suspended, with no indication of the older son's response to his father's urging. The final word belongs to the father, his affirmation of a life restored, and his call to celebration. So the parable's open-endedness (see the discussion of open-ended stories earlier in this chapter) is perhaps deceiving. The only appropriate response to the parable's rhetoric is to join the feast.

And that observation brings us back to the scene that Luke has provided for the parable. With this parable's plot-extending third act featuring the older son and his understandable protest, Jesus makes contact with the viewpoint of his sharpest critics. He has oriented his ministry around the plight of the lost, the outsider, the sinner, those who need to be restored—not around the healthy and the righteous (cf. 5:31–32). Yet with this complex parable, he signals that he has not written off the Pharisees but still seeks to convince them. "In his ministry, Jesus shares with his Torah-observant critics a commitment to grace embodied in a reordered life (5:32; 15:7, 10; imaged also in the younger son's return [15:17–20]), but . . . the reordered life (repentance) that Pharisees also applaud may follow the offer of gracious acceptance rather than precede it."[55] Within the story, the parable of the father and his two sons leaves the outcome with the Pharisees: can they move past their protest at Jesus' acceptance of the lost and take a seat at the feast too?

In 18:9–14, Jesus issues a parable about two men at prayer and addresses it to generic listeners "who trusted in themselves that they were righteous and regarded others with contempt" (v. 9). One worshiper, a Pharisee, perfectly captures the profile of Jesus' target audience. His prayer appears to reflect a life of above-and-beyond, Torah-keeping virtue, yet his prayer, Jesus asserts, does not find favor with God. The problem is that, though framed as gratitude to God, his mostly self-referential, self-congratulatory prayer

---

54. Contemplating his return home and rehearsing the speech he will deliver to his father, the prodigal son anticipates that he will ask to be added to his father's workforce (15:19). Yet in the reunion scene, the son never delivers that line (v. 21), though some manuscripts do include it (likely a later expansion of the text). However readers interpret that silence (or gap), the contrast between the welcome the son deserves and the welcome the father extends—restoration to status as son—is difficult to miss.

55. Carroll, *Luke*, 319.

presumes his moral superiority over others, and specifically over a fellow worshiper, a sinful tax collector. The eloquence of the tax collector's prayer is its concise candor: simply "God, be merciful to me, a sinner!" (v. 13), nothing more.[56] Yet he is the worshiper whom God validates as just, who receives vindication (*dedikaiōmenos*, a divine passive, in v. 14). By the end of the story, then, the two worshipers have exchanged roles—another inside-out status inversion of righteous Pharisee and sinful tax collector. The Pharisee's prayer reveals the disdain he feels toward others to whom he regards himself as morally superior (recalling v. 9). He too needs mercy, though he fails to recognize that need. So it is, as well, with Jesus' righteous detractors in the Lukan narrative.

In Luke's Gospel, God's reign is redrawing the social maps by which people have found their orientation in the world; the salvation that Jesus both announces and enacts entails inside-out status inversions. Will insiders thrust to the margins by their failure to accept Jesus' mission remain there? Or will they, in their new status as the lost, now spark celebration in heaven by their restoration?

Inside-Out Reversals: Samaritans

The horizontal status reversals in Luke's narrative center on the theme of sinners and the righteous (or Pharisees), but they extend to include Samaritans and Gentiles, although Luke defers to book 2 fuller development of the theme. Samaritans, inhabitants of the region between Galilee and Judea and descendants of the former northern kingdom of Israel after its conquest by the Assyrians (722 BCE), were viewed negatively by Galileans and Judeans alike. (Samaritans regarded the Samaritan Pentateuch as authoritative Scripture and the temple on Mount Gerizim [or the location of its ruins], not the temple on Mount Zion, as sacred space.) Animosity between Samaritans and Jews was well established by the first century and is documented in many literary works.[57]

Whether or not Luke's readers know any of the history of tensions between the two, 9:52–55 tutors them on the subject. When Jesus dispatches disciples into villages in Samaria as an advance team to prepare for his own arrival, they are not welcomed (vv. 52–53). Why not? "Because," the narrator explains, "his face was set towards Jerusalem" (v. 53; cf. the description of Jesus' resolve in v. 51). However, Jesus refuses to endorse James and John's wish for the Samaritan villages' annihilation, the first signal that he has other and better plans for the region and its people.

---

56. The tax collector's prayer is brief (six words in Greek), but the description of his body language is lengthier (nineteen words). By contrast, the Pharisee is verbose (a prayer of twenty-nine words, including five first-person verbs).

57. E.g., Ezra 4; Neh 2:19; 4:2–9; Sir 50:25–26; T. Levi 5–7; Josephus, *Ant.* 9.14.3; 11.2.1; 11.4.3–6, 9; 11.7.1–7; 12.5.5; 13.3.4; 18.2.2; 20.6.1–3; Jub. 30; John 4:9, 20–22.

Twice in Jesus' later activity, Samaritans figure in positive ways, each time exemplifying the horizontal-reversal pattern. First, in a parable responding to a lawyer's question about the scope of the commandment to love neighbors, Jesus presents a traveling Samaritan—not a priest or a Levite—as model of effective, compassionate care for a man lying beaten and helpless along the road from Jerusalem to Jericho (10:30–35). Second, in an episode suggestively set in a liminal zone "between Samaria and Galilee" (17:11), only one man healed of a leprous condition comes back to Jesus to express gratitude and to praise God for the gift of healing. Only then does the narrator reveal the man's identity as a Samaritan, and Jesus wonders aloud why only such an outsider—a "foreigner"—returned in gratitude (17:11–19). The label expresses the border crossing in play, but the restored Samaritan's exemplary response to the experience of healing benefaction anticipates the later successful mission among Samaritans narrated in Acts 8. Guided by the Holy Spirit, Jesus' followers press beyond established borders, expanding membership in the people of God.

Luke's Samaritans

- "Fire from heaven to consume them"? Samaritan villages refuse Jesus' representatives. (9:52–55)
- In parable, a Samaritan exemplifies the life-giving other-regard the Torah commends. (10:25–37)
- Only a Samaritan, "this foreigner," comes back to honor God and thank Jesus for healing. (17:11–19)
- Successful mission in Samaria. (Acts 8)

Inside-Out Reversals: Gentiles and the Jewish People

Luke's Gospel highlights the rootedness of the story, and of Jesus and the movement he launched, in Jewish Scripture and history; this narrative interest is signaled clearly in the stories and speeches of chapters 1–2. Yet Luke's two books present a complicated account of the relation of Jesus and his followers to the Jewish people and their religious traditions and practices.[58] The narrative offers Jesus as Israel's Messiah and Savior, long awaited by a people who drew encouragement from ancient promises to David (e.g., Luke 1:31–33, echoing 2 Sam 7:12–16). But the outcome of Jesus' ministry, prefigured

---

58. A provocative recent treatment of the topic is that of Amy-Jill Levine, "Luke and the Jewish Religion," *Int* 68 (2014): 389–402. Levine argues that Luke's view of contemporaneous Jews and of Jewish tradition and practices is entirely negative. Luke's perspective on Jews and Jewish religion has been vigorously debated. See, e.g., Robert L. Brawley, *Luke-Acts and the Jews: Conflict, Apology, and Conciliation*, SBLMS 33 (Atlanta: Scholars Press, 1987); Joseph B. Tyson, *Luke, Judaism, and the Scholars: Critical Approaches to Luke-Acts* (Columbia: University of South Carolina Press, 1999); idem, *Images of Judaism in Luke-Acts*.

by his rejection in his hometown, is mixed at best. The hybrid parable of the pounds and the rejected-but-vindicated throne claimant (Luke 19:12–27) serves metaphorically as interpretive commentary on the Messiah Jesus' imminent reception in Jerusalem; likewise, his royal claim is about to be repudiated there by his own fellow "citizens," only to be validated (by God) after a long journey (death, resurrection, exaltation). And as another parable, featuring rebellious vineyard tenants (20:9–16), anticipates, Jesus is ultimately rejected by the local Judean-Jerusalem elite and consigned by Governor Pilate to death by crucifixion, for which they lobbied, along with the assembled crowd they have incited (23:13–25). Any messianic claims for Jesus are roundly rejected by the temple-based leadership (22:66–71; 23:35).

Yet while Simeon's oracle imagines revelatory light coming to Gentiles, it also speaks of glory for Israel (2:31–32). The turn the story eventually takes in book 2, opening membership in the movement to Gentiles, does not abandon Israel or Jewish Scripture and tradition but instead continues Israel's story.[59] Here, Luke's narrative suggests, the people of God fulfill their vocation, from the foundational promise to Abraham onward, to convey blessing to the nations, to all earth's families (Acts 3:25, drawing from Gen 12:3; 22:18; 26:4).

Already the Gospel signals this future direction of the story. In addition to Simeon's oracle (esp. Luke 2:32), the narrator's prophetic-scriptural script for the Baptizer's mission quotes not just Isaiah 40:3 (as in Mark 1:3) but also Isaiah 40:4–5, thus including "all flesh" (all humankind) in the salvation that God intends (Luke 3:5–6 RSV). In Jesus' own (unsuccessful) mission launch, he implies that his Spirit-empowered, prophetic-messianic mission, after the pattern of Elijah and Elisha, will reach outsiders—even Gentiles—with God's favor (4:25–27). Although Jesus' public ministry is almost entirely restricted to Jewish people, there are two striking exceptions: the healing-at-a-distance of a centurion's slave (7:1–10) and the liberation of a Gerasene tomb dweller long oppressed by a Legion of demons (8:26–39).[60] Jesus' praise of the Roman soldier's tenacious, expectant faith expresses with dramatic emphasis the narrative's inside-out reversal pattern. "Not even in Israel," Jesus remarks, perhaps with hyperbole, "have I seen such faith" (7:9). There will be more of that to come in the Gospel's narrative sequel.

Repeatedly confronted with his ministry's mixed reception (with well-established teachers such as Pharisees, scribes, and synagogue leaders being his usual detractors), Jesus later projects that divided response—and its consequences—into the eschatological future. He fields a leading question: "Lord, will only a few be saved?" (Luke 13:23). His answer avoids quantifying the number of the saved but does image a narrow door through which

---

59. The episode of Peter's conversion to bring the gospel message to Cornelius's household is the pivotal moment orchestrated by God (Acts 10:1–48).

60. As noted earlier in this chapter, Luke omits the peculiar Markan episode of Jesus' encounter with a Greek-Syrophoenician woman (Mark 7:24–30).

many will not be able to enter (v. 24). Then he pictures a homeowner who refuses to open his door and home to frantically knocking would-be guests; their evil practices have undercut their association with him, even in the intimacy of shared meals (vv. 25–27). Jesus then warns his audience against the complacent presumption that they will be among those admitted to the eschatological banquet (the realm of God; cf. 14:15). Indeed, people will come from everywhere (else) to feast with the patriarchs and the prophets, while "you yourselves [are] thrown out" (13:28–29). This is inside-out status reversal of the most extreme kind, a point Jesus clinches with a concluding statement that "some" (interestingly not all, only some) of those who are "first" and "last" will exchange positions (v. 30). Jesus conducts a ministry as Israel's prophet-Messiah that only some of the people accept. The thread runs right through to the end of the narrative: the crucifixion scene juxtaposes the mocking Judean governing elite and the chest-pounding, remorseful general public (23:35, 48). This sets the stage for the call to repentance issued by the apostles in the speeches of Acts (e.g., 2:38; 3:19; cf. 5:31), with its dramatic results (e.g., the thousands of 2:41), alongside the resumption of hostility from the temple-based Judean elite (Acts 4–5, 7).

The Pharisees are Jesus' chief critics throughout the narrative, until his collision with the Jerusalem power base (after their last mention, in Luke 19:39–40, they do not surface again until Acts 5:34). Yet they sustain cordial, if sometimes tense, relations with Jesus, and in their interactions with him they continue to do what Jewish teachers who are devoted to understanding and faithfully living the Torah typically do: they vigorously debate the interpretation and appropriation of God's Torah. The critiques that pass between them are mutual, reciprocal, and sometimes harsh—such as Jesus' pointed remarks in Luke 11:39–44; 16:14–15. It is not Pharisees but the elite priestly circle, controlling the temple system, whose opposition to Jesus leads to his arrest and execution (19:47; 20:19; 22:2, 52, 66–71; 23:10).[61] They regard him as a serious threat to their control and to the stability and fragile peace of Jerusalem and its environs imposed by the Roman occupation. Ironically, Luke has Jesus lament the city's failure to recognize, hence its refusal to acknowledge, the divine visitation in connection with his ministry, the result being a missed opportunity for peace (19:41–44). With collaboration from the apostle Judas and then the authorization of the Roman governor, they succeed in removing the perceived threat.

Over the course of the Acts narrative, Jewish audiences—initially attracted to the message and appeal of the apostles—become more and more

---

61. Acts 23:6–9 shows that Luke is aware of the presence of Pharisees among the elite scribes in the Jerusalem council—who would therefore have been expected to play a role in the passion drama, as in the other Gospels (e.g., Matt 27:62; John 18:3; cf. Mark 12:13). So the absence of any explicit mention of the Pharisees in the Gospel of Luke, after 19:39–40, suggests that the character sketch for this group has been shaped by particular rhetorical interests. See further John T. Carroll, "Luke's Portrayal of the Pharisees," *CBQ* 50 (1988): 604–21.

antagonistic to the emerging movement. More than once, Paul is prompted to redirect his preaching to Gentiles (Acts 13:44–48; 18:5–6; 19:8–10; 28:23–28), though for Luke this is not simply a matter of Paul's choice. Rather, Paul operates under the divine mandate to include Gentiles in his mission (9:15), and this is not his innovation, nor Peter's, but the divine initiative in fulfillment of ancient promise (13:46–47; 15:14–18). The concluding scene of Luke's two volumes places Paul in Rome, speaking first to an interested audience composed of Jews, then, after their mixed response, to anyone who will come to him (in his own lodging, while in custody) to hear his message (28:16–31). His last recorded speech quotes Isaiah 6:9–10 to explain from Scripture why many Jewish listeners resist the message (Acts 28:25–27), then affirms that its future lies with the mission among Gentiles: "this salvation has been sent to the Gentiles [nations, *ethnē*]; they will listen" (28:28). Nevertheless, Paul continues to speak of Israel's hopes (28:20), which he closely binds to the resurrection (23:6; 24:15; 26:6–8)—God's vindication of the crucified Messiah Jesus (13:27–30; cf. 2:22–24, 36; 3:12–15; 5:30–31).

No less than Matthew, though perhaps in an urban environment less thoroughly shaped by Jewish people, traditions, and religious practices, Luke's Gospel and Acts betray an intense struggle for identity in relation to the Jewish heritage and its promises and hopes. Luke's narrative offers a picture of the emerging Christian movement as legitimate heirs of this heritage. The Gospel tells the first part of that story, and book 2 amplifies the moves already made in book 1 to revise conventional understandings of the composition and character of God's people Israel.

Luke and Empire: Capitulation, Cooperation, Subversion, or Ambivalence?

"Give to the emperor the things that are the emperor's, and to God the things that are God's" (Luke 20:25): what exactly is the relation between these two claims and allegiances? The Roman Empire figures prominently in Luke-Acts, but there has been vigorous debate about Luke's appraisal of the empire.[62] Does the narrative present a positive view of Rome, at least in part to defend early Christian groups noticed by Roman observers?[63] Or perhaps to commend to Christian groups a constructive engagement with the empire?[64] Does Luke, then, picture the Christian movement's relation to

---

62. For more detailed discussion, see the excursus on "The Reign of God and the Roman Empire in Luke's Gospel" in Carroll, *Luke*, 398–404, and the literature cited there; also, most recently, Kuhn, *Kingdom according to Luke and Acts*, 258–70.

63. This is the view, e.g., of Henry Joel Cadbury, *The Making of Luke-Acts*, 2nd ed. (London: SPCK, 1958; repr., Peabody, MA: Hendrickson Publishers, 1999), 308–16; Hans Conzelmann, *The Theology of St. Luke*, trans. Geoffrey Buswell (New York: Harper & Row, 1961), 137–49.

64. E.g., Paul Walaskay, *"And So We Came to Rome": The Political Perspective of St. Luke*, SNTSMS 49 (Cambridge: Cambridge University Press, 1983); Esler, *Community and Gospel*. Esler suggests that Luke's community may have included Roman administrative and military officers. For such readers, the Gospel affirms that participation in the Christian group and service to the empire are compatible (ibid., 210, 217–19); cf. Helen K. Bond, *Pontius Pilate in History and Interpretation*, SNTSMS 100 (Cambridge: Cambridge University Press, 1998), 162.

the empire in terms of alliance and cooperation? Or is Luke instead a severe critic of the imperial economic-religious-political system?[65] Indeed, does Luke's narrative color Rome evil, inviting readers to see Rome as the agent of Satan's world domination?[66]

As this array of interpretations would lead one to expect, Luke's narrative holds complicated, ambiguous (or ambivalent) images of the empire and its representatives. From the outset, Luke clearly sets the story within the Roman world, mentioning two emperors (Augustus, 2:1; Tiberius, 3:1), as well as the governor who administers Judea (Pontius Pilate) and three tetrarchs (Herod Antipas, Herod Philip, and Lysanias, 3:1–2). When Augustus orders a universal census (a tool of Roman control and exploitation), Joseph and Mary do their part (2:1–5). Luke's Jesus knows the power of the imperial system to collect taxes (20:20–26) and through its armies to vanquish cities and ravage temples (19:43–44; 21:5–6, 20–24). Luke's second book ends with Paul under Roman custody, waiting for his judicial appeal to be heard by the emperor (Nero, though he is not named). Like Jesus before him, Paul collides with agents of Roman power: provincial governors, centurions, and the high priest and his council at Jerusalem, co-opted to serve Roman political interests (Luke 22–23 and Acts 21–28). The shadow of empire falls over Luke's story from beginning to end.

Roman military officers are typically portrayed favorably, especially the centurions of Luke 7:1–10; 23:47; Acts 10:1–48; 13:6–12; 27:1–44 (tribunes appear in Acts 21:31–40; 22:24–29; 23:16–30). Agents of the system of tax collection are viewed negatively by everyone except Jesus (Luke 5:27–32; 7:29–35; 15:1–2; 19:1–10). Roman governors are called upon to intervene in and settle judicial cases involving Jesus (23:1–25) and Paul (Acts 18:12–17; chs. 24–26). Their assessment: Jesus and his followers are not guilty as charged and pose no threat to Roman order. There is considerable irony here. The sovereignty of God and the authority of the *kyrios* (Lord) Jesus *do* mean that Roman power is not supreme. On this point, Paul's accusers among Jewish residents in Thessalonica are more astute: "[Paul and his associates] are all acting contrary to the decrees of the emperor, saying that there is another king named Jesus" (Acts 17:7). However, unlike others who violently resist Roman military occupation (notably Theudas and Judas in Acts 5:36–37), Jesus and his followers do not advocate violent resistance to the empire. At the same time, they acknowledge a sovereign and a dominion other than Rome's.

Rather than paint Jesus and the early Christian movement as either rebels, at one extreme, or accommodating collaborators, at the other, Luke's narrative is more subtle. Understanding of the geopolitical context and the

65. E.g., Joel B. Green, *Theology of the Gospel of Luke*, NTT (Cambridge: Cambridge University Press, 1995), 119–21.

66. See Kazuhiko Yamazaki-Ransom, *The Roman Empire in Luke's Narrative*, LNTS 404 (London: T&T Clark, 2010), 82, 97, 200–202.

constraints it places upon Luke and his audience is helpful. Domination by a colonizing power like Rome makes violent resistance futile, but this does not mean that passive acceptance and capitulation is the only remaining option. Between open rebellion and submission, a dominated group may find a safer, more indirect way to resist domination and so reclaim a measure of dignity.[67] Out of public earshot, critique of empire can be voiced, and in public exchanges coded communications can deliver the same message, though not all who hear will *get* it (what Scott terms resistance by means of a "hidden transcript").

A postcolonial analysis rejects any simple opposition between two binaries, the colonizing power (the Roman Empire, in this case) and the group over which it exercises domination. Rather, in the context of empire, a dominated group identifies with the dominant power, but only in part. It may mimic the oppressor but at the same time inject parody or mockery of the powerful. A hybrid space emerges: a "third space" can be constructed in which speech and practices, and the values they encode, differ from those shaped by the binary opposition between the dominant and dominated groups.[68] In the setting of an empire such as Rome's, with its overwhelming military, economic, and political power (all undergirded by religious ideology—these were all intertwined in the Roman world), effective overt resistance was scarcely imaginable (as the revolutionaries in the war begun in 66 CE, like so many other freedom fighters before and after them, eventually learned). If Luke were of a mind to foster resistance to the dominant Roman cultural system, it would need to take the form of indirect resistance. Especially if the author was a person of some status, one would expect his narrative discourse about empire to mix indirect or hidden, coded resistance with expressions of ambivalence, including a measure of mimicry, cooperation, and constructive engagement.

How, then, does Luke's narrative portray the empire? Rome wields its power in the global force field in which Satan, too, operates (Luke 4:5–6), and in contest with the sovereignty of God. So it is important to probe the ways in which these powers interact. Moreover, in the midst of such contested power, how does Luke's story picture the construction of a third space, the formation of a community that lives by a different set of norms, shaped by the aims, commitments, and distinctive practices of God's realm?

67. Here I am drawing upon the work of James C. Scott, *Domination and the Arts of Resistance: Hidden Transcripts* (New Haven, CT: Yale University Press, 1990). Ordinarily a subordinate group has "vested interest in avoiding any *explicit* display of insubordination"; however, some degree of resistance is in their interest so as to "minimiz[e] the exactions, labor, and humiliations to which they are subject" (ibid., 86).

68. Here I am drawing from Homi K. Bhabha, *Location of Culture* (London: Routledge, 1994), 85–92, 120–21 (parodic mimicry); 85–92 (indirect, ambivalent resistance); 34–39, 217–23 (third space). Yong-Sung Ahn examines Luke 19:45–23:56 through a postcolonial lens in *The Reign of God and Rome in Luke's Passion Narrative: An East Asian Global Perspective*, BibIntS 80 (Leiden: Brill, 2006).

Narrative beginnings orient readers to what is ahead and intimate its import. If this is so, Luke 1–2 provides crucial orienting—and disorienting—signals for Luke's audience within the world Rome rules, in which the emperor is supreme. Mary's Song voices praise of God as "Savior" (*sōtēr*, 1:47), redirecting a title of honor typically reserved for emperors (Luke 2:11 also names Jesus "Savior"). Even more radical is the way she images God's project of salvation: it completely reconfigures the power field, demoting rulers and the wealthy and elevating those who lack power, status, and resources (1:51–53). Within the story setting, this revolutionary picture of an "alternative reign"[69] is offstage, hidden-transcript rhetoric spoken in private conversation between two women. But as an opening God's-eye comment on power, it is voiced again in the much more public space of Luke's Gospel.[70]

Another inspired prayer-hymn, spoken by John's father Zechariah, also refigures power relations for God's people within the Roman world: they will be liberated from their "enemies" (1:71, 74), and through a messianic deliverer God will provide "peace" (1:79), parodic reversal of the "peace" imposed by Rome in the celebrated Pax Romana. After Jesus' birth, Simeon delivers an oracle that associates salvation with this newborn child, encompassing glory for Israel and light for the nations (2:32). Rome's gifts to the world are now credited instead to Israel's God. Though in a private message to Jesus' parents, Simeon is speaking in the Jerusalem temple, where immense economic and political power is centered.

Heaven also gets into the act, as Gabriel's birth announcement to Mary, previewing the significance of the child to whom she will give birth, revises the power arrangements in Judea. No longer is Herod the true king of Judea (1:5), for in fulfillment of ancient promise to King David, the Son of God will occupy his throne (1:32–33, recalling 2 Sam 7:12–16). Luke 3 then provides a roster of the rulers in empire-controlled Palestine at the time of John's prophetic ministry of baptism (vv. 1–2), but the reimaging of power relations in chapters 1–2 means a revaluation of the position of all these rulers—even the emperor Tiberius. Jesus alone is the divinely authorized *kyrios* (Lord) and *sōtēr* (Savior).[71]

As Jesus launches his mission, he does so in tune with his mother's

---

69. Warren Carter, "Singing in the Reign: Performing Luke's Songs and Negotiating the Roman Empire (Luke 1–2)," in *Luke-Acts and Empire: Essays in Honor of Robert L. Brawley*, ed. David Rhoads, David Esterline, and Jae Won Lee, PTMS 151 (Eugene, OR: Wipf & Stock, 2011), 23–43, esp. 42–43.

70. All the more so if Esler is right that Luke's audience would have included at least some Roman administrative and military officials (*Community and Gospel*, 210, 217–19).

71. In both inscriptions and literary works, Roman emperors (among them Augustus, Tiberius, Claudius, Nero, Vespasian, Domitian, and Trajan) are acclaimed as *sōtēr* (savior; *salus* in Latin). See Gary Gilbert, "Roman Propaganda and Christian Identity in the Worldview of Luke-Acts," in *Contextualizing Acts: Lukan Narrative and Greco-Roman Discourse*, ed. Todd Penner and Caroline Vander Stichele, SBLSymS 20 (Atlanta: Scholars Press, 2003), 233–56, esp. 237–42.

revolutionary song (Luke 4:18–19; 6:20–26; cf. 1:51–53). He has unparalleled authority as the one through whom God's sovereign rule is now active in the world, but it is power with a difference. He embraces outsiders, heals persons afflicted with sickness and disability, honors those lacking status and resources, at the same time challenging the primacy of household role definitions and the preoccupation with status and honor, evident in such customary practices as benefaction and patronage, reciprocity, and retaliation (e.g., 6:27–36; 9:59–62; 14:7–24, 25–33; 22:24–30). Luke's account of the ministry of Jesus, therefore, amounts to vigorous criticism of the cultural system over which the empire presides.

Luke's Challenges to the Roman Cultural System

- Primacy of household and its conventional roles
- Importance of status and of honor maintenance through
    — Benefaction and patronage
    — Reciprocity
    — Retaliation
- Emperor as sovereign
- "Peace" enforced through military occupation

The peculiar messianic vocation that Jesus embraces was not self-evident, however, to judge from the testing ordeal in the desert, where Jesus wrestles with other notions of power at the prompting of Satan (4:1–13). Jesus has the Holy Spirit's presence as resource, so the outcome is not truly in doubt; nevertheless, at the center of three (representative) tests stands the evil one's offer of dominion over all nations (4:5–6). This offer implies that behind the world rulers then in power—supreme among them, the Roman Empire—lurks the malevolent activity of Satan. Moreover, it links power like Rome's rule over the nations with idolatry—not a huge leap, given the extravagant claims for Rome and its emperors in the imperial propaganda[72] and in universal histories like those of Polybius, Dionysius of Halicarnassus, and Diodorus of Sicily.[73] Jesus refuses the lure of world dominion, however,

---

72. Perhaps no example of this propaganda is more revealing than the Priene Inscription (9 BCE), in which Greeks of the Roman province of Asia celebrate Augustus as Savior and Benefactor and label "the birthday of the god [Augustus]" as the "beginning of good tidings for the world" (ET adapted from M. Eugene Boring, Klaus Berger, and Carsten Colpe, *Hellenistic Commentary to the New Testament* [Nashville: Abingdon Press, 1995], 169).

73. The narrative ascribes these claims to Satan, in the setting of wilderness isolation. This is not an open declaration of revolt by Jesus (or Luke), and the fact that the devil is the speaker raises a question about the credibility of the statement. Still, the exchange forces a choice on Jesus: allegiance to an evil power with which the nations are entangled, or to God. The *Histories*

opting for devotion to God alone; the ensuing account exhibits Jesus' unfailing alignment with the aims and character of God's realm. Rather than wield power to dominate others, he will use it to set them free from oppressive forces (sickness, demons, sins, debts). And he will choose to serve others in humility rather than lord it over them (22:24–30).

As Luke's Gospel adopts language of empire (*basileia*, reign, kingdom; *thronos*, throne; *exousia*, authority, power), there is a measure of imperial mimicry. Ironic parody, however, colors Luke's use of such language. No potent armies here—only two (ambiguous) swords (22:38; cf. vv. 49–52)—and no thrones either, just a cross from which to "reign" as "King of the Jews" (23:36–38; cf. v. 42). The narrative pictures a community in which the vulnerable and powerless, the young and the poor, those on the outside and underside of society, receive honor. Jesus' followers with wealth and privilege relinquish it and focus on the needs of others rather than self-promotion.

Luke's narrative invites its audience to imagine and enter a third space in which a distinctive set of practices prevails, informed by a countercultural understanding of power and status. The ideology of empire does not dominate in this space, though there is no call for overt revolution (the radical rhetoric of Mary's Song notwithstanding). Despite the implied connection between Roman imperial domination and Satan's authority (4:6), however, the narrative offers an ambiguous profile of Rome. There are virtuous, God-honoring centurions (Luke 7:1–10; Acts 10:1–48; cf. Luke 23:47). Roman judicial procedures are administered by flawed officials, yet they have the potential to protect the rights of Roman citizens and sometimes exonerate Jesus' followers (e.g., Acts 19:35–41). The empire cannot finally obstruct the success of their mission to the whole world. Indeed, Roman power becomes a vehicle to accomplish divine purposes. The presentation of Rome and its co-opted agents of local domination is therefore ironic. Despite the empire's enormous capacity to destroy—apparent in Jesus' arrest and execution, serving the "power of darkness" (Luke 22:53), and later in the devastation of holy temple and city—God can make use of imperial power to accomplish purposes of liberation and salvation.

Challenged to take a public stand on payment of the tribute tax to Rome, Jesus sidesteps the either-or trap set for him—say yes and alienate the crowd, say no and be liable for treason—by affirming obligations both to Rome and to God (Luke 20:20–26; cf. 23:2). On the face of it, this appears to be an ambiguous response: how does one weigh these two (at least sometimes) competing claims? Which allegiance should win out in the case of conflict

---

of Polybius (2nd c. BCE), the *Roman Antiquities* of Dionysius of Halicarnassus, and the *Library of History* by Diodorus of Sicily—all present world history in a way that highlights Rome's supremacy. In Luke's story, Roman hegemony yields to the reign (and people) of God. Bonz offers a perceptive analysis of the challenge that Luke's narrative poses to Roman imperial ideology (*Past as Legacy*).

between them: loyalty to Caesar or loyalty to God? By this point in the story, attentive readers have an advantage over Jesus' opponents who have tried to set the trap. The relation of the two obligations is actually quite clear: commitment to serve God overrides all other commitments, even loyalty to the emperor. One can faithfully serve only one master (16:13). The way Jesus has framed his answer encodes ambiguity, but in Luke's full story the audience meets an ideology (better yet, a theologically informed ethic)—a set of norms, values, commitments, and practices—that runs counter to Roman hegemony.

The exchange in Luke 20:20–26 displays Jesus' wit, but his adversaries use his answer against him anyway, during Pilate's interrogation (23:2). Pilate's peremptory examination of the prisoner, though, leads him to the judgment that Jesus is not guilty of any of the charges being leveled against him: opposing payment of the tribute tax, claiming to be king, and inciting the people with his teaching (23:2, 5). Yet at the end of the proceedings, Pilate fails to administer justice; although he repeatedly pronounces Jesus innocent (vv. 4, 14–15, 22), he orders his execution "as they wished" (v. 25). After Jesus' death on the cross, the centurion at the site adds one more Roman officer's validation of Jesus as *dikaios* (righteous, just, 23:47 mg., CEB). The narrative exposes the governor's failure; not Roman governance but Jesus is being portrayed as just.[74]

Luke's narrative exposes flaws in the Roman system: the gap between Greco-Roman cultural values, norms, and practices and those of God's dominion is wide. Rome's military and political supremacy is evident, however. And although Mary's Song does sound revolutionary chords, the Lukan audience hardly perceives the Gospel as a call to arms, urging open, violent resistance to the empire. For Jesus' followers, he (not the emperor) is the true sovereign (*kyrios*), and he insists on uncompromising commitment to God's work and ways. But Luke does not push them down the path toward open rebellion.

Luke's two books show ambivalence about Roman authority and do not advocate rebellion. Yet the claim that *this* history, not Rome's, is the world history that holds the future is bold in the setting of the Roman Empire. This is not sedition, but it is serious "cultural disruption"; it is not a "platform for revolution"[75] but an invitation to a peculiar community and a distinctive way of life—a third space in which the claims, values, and commitments of God's reign can be embodied in practice. Roman military and political supremacy will eventually give way to God's reign, but not until the eschatological

---

74. In Acts, too, the local governing elite sometimes violate norms of justice: Philippian magistrates mistreat Paul, a Roman citizen (16:35–39), and the priestly elite at Jerusalem plot Paul's murder while he is in custody (23:12–15; 25:1–4).

75. C. Kavin Rowe, *World Upside Down: Reading Acts in the Graeco-Roman Age* (New York: Oxford University Press, 2009), 149–50.

future. Meanwhile, to judge from the Gospel's narrative sequel, the destabilizing potential of the countercultural communal vision that marks Jesus' ministry does not materialize completely. That potential remains encoded within the narrative, ready for later readers to perceive and activate.

Concluding Reflection: The Aims and Impact of Luke's Narrative

What would a community shaped by the theological convictions and ethical commitments of Luke's Gospel look like? How well do its aims, whether stated in the preface or implied by the ensuing narrative, square with its rhetorical impact on first-century and twenty-first-century readers? One way to answer these questions is to examine the performance of Jesus' followers in the Gospel's narrative sequel. While they do not perfectly enact Jesus' vision for the community of disciples, there are important connections.[76] The sovereignty of God is boldly proclaimed in the context of empire (e.g., Acts 5:29–32; 10:34–43; 17:22–31; 28:23). Wealth is shared to address the needs of all (e.g., 2:43–47; 4:32–37), and health is restored to persons who are sick or experience disability (e.g., 3:1–10; 5:12–16). With prodding from the mission-directing Spirit of God, the apostolic community embraces outsiders (e.g., Samaritans in 8:4–25; Gentiles in 10:1–11:18; 15:1–21). Even though this surely idyllic profile of the Acts community may somewhat dull the sharp, countercultural, radical edge of Jesus' performance of God's reign in word and act, the narrative does offer many images of full-bodied conversion of imagination and practice that respond faithfully to the message of the gospel.[77] Still, an audience that revisits the Gospel narrative after hearing the story related in book 2 may well discern important gaps between promise (of the Gospel) and performance (in Acts)—and not just in the extremes of failure represented by deceiving Ananias and Sapphira (5:1–11) and greedy Simon Magus (8:18–24).

The narrative roots the message and the people in the story and Scriptures of Israel and celebrates the fulfillment of hopes instilled by that story and those Scriptures. But if Luke is to be believed, this is the story not just of a particular people but of all peoples, to the farthest reaches of the earth (Acts 1:8). It is an expansive vision of a multiethnic, multicultural people of God, of Abraham's children equipped to fulfill their vocation in and to

76. This point is emphasized by Luke Timothy Johnson, with special focus on the continuity between the prophetic character of the Lukan Jesus' ministry and the portrayal of the early church in Acts (*Prophetic Jesus, Prophetic Church: The Challenge of Luke-Acts to Contemporary Christians* [Grand Rapids: Wm. B. Eerdmans Publishing Co., 2011]).

77. For a provocative, multidisciplinary probing of the topic of conversion in Luke and Acts, drawing from the neurosciences and cognitive metaphor theory, see Joel B. Green, *Conversion in Luke-Acts: Divine Action, Human Cognition, and the People of God* (Grand Rapids: Baker Academic, 2015).

the whole world. So from the start of Jesus' ministry as God's prophet and Israel's Messiah, people are stretched beyond their comfort zones: carefully constructed and well-established social boundaries are challenged and sometimes simply transgressed. The divine hospitality, mirrored in Jesus' word pictures and meals and acts of forgiveness and healing, is provocatively boundary crossing and inclusive.

With restoration of the lost, solidarity with the dishonored and dishonorable, and the elevation of the low-status and impoverished, God's work of salvation is fashioning a different kind of community. All of this means both continuity and discontinuity in the long history of God's people, reaching from Abraham to the present. Through surprising twists and turns, across improbable thresholds, it is the faithful, covenant-keeping, promise-honoring God who is driving the history. What appear to be innovations turn out to be Torah and Prophets sprung to life anew for a new day and setting. Unlike the other Gospels, Luke explicitly narrates (in Acts) the movement of Jesus' followers into that new day and setting, in a mission that bridges to the time and activity of Luke's audience.

As they reflect on this long story and this very large world stage, they have much challenge to consider, not least countercultural teaching about status seeking, wealth, and patronage. The repeating images of vertical status reversal are not designed to put the wealthy and secure at ease! Luke's narrative is forming and informing a third-space community that will share resources, honor the least, restore the lost, and love the outsider, even the enemy, eschewing retaliation and the lure of power. So what will this mean for group members (or potential members) who enjoy a measure of power, influence, and comfort? What will commitment to this group and cause ask of them? What will it demand of them in relation to others in the group and beyond? Participation in a heterogeneous, culturally diverse group in which important differentiating lines of status, privilege, and power have become so blurred will be challenging on all sides—whether in the setting of imperial Rome in the late first or early second century or the tense geopolitical realities of the early twenty-first century.

Early in this chapter I suggested that Luke's literary project is an exercise in legitimation. Indeed, although some of the claims it advances may seem improbable and may appear to entail significant and discordant discontinuities (not least the death of the Messiah and the movement's growing disfavor with many Jews and the incorporation of many Gentiles), this is— for Theophilus and others hearing the narrative with and after him if they accept it as reliable teaching—the continuing story of Israel and the saving activity of Israel's faithful God. So it is an identity-nourishing narrative that also addresses questions of theodicy: in such a history as this, what can God possibly be up to? (Readers today may also query: In a world like ours, what can God possibly be up to?) Yet at the same time, it is a narrative deeply concerned with human response to the divine presence in human history, a narrative invested in forming the moral character of a very peculiar people. To this multiethnic, multicultural people drawn from every social level and life circumstance in all nations, God has entrusted the Spirit leading and Spirit empowerment to embody in their life together the ongoing vitality of God's dominion—until the Messiah/Lord returns "in the same way as you saw him go into heaven" (Acts 1:11b). So, in the meantime, "why do you stand looking up toward heaven?" (v. 11a). For now, the work, the witness, the practices of faith and nurture of this border-crossing community are right here on earth.

6. The Gospel according to John

From its first appearance, the Gospel of John has stood out as a unique—and remarkable—narrative about Jesus. For many readers across the centuries, the comment of Clement of Alexandria has rung true: "John, last of all, conscious that the outward facts had been set forth in the Gospels [i.e., the Synoptics], was urged on by his disciples, and divinely moved by the Spirit, composed a spiritual Gospel" (as reported by Eusebius, *Hist. eccl.* 6.14.7). There are important points of contact between John and the other canonical Gospels, but readers who come to this story after engaging the accounts of Matthew, Mark, and Luke cannot fail to be struck by the differences in John's rendition. Here are just a few of the most obvious differences:

- *Space and time* are figured differently: Jerusalem and Judea emerge as the clear focus of Jesus' activity, which spans three Passovers (cf. the singular Passover in the Synoptics), hence more than two years.
- *Thematic focus* and the customary *idiom and vocabulary* of Jesus diverge dramatically as well: the prominent Synoptic image of the *basileia tou theou* (reign/realm of God) disappears almost completely, its place largely assumed by eternal life; and Jesus' predilection for brief, witty aphorisms and parables yields in John to extensive monologues and contentious debates in which Jesus' own identity and role become the central concern. As in Mark, Jesus is often misunderstood by other characters, but much of the time John's Jesus seems deliberately to provoke misunderstanding with a series of riddles.
- While John, like the other Gospels, presents *Jesus as a healer*, stories of his healing activity are fewer in number but receive substantial elaboration—as "signs" (*sēmeia*) that point to the identity and significance of Jesus himself and exemplify the benefactions that he provides to all who have faith, even as other observers vigorously contest his articulation of their meaning. (Notably, John also does not report any encounters with the demon-possessed among the healing miracles.)
- *On Trial*. As in the other New Testament Gospels, Jesus' public ministry culminates in his crucifixion, by order of the governor Pontius Pilate, but no account of a formal interrogation by a council convened by the high priest precedes Pilate's judicial examination of the prisoner. Instead, Jesus' entire ministry is cast as a sustained trial in which his actions and claims are examined by leaders (esp. Pharisees) among

his Jewish contemporaries. The event precipitating his arrest is not a disruptive act in the temple but the restoration of life to Lazarus. (Also, the crucifixion occurs at midday *before* the Passover evening rather than on the day following, as in the Synoptics.)

- The *ministry-spanning* debates about the meaning and significance of Jesus' words and actions fit within a sharply dualistic framework in which an array of opposites are paired: light and darkness, life and death, truth and lie (falsehood), from above and from below, and so on.

Where on earth did such a remarkable version of the story of Jesus come from?

Historical Questions

Who?

As with the Synoptic Gospels, the developing Christian tradition first securely attaches an author's name to this "Fourth" Gospel,[1] as far as we can tell, well into the second century CE. Writing around 180, Irenaeus credits the publishing of a Gospel—in the city of Ephesus—to John "the disciple of the Lord, who had also leaned on his breast" (*Haer.* 3.1.1), identifying the author as the beloved disciple, who plays a prominent role in the narrative beginning in the Last Supper scene (John 13:23–25). Elsewhere Irenaeus clearly assumes that this disciple named John is the apostle John, son of Zebedee (*Haer.* 3.3.4). He appears to share this assumption with a gnostic writer whom he criticizes, Ptolemy, who was associated with the school of Valentinus (*Haer.* 1.8.5).

One of the intriguing details in the reception history of the Fourth Gospel is that the earliest known commentary on John was written by another Valentinian gnostic, Heracleon. He too appears to have thought that the Gospel was composed by "John, the disciple of the Lord" (according to Origen in *Comm. John* 6.3). In view of the popularity of this Gospel among second- and third-century groups that the emerging "Great Church" left behind as heretical—notably Valentinian gnostics and also Montanists, who especially prized John's teaching regarding the Paraclete/Spirit—it was no doubt important that the Gospel find a comfortable authorial home in the circle of the apostles. Hence, if the tag "John, the disciple of the Lord" originally pointed not to the apostolic figure but to "John the presbyter [elder],"[2]

---

1. Scholars working on the Gospel according to John often refer to it as the Fourth Gospel, and for stylistic variation I will sometimes do so in this chapter, yet without assuming that John was the last of the four canonical Gospels to be composed. This is possible but not certain, given the complexity of the interactions among Synoptic and Johannine traditions in the formation history of these Gospels.

2. This is vigorously argued by Richard J. Bauckham, *The Testimony of the Beloved Disciple: Narrative, History, and Theology in the Gospel of John* (Grand Rapids: Baker Academic, 2007), 33–72.

the transfer in authorship credit to John, son of Zebedee, is intelligible (even though he is explicitly mentioned only in John 21:2, and even there only as "son of Zebedee").

Certainly, in its full form (of twenty-one chapters), the Gospel supplies strong evidence that it presents (or at least claims to present) reliable teaching grounded in the eyewitness testimony of the "disciple whom Jesus loved" (see John 19:35; 21:20, 24). That mysterious character remains anonymous throughout the narrative (he is mentioned in 13:23; 19:26–27, 35; 20:3–10; 21:7, 20–23; probably also in 18:15, "that disciple"). A final-stage narrator's or editor's "we" attributes the writing of the Gospel to that anonymous disciple (21:24), although the "we" narrator's voice-over in the crucifixion scene accents this disciple's role as authoritative eyewitness for at least this portion of the narrative rather than as author (19:35). This anonymous character probably represents an actual disciple known to the Gospel's first audience; nevertheless, the eyewitness role he plays is a technique of narration that gives "an impression of verisimilitude" and "legitimate[s] the narrator's perspective on the significance of the person of Jesus"; his status as one especially loved by Jesus guarantees the "credibility and reliability of his witness."[3]

An intriguing alternative explanation of the initial linking of the Gospel to the name of John suggests that the connection may have arisen from a (mis)reading of passages highlighting the testimony of the baptizing witness John, which is pivotal in the prologue (1:6–8, 15) and prominent early in the narrative (1:19–37; 3:23–30; cf. 5:32–36).[4] Whatever explains the origin of the tradition that John (whether presbyter or apostle) composed the Fourth Gospel, the authorship of this account, like its Synoptic Gospel counterparts, is anonymous.[5] Evaluating the reliability of its testimony to Jesus' career, ostensibly resting on the eyewitness testimony of an intimate associate of Jesus, the "disciple whom Jesus loved," must follow careful analysis of the narrative's content.

The implied author of the narrative is able to record events in and around Jerusalem and tells the story in a fashion that has affinities with the sharp dualism of the Dead Sea Scrolls, though the differences from the scrolls do

---

3. Andrew Lincoln, *The Gospel according to Saint John*, BNTC 4 (Peabody, MA: Hendrickson Publishers, 2005), 24–25.

4. See J. Ramsey Michaels, *The Gospel of John*, NICNT (Grand Rapids: Wm. B. Eerdmans Publishing Co., 2010), 16–17.

5. For detailed discussion of the authorship of the Fourth Gospel, see C. K. Barrett, *The Gospel according to St. John: An Introduction with Commentary and Notes on the Greek Text*, 2nd rev. ed. (Philadelphia: Westminster Press, 1978), 100–109; Raymond E. Brown, *The Gospel according to John*, 2 vols., AB 29–29A (Garden City, NY: Doubleday, 1966–70), 1:lxxxvii–cii; Rudolf Schnackenburg, *The Gospel according to St. John*, 3 vols. (New York: Crossroad, 1982), 1:75–104; Michaels, *Gospel of John*, 5–24; Bauckham, *Testimony of the Beloved Disciple*, 33–72. Also, see R. Alan Culpepper, *John, the Son of Zebedee: The Life of a Legend* (Columbia: University of South Carolina Press, 1994).

not suggest any direct association between the two.[6] The narrative is permeated by conflict between Jesus and his followers, on the one hand, and "the Jews," on the other; three times the Gospel pictures or projects conflict so intense that it issues in severance from the synagogue (*aposynagōgos* in 9:22; 12:42; 16:2; cf. 9:35). John often alludes to or quotes the Jewish Scriptures (explicit citations of OT texts being reserved for the passion narrative), and frequent references to various Jewish festivals provide much of the narrative structure: Passover in 2:13, 23; 6:4; 11:55; 12:1; 13:1; 18:28, 39; 19:14; Booths in 7:2; Hanukkah (Dedication) in 10:22. Moreover, Moses and Abraham are invoked as key scriptural witnesses to Jesus (see 1:45; 5:45–46; 8:56)—and in settings of controversy suggesting that the claim to Jewish tradition John is staking is vigorously contested in the world of the author and earliest audience.

When and Where?   The papyrus manuscript P[52], which contains an excerpt of John 18 (fragments of vv. 31–33, 36–38), dates from the first half of the second century CE. Thus at least some version of the Gospel must have appeared no later than the early second century. It has been common to assume that a writing advancing such a "high" Christology (Jesus' identity with God), and appearing to reflect a rupture in the synagogue over Johannine theological claims, must be the latest of the canonical Gospels, especially if it shows familiarity with one or more of the other Synoptics. However, notions of progressive development in Christology are dubious: consider, for example, the robust Christology conveyed already at mid-first century in the "Christ hymn" of Philippians 2:6–11! Moreover, conflict within synagogues that led to voluntary or forced separation occurred at varying paces and levels of intensity in various locations and cannot provide a reliable index to a book's dating. And if the Fourth Gospel draws from traditions that overlap and interact with the traditions that have been taken up in the Synoptics, but does not depend on one or more of these accounts as sources, it is conceivable that at least some version of John (perhaps before a revision that appended ch. 21?) appeared before Luke or (less likely) Matthew. Still, a date late in the first century, and later than at least Mark and Matthew, is as likely as any other.

Like P[52], two other early manuscript witnesses to the Fourth Gospel, the Bodmer papyri identified as P[66] and P[75] (early 3rd c. CE), were discovered in Egypt. Since most surviving New Testament papyrus manuscripts were preserved in the arid climate there, however, an Egyptian source for John's composition, while possible, is not assured. Early Christian tradition places the composition of the Fourth Gospel in Ephesus (e.g., Irenaeus, *Haer.* 3.1.1), but this too is far from certain.[7] Some scholars are inclined to accept the

6. Cf. Brown, *Gospel according to John,* 1:lxiii: the affinities between the Fourth Gospel and the Dead Sea Scrolls suggest not direct literary dependence but "familiarity with the types of thought exhibited in the scrolls."

7. Michaels judges the evidence for Ephesus "rather thin" but still deems that site a "reasonable guess" (*Gospel of John,* 37).

traditional site of Ephesus for John's final composition yet also acknowledge the presence of elements suggesting closer proximity to Palestine, such as the following:

- Familiarity with specific aspects of Palestinian topography[8]
- Emphasis on Jewish festivals as a structuring device for the narrative (as noted above)
- Affinities with features of the Dead Sea Scrolls[9]
- The Gospel's intensive debates regarding interpretation and practice of the Torah, with particular interest in the witness of Scripture to Jesus' messianic identity[10]

Several scholars have therefore proposed scenarios that involve a complex history of composition and reception and that follow the Johannine group from an original home in Palestine or Syria to the Roman province of Asia and its most important city, Ephesus.[11] Such a complex chronology and journey for the Gospel and its author and earliest audiences is possible but not provable. The analysis of John's narrative presented in this chapter assumes its setting within the Roman Empire, probably in a city in the eastern part of the empire, and a likely final composition date in the late first or early second century—yet without placing interpretive weight on more specific guesses about date or place(s) of initial dissemination.[12]

8. See Paul N. Anderson, *From Crisis to Christ: A Contextual Introduction to the New Testament* (Nashville: Abingdon Press, 2014), 163–64; idem, *The Riddles of the Fourth Gospel: An Introduction to John* (Minneapolis: Fortress Press, 2011), 195–220; Marianne Meye Thompson, *John: A Commentary*, NTL (Louisville, KY: Westminster John Knox Press, 2015), 18–19.

9. Notice the essays gathered in *John and the Dead Sea Scrolls*, ed. James H. Charlesworth (New York: Crossroad, 1990); and *John, Qumran, and the Dead Sea Scrolls: Sixty Years of Discovery and Debate*, ed. Mary L. Coloe and Tom Thatcher, EJL 32 (Atlanta: SBL Press, 2011). There are also affinities between the Fourth Gospel and the Odes of Solomon; see Schnackenburg, *Gospel according to St. John*, 1:143–45.

10. See, e.g., 5:9–16 (Sabbath observance); 5:45–47 (Moses invoked as witness to Jesus); 6:25–60 (manna and bread from heaven); 7:14–24 (Sabbath and circumcision); 7:37–43 (the Messiah's origins); 8:12–20 (legitimate testimony); 8:31–59 (status as children of Abraham).

11. An influential proponent of such a scenario is Raymond E. Brown; see, e.g., *Gospel according to John*, 1:xxxiv–xxxix; idem, *Community of the Beloved Disciple*. More recently, Paul Anderson has offered a similar historical reconstruction: *The Christology of the Fourth Gospel: Its Unity and Disunity in the Light of John 6*, WUNT 2/78 (Tübingen: Mohr Siebeck, 1996), 245–48; idem, *The Riddles of the Fourth Gospel: An Introduction to John* (Minneapolis: Fortress Press, 2010), 134–41. The Letters 1–3 John, esp. 1 John, share common vocabulary and conviction with the Fourth Gospel and probably afford a glimpse of later internal struggles within the Johannine groups, which—despite Jesus' "new commandment" to "love one another" (John 13:34; 15:12, 17) and despite his fervent petition for the unity of his later followers (17:20–23)— unraveled and eventually splintered over divergent christological beliefs and uncharitable views toward one another (e.g., 1 John 2:18–19; cf. 4:20; 2 John 7–11; 3 John 9–10).

12. Recognizing the indeterminacy regarding dating and provenance in internal and external evidence alike, Barrett offers the range of 90–140 CE for the Gospel's composition (*Gospel according to John*, 127–28) and, while assessing the case for Ephesus as "not strong" (129), concedes that a convincing case cannot be made for other sites such as Alexandria and (Syrian) Antioch and that the hypothesis of origin in Ephesus at least permits "conjectural" attempts to address the question of the author's identity (131). One must be wary of building a castle with such a flimsy deck of cards.

What?

Like the Synoptics, John employs literary conventions associated with Greco-Roman biography[13] but does so in its own, sometimes peculiar way. As Attridge has emphasized, the various conventional forms deployed in the Johannine narrative have consistently undergone "genre bending."[14] Emphasizing the motif of contested testimony that pervades the account of Jesus' public activity in the Fourth Gospel, Lincoln suggests that John employs the genre of biography (*bios*) not simply to relate the story of Jesus on trial but also to provide compelling testimony to him. This *bios* presents a plot that is "dominated by the motif of the trial"; like other ancient biographies, it has "an apologetic and polemical function," and "biography draws out the significance of Jesus' career in a context where this significance is under dispute."[15]

Exactly what that dispute was, and where and with whom, has been much discussed. Especially influential in the last half century has been the proposal of J. Louis Martyn that the Fourth Gospel tells the story of Jesus' conflict with "the Jews"—even picturing the outcome of expulsion from the synagogue (9:22, 35; 12:42; 16:2)—in a way that retrojects into his lifetime and ministry a wrenching conflict that actually occurred later in the experience of the Johannine community.[16] While specific details of Martyn's historical reconstruction have received vigorous critique—especially his focusing the synagogue conflict through the lens of the Birkat Haminim (invoking a "curse on the heretics" in the course of the liturgical prayer Eighteen Benedictions)—the basic approach remains plausible and interpretively fruitful.

Excursus: J. Louis Martyn's Reconstruction of the Setting of the Fourth Gospel: Critical Appraisals

Among Martyn's critics, considerable attention has been devoted to his handling of historical evidence relating to the Birkat Haminim.[17] Reinhartz argues that the narrative of John reflects not only severe conflict between Jesus believers and the synagogue but also more positive interactions, and therefore that the Johannine

---

13. See, e.g., Richard A. Burridge, *What Are the Gospels? A Comparison with Graeco-Roman Biography* (Cambridge: Cambridge University Press, 1992), 220–39.

14. Harold Attridge, "Genre Bending in the Fourth Gospel," *JBL* 121 (2002): 3–21. Attridge summarizes John's genre-bending moves eloquently: "Revealing words reveal riddles; realistic similitudes become surreal; words of testimony undercut the validity of any ordinary act of testifying; words of farewell become words of powerful presence; words of prayer negate the distance between worshiper and God; words that signify shame, death on a cross, become words that enshrine value, allure disciples, give a command, and glorify God" (21).

15. Andrew T. Lincoln, *Truth on Trial: The Lawsuit Motif in the Fourth Gospel* (Peabody, MA: Hendrickson Publishers, 2000), 169–71, esp. 171.

16. J. Louis Martyn, *History and Theology in the Fourth Gospel*, 3rd ed. (Louisville, KY: Westminster John Knox Press, 2003; orig., Nashville: Abingdon Press, 1968).

17. See, e.g., Reuven Kimelman, "'*Birkat Ha-Minim*' and the Lack of Evidence for an Anti-Christian Jewish Prayer in late Antiquity," in *Jewish and Christian Self-Definition*, vol. 2,

community's relation to the synagogue was much more ambiguous than Martyn thought.[18] Recently a quite different tack has been taken by Bernier, who contends that the exercise of discipline separating persons from synagogue participation, contrary to Martyn's assumptions, is in fact attested for the period of Jesus' lifetime.[19] These varying criticisms notwithstanding, many interpreters of John's Gospel continue to find Martyn's two-level reading of the conflict with "the Jews" in this narrative instructive.[20] Martinus de Boer puts the point sharply: the problem "is not 'the Jews' as a group or a people but hostile, murderous behavior directed at God's Jewish envoy and his Jewish followers"; the designation "the Jews" is "probably an ironic acknowledgment of the claim on the part of Jewish authorities in the synagogue to be the authoritative arbiters of a genuinely Jewish identity."[21]

Raimo Hakola reverses the direction of the argument. Rather than seeing the Fourth Gospel as responding to hostility from the rabbis or synagogue, Hakola suggests "that the Johannine Christians themselves interpreted their faith in Jesus in such a way that it led them on a collision course with basic matters of Jewishness."[22] The dualism in John "may be taken as both a result of the growing alienation of the Johannine group from its surrounding society and as an attempt to intensify this alienation."[23] Moreover, the character of Jesus in John "can be seen as a self-expression of a community which was willing to see itself as the culmination of Jewish tradition although it had turned away from central aspects of this tradition. In the symbolic universe of the Johannine Christians, Jesus the Jew and the Messiah formed a bridge between their Jewish heritage and their actual alienation from Jewish identity."[24]

Drawing from the social sciences in addition to literary and historical analysis, Neyrey sees the conflict proceeding in both directions; he holds that the Fourth Gospel's "high Christology" both "developed in a situation of conflict" and "was in turn shaped by the mounting conflict it provoked. The synagogue could never tolerate claims such as were made about Jesus."[25] Neyrey's nuancing of the Martyn proposal is

Aspects of Judaism in the Graeco-Roman Period, ed. E. P. Sanders, with A. I. Baumgarten and Alan Mendelson (Philadelphia: Fortress Press, 1981), 226–44, 391–403; Daniel Boyarin, "Justin Martyr Invents Judaism," *Church History* 70 (2001): 427–61.

18. Adele Reinhartz, *Befriending the Beloved Disciple: A Jewish Reading of the Gospel of John* (New York: Continuum, 2001), 37–40.

19. Jonathan Bernier, Aposynagōgos *and the Historical Jesus in John: Rethinking the Historicity of the Johannine Expulsion Passages*, BibIntS 122 (Leiden: Brill, 2013), 72 and passim.

20. Among many others, see David Rensberger, *Johannine Faith and Liberating Community* (Philadelphia: Westminster Press, 1988); Lincoln, *Gospel according to St. John*, 82–84; Francis J. Moloney, *The Gospel of John*, SP 4 (Collegeville, MN: Liturgical Press, 1998), 2–4; Martinus C. de Boer, "The Depiction of 'the Jews' in John's Gospel: Matters of Behavior and Identity," in *Anti-Judaism and the Fourth Gospel*, ed. Reimund Bieringer, Didier Pollefeyt, and Frederique Vandecasteele-Vanneuville (Louisville, KY: Westminster John Knox Press, 2001), 141–57.

21. De Boer, "Depiction of 'the Jews' in John's Gospel," 142.

22. Raimo Hakola, *Identity Matters: John, the Jews and Jewishness*, NovTSup 118 (Leiden: Brill, 2005), 216.

23. Ibid., 217.

24. Ibid., 218–19.

25. Jerome H. Neyrey, *An Ideology of Revolt: John's Christology in Social-Science Perspective* (Philadelphia: Fortress Press, 1988), 211.

helpful, though he probably underestimates the tolerance of early Judaism for variant theological positions.[26]

John's narrative does not invent the theme of conflict between Jesus and other Jewish teachers, which is amply attested in the Synoptic Gospels as well. However, John intensifies the conflict, dramatically increases its stakes, and focuses it sharply on christological claims, especially concerning the relation of Jesus as Son to God as Father and the "divine identity" of Jesus with God—in tensive interaction with the Jewish commitment to one God alone. All of this is framed in a way that reflects the later beliefs and experiences of the Johannine groups rather than Jesus' own career. In principle, the same process shaped the other canonical Gospels, whose presentations of Jesus' ministry are also refracted through later beliefs and circumstances. Yet the christological preoccupations on which John's account centers set John apart. Later conflicts *within* the Johannine groups also evidently revolved in large measure around differing understandings of the identity and status of Jesus—as Son of God who lived as an embodied self and really suffered (e.g., 1 John 2:18–23; 4:1–6; 5:6–12). This historical development, in which synagogue conflicts largely over christological claims morphed into bitter intramural strife, lends additional plausibility to the hypothesis that the Johannine narrative encodes the later experience of Johannine groups.

The Question of John's Relation to the Synoptic Gospels

The opening paragraphs of this chapter identified several of the most obvious differences between John's narrative and its Synoptic counterparts. John's Gospel marches to the beat of a different drummer than the Synoptic percussion section. At the same time, however, there are significant and often intriguing convergences and connections between John and one or more of the Synoptics. John too presents Jesus as a Messiah who teaches and heals, gathers around him a group of disciples, and enters into conflict with Jewish leaders. The Fourth Gospel reports some of the same events, such as the miraculous feeding of a large crowd, followed by Jesus' walking on water (6:1–21); an anointing of Jesus by a woman (12:1–8); a triumphal entry into Jerusalem (12:12–16); an angry gesture in the temple, overturning the tables of the money changers (2:14–17); betrayal by Judas, arrest, threefold denial by Peter, judicial interrogation by Pilate, and crucifixion as "King of the Jews" (chs. 18–19); and resurrection appearances (chs. 20–21, though

26. On this point, see Daniel Boyarin, *The Jewish Gospels: The Story of the Jewish Christ* (New York: New Press, 2012).

apart from Mary Magdalene's role as first witness in 20:1–2, the details are mostly different).

Probing more closely, one finds a number of intriguing connections between John and Mark, and especially between John and Luke. To illustrate, I will identify several points of contact between the Fourth Gospel and Luke:[27]

- *Luke 7:36–50 and John 12:1–8.* Although John's version bears closer resemblance thematically and in narrative placement to the parallel episodes in Mark and Matthew, only Luke and John share the detail that a woman anoints Jesus' feet rather than his head and then dries them with her hair (Luke 7:38; John 12:3).
- *Luke 9:10–22 and John 6* differ from Mark and Matthew by narrating only *one feeding miracle*, followed closely by Peter's confession regarding Jesus' identity.
- *The passion narratives in Luke and John* share several features that diverge from Mark and Matthew, among them the following: Judas's act of betrayal is attributed to intervention by Satan (Luke 22:3; John 13:27); a sword strikes the *right* ear of the high priest's slave in the arrest scene (Luke 22:50; John 18:10); no flight of the disciples is mentioned (Luke 22:53; John 18:11–12); no witnesses are summoned in a Jewish proceeding against Jesus, before his conveyance to Pilate; Pilate three times affirms Jesus' innocence (Luke 23:4, 14, 22; John 18:38; 19:4, 6); and Jesus' antagonists voice a double shout "Crucify! Crucify!" (though in different verb tenses; Luke 23:20–23; John 19:4–6).
- *The literary cartography of Luke and John* presents converging geographic notices. Each Gospel signals positive interest in Samaria as a productive mission site in the early years of the movement (Luke 10:30–35; 17:11–19 [reversing 9:52–55]; Acts 8; John 4:1–42). And both Luke and John locate the resurrection-appearance narratives in the vicinity of Jerusalem, not in Galilee (as in Matt 28 and, in prospect, Mark 16). John 21 does, however, shift the setting to Galilee—specifically, the Lake of Tiberias (= "Lake Gennesaret" [Luke] or "Sea of Galilee"), a fitting locale given the fishing expedition the narrator offers as the occasion for a renewed disciple summons to Peter.[28]
- *In the resurrection-appearance stories,* despite the wide variation in the four canonical Gospels, there are fascinating resemblances between John 20–21 and Luke 24 (and 5:1–11). For example, both John 20:3–6

27. On the points of contact between John and Mark, see, e.g., Barrett, *Gospel according to St. John*, 43–45.

28. Mark A. Matson provides a thorough catalog of features common to Luke and John (*In Dialogue with Another Gospel? The Influence of the Fourth Gospel on the Passion Narrative of the Gospel of Luke*, SBLDS 178 [Atlanta: SBL Press, 2001], 91–163).

and Luke 24:12 relate a disciple's sprint to the empty tomb (in Luke, Peter runs; in John, the beloved disciple runs ahead of Peter), followed by a stooping to peer into the tomb and a glimpse of linen (burial) cloths (featuring Peter in Luke, the beloved disciple in John). Several common or similar motifs appear in John 20:19–29 and Luke 24:36–49: the disciples' fear, doubt or disbelief, and joy; a narrative interest in demonstrating the continuity between the (embodied) crucified and resurrected Jesus; and the granting of the Spirit, whether experienced within the scene (John) or anticipated (Luke). Yet there is limited vocabulary and phrasing common to the two narratives, and Luke and John develop the similar motifs in different ways. Moreover, in both John 21:1–14 and Luke 5:1–11, Jesus choreographs a large catch of fish in a scene that includes a group of disciples, among them Peter, but there is almost no identical phrasing in the two passages, and they are placed in different narrative settings.

What is one to make of this complex pattern: occasional, striking agreements in detail or phrasing in accounts that otherwise differ so substantially and deliver such contrasting profiles of Jesus' character and voice?[29] Does John's narrative presuppose one or another of the Synoptic narratives? If so, why doesn't John's author conform the account more closely to Synoptic sources, in a way comparable to the patterns of borrowing we encounter in the case of the Synoptics (however the precise interrelationships among them are conceived)? Or does John, or some stage in the emerging Johannine tradition, know of *traditions* that underlie one or more of the Synoptic Gospels but not the completed Gospel narratives? Or should one reverse the direction of influence, crediting John's Gospel or some stage of its formation as a source drawn upon by one or more of the Synoptics? (Such a case can most plausibly be made for Luke.)

Complicating the analysis are the fluidity of the textual transmission of the first Christian Gospels, including some textual interpolations aimed to achieve greater conformity among the Gospels, and the complexity of the compositional and redactional histories of the individual narratives. Given those "moving targets," how can one with any confidence and persuasiveness chart the direction of influence between a Synoptic Gospel and John? My own inclination is to prefer explanations of similarities between John and one or more Synoptic Gospel as the result of interacting traditions, but the matter is far from certain. Even if John's author had access to one or more of the other canonical Gospels in something resembling their present

29. Orientation to an enormous body of literature on John and the Synoptics may be gained by sampling D. Moody Smith's and Frans Neirynck's multiple contributions, spanning several decades, and the literature cited therein. Especially helpful is Smith, *John among the Gospels*, 2nd ed. (Columbia: University of South Carolina Press, 2001).

form, however, it makes best sense to read John's account as the distinctive narrative that it is, without seeking at every point of divergence from the other Gospels to explain the differences in terms of specific editorial moves by the Fourth Evangelist.

Literary Design

John's narrative falls into roughly two halves. After an opening prologue that introduces major themes of the account to follow (1:1–18), we see the following:

- John 1:19–12:50 presents the public ministry—the works (*erga*) or signs (*sēmeia*) and words (*logoi*)—of Jesus.
- John 13:1–20:31 prepares the disciples (and readers) for Jesus' death/ departure in an extensive set of farewell-discourse monologues and dialogues (13:1–17:26), then narrates his arrest, trial, crucifixion, and resurrection encounters with his disciples (18:1–20:29).

An epilogue (20:30–31) extends through 21:25 in the canonical form of the Gospel; John 21 narrates the resurrected Jesus' final encounter with several followers, a scene that resolves important suspended narrative concerns— especially the rehabilitation of Peter, the future leadership roles of Peter and the beloved disciple, and the disciple group's mandate for mission beyond its boundaries. Each major half of the Gospel ends with a section that focuses on the nexus of signs, belief (or unbelief), and life (12:37–50; 20:30–31).[30]

After providing an outline of the Gospel's structure, I will walk readers through the narrative in considerable detail, drawing attention to several techniques of narration and highlighting prominent motifs and concerns. Afterward I will briefly develop some of these strategies of narration: riddle and misunderstanding, explanatory comments, metaphor, duality or polarity, revelation through signs, and revelation through discourse and debate.

Outline of the Literary Structure of John's Gospel

1:1–18	Preface (overture) placing the story in cosmic-eternal context and sounding major themes of the Gospel
1:19–12:50	Jesus' ministry of work (sign) and word in Galilee and especially Judea
1:19–51	John the baptizing prophet's witness to Jesus and the first recruitment of disciples
2:1–4:54	Signs, enigmatic teaching, and Samaritan witness

---

30. See Thompson, *John*, 16.

- Sign at Cana in Galilee: Wedding wine (2:1–12)
- Symbolic act in the temple and signs in Jerusalem (2:13–25)
- "Nick at night": Revelation in the dark and coming to the light (3:1–21)
- Another round of testimony from the baptizing prophet John—his voice blending with the narrator's (3:22–36)
- Jesus finds a Samaritan witness at Jacob's well (4:1–42).
- Sign at Capernaum (from Cana) in Galilee: restored health for a royal official's son (4:43–54).

5:1–10:42	Jesus performs and interprets signs, and both word and deed provoke intensifying opposition.
11:1–12:50	Jesus performs a climactic sign, restoring life to Lazarus—eliciting both faith and the Judean council's decision to have him killed—and concludes his public activity.
13:1–17:26	In symbolic gesture and lengthy discourse with dialogue, Jesus prepares his intimate followers—friends—for his departure and prays for their unity and their well-being in future mission under duress.
18:1–19:42	Jesus is arrested, is interrogated by the elite priest Annas and especially the Roman prefect Pilate, and is exalted through crucifixion-death.
20:1–31	Empty tomb and resurrection appearances to disciples, with a first epilogue
21:1–25	Final resurrection appearance, rehabilitation of the denying disciple Peter, and a second epilogue

Reading through the Story

John's Gospel does not open with the baptism of Jesus by John (as Mark does), or with a genealogy tracing Jesus' roots back to Abraham (as Matthew does), or with the birth and infancy of John the Baptizer and Jesus (as Luke does). Instead, John begins at the beginning, the beginning of the *kosmos*: "In the beginning was the Word [*Logos*], and the Word was with God, and the Word was God. He was in the beginning with God. All things came into being through him" (1:1–3). The echo of the opening of Genesis is difficult to miss. As in the biblical account of creation, God creates through speech; the audacious claim of the Johannine prologue is that God's life-creating speech act, which called the entire universe into existence, is to be identified with the Word-become-human-flesh, to whom the rest of the Gospel narrative will bear witness: Jesus of Nazareth. From the outset John makes clear who Jesus is: he is the revealer of God, the very mind (so to speak) of God.

Opening the Story: Revealing Jesus' Identity in John 1:19–51

- Lamb of God, who takes away the world's sin (v. 29)
- Son of God (v. 34)
- Rabbi, Teacher (v. 38)
- Messiah, Christ (v. 41)
- Son of God, King of Israel (v. 49)
- Human One, Son of Humanity (v. 51)

And the beginning of the *story* does not conceal Jesus' identity.[31] As the first set of characters crosses the Johannine stage, Jesus accumulates an impressive list of honor-conferring labels in 1:29–51: "Lamb of God, who takes away the sin of the world" (v. 29);[32] "Son of God" (v. 34); "Rabbi" (= "Teacher," v. 38); "Messiah" (= "Christ," v. 41); "Son of God, King of Israel" (v. 49); "Human One [Son of Humanity]," v. 51). The audience already discovers that who Jesus is—his identity and significance—is a, if not *the*, central issue in John's Gospel.

Jesus begins his ministry in Galilee with a wedding-feast miracle of turning water (stored in stone jars for ritual washing/purification) into vintage wine (2:1–11). This "first sign" of his glory leads his disciples to believe in him. The implication of a richly symbolic act appears to be that the time of the eschatological feast, the era of definitive salvation, when the wine will be abundant, has arrived (note connections to the imagery in such passages as Amos 9:13–14; Hos 14:7; cf. 1 En. 10:19; 2 Bar. 29:5). Irony is in play, however, because the scene also introduces a prominent Johannine motif: Jesus protests to his mother, "My hour has not yet come" (John 2:4). Readers eventually learn that this hour is the crucifixion—the parodic exaltation of Jesus, who does after all, in this most improbable of ways, even now bring the abundant life of the new age into the world (trace "the hour" thread in John 7:30; 8:20; 12:23, 27; 13:1; 17:1; cf. 4:21, 23; 5:25, 28; 16:2, 4, 21, 25, 32; 19:27).

---

31. Thus John's strategy of christological presentation contrasts sharply with Mark's messianic mystery (see ch. 3 above). However, for all the explicitness and directness of John's christological affirmations spoken within the hearing of the story's characters, in the Fourth Gospel no less than in Mark, Jesus' true identity and significance are more often misunderstood than comprehended and embraced. See the discussion below of Jesus' riddles and the motif of misunderstanding.

32. Two distinctive details of John's passion account reinforce this initial identification of Jesus by the baptizing prophetic witness John: (1) the timing of Jesus' death on the day of Preparation for the Passover (19:14, 31, 38–42), thus coinciding with the ritual slaughter of the Passover lambs, rather than the next day, as in the Synoptics; and (2) explicit mention that, as with lambs slaughtered for the Passover meal, none of Jesus' bones are broken during his crucifixion (19:31–37, with quotation of Ps 34:20 in John 19:36; cf. Exod 12:46).

At Passover in Jerusalem (2:13; the first of three Passover festivals in the course of the narrative: see also 6:4; 13:1), Jesus then purges the temple courtyard of merchants and speaks of himself as God's temple, given to destruction but then rebuilt (in resurrection). He performs a number of unnarrated signs, eliciting the faith of many observers (2:23). Yet we are told that Jesus did not trust their faith (2:24). Sign-dependent faith is vulnerable—a theme to which the narrative will return (4:48; 6:2, 14, 26, 30; 12:37; 20:29–30).

Throughout the ensuing narrative (in chs. 3–12), through signs (miracles pointing to Jesus' significance) and provocative teaching, Jesus reveals himself. What he discloses, again and again, is that he is uniquely God's revealer and authorized agent, the Son sent from the Father (God), the one who speaks words from God and does the work of God, the one with power to give life.[33] Some who observe his actions and hear his words believe (e.g., 4:39, 41–42, 50, 53; 6:69; 7:31; 8:30; 9:38; 10:42; 11:27, 45, 48; 12:42). But, more and more, Jesus' words and deeds incite conflict. To be sure, the resuscitation of Lazarus inspires faith in many (11:45), yet that outcome prompts fear in the temple-based Judean leadership and their resolve to eliminate what they perceive as a national-security threat (11:46–53). The culmination of Jesus' ministry of signs, finally, is the unbelief of many of his contemporaries; some among the leadership group do believe, yet they hesitate to make this a public commitment (12:37–42).

The claims Jesus makes for his unique role and relation to God ("the Father who sent him"), then, win him enemies; even many (most?) who have believed eventually fall away at his "hard words" (6:60, 66; 8:31–59). So the narrative of Jesus' signs and interpreting words takes on the character of a downward-spiraling cycle of antagonistic exchanges—indeed, a prolonged trial in which Jesus' examiners, typically the leader group composed of Pharisees, respond to his actions and teaching with intensifying hostility.[34]

The flurry of attention-getting signs by Jesus at the Passover festival in Jerusalem prompts the Pharisee Nicodemus, a distinguished "teacher of Israel"[35] (3:10), to approach him by night (3:2). Yet even prominent, erudite Nicodemus cannot understand what Jesus says to him. Blending the literary devices of verbal irony and misunderstanding, both of which appear often in John (see below), this scene bringing together two such different teachers communicates over the head of Nicodemus to the reader by playing with

---

33. Jesus' words communicating on behalf of God: 3:34; 12:49–50; 14:10, 24; 17:8. Jesus as Son sent from the Father, with agency to represent God: 3:17, 35; 5:17, 19–20, 23–24; 6:37–38, 44; 8:26–27, 42; 10:30, 36–38; 14:11, 24; 16:15; 17:7. Jesus as giver of the (eternal) life that comes from God: 3:15–16, 36; 5:21, 25–26; 6:27, 33, 40, 47, 54; 10:10, 28; 11:25–26; 17:2–3.

34. For development of the view that John casts Jesus' entire ministry (esp. in Judea) as a trial, see Lincoln, *Truth on Trial*; George L. Parsenios, *Rhetoric and Drama in the Johannine Lawsuit Motif*, WUNT 2/258 (Tübingen: Mohr Siebeck, 2010).

35. "Teacher" (*didaskalos*) follows the article, so the phrase might be translated "*the* teacher of Israel." The sense is that Nicodemus is an important, recognized teacher.

dual meanings of the Greek adverb *anōthen*. What does Jesus mean when he speaks of the necessity of birth *anōthen*, if one is to be able to see—hence, experience—God's realm (3:3)?[36] With temporal nuance, the sense would be birth *again* (a second time)—and this is how Nicodemus understands the assertion and thus rejects it as absurd (v. 4). With spatial nuance, however, the meaning would be birth *from above*. The following image of rebirth by water and especially Spirit (vv. 5–8) confirms that this is the kind of rebirth Jesus has in mind. Participation in God's domain requires spiritual rebirth, and the gift of this new (or renewed) life in John has its source "above," in God. Jesus has come both to disclose and to bestow this life. But Nicodemus fails to comprehend. John is not finished with this character, however, and the two later appearances of this leading Pharisee suggest some movement for Nicodemus from the dark of night—symbolically, lack of (in)sight— toward belief (see 7:50–51; 19:39–42).[37]

In tandem with the Nicodemus scene, John 4 presents a remarkable study in character contrasts. While the scholar Nicodemus remains in the dark about Jesus' words, a doubly marginalized character—a Samaritan woman— engages Jesus in serious theological dialogue at Jacob's well and emerges from the encounter not with a husband (the stereotypical outcome of such chance meetings at a well: e.g., Jacob and Rachel in Gen 29:1–12; Moses and Zipporah in Exod 2:15–22) but with something better: faith in Jesus and success as a witness to her whole village on his behalf (John 4:5–42).

Seeing Signs and Believing (or Not)
1. Vintage wedding wine from water for purification rites (2:1–11) — Many signs in Jerusalem yield untrustworthy faith. (2:23–25; 3:2)
2. "Unless you see signs and wonders": Healing for a royal official's son (4:46–54)
3. A Sabbath stroll for a paralyzed man (5:1–9)
4. "Bread from heaven": Enough food for a multitude, but do they want it? (6:1–15, 22–71)
5. "It is I; do not be afraid": A walk on the lake (6:16–21)
6. Blind from birth, but no longer: More Sabbath controversy for the "light of the world" (9:1–41)
7. "I am the resurrection and the life": Lazarus restored to life—and the council resolves to put Jesus to death (11:1–53)

---

36. Only here and in v. 5 does the Fourth Gospel employ the phrase *basileia tou theou* (reign or realm of God), the core symbol of the Synoptic Jesus' message, though the kingship of Jesus does figure prominently in the interrogation by Pilate and the crucifixion (18:33, 36–37, 39; 19:3, 19–22).

37. The ambiguity of John's presentation of Nicodemus has fascinated interpreters. For a sample of character studies, see, in addition to commentaries on John's Gospel, Rensberger, *Johannine Faith and Liberating Community*, 37–41; Jouette M. Bassler, "Mixed Signals: Nicodemus in the Fourth Gospel," *JBL* 108 (1989): 635–46; Craig R. Koester, *Symbolism in the Fourth*

The following episode turns from faith prompted by words of testimony to faith associated with the performing of signs, when Jesus heals the son of a member of the elite, a "royal official" (4:46–54). At the close of the scene (v. 54), the narrator mentions that this is the "second sign" Jesus performed in Galilee after his return from Judea (where he encountered Nicodemus in ch. 3), thus framing the entire section 2:1–4:54 with bookends of Galilean-Cana signs. Like the intervening Jerusalem-based signs, however, this second sign at or near Cana raises a critical question about the genuineness of faith that depends on the observation of the extraordinary, of signs (recall Jesus' suspicion of sign-induced faith in 2:24). "Unless you see signs and wonders you will not believe," Jesus challenges the petitioning official (4:48). The father persists in his plea for help for his son, however, and Jesus says that he will live (vv. 49–50a). At this word, the narrator informs us, the man believed (v. 50b): his is not, after all, vulnerable, sign-dependent faith. The fact that repeated mention of belief follows discovery of the son's restored health (vv. 51–53) suggests that the relation of faith to observed signs is complicated in this narrative. John's audience will listen for further elaboration of this motif as the narrative proceeds—and will not be disappointed, beginning already in the next chapter. It will turn out, again and again, that Jesus' signs and his interpretation of them elicit divergent responses, ranging from faith to outrage.

Opposition to Jesus begins in earnest in John 5, sparked by his healing of a long-disabled man (5:1–9). When he directs the man, "Stand up, take your mat and walk" (v. 8), and he does exactly that, observers ("Jews") accuse the man of breaking the Sabbath (v. 10; the narrator delays mention of the Sabbath timing of the event until v. 9b). He in turn points the finger at Jesus, who had told him to carry his mat (vv. 11, 15). These Sabbath defenders thus begin to actively pursue (or persecute, *ediōkon*) Jesus (v. 16). Concern with appropriate conduct on the Sabbath quickly fades from view when Jesus sidesteps the question of lawbreaking and instead claims to be sharing in the activity—even on the Sabbath—of his "Father" (v. 17). The critics of Jesus react with rage, charging that by calling God "Father," Jesus has placed himself in a position "equal to God" (v. 18). Jesus then launches into a lengthy discourse in which he (1) amplifies his claim to a unique relation with God, as the Son sent by the Father with full authority to give life—even resurrection life—and to judge (vv. 19–30), and (2) then invokes witnesses on his behalf: John the Baptizer, the works Jesus performs, the Father, Scripture, and Moses (vv. 31–47). It is as if Jesus, on trial, is assembling his character

Gospel: Meaning, Mystery, Community, 2nd ed. (Minneapolis: Fortress Press, 2003), 45–48; Susan E. Hylen, *Imperfect Believers: Ambiguous Characters in the Gospel of John* (Louisville, KY: Westminster John Knox Press, 2009), 23–40; R. Alan Culpepper, "Nicodemus: The Travail of New Birth," in *Character Studies in the Fourth Gospel: Narrative Approaches to Seventy Figures in John*, ed. Steven A. Hunt, D. Francois Tolmie, and Ruben Zimmermann, WUNT 2/314 (Tübingen: Mohr Siebeck, 2013), 249–59.

witnesses. However, by the time he finishes his speech—"If you believed Moses, you would believe me, for he wrote about me. But if you do not believe what he wrote, how will you believe what I say?" (vv. 46–47)—it is clear that the dialogue has become a monologue. No listeners respond.

Not until John 7, that is. At another festival in Jerusalem (Booths = Tabernacles), Jesus responds to the charge that his conduct on the Sabbath (recalling 5:1–9) amounts to lawbreaking (7:21–24), and his detractors voice indignation at his assertions of unique relation to God as his Father and his role as supreme agent commissioned and sent by God. In a rapid-fire volley of conflicting perspectives, Jesus offers words of provocative explanation and self-defense; a divided audience response intersperses occasional sparks of teaching- or signs-inspired belief (7:31, 40–41; cf. vv. 45–48) with a string of accusations and expressions of bewilderment and hostility (7:12, 20, 25–27, 30, 35–36, 41–43).

First, though, Jesus performs another sign—a crowd-feeding miracle in Galilee at the time of Passover (6:1–13)—to which the well-nourished crowd responds by seeking to acclaim Jesus as prophet-king (vv. 14–15). But after Jesus takes a stroll on the lake and ushers his disciples safely to land in their storm-tossed boat (6:16–21), he explains the feeding sign's meaning. He himself is "bread from heaven," the "bread of life" that nourishes eternally (6:32–35, 48, 51, 58), surpassing the only-temporary gift of manna, renewed daily in the wilderness wandering that followed the first Passover (vv. 31, 49, recalling the manna narrative in Exod 16). As if this Moses-and-manna-surpassing claim to be the source of permanent, life-giving nourishment were not audacious enough, Jesus presses further, declaring that the only way to gain enduring life is to devour his flesh and drink his blood (John 6:51–58). Understandably, the crowd, including most of Jesus' followers, recoils from these gruesome images (vv. 60, 66). Understandably—but not understanding. This chapter is laced with irony and misunderstanding (see the discussion of these techniques below); the Eucharist-familiar reader will hear the language of eating Jesus' body and drinking his blood figuratively. In a narrative that highlights the motif of signs and the divergent responses they elicit, John's audience will also be struck by the humorous irony in the crowd's insistent request that Jesus perform a sign like the gift of manna (6:30–31)—right after he has completed the feeding miracle (= sign)! The favorable impression left by their experience of the sign (recall v. 14), prompting a petition that Jesus "give us this bread [the life-nourishing bread from heaven] always" (v. 34), swiftly vanishes.

Chapters 8 and 9 present another round of debate and (intensifying) conflict (8:12–59),[38] followed by a remarkable act of Jesus (a sign) that generates

---

38. John 7:53–8:11 narrates Jesus' redirecting of judgment from a woman accused of adultery to her accusers. This story is lacking in the best early manuscripts of the Fourth Gospel and in some manuscripts is even located in Luke's Gospel (following Luke 21:38 or 24:53). It survived as a free-floating early tradition that found various homes in the Gospels. Its language and motifs do not belong in John's narrative.

divergent responses: the gift of sight to a man blind from birth, and its aftermath (9:1–41). Jesus' claim to be the "light of the world," the source of life-giving light (8:12), sparks debate. Pharisees listening to him reject what they regard as self-testimony, which thus lacks validity (v. 13, an image again suggesting a judicial proceeding against Jesus). Combining the roles of "witness" and "judge," Jesus counters by claiming that God (the "Father") joins him in testimony on his behalf, and that whatever judgment Jesus may pronounce in fact represents the divine judgment (vv. 14–18).

Despite a whisper of believing assent to Jesus' teaching (8:30), the vigorous debate that ensues becomes increasingly adversarial. Indeed, by story's end even "Jews who had believed in him" (v. 31) evidently come to view him as a blasphemer, for they pick up stones to kill him (v. 59). They have invoked Abraham as their father, a paternity that Jesus contests because only the devil, not Abraham, can be the father of their murderous rage against him (vv. 39–41, 44–45). They reciprocate by labeling him a demon-possessed Samaritan (v. 48). Abraham, Jesus avers, actually takes delight in Jesus' coming as the one whom God honors (v. 56); even more, "before Abraham was, I am" (v. 58). Like other "I am" statements of Jesus in John that lack a predicate (see the discussion of this formula below), this one clearly identifies Jesus closely with the God who self-identified to Moses as "I AM" (Exod 3:13–14; cf. Isa 43:10, 13, 25). No wonder Jewish auditors, whether former Jesus believers or not, take offense!

Chapter 9 returns to the image of Jesus as light for the world, the source of truth. Again a sign Jesus performs discloses who he is and what he offers, but it is evaluated in quite different ways. Another character study in contrasts links the man born blind to the paralyzed man of John 5. Thanks to Jesus' intervention, both men receive restored physical capacity on the Sabbath; in each case the narrator delays mention of the Sabbath timing of the event until after the healing has occurred (5:9; 9:14). Both men are drawn into a series of interrogations by Judean elite hostile to Jesus; in John 9 the Pharisees are the key players (*Ioudaioi*, "Jews," in ch. 5). But the two men acquit themselves quite differently under pressure. Unlike the man in chapter 5, and also unlike parents who are overcome by fear of being expelled from the synagogue when they are questioned (9:18–23), the man born blind stands up assertively to hostile interrogation (vv. 13–17, 24–34); indeed, his follow-up conversation with Jesus and his replies to hostile Pharisees document a journey toward deeper understanding, clearer vision (not just physical but spiritual), and genuine faith (v. 17 → v. 38). At scene's end, the once-blind man sees while the Pharisees, who claim to be able to see, win Jesus' rebuke as persons who refuse to discern the truth and are therefore culpable (vv. 40–41).[39]

39. By framing the whole scene with the image of "sin," the narrator employs the technique of inclusio to good effect in ch. 9. Confronted with a man unable to see since his birth, the disciples query whether his own or his parents' sin is to blame (9:2). Jesus rejects the assumption behind the question: the disability is not a matter of anyone's sin but rather an opportunity for

The narrator marks no change in audience in John 10, so the lengthy monologue of 10:1–18 ostensibly continues to address the Pharisees. Mixed metaphors present Jesus both as the gate of the sheepfold (vv. 7, 9) and, more prominently, as the authentic shepherd. In contrast to persons hired to tend a flock of sheep, the shepherd deeply cares for his sheep, to the point of sacrificing life itself to defend them (vv. 11–16). As just such a shepherd, which is a biblical metaphor of leadership for the people (e.g., Num 27:16–17; Ezek 34:1–31; cf. Mic 2:12–13), Jesus freely offers his own life for the sake of "abundant life" for his sheep, his people (John 10:10–11, 15, 17–18). His death to benefit others will not be something imposed upon him but his own choice, and even death will not permanently hold him (vv. 17–18). Also like a true shepherd, Jesus knows his sheep by name, and they recognize his voice (vv. 3–5); although Jesus' auditors within the story do not grasp the point of the image (v. 6), John's audience may find reassurance because they are *known* by their Lord, and they are equipped—by the Gospel itself and, they will soon discover, the Spirit/Paraclete—to hear his voice in the words the Gospel records.

Finally the narrator mentions the audience's response in 10:19, and once again Jesus' words create division. Some regard Jesus as speaking like a crazy, demon-distorted man (v. 20; cf. 8:48), but others, recalling the sign of his provision of sight to a man born blind, disagree (10:21). Verse 22 places the ensuing dialogue in the Jerusalem temple at the Feast of Dedication (Hanukkah), which commemorates the rededication of the temple by Judas Maccabeus in 164 BCE, after Antiochus IV (Epiphanes) had desecrated the temple. "Jews" press Jesus for plain talk about his rumored messiahship (v. 24), but when he instead insists that the testimony of his works should suffice (v. 25) and claims identity with the Father ("The Father and I are one," v. 30), the result, again, is outrage, and they heft stones to put him to death, implicitly for blasphemy (v. 31; Jesus makes this explicit in v. 36). But he resumes testimony in his defense, or rather Jesus repeats his appeal to the testimony his works provide (vv. 32–38) and his claim to be one with God ("The Father is in me and I am in the Father," v. 38). The outcome: an unsuccessful attempt, yet again, to arrest Jesus (v. 39), though pockets of belief, recalling the Baptizer's witness to Jesus, persist (vv. 40–42).

The pattern of a dramatic sign issuing in divergent reactions occurs once more in John 11, but this time in a climactic fashion that moves the narrative decisively toward Jesus' death. The passage opens by introducing its trio of central characters: Lazarus, who is beset with illness and then dies, and his sisters Mary and Martha, who mourn his death and engage Jesus

---

God's glory to be seen (v. 3). The story concludes with the Pharisees' assertion that they can see, which Jesus turns against them as evidence that in fact they persist in sin (vv. 40–41). One further reference to sin in the passage is ironic: like Jesus in his conversation with the disciples, the Pharisees link sin and divine glory, but they (wrongly) regard Jesus as a sinner distanced from the glory of God (v. 24).

in dialogue.[40] They send word to him that Lazarus, "whom you love," is ill (11:3). Suspense builds when Jesus intentionally delays travel to Bethany (vv. 4–6), confident that the illness will issue not in death but in honor for God (v. 4). Also, he must overcome his disciples' reluctance to return to Judea, where mortal danger looms (vv. 7–16), as well as their confusion about Lazarus's circumstance—until Jesus plainly says, "Lazarus is dead" (v. 14). Thomas's concession signals the profound irony of the rest of the chapter: "Thomas, who was called the Twin [which the name "Thomas" means], said to his fellow disciples, 'Let us also go, that we may die with him'" (v. 16). Death and life are fully in play, yet they are not what they appear to be.

First Martha and then Mary lament his arrival too late to help their brother (vv. 21, 32), though Martha's protest is tinged by hope (v. 22) that is missing from her sister's complaint. Martha also voices belief in a future resurrection and affirms Jesus' identity as Messiah, Son of God (vv. 24, 27); his reply, however, corrects Martha's temporal perspective while at the same time instructing and reassuring John's audience: "I am the resurrection and the life. Those who believe in me, even though they die, will live, and everyone who lives and believes in me will never die" (vv. 25–26). Jesus proceeds to give Lazarus a "shout-out" (of the tomb) and restores his life (v. 43). Lazarus is unbound from his burial linen (v. 44): it is not about death but instead about God's glory, bound up with belief in Jesus as the one sent by the Father (vv. 40–42). And such an impressive, culminating sign performed by Jesus indeed generates faith in many of Jesus' fellow Jews (v. 45).

There is still more and deeper irony just ahead, however. Precisely because the raising of Lazarus captures wide attention and engenders (sign-based) belief, the elite leadership group in Jerusalem (leading priests and Pharisees) convenes and without a formal trial and in the absence of the accused reaches a consensus judgment that determines his fate.[41] As the ones co-opted by the empire, in collaboration with the Roman governor and army, to keep order in Jerusalem and its environs, they have an understandable concern: "If we let him go on like this, everyone will believe in him, and the Romans will come and destroy both our holy place and our nation" (11:48). This is not a necessary outcome, however: the "high priest that year,"[42] Caiaphas, lays out the stratagem that will avert political disaster: "It

---

40. John 11:1 sets the scene for the raising of Lazarus by mentioning his illness at Bethany, "the village of Mary and her sister Martha." Verse 2 elaborates, describing Mary as "the one who anointed the Lord with perfume and wiped his feet with her hair." This foreshadowing of an event yet to be narrated would not be awkward for readers who already know the tradition of the anointing.

41. Recall Nicodemus's concern about due process in a judicial proceeding: "Our law does not judge people without first giving them a hearing to find out what they are doing, does it?" (7:51). The culmination of Jesus' "trial" by the Judean authorities in ch. 11 again ignores this judicial principle.

42. Odd phrasing, as if the role of high priest were an annual appointment; actually, Caiaphas served as high priest for nearly two decades (18–36 CE).

is better for you to have one man die for the people than to have the whole nation destroyed" (v. 50). John's audience will not miss the irony: Caiaphas speaks truth, but the reality inverts his intended meaning. The resolve of the council, sealed in this scene (v. 53), indeed sets in motion the events that lead to Jesus' death, but he has already embraced that destiny for himself (10:17–18), and he has done so to save the nation—and others besides (11:51–52)—in a manner very different from what Caiaphas imagines.[43] The narrator credits Caiaphas with speaking prophetically; perhaps so, but only in spite of his own prudential thinking.

The irony of the narrative is thick: Jesus raises Lazarus from the dead, an event that shows Jesus is the one who gives life (eternal life, available even now, not just in the remote resurrection future), yet this act leads directly to his own death, which, for John, is the event by which the life that Jesus gives comes in full force—"life . . . abundant" (10:10). With access to the full narrative, and with benefit of hindsight, John's audience knows what Caiaphas cannot discern.

In chapter 12, in the aftermath of the council's decision to have Jesus killed, his "hour" finally arrives. The episodes in this concluding section of Jesus' public ministry present kaleidoscopic images of belief and unbelief. The spotlight first falls on Lazarus's sister Mary, whose extravagant gesture of honor bathes Jesus' feet with expensive perfume and fills the house with its aroma. The act incites Judas's fury—the Fourth Gospel casts him as a thief whose protest against this waste is dishonest (12:4–6)—but Jesus reframes it as an advance anointing for burial (12:1–8). To the consternation of Pharisees, an enthusiastic crowd then acclaims the "King of Israel" as he enters Jerusalem in (humble) triumph (12:12–19, echoing Zech 9:9). "Greeks" in search of Jesus approach, prompting him to declare that his moment, his hour, has come (12:20–23; cf. 13:1). This hour of glory is ironic: it will take the form of his being lifted up on a cross, the epitome of humiliation in human terms (12:23, 32–33). In a nod to the Synoptic tradition of anguished prayer in Gethsemane, John's Jesus pauses to ask whether he should ask God to be rescued from the hour of danger that looms, but his answer is immediate: of course not, for this is what he has come to do (v. 27). There is irony, too, in the Pharisees' resigned exasperation, as they complain that "the world has gone after him" in the "buzzfeed" after the raising of Lazarus (v. 19). Irony appears in two respects: (1) the narrator's very next move is to bring Greeks on the scene, anticipating the eventual fulfillment of Jesus' remark that he has "other sheep that do not belong to this fold" (10:16); yet also (2) the sign-generated belief the Pharisees lament will prove to be short-lived (12:37–41), and "many," including some of the elite leaders, do believe

---

43. The concern to reassert control by eliminating the threat Jesus poses later extends also to Lazarus, whose physical presence is a continual reminder of Jesus' signs and thus a prompt for faith in Jesus (12:10–11).

but fear to go public with their faith because of the consequences: removal from the synagogue community (v. 42).[44]

Jesus offers a brief recapitulation of central themes of his public ministry, as it comes to a close (12:44–50):

- Jesus is the one sent from the Father, and thus his supreme agent and representative.
- Jesus is the source of light amid the world's darkness.
- Belief in Jesus is crucial.
- Judgment and salvation result from people's response to Jesus' message.
- The core message God has entrusted to Jesus concerns eternal life.

There is no particular audience for this summary of Jesus' teaching and ministry; he is shouting out through the story to John's readers, on the cusp of the passion narrative—his death/departure and return to the Father.

Recap: Central Themes of Jesus' Ministry (John 12:44–50)

- Jesus, sent from the Father: God's agent
- Jesus the source of light
- Belief in Jesus is crucial
- Judgment and salvation result from response to Jesus' message
- Core message: Eternal life

The Passover festival approaches (13:1, the third mentioned in the narrative), and Jesus, aware that his time has come, retreats to be with his disciples and to prepare them for his departure. One of them will play a direct role in aiding an exit strategy that will, ironically, achieve the conflicting aims of Satan, of Rome and its allies among the Judean elite, of Judas, and also of Jesus! The narrator gives the audience an inside view of the devil's intentions, which single out Judas for the part of betrayer (13:2). Jesus' last meal with the disciples becomes the occasion for a farewell discourse (chs. 13–16) that reassures the disciples: when Jesus leaves them, the Paraclete

---

44. Together with 9:22, 34–35 and 16:2, this passage has often been viewed as anachronistic, reading back into the lifetime of Jesus separation of Christ believers from the synagogue (whether forced exclusion or voluntary departure) that only occurred much later. The influential proposal of J. Louis Martyn along this line (*History and Theology in the Fourth Gospel*) has been subjected to sharp critique in recent years, but I find the basic approach, if not all the details, convincing. See the excursus above, "J. Louis Martyn's Reconstruction of the Setting of the Fourth Gospel: Critical Appraisals."

(*paraklētos*), John's distinctive name for the Spirit—the Advocate, the Comforter, the Encourager—will continue his work among them. And he prays for their unity (ch. 17). The first part of the "discourse," however, is nonverbal, a richly symbolic gesture. Jesus stoops low to wash the feet of his disciples (even the one he knows will betray him: 13:10–11), an act of lowly service that belies his status and honor as their Teacher and Lord (vv. 3–11). No wonder Peter at first strenuously resists. (The humor and hyperbole in vv. 6–10 are entertaining!) This gesture and the words of instruction and assurance that follow, to the end of chapter 17, express Jesus' profound love for "his own," as he prepares to leave them (13:1).

Jesus has washed his disciples' feet, a symbolic purification in advance of his self-giving in death, but he develops the gesture's meaning primarily as a model of humble service for emulation by his followers (vv. 12–17).[45] He then makes a solemn scene somber by predicting that despite the intimacy of the occasion, one of the close friends gathered to share this meal would betray him (vv. 18–21). Jesus is completely aware of what is happening. Bewildered, the disciples query which of them it might be, and Peter asks another disciple, "the one whom Jesus loved" (v. 23), to take advantage of his position next to Jesus to find out. Jesus confirms for John's audience both *that* he knows and *who* the betrayer is, though the disciples remain in the dark (vv. 22–30). This is not new information for readers, who learned much earlier about Judas's perfidy (6:71; 13:2), but the disciples present with Jesus in the room do not understand (13:28–29). So begins the peculiar revelatory role of this anonymous, beloved disciple unique to John's narrative, who is introduced here for the first time and remains prominent to the end of the Gospel as its key witness (see 18:15–16; 19:26–27, 35; 20:2–9; 21:7, 20–24).

Whatever Satan's part in the drama—after Jesus hands Judas his piece of bread, Satan "enters" Judas (13:27a)—it is Jesus who is in control. He directs Judas: "Do quickly what you are going to do" (v. 27b), and Judas leaves at once. Given the importance of the metaphors of light and darkness in the narrative (1:4–9; 3:19–21; 5:35; 8:12; 9:5; 11:9–10; 12:35–36, 46; cf. 3:2, "night"), John's audience will not miss the deep meaning of the narrator's terse description: "And it was night" (13:30). Darkness prevails, or so it seems (recall 1:5). However, Jesus' next remark suggests that the conspiracy of Judas and Satan is in fact powerless; the events underway, contrary to all appearance, bring honor to Jesus (the Human One) and to God (13:31–32). From this point to the end of chapter 16, Jesus in speech and dialogue readies the disciples (minus Judas) for what lies ahead.

---

45. Luke's Last Supper narrative lacks the footwashing scene but scores a similar point; there too Jesus presents his humble service, despite his superior status, as an example for his disciples to emulate in their own future leadership (Luke 22:24–27).

Main Themes in the Farewell Scene (John 13–17)
• The "new" love command
• Departure and (temporary) return
• Permanent return: "Another Paraclete"
• Abiding in Jesus
• Jesus represents God to the world
• Belief in God, and in Jesus whom God sent
• Peace and joy for the distressed
• Assurance for future requests
• Hostility from "the world"
• "Ruler of this world" defeated

Although 14:31 seems to signal the end of the farewell discourse with dialogue, Jesus proceeds to speak for three more chapters. This literary seam has led many to conclude that the original discourse was expanded in a second edition.[46] However complex the compositional history of this section of the Gospel (not recoverable), it possesses a remarkable thematic coherence. Jesus keeps hammering away at a set of key themes, often speaking through the disciples' confusion to instruct John's readers:

- The "new" love command (13:34–35; 15:10–14, 17; cf. 14:15, 21)
- Jesus' departure and (temporary) return (13:33, 36–37; 14:2–6, 12, 18–19, 28; 16:4–7, 10, 16–19, 28)
- Jesus' permanent return in the form of (another) Paraclete (14:16–17, 25–26; 15:26; 16:7–15)
- Disciples abiding in, remaining connected to, Jesus (14:17 [Spirit], 23; 15:1–10 [vine metaphor])
- Jesus' identity with the Father, whom he represents in the world (14:7–13, 20–24, 31; 15:8–10; 16:15, 25–28, 32)
- Belief in God, coincident with belief in Jesus, whom God sent (14:1, 11–12, 29; 16:27, 30–31)
- Peace and joy for troubled, sorrowful hearts (14:1, 27; 16:20–22, 33)
- Assurance that disciples' future requests will be granted (14:13–14; 16:23–24)
- Hostility and hatred toward the disciples from the "world" (15:18–25; 16:1–4, 32–33)
- The "ruler of this world" judged and vanquished (14:30; 16:11; cf. 16:33).

46. E.g., Brown, *Gospel according to John*, 1:xxxvii; 2:656–57; cf. Barrett, *Gospel according to John*, 454–55, 470; Schnackenburg, *Gospel according to St. John*, 3:89–93.

Jesus speaks without interruption in 17:1–26, with the divine Father as his audience. Or rather, since God does not need to be told what Jesus has to say (cf. 11:41–42; 12:28–30), this prayer addresses the Gospel audience. Once again, Jesus recapitulates central themes of the whole narrative:

- The arrival of the "hour" links Jesus' glory to his death. (17:1)
- Jesus has authority, as the one sent from God, to confer eternal life. (vv. 2–3, 8)
- Jesus has performed the "work" God gave him to do and spoken the words God gave him to speak. (vv. 4, 7–8)
- Jesus shares glory with God from before the world's creation. (v. 5, recalling 1:1–3; cf. 17:24)
- Jesus has revealed God (the "name") to the ones God has given to him. (vv. 6, 9–10)[47]
- The ones who have believed, like their Teacher and Lord, will encounter hostility from a world to which they do not ultimately belong. (vv. 14–16)

"They do not belong to the world" (v. 14). Nevertheless, Jesus' followers are to be sent into that hostile space with a mission and a message (v. 18; cf. 20:21). Much of the language of the prayer has a sectarian quality, consistent with the dualism that pervades the Gospel (e.g., light vs. darkness; truth vs. lie; from above vs. from below, life vs. death). Yet for the disciples (sent by Jesus), as for Jesus himself (sent from the Father), the world—for all its hostility to the truth and those who testify to it—remains the arena for mission, a space from which God's love refuses to withdraw.

A prominent concern of the prayer, however, is the unity of Jesus' followers (17:11, 21–23). Their unity has its basis in the unity of Jesus and the Father, and in the mutual love that binds them. Yet it is a matter of fervent petition because even though Jesus has commanded that they love one another and affirmed that they abide in the love that Jesus shares with the Father, and even though "they are one" as Jesus and the Father are one, their unity will be vulnerable. Their experience in the world and within their own community(ies) will sorely test their love for one another. Indeed, it will prove fragile. If the letters of John give a series of snapshots of later developments in the Johannine community(ies), the afterlife of this prayer of Jesus will reveal not unity but division, not harmony but schism (e.g., 1 John 2:18–19; cf. 4:20; 2 John 7–11; 3 John 9–10).

---

47. The imagery of the prayer in John 17 (esp. vv. 6–8) offers a more positive picture of the disciples than in much of the preceding narrative. This dissonance reflects the transitional, bridging role of the passage, which points beyond the present moment to the future that the disciples will experience. In that future, a thrice-denying Peter will be restored (21:15–19), the Spirit breath of Jesus will animate the disciples' mission (20:21–23), and the Paraclete/Spirit will teach and guide them (14:25–26; 16:13–15).

Since prayer is a vehicle of theology, it is instructive to ask what theological perspective Jesus articulates in John 17. True to the Gospel as a whole, the passage presents a robust Christology: Jesus is the Son whom the Father has sent into the world to speak and act on God's behalf and with authority from God. Jesus and God are unified, therefore, in will and word and action. Yet they are not collapsed into one. After all, Jesus petitions God, even as he knows that God hears and honors him. (The Johannine prologue speaks of the Word as God but also as "with God," hence distinct from God [1:1].) Moreover, Jesus prays to "the only true God" (17:3), recalling the core Jewish affirmation also articulated in 5:44. Jesus does not seek his own glory but desires that honor accorded him serve God's glory (17:1; cf. v. 5). Christology is subsumed under theology in John's Gospel; as Jesus also puts it, "The Father is greater than I" (14:28).

After such a lengthy interlude with Jesus and his intimate friends ("his own," 13:1), on retreat from the hostile forces surrounding them, 18:1–12 swiftly brings Jesus and his disciples face-to-face with the betrayer and with a massive army that arrests him (a whole cohort [*speira*], which would have numbered six hundred soldiers!). The narration of the arrest scene puts Johannine symbolism and irony on vivid display. Judas and the soldiers bring "lanterns and torches" along with their weapons (v. 3). Of course they must do so: Judas earlier left the table of his Lord and went into the dark of "night" (13:30), and human-contrived illumination is necessary for those who reject the "light of the world" (see 8:12; 9:5). When Jesus asks the throng whom they are seeking (*zēteite*, in vv. 4, 7)[48] and they say (twice) "Jesus of Nazareth" (vv. 5, 7), he replies "I am" (*egō eimi*, vv. 5, 6, 8). More than "I am that guy," the expression carries the potency of a divine-identity formula (see Exod 3:13–14; Isa 43:10, 13, 25), as the soldiers' reaction demonstrates: "They fell to the ground" (John 18:6). While the arrest unfolds, it is evident that the one now taken into custody as prisoner is, in fact, directing the action. As he earlier announced, he goes to his death not as a passive victim but with purpose (10:17–18). So in this moment: "Am I not to drink the cup that the Father has given me?" (18:11). He even secures safe passage for his followers (vv. 8–9), despite a violent gesture of resistance by Peter (vv. 10–11).[49]

The bound prisoner is escorted to Annas, the high priest Caiaphas's father-in-law, but (in a significant departure from the Synoptic pattern)

---

48. "Seeking" Jesus is an important motif in the narrative. Parsenios distinguishes between friendly and hostile seeking or pursuit of Jesus in the Fourth Gospel (*Rhetoric and Drama*, 49–85). Hostile seeking is a form of judicial investigation (ibid., 49–50). For neutral or favorable seeking of Jesus, see 1:38; 7:11, 34; 11:56. For instances of "seeking to kill [or stone]," see 5:18; 7:1, 19–20, 25; 8:37, 40; 11:8; also, seeking to arrest in 7:30; 10:39. Thus the arresting cohort finally succeeds where previous attempts to seize Jesus have been thwarted. One can also seek glory or honor (7:18), but genuine honor is something that one seeks for God (7:18), or that God seeks on one's behalf (5:44; 8:50 [for Jesus]).

49. Only John's account identifies Peter as the one who strikes this blow at the arrest, and only John names the victim: Malchus (18:10). Like Luke, John specifies that it is the "right ear" that is wounded (cf. Luke 22:50).

no council is convened by the high priest for a judicial examination.[50] John 18:13–27 interweaves Peter's threefold denial of his discipleship (vv. 15–18, 25–27)[51] with Annas's interrogation of Jesus (vv. 19–23) and his delivery to Caiaphas (v. 24). Caiaphas plays a minimal role in the process;[52] the "high priest" who interrogates Jesus "about his disciples and about his teaching" can only be Annas (v. 19). Jesus refuses to answer the inquiry and challenges his elite priestly interrogator to interview those who have heard his teaching in both synagogue and temple (vv. 20–21). A member of the temple police force strikes Jesus for such an impudent response to the high priest (v. 22), and Annas is finished with the prisoner.

Dominating John's passion account is the dramatic, intricately constructed seven-scene encounter between Jesus and the local administrative face of Roman control, the governor Pilate, which extends from 18:28 through 19:16a. The seven scenes exhibit careful dramatic staging, which moves Pilate back and forth between the prisoner (inside the governor's palace) and his accusers (outside), who are named simply "the Jews," apart from one specific reference to "the chief priests and the [temple] police" (19:6) and once to "chief priests" (19:15). The opponents of Jesus remain outside in order to avoid ritual defilement that would prevent their participation in the Passover celebration (18:28). John's audience follows Pilate's movements and assesses his quite different interactions with Jesus and his accusers.

Scene 1: Outside—Pilate and Jesus' accusers (18:28–32)

When Pilate receives a vague answer to his query about the accusation being leveled against Jesus, he replies curtly, "Take him yourselves and judge him according to your law" (vv. 29–31a). "The Jews [*Ioudaioi*]," though, concede the judicial constraints they face and in the process reveal their objective: "We are not permitted to put anyone to death" (v. 31b). A narrator's aside explains: "This was to fulfill what Jesus had said when he indicated the kind of death he was to die" (v. 32)—that is, exaltation on a cross (see 3:14; 8:28; 12:32–33).

Scene 2: Inside—Pilate and Jesus (18:33–38a)

Pilate's initial interrogation of Jesus centers on the question whether he is "the King of the Jews" (vv. 33, 37), and on the character of his reign or dominion (vv. 36–37).[53] Jesus acknowledges that he has a "kingdom,"

---

50. Annas was long a powerful elite priestly figure; he served as high priest for a decade (6–15 CE), and after he was deposed by the governor Gratus, five of his sons were appointed high priest in succession, in addition to his son-in-law Caiaphas.

51. Peter's "I am not" (*ouk eimi*, 18:17, 25) contrasts with Jesus' "I am" (*egō eimi*).

52. In contrast to the important part Caiaphas is given in 11:47–53, about which the narrator provides a reminder in 18:13–14.

53. In 18:34 Jesus' question to Pilate exposes a gap (or textual indeterminacy) in the narrative that readers may also be pondering: "Do you ask this on your own, or did others tell you about me?" Pilate partially fills the gap with missing information: "Your own nation and the chief priests have handed you over to me. What have you done?" (v. 35). The reply implies that the elite priests informed Pilate that Jesus claimed royal status.

though it is "not from this world" (v. 36)—that is, its origin and character derive from somewhere else ("from above," John's audience surmises). He then describes his reign in terms of commitment to speak truth and thus the universal sway he holds: "Everyone who belongs to the truth listens to my voice" (v. 37). Pilate counters with the rhetorical question "What is truth?" (v. 38) and does not pause to hear an answer. Face-to-face with the one who speaks and embodies truth (e.g., 14:6), Pilate does not "listen to [his] voice" but shows contempt for him (18:37).

Scene 3: Outside—Pilate and "the Jews" (18:38b–40)

Pilate declares his finding: Jesus' accusers have "no case." But rather than simply discharge Jesus, he invokes the custom of a symbolic Passover prisoner release (Passover being a festival commemorating liberation from Egypt)[54] and—in a gesture that it is difficult *not* to see as taunting Jesus' elite accusers—proposes, "Do you want me to release for you the King of the Jews?" (v. 39). The Judean leaders ask instead for the release of Barabbas, labeled "a bandit" (i.e., rebel) in a narrator's aside (v. 40).

Scene 4: Inside (choreographed movement implied)— Pilate, soldiers, and Jesus (19:1–3)

At the center of the Roman proceeding against Jesus stands a scene of "judicial torture."[55] Pilate has Jesus beaten (19:1); the Greek construction actually has Pilate as the subject of the verb; even though readers surely understand that he ordered others to carry out the beating, the phrasing emphasizes the governor's agency. Soldiers then heap additional insult on the injury, weaving a wreath of thorns and crowning Jesus with it. Fitting him in royal garb (a purple robe), they mock him: "Hail, King of the Jews!" (vv. 2–3). John's audience knows that the soldiers unwittingly speak truth, or at least a part of it (Jesus' kingship is limited neither to one nation nor to this world; cf. 18:36). Jesus may be wearing (royal) purple, but the scene graphically shows the Roman Empire's true colors.

Scene 5: Outside—Pilate and chief priests with temple police (19:4–8)

Pilate now repeats his earlier judgment: "I find no case against him" (v. 4). He has King Jesus brought out, sporting his crown of thorns and the purple robe, and presents him: "Here is the man!" (v. 5; no ordinary man but the Son of Man, or Human One, readers might clarify). Not deflected from their goal by Pilate's provocation, the chief priests and (temple) police demand

---

54. This custom, which in John as in the Synoptic Gospels results in the release of the rebel Barabbas rather than Jesus, is not otherwise attested in extant sources.

55. See Tom Thatcher, *Greater than Caesar: Christology and Empire in the Fourth Gospel* (Minneapolis: Fortress Press, 2009), 66; here agreeing with Stephen D. Moore, *Empire and Apocalypse: Postcolonialism and the New Testament*, The Bible in the Modern World (Sheffield: Sheffield Phoenix, 2006), 61–63. Rensberger, too, views Pilate's actions as aiming to "humiliate 'the Jews' and to ridicule their national hopes" (*Johannine Faith and Liberating Community*, 92).

that Jesus be crucified (v. 6a). Yet Pilate (as in 18:31) tells his adversaries to handle the matter ("*You* crucify him!" [AT]) and repeats for a third time his finding that they have "no case" (19:6b). Since Pilate knows full well that they do not have authority to carry out the crucifixion (recall 18:31), this is further taunting by the governor. The Jews (i.e., their elite leaders), however, insist that their law requires his death, "because he has claimed to be the Son of God" (19:7), a new piece of evidence that concerns Pilate. His earlier cynicism is now joined by a measure of fear, driving him back inside to interrogate Jesus one last time.[56]

Scene 6: Inside—Pilate and Jesus (19:9–11)

Not realizing what a key question he is raising, Pilate probes Jesus' origins—"Where are you from?"—but is met with silence (v. 9; on the "where from" question, see 1:45–46; 3:31; 7:27–28; 8:14, 23). Irked, the prefect presses the prisoner to answer: "Do you not know that I have power to release you, and power to crucify you?" (v. 10). Jesus now does respond, but only so as to put Pilate's power in perspective: "You would have no power over me unless it had been given you from above [Jesus' place of origin, by the way!]; therefore the one who handed me over to you is guilty of a greater sin" (v. 11).[57]

Scene 7: Outside—Pilate, Jesus, and "the Jews" (19:12–16a)

Once more Pilate tries to release Jesus; but the Judean leaders counter with pressure of their own: "If you release this man, you are no friend of the emperor. Everyone who claims to be a king sets himself against the emperor" (v. 12). So the prefect brings Jesus back outside and sits (or seats Jesus)[58] on

56. The Greek phrase in 19:8 may be translated "more afraid than ever" (so NRSV); "very [much] afraid" (so Barrett, *Gospel according to John*, 542; cf. Brown, *Gospel according to John*, 2:877); or "rather, [he became] afraid" (so Michaels, *Gospel of John*, 933); similarly, Rensberger: "he became fearful instead" (*Johannine Faith and Liberating Community*, 94). This last rendering makes the best sense to interpreters who regard the Johannine Pilate as a calculating leader who is manipulating the parties in this scene to achieve his own ends—mocking Jesus and taunting the Judean elite, and successfully drawing out of the latter an unequivocal affirmation of loyalty to the emperor (19:15). For readings of Pilate's character along this line, see, e.g., Warren Carter, *John and Empire: Initial Explorations* (New York: T&T Clark, 2008), 289–314; Cornelis Bennema, *Encountering Jesus: Character Studies in the Gospel of John*, 2nd ed. (Minneapolis: Fortress Press, 2014), 317–28; Rensberger, *Johannine Faith and Liberating Community*, 92–95. Bennema judges Pilate's success a "hollow victory."

57. Who is "the one who handed me over to you" (19:11): Judas, or Caiaphas and his circle? The verb *paradidōmi* could be translated "hand over" or "betray"; with the latter sense it practically supplies Judas's middle name (6:71; 12:4; 13:2, 11, 21; 18:2, 5). However, Jesus' elite-priestly opponents use it of themselves in the former sense (18:30). In neither case, though, is Pilate exonerated, even if his is said to be a "lesser" sin.

58. The Greek of 19:13 is ambiguous. The verb *ekathisen* can be taken as intransitive (Pilate sat) or transitive (Pilate positioned Jesus). Either sense of the verb fits the Johannine irony in the scene: Jesus is the one judging Pilate, not the other way around. The irony is obviously most blatant if Pilate mocks Jesus by placing him on the seat where judgment is pronounced. See Lincoln, *Truth on Trial*, 132–35.

the judge's bench (v. 13). A narrator's aside injects an important time notice: it is about noon on "the day of Preparation for the Passover" (v. 14a); on this afternoon the Passover lambs are ritually slaughtered (recall the baptizing prophet's testimony that Jesus is the "Lamb of God" who removes the world's sin [1:29], and Jesus' claim to be the one who truly liberates [8:31–36]).

Irony reigns when Pilate then declares, "Here is your King!" (19:14b). This provokes renewed shouts for crucifixion, met by Pilate's mocking rejoinder: "Shall I crucify your King?" (v. 15). The chief priests take the bait, giving Pilate an unqualified assertion of their complete loyalty to the empire, words that must have been music to a Roman prefect's ears: "We have no king but the emperor" (v. 15c). Yet this pledge contradicts the core Jewish conviction that God (alone) reigns as "King" (e.g., Judg 8:23; 1 Sam 8:7; Pss 145:1; 146:10; 149:2; Isa 26:13). Pilate then hands Jesus over—or back (recall 18:30)—to the Judean leaders to be crucified (v. 16).

The pace of the narrative slows dramatically beginning in 13:1. John 1–12 presents public activity of Jesus spanning more than two years. Then, after five chapters narrating only Jesus' final meal with his disciples and the farewell discourse with dialogue there (chs. 13–17), the scene featuring the interrogations by Pilate stretches over nearly thirty verses (18:28–19:16a). The events reported to the end of John 19 all occur before nightfall that same day.[59] So when the "hour" finally arrives, it passes swiftly.

Distinctive Features of John's Crucifixion Narrative

- Jesus carries his own cross.
- Charge ("King of the Jews") in three languages.
- Explicit claims to Scripture fulfillment.
- Jesus' loved ones nearby, and Jesus forms a new "family."
- Eyewitness testimony: blood and water.
- Nicodemus helps Joseph of Arimathea give Jesus a burial with dignity.

The crucifixion of Jesus—contrary to every meaning this brutal mode of execution carried in Jesus' (and John's) world—is Jesus' hour of glory, his exaltation. Here he accomplishes the purpose of his coming into the world: giving his life so that abundant life may come to others (10:10–11, 15, 17–18), and returning to the Father who sent him (7:33; 16:5). This moment of death in dishonor that is in fact life in glory represents the supreme irony of the Gospel narrative. Thatcher describes well the ideology that informed the Roman Empire's frequent practice of crucifixion. Each cross "reenacted

---

59. On the temporal pacing of the narrative, see James L. Resseguie, *The Strange Gospel: Narrative Design and Point of View in John*, BibIntS 56 (Leiden: Brill, 2001), 187.

Rome's conquest of the victim's nation"; crucifixion violence "went beyond physical punishment to symbolic annihilation, with the destruction of the victim's flesh narrating Rome's capacity to suppress every threat to the state's entire sovereignty."[60] But in John's crucifixion narrative, Jesus rather than Rome is sovereign. In 19:30, his last words, "It is finished [AT: completed, accomplished]," "completely [reverse] the public meaning of crucifixion by allowing Christ to speak from a posture of absolute authority."[61] Not Jesus but "the ruler of this world" (in cosmic terms, Satan, but in human and political terms, the emperor) is conquered here (see 1:31; 14:30; 16:11).

Several distinctive features of John's crucifixion narrative are noteworthy:

- Jesus carries the cross (crossbeam) by himself (19:17); no Simon of Cyrene is needed here!
- The capital charge "Jesus of Nazareth, the King of the Jews" is inscribed in three languages (Hebrew, Latin, and Greek); Pilate ignores the chief priests' appeal to revise the placard to say that Jesus *claimed* to be king (vv. 19–22).
- In just a few verses, readers meet a cascade of explicit Scripture-fulfillment citations: soldiers casting lots for Jesus' robe (v. 24; cf. Ps 22:18); Jesus' thirst (John 19:28; cf. Ps 69:21); no bones are broken and instead his side is pierced (John 19:36–37; cf. Exod 12:46; Ps 34:20; Zech 12:10).
- Jesus has loved ones close enough to his cross to speak with them; among them he constitutes a new family, directing his mother to join the household of the beloved disciple (John 19:25–27).
- The narrator highlights the eyewitness account (evidently by the beloved disciple) observing blood and water from Jesus' side after it has been pierced (vv. 34–35).
- The prominent Pharisee-teacher Nicodemus (now a "disciple" in "secret") assists Joseph in burial rites, using an enormous quantity of spices (vv. 38–41).

Jesus dies on a cross, an event not imposed on him but freely embraced as a self-surrender of life for the purpose of giving life to the world, thus culminating the activity of his entire ministry, in word and sign, of calling people to faith and granting life to all who accept him. The world ruler—Rome, but in cosmic perspective Satan—appears to win at "Skull-Hill" (19:17 AT), yet truth is not what it appears to be. Two Judean leaders, elite men emerging from the circle of Jesus' opponents, put the exclamation point on the close of his life, providing the dignity of burial with honor and with one hundred pounds of spices; for John's audience, all this underscores the profound irony of the whole sequence of events.

60. Thatcher, *Greater than Caesar*, 93.
61. Ibid., 114.

The more decisive exclamation point, however, comes from God, who signals unambiguously that this is not, after all, the close of Jesus' life. As in the Synoptics, Mary Magdalene (alone, according to John) comes to a tomb that is now empty.[62] In an entertaining interlude between her discovery of the empty tomb (20:1–2) and her personal encounter with the risen Jesus (vv. 11–18), Peter and the beloved disciple race to the tomb and also find the tomb empty, except for burial linens left lying there (vv. 3–10). In what reads like a contest between these two Jesus followers, the disciple whom Jesus loved is the first to reach the tomb and reach resurrection belief (vv. 4, 8).

Verses 11–18 then narrate Mary Magdalene's encounter with Jesus. The scene opens in a fashion reminiscent of the Synoptic accounts, with two angels in white asking Mary Magdalene, now back outside but gazing into the tomb, why she is weeping (vv. 11–13).[63] She repeats her understanding that the body has been "taken away." The angels do not speak further; fittingly for the Fourth Gospel, it is unmediated encounter with Jesus himself that ushers Mary Magdalene from grief to belief. He repeats the angels' query "Why are you weeping?" (v. 15), then responds to her mistaking him for the gardener by simply addressing her by name—"Mary!"—and she recognizes him through his voice (v. 16), as indeed the true shepherd's sheep know him when he calls them by name (10:3–4).[64] He is soon to ascend, returning to his Father, and rather than try to hold on to him, she should tell the rest of the disciples what she has heard (20:17–18).

Still on Easter, Jesus makes an evening appearance to the disciples—significantly, minus Thomas—and twice gives them the greeting and wish for peace, not a trivial matter for a group huddled behind secure doors for fear of hostile opponents (20:19–23). Now, however, Jesus extends to them the same sending language that has been a primary image for Jesus' own work (as the Son sent from the Father): "As the Father has sent me, so I send you"

62. In Mary Magdalene's report to Peter and the beloved disciple, she mentions that "we do not know" where the body taken from the tomb has been placed (20:2). This hint that she did not come to the tomb alone may show that the author of the Fourth Gospel was familiar with Synoptic-like traditions (if not one or more of the Gospels themselves) that include more women at the tomb than just Mary Magdalene; cf. Matt 28:1 (two women); Mark 16:1 (three); Luke 23:55–24:10 (a larger number).

63. The details vary in all four canonical presentations of the scene, but the same basic pattern pertains in them all: one or two figures (human or angelic) dressed in white or dazzling garb begin speaking with the women by countering their emotional distress (their fear is mentioned in each of the Synoptics, weeping in John). In Luke and John, the woman (women) is (are) asked a "why" question; however, in John it is not the angels but instead the risen Jesus who speaks the words that move her from sorrow and confusion to belief (move them: in Matt 28:5–7; Mark 16:5–7; Luke 24:4–7).

64. See Kasper Bro Larsen, *Recognizing the Stranger: Recognition Scenes in the Gospel of John*, BibIntS 93 (New York: Brill, 2008), 190–91. Larsen observes that the recognition scene in 20:1–10 proceeds from seeing through telling and hearing back to seeing. In 20:11–29, however, seeing leads to telling, and then hearing concludes the scene. When Jesus is no longer physically present (e.g., the situation of John's audience), telling and hearing are the only modes of communication available (ibid., 191)

(v. 21). He follows the declaration with the empowerment to carry out this daunting task, breathing his Spirit breath (*pneuma*) on them: "Receive the Holy Spirit" (v. 22)—no need to wait for Pentecost in John's story! The wise discernment with which the Spirit/Paraclete will endow Jesus' followers will be much needed if they are to exercise the authority and charge the risen Jesus now gives the disciples: forgiving or retaining the sins of community members (v. 23).

But what about Thomas, the Twin? When he rejoins the other disciples, they repeat Mary Magdalene's witness: "We [I] have seen the Lord" (v. 25a; cf. v. 18). He is skeptical, however: "Unless I see the mark of the nails in his hands, and put my finger in the mark of the nails and my hand in his side, I will not believe" (v. 25b; the phrase "I will [certainly!] not believe" employs the subjunctive mood with a double negative to express emphatic negation). Will faith that depends or insists on sight prove possible after Jesus' departure? For persons who come after Thomas, faith will rest not on sight but instead on hearing the testimony of others (v. 29). Throughout the Johannine narrative, sight/sign-dependent faith has emerged as vulnerable. In the case of Thomas, though, Jesus does not withhold what the "Twin" has demanded. Jesus joins the gathered company again and, recalling Thomas's earlier words, urges him to touch the body of the risen Lord, still marked with crucifixion wounds (v. 27). Thomas, though, does not after all need to touch: he has seen and heard enough—and the encounter with Jesus evokes from the Twin the most sublime christological confession of the Gospel: "My Lord and my God!" (v. 28).

John 20 closes with a two-verse epilogue that acknowledges the selectivity in its account of the signs Jesus performed and states the work's primary aim: to engender life-bestowing faith in Jesus "the Messiah, the Son of God" (vv. 30–31).[65] Whether or not the Gospel originally, and aptly, ended at 20:30–31, the canonical form of John includes another chapter recording a final resurrection appearance by Jesus to a group of seven disciples,[66] concluding with a second two-verse epilogue (21:24–25; as in 20:30–31, this

65. There is considerable manuscript support for the subjunctive verb translated "that you may come to believe" in the NRSV of 20:31. The NRSV opts for an aorist subjunctive of purpose (*pisteusēte*); however, many commentators prefer the present subjunctive *pisteuēte*, with the sense of continued believing. See, e.g., Brown, *Gospel according to John*, 2:1056, 1059–60; Barrett, *Gospel according to John*, 575; Schnackenburg, *Gospel according to St. John*, 3:338. In my view, while the Fourth Gospel does not preside over the formation of a community completely walled off from the world but one that is sent into that world with a mission of witness, the narrative speaks primarily to an audience that already believes.

66. Six join Simon Peter on a fishing outing (21:1–4): Thomas (the Twin), Nathanael (cf. 1:45–51), the sons of Zebedee (James and this John are not mentioned by name here or elsewhere in the Fourth Gospel), and two anonymous disciples—one of whom must be "the disciple whom Jesus loved," who figures in the story beginning in 21:7. That this entails an abandonment of discipleship and a return to the occupation of fishing seems unlikely, at least in the canonical version of the story, which follows the resurrection appearances and Spirit endowment of ch. 20. In any case, the episode does explicitly restore Peter to the status of disciple (21:15–19).

second epilogue mentions that the book presents only a selection of Jesus' activity). The setting of the last episode in the Gospel has shifted from Jerusalem back to Galilee.

The fishing expedition and breakfast scene in 21:1–14 bear intriguing resemblance to Luke 5:1–11. Though placed in different narrative settings in the two Gospels and containing almost no identical phrasing, these two fishing tales have motif elements in common. Jesus directs a dramatic, large catch of fish (described with some variation of *plēthos ichthyōn*, "lots of fish," 21:6 AT) after failed attempts by a group of disciples to secure a catch. In both accounts Peter plays a central role yet is part of a larger fishing company.[67] John 21 expands the fishing miracle, adding recognition and shared-meal motifs that fit the postresurrection context. Within that setting, the meal component of the story corresponds to Luke 24:41–43, but the passages do not show verbal contact, and Jesus plays different roles in the two—hosting an impromptu breakfast in John 21, asking for food in Luke 24.[68]

Prominent in this concluding chapter of the Fourth Gospel is the final development of two key Johannine characters, Simon Peter and the disciple whom Jesus loved. John 21:15–19 explicitly rehabilitates Peter, restoring his status and identity as disciple, after he has denied being a disciple following Jesus' arrest (18:17, 25, 27). In answer to Jesus' repeated question "Simon son of John, do you love me?" Peter three times affirms his love for Jesus, even as he had denied his discipleship three times. Each time Jesus charges Peter to feed or care for his sheep, thus focusing his renewed disciple vocation on a pastoral function. While the beloved disciple will continue Jesus' work of revelation witness, Peter will carry on the role of shepherd.[69] Jesus also offers Peter a preview of his death as an old man (vv. 18–19a), then reissues the summons "Follow me" as a disciple (v. 19b).

Peter, hearing of his own eventual demise as a martyr, asks Jesus about the beloved disciple: "Lord, what about him?" (v. 21). The sometimes playful, sometimes dead-serious rivalry between the two (see 13:23–26; 18:15–16; 20:3–10; 21:7) comes to closure at story's end. "If it is my will that he remain until I come, what is that to you?" Jesus replies to Peter. He then

67. In John 21, Peter is joined by six others (see n. 66); in Luke 5:1–11, Peter's fishing team includes James and John, the sons of Zebedee.

68. Cf. also the Emmaus meal at which Jesus, the invited guest, becomes host (Luke 24:28–32)—thus closer to the role given Jesus in John 21:12–13. The number of fish caught (153) has been the subject of much speculation; for a vigorous recent attempt, see Bauckham, *Testimony of the Beloved Disciple*, 271–84. Bauckham observes that the word *sēmeion* ("sign") occurs 17x in John (ibid., 281). Three other key Johannine words that appear with *sēmeion* in John 20:30–31 (all for the last time in the Gospel) are *pisteuein* ("believe," 98x), *Christos* ("Christ," 19x), and *zōē* ("life," 36x)—a total count of 153, which also is the sum of the consecutive numbers 1 through 17. These are fascinating numerological details, but I do not find the proposal convincing or interpretively meaningful. Bauckham also suggests that the number has intertextual connection to passages in Ezekiel: the Hebrew names Gedi and Eglaim, which appear in Ezek 47:10, have numerical values of 17 and 153, and Ezek 47:10 refers to the spreading of nets and fish of many kinds (ibid., 278–80).

69. See ibid., 83–87.

repeats, "Follow me!" (v. 22). Verse 23 mentions rumors that the beloved disciple would not die before Jesus' return but also clarifies that this is a mishearing of Jesus' statement. What does "remain until I come" (v. 23) is the testimony that the beloved disciple has left behind him, which "we know" to be "true" (v. 24). If the Gospel's second epilogue is to be believed, it is this anonymous disciple's voice that supplies the authoritative witness on which the Gospel is based.

Techniques of Narration

The narrative of John's Gospel makes extensive use of various techniques of storytelling that engage and instruct the audience. Like Mark but to an even greater degree, John employs strategies of implicit, or indirect, communication. Often in the Fourth Gospel, the text says much more than it seems to be saying. One needs to read this story at a higher (or deeper) level than the surface meaning of the words—and on another plane than the characters whom Jesus encounters in the story hear him—in order to "get" it. Here I focus attention on the literary techniques of (1) riddle and misunderstanding, (2) explanatory comments by the narrator, (3) irony, and (4) metaphor.[70] Each technique creates a special bond between author and reader, a community of understanding not shared by the characters in the story. This shared understanding, at a level not attained by the story's characters, leads the reader toward embracing the author's perspective—and that means, above all, his claims for Jesus. I will then briefly consider three additional ways in which the narrative "reveals" its truth to readers: (1) an unrelenting dualism or polarity of language that clearly locates John's audience in the world, (2) signs that Jesus performs, and (3) discourses with dialogue through which Jesus presents his teaching.

Techniques of Narration in John's Gospel
• Riddle and misunderstanding
• Explanatory comments by the narrator
• Irony
• Metaphor
• Duality, or polarity
• Revelation through signs
• Revelation through discourse and debate

70. The treatment of these literary techniques in this section of the chapter will be brief; the walk through the narrative above has already surfaced much of this material. R. Alan Culpepper's pioneering narratological exploration of these literary techniques is still illuminating (*Anatomy of the Fourth Gospel: A Study in Literary Design* [Philadelphia: Fortress Press, 1983], 149–202).

The Johannine Jesus is a persistent riddler. Riddles, conveyed in compact narrative units (often unfolded in riddling sessions), pose (or imply) questions in language that deliberately conceals as well as discloses; the audience may or may not be able to solve the riddle. Indeed, in the riddles that pervade John's narrative, typically the character hearing the riddle does not solve it. Whether through riddle or enigmatic or ironic statement, Jesus repeatedly befuddles characters he encounters. Through their misunderstanding, however, readers arrive at clearer, deeper understanding.

Riddles

John again and again presents Jesus "posing a dilemma that needs to be solved";[71] he purposefully uses ambiguity in language in a way that confuses listeners. The result is a divided audience of insiders who understand and outsiders who do not. Here are just a few examples among many in the Fourth Gospel:

- *Riddle*: Jesus says, "I am the living bread that came down from heaven. Whoever eats of this bread will live forever; and the bread that I will give for the life of the world is my flesh." (6:51)
- — *Listener Response* (confusion): "The Jews then disputed among themselves, saying, 'How can this man give us his flesh to eat?'" (v. 52)
- *Riddle*: Jesus says, "I am going away, and you will search for me, but you will die in your sin. Where I am going, you cannot come." (8:21)
- — *Listener Response* (confusion): "Then the Jews said, 'Is he going to kill himself? Is that what he means by saying, "Where I am going, you cannot come"?'" (v. 22)
- *Riddle*:

  [Jesus says,] "Very truly, I tell you, anyone who does not enter the sheepfold by the gate but climbs in by another way is a thief and a bandit. The one who enters by the gate is the shepherd of the sheep. The gatekeeper opens the gate for him, and the sheep hear his voice. He calls his own sheep by name and leads them out. When he has brought out all his own, he goes ahead of them, and the sheep follow him because they know his voice. They will not follow a stranger, but they will run from him because they do not know the voice of strangers." (10:1–5)

---

71. Warren Carter, *John: Storyteller, Interpreter, Evangelist* (Peabody, MA: Hendrickson Publishers, 2006), 116. Tom Thatcher observes (*Jesus the Riddler: The Power of Ambiguity in the Gospels* [Louisville, KY: Westminster John Knox Press, 2006], 3), "Riddles use language that is confusing in an intentional and artistic way." Riddles "obscure their referents through controlled ambiguity, the artful use of language that could reasonably refer to more than one thing." A riddle "is a question that purposefully suggests several possible answers and leaves it to the audience to guess which answer is the right one."

— *Listener Response* (confusion): "Jesus used this figure of speech [or riddle: *paroimia*] with them, but they did not understand what he was saying to them." (v. 6)

• *Riddle*: "Jesus said to [Martha], 'Your brother will rise again.'" (11:23)

— *Listener Response* (partial understanding): "Martha said to him, 'I know that he will rise again in the resurrection on the last day.'" (v. 24; Jesus proceeds to correct the temporal perspective in vv. 25–26)

• *Riddle*: Jesus says, "A little while, and you will no longer see me, and again a little while, and you will see me." (16:16–24, esp. v. 16)

— *Listener Response* (confusion): "Then some of his disciples said to one another, 'What does he mean by saying to us, "A little while, and you will no longer see me, and again a little while, and you will see me" . . .?' They said, 'What does he mean by this "a little while"? We do not know what he is talking about.'" (vv. 17–18)

• *Then More Riddles*:

[Jesus says,] "Very truly, I tell you, you will weep and mourn, but the world will rejoice; you will have pain, but your pain will turn into joy. When a woman is in labor, she has pain, because her hour has come. But when her child is born, she no longer remembers the anguish because of the joy of having brought a human being into the world. So you have pain now; but I will see you again, and your hearts will rejoice, and no one will take your joy from you.

"On that day you will ask nothing of me. Very truly, I tell you, if you ask anything of the Father in my name, he will give it to you. Until now you have not asked for anything in my name. Ask and you will receive, so that your joy may be complete.

"I have said these things to you in figures of speech [or riddles: *paroimiai*]. The hour is coming when I will no longer speak to you in figures, but will tell you plainly of the Father." (16:20–25)[72]

What is the effect of such riddles on John's audience? Riddles that remain unexplained would puzzle first-time readers, just as they do the story's characters. As a result, readers will be prompted to think about their meaning and continue reading with the aim of eventual discernment; such enigmas "are meant to tease initially uncomprehending readers into theological enlightenment."[73] In the process, they will become aligned with the wisdom of Jesus conveyed through the narrative, insiders to truth in ways not possible within the story for its characters.[74]

---

72. As Carter points out, in 16:25 Jesus announces an end to riddles with another riddle (*John: Storyteller, Interpreter, Evangelist*, 118).

73. Bauckham, *Testimony of the Beloved Disciple*, 121.

74. For full discussion of John's use of the riddle form, see Tom Thatcher, "The Riddles of Jesus in the Johannine Dialogues," in *The Gospel of John and Christian Theology*, ed. Richard Bauckham and Carl Mosser (Grand Rapids: Wm. B. Eerdmans Publishing Co., 2008), 263–77; idem, *The Riddles of Jesus in John: A Study in Tradition and Folklore*, SBLMS 53 (Atlanta: SBL Press, 2000); idem, *Jesus the Riddler*.

Misunderstanding

Through the ambiguity of riddles spoken by Jesus and in other ways, John's Gospel repeatedly uses the literary device of misunderstanding: Jesus makes a statement; the character to whom he is speaking misunderstands, which conveniently gives Jesus the opportunity to explain his meaning in a way that takes the discussion to a higher (or deeper) level—all for the reader's instruction.[75] A parade example is the conversation with Nicodemus. This distinguished "teacher of Israel," Nicodemus, misunderstands when Jesus says, "Truly, truly, I tell you, unless one is born *anōthen* [ambiguity here: is the nuance temporal or spatial, "anew/again/a second time" or "from above"?], that person cannot see the realm of God" (vv. 3–4 AT). Jesus explains: "To enter the realm of God, one must be born of water and Spirit" (v. 5 AT). Readers discern—Nicodemus does not (yet)—that participation in *God's* world requires, beyond the observance of ritual, a spiritual renewal, a being born *from above*.

Again and again, various character groups misunderstand what Jesus says. Jewish *leaders* in Jerusalem misunderstand a statement about the temple's destruction and then Jesus' rebuilding it in three days, which disciples later (after Easter) understand as symbolic (2:19–22). But listeners at the time do not get it: "This temple has been under construction for forty-six years, and will you raise it up in three days?" (2:20).

Disciples, too, misunderstand—and often! When they do, Jesus ordinarily says more, which they may or may not comprehend, but either way the audience of the Gospel receives this amplified teaching. Here are two examples: after Jesus' encounter with the Samaritan woman, the disciples urge him to eat, but he replies, "I have food to eat that you do not know about" (4:32, a riddle). The disciples process these words on a literal plane and so mishear: "Surely no one has brought him something to eat?" (v. 33). Jesus explains the saying as metaphor: "My food is to do the will of him who sent me and to complete his work" (v. 34). Later, in preparation for a trip to Bethany, Jesus tells the disciples, "Our friend Lazarus has fallen asleep, but I am going there to awaken him" (11:11). Again they hear Jesus on a literal plane: "Lord, if he has fallen asleep, he will be all right" (v. 12), but the narrator clarifies that the statement is metaphorical: "Jesus, however, had been speaking about his death" (v. 13). On this occasion, he decodes for them: "Then Jesus told them plainly, 'Lazarus is dead'" (v. 14).

The *crowds* also misunderstand Jesus. For example, they stumble when trying to interpret his saying about being "lifted up from the earth" (12:32). This time the narrator gives the true sense of these ambiguous words ("to indicate the kind of death he was to die," v. 33) *before* the crowd responds

---

75. For further discussion of the Johannine technique of misunderstanding, see Culpepper, *Anatomy of the Fourth Gospel*, 152–65; Carter, *John: Storyteller, Interpreter, Evangelist*, 114–16; Andreas J. Köstenberger, *A Theology of John's Gospel and Letters*, Biblical Theology of the New Testament (Grand Rapids: Zondervan. 2009), 141–45.

with confusion: "We have heard from the law that the Messiah remains forever. How can you say that the Son of Man must be lifted up? Who is this Son of Man?" (v. 34). They do understand that Jesus is alluding to his coming death and experience cognitive dissonance when trying to square that image with their notion of the Messiah. As the episode ends, confusion progresses to disbelief (as in 6:32–58). In John 8, too, misunderstanding of provocative speech by Jesus proceeds to disbelief. When he speaks of his departure—"I am going away. . . . Where I am going, you cannot come" (8:21)—his Jewish auditors are puzzled: "Is he going to kill himself? Is that what he means by saying, 'Where I am going, you cannot come'?" (v. 22). As the dialogue continues, the narrator observes that "they did not understand" Jesus' reference to the Father (God) as "the one who sent me" (vv. 26–27). Verse 23, in Jesus' voice, gives the reason for such pervasive misunderstanding: "You are from below, I am from above; you are of this world, I am not of this world" (reflecting John's cosmic dualism).[76]

This repeating pattern of misunderstanding lifts John's audience to a privileged position above the limited comprehension of the characters who interact with Jesus. In this way readers learn *how* to read the story, how to understand Jesus at a more profound level—to "believe." The audience of the Gospel gains deeper understanding of Jesus' message and therefore of his person, significance, and mission.

Narrator's Explanations

Characters who interact with Jesus may struggle to understand what he says, but the narrator repeatedly offers explanations of words and events in a way that guides the Gospel audience toward understanding.[77] A few examples from John 1–4 and from the crucifixion scene illustrate this technique:

- In rapid succession, three narrator's asides translate Aramaic or Hebrew terms: "Rabbi (which translated means Teacher)" (1:38); "Messiah (which is translated Anointed)" (1:41); and "Cephas (which is translated Peter)" (1:42).
- In 2:21–22, the narrator explains Jesus' enigmatic statement about the temple's destruction: "But he was speaking of the temple of his body. After he was raised from the dead, his disciples remembered that he had said this; and they believed the scripture and the word that Jesus had spoken."

76. Among many other instances of the misunderstanding pattern in John's narrative, see, e.g., 4:10–15; 6:32–42, 51–58; 8:21–24, 31–38, 51–58; 10:1–18; 12:27–30, 32–36; 13:36–38; 14:4–9 (a riddling session); 16:16–19 (another riddling session).

77. See Carter, *John: Storyteller, Interpreter, Evangelist*, 110–11; Köstenberger, *Theology of John's Gospel and Letters*, 135–41. Among the types of explanations Köstenberger identifies are translation of Aramaic/Hebrew terms, explanation of Palestinian geography, explanation of Jewish customs, references to Jesus' insight or prescience or to God's providential ordering of events, references to characters or events mentioned earlier, references to fulfillment of Scripture or of Jesus' words, and clarification of the meaning of statements made by Jesus or others.

- In 4:1–2, the narrator clarifies that Jesus did not actually baptize people: "Now when Jesus learned that the Pharisees had heard, 'Jesus is making and baptizing more disciples than John'—although it was not Jesus himself but his disciples who baptized—he left Judea."
- When Jesus encounters a Samaritan woman at Jacob's well and asks her for a drink, a narrator's aside twice gives clarifying explanation: "His disciples had gone to the city to buy food" (4:8) and "Jews do not share things in common with Samaritans" (4:9; NRSV places both of these asides in parentheses).
- In 4:44, a narrator's aside that makes contact with the Synoptic tradition explains Jesus' movement into Galilee: "for Jesus himself had testified that a prophet has no honor in the prophet's own country."
- After the death of Jesus, the soldiers refrain from breaking his legs and one of them instead pierces his side with a spear, "and at once blood and water came out" (19:33–34). The narrator then comments, "(He who saw this has testified so that you also may believe. His testimony is true, and he knows that he tells the truth.) These things occurred so that the scripture might be fulfilled, 'None of his bones shall be broken.' And again another passage of scripture says, 'They will look on the one whom they have pierced'" (vv. 35–37). The narrator's intervention in the story here underscores its reliability through the double appeal to the anonymous disciple's witness and to the fulfillment of Scripture.

Irony

Irony—including both verbal and dramatic or situational irony—is prominent in John's Gospel (even more than in Mark; see ch. 3 above).[78] Irony is present when an event or statement carries potential meaning on two levels, with the meaning on one level being contradictory to that on the other level, and when there is some element of unawareness (on the part of the "victim" of the irony).

Particularly thick with irony is the raising of Lazarus and its aftermath in chapter 11. Lazarus's death brings life, which leads to the Jerusalem elite's resolve to have Jesus put to death, which—in John's telling of the story—means abundant life for the world. The narrator rivets attention on the irony of the high priest Caiaphas's call for the death of one man to save the nation, an unwitting prophetic speech that carries meaning wholly other than what he intends and imagines (11:49–50). Such Johannine victims of irony remain

---

78. See, e.g., 6:42; 7:27–28, 35–36; 8:22 (cf. 10:17–18); 11:16, 48–50; 18:33, 39; 19:3, 5, 14–15. For discussion of Johannine irony, see Paul D. Duke, *Irony in the Fourth Gospel* (Atlanta: John Knox Press, 1985); Gail R. O'Day, *Revelation in the Fourth Gospel: Narrative Mode and Theological Claim* (Philadelphia: Fortress Press, 1986); Culpepper, *Anatomy of the Fourth Gospel*, 165–80; Carter, *John: Storyteller, Interpreter, Evangelist*, 118–22; Köstenberger, *Theology of John's Gospel and Letters*, 150–55.

unaware of the truth "from above," but if John's readers do "get" it, they are lifted above the view of the uncomprehending characters and drawn toward the perspective of the Gospel's author, as discerned in the voice of the narrator and especially that of Jesus.

As in the example of Caiaphas (11:49–50), John often has Jesus' conversation partners and especially his adversaries unwittingly speak the truth about him. For example, early in the conversation with Jesus, the Samaritan woman asks him, "Are you greater than our father Jacob?" (4:12 RSV). Later "the Jews" challenge what they regard as an inconceivable status claim: "Are you greater than our father Abraham?" (8:53). And Pilate declares, "Behold your King!" (19:14 RSV; other ironic declarations of Jesus' royal status in 18:39; 19:3, 15, 19). John's audience recognizes the truth in these rhetorical questions and statements, even if the character speaking does not (or in the case of the Samaritan woman, does not yet).

In fact, the whole passion narrative is laced with irony. Jesus, the "light of the world," is met by a band of soldiers and officials who need torches when they come to arrest him—vivid display of the point that they "walk in darkness" (8:12). Pilate, ostensibly the one in charge of the trial of Jesus, comes under judgment by the very one who stands before him as the embodiment of truth, a truth that Pilate cannot see. Finally (as in the other Gospels), there is the supreme irony: Jesus is executed for being precisely what he truly is: "King" (John highlights the irony in 19:19–22). And the elite priests, in order to achieve their goal, must, in the process of denying Jesus' kingship, also deny the sovereignty of God (19:15). As Culpepper comments, "The implied author does not wink or smile. Is that grim satisfaction or tears in his eyes?"[79]

The from-above Christology of the Fourth Gospel means that the whole life of Jesus is a matter of profound irony—he and his words and actions are not what they seem, or are much more than they seem. The multiple levels of meaning encompass heaven and earth, and everyone ("the world") who operates "from below" is unaware of the truth, as epitomized by Pilate's peremptory dismissal "What is truth?" (18:38). And because God's purpose to confront the world with truth in the person of the Son whom he has sent, and to offer life for all who believe, is effectual and not to be thwarted by even the most potent opposition, the plot of the entire narrative is ironic.[80] Rome and its allies among the Jerusalem elite—not to mention Satan—succeed in eliminating a threat to their power and control. Yet even his death on a cross, contrary to all appearances, means that the world ruler has been vanquished and that abundant life now comes to all who accept it.

79. Culpepper, *Anatomy of the Fourth Gospel*, 169.
80. As Lincoln puts it, "The irony of the opposition's counterplot is that, in its success in putting Jesus to death, it brings about the resolution of the main plot" (*Truth on Trial*, 18). Indeed, each of the canonical Gospels in its own way presents Jesus in a deeply ironic way, through the focusing lens of the cross.

Metaphor

The Fourth Gospel presents a wide range of metaphors that inform audience appreciation of the identity and significance of Jesus and convey the truth Jesus embodies. Jesus "is" bread (food), a spring of flowing water, light, a vine, a gate, and a path.[81] This array of metaphorical images supports the claim of the narrative that Jesus is the source of life. Jesus has divine authority to give life (e.g., 5:26), a claim that is reinforced by the presentation of many of these metaphors in "I am" statements, where the "I am" recalls God's self-identification to Moses as "I AM" (Exod 3:13–14; cf. Isa 43:10, 13, 25).[82] Jesus says he is "the bread of life" (6:35, 48; cf. 6:41, 51, bread "from heaven"), "the light of the world" (8:12; 9:5), "the gate for the sheep" (10:7, 9), "the good shepherd" (10:11, 14), "the resurrection and the life" (11:25), "the way" (14:6, "and the truth, and the life"), and "the vine" (15:1, 5).

Johannine Metaphors Employing "I am" Statements	
• Bread of life (or from heaven)	• Resurrection and the life
• Light of the world	• The way, the truth, the life
• Gate for the sheep	• Vine
• Good shepherd	

Duality (Polarity)

In John, an array of metaphors converge in the governing image of Jesus as the one uniquely authorized by God for the mission of bestowing life in and for the world. Nevertheless, the world divides in response to the gift he bears; many do not accept it, an outcome clearly previewed in the Johannine prologue (1:10–11). It is not surprising, therefore, that many of the metaphors that present the life-giving character of Jesus' mission have a "shadow" side, participating in the duality or polarity that pervades the entire narrative:[83]

- From above ↔ from below
- Not from this world ↔ from this world

---

81. These Johannine metaphors are typically discussed under the rubric of symbol. See, e.g., Koester, *Symbolism in the Fourth Gospel*; Culpepper, *Anatomy of the Fourth Gospel*, 180–98. Symbols stand in for the thing (concept, etc.) they represent, but in metaphor the listener is prompted to think of one thing in terms of another. Here is how this figurative language typically works in John's Gospel. Readers gain insight into the meaning of Jesus and what he provides through reflection on the metaphor. Often the specific entailments of the metaphor that are relevant to the comparison are left unstated, though occasionally these are fleshed out. For example, the image of Jesus as "the bread of life" in John 6 invokes the metaphor "believing in Jesus is eating bread," and Jesus explicitly mentions the central entailment of eating to receive life-sustaining nourishment (6:35, 50–51). However, Jesus amplifies the metaphor in spiritual terms: the bread is *from heaven*, offers *eternal life*, and is to be identified with Jesus' own *flesh*.

82. On the "I am" sayings in John, see Thompson, *John*, 156–60.

83. On John's dualistic language, see Köstenberger, *Theology of John's Gospel and Letters*, 282–92; Carter, *John: Storyteller, Interpreter, Evangelist*, 86–106.

- Believe ⟷ not believe
- Save ⟷ condemn/judge
- Life ⟷ death
- Light ⟷ darkness
- Love ⟷ hate
- Truth ⟷ falsehood
- Flesh ⟷ spirit

Embroiled in controversy with Judean contemporaries in John 8 and in testy exchange with the Roman governor Pilate, Jesus names the core polarity:

- "You are from below, I am from above; you are of this world, I am not of this world." (8:23)
- "You would have no power over me unless it had been given you from above." (19:11)

Jesus comes "from above," from the Father, sent into the world that God created and loves to represent God and to speak and act for God. Some see it, believe, and accept the gift offered; others, however, turn away (clearly imaged in 3:16–21). There is no fence one can straddle to avoid or defer decision, though such characters as Nicodemus and Thomas do hint that there is possibility of moving *toward* genuine faith from a position of confusion or skepticism.

In John's narrative, the global scale of the collision between worlds is evident in the role played by Rome, represented by Pilate. Yet the cosmic scale of the conflict is seen in Satan's attempts to orchestrate the annihilation of God's Son and his life-bestowing mission. The ambiguity of the phrase "ruler of this world" (12:31; 14:30; 16:11)—the figures of Rome and Satan can both be glimpsed, depending on how one turns the image—invites John's audience to view its own place in the world, and in eternity (in space-time, one might say today), in a new way. Whatever hostility John's readers may encounter because of their commitment, they will see and know the big picture.[84] They will find reason—and, with the aid of the Paraclete, *capacity*—to "abide," to persevere, in this commitment (6:56; 8:31; 15:1–10).

Drawing on the work of Halliday, Warren Carter holds that John's dualistic language "constitutes an antisociety in tension with, and counter to, dominant values"; this language "reflects, creates, and maintains an alternative identity and understanding of the world."[85] Nowhere is this more

---

84. As Warren Carter puts it, the Johannine polarity (belonging to God vs. belonging to the devil) concerns "origin and commitments in relation to two superhuman powers" (*John: Storyteller, Interpreter, Evangelist*, 89) or "two cosmic superpowers" (ibid., 90).

85. Ibid., 88. See M. A. K. Halliday, *Learning How to Mean: Explorations in the Function of Language* (London: Edward Arnold, 1971). Similar readings of John as employing "antilanguage" are offered by Bruce J. Malina and Richard L. Rohrbaugh, *Social-Science Commentary*

apparent than in Jesus' prayer in John 17, which envisages the formation of a community of disciples who live in an antagonistic world and are called to embrace a mission as witnesses within it, but fundamentally do not belong to it. Their identity, character, and future are defined from beyond, and this orients them within hostile space as an alternative community. By their love for one another, they will demonstrate that they belong to the Lord as his disciples (13:35).

Revelation through Signs

Since this story so emphasizes the distinction between God's world ("above") and the humanly constructed world ("below"), genuine knowing, or truth, depends on revelation. From the beginning, John's audience recognizes that the possibility of knowing (truth) stems from Jesus' identity and role as the *Logos*, God's own self-communication to the world of God's creation (1:1–3). Jesus discloses God's character and aims in both work and word. Doing the work of God, Jesus performs signs (*sēmeia*); he does not leave the work uninterpreted but explains what it means and discloses the truth to which it points.[86] Much of the interest generated by the narrative, though, concerns not what Jesus does or says but how observers respond. Sometimes the signs, with their interpretation by Jesus, elicit faith. But sometimes they—or the explication that follows—provoke resistance, even hostile opposition.

Along with generic narrative summaries of signs performed by Jesus, and the response they generate (e.g., 2:23–24; 3:2; 6:2, 26; 7:31; 12:37; 20:30–31), John presents a set of discrete episodes:

- *Water transformed* into festive wedding wine is emblematic of the abundant blessing of the era of salvation now dawning (2:1–11).
- — *Outcome*: Disciples believe (2:11)—and the fabulous wine no doubt produces a very happy wedding party too!
- *Healing and restored life* for the child of a royal official raise the probing question whether faith that depends on signs is genuine (4:46–54).
- — *Outcome*: After Jesus has placed a question mark beside belief that depends on signs (4:48; cf. 2:23–24), the father—both before and after the healing—proves to have faith (4:50, 53), and his whole household comes to believe.
- *Disability* (walking impairment) *is healed* (5:1–9; complication of Sabbath timing).
- — *Outcome*: Jesus' claim to be acting as agent of his Father, God, sparks a reaction of rage, and he further elaborates the sign in terms of the authority he has received from God to grant life and to judge.

---

on the Gospel of John (Minneapolis: Augsburg Fortress, 1998); and Norman R. Peterson, *The Gospel of John and the Sociology of Light: Language and Characterization in the Fourth Gospel* (Valley Forge, PA: Trinity Press International, 1993).

86. On the signs in John, see Thompson, *John*, 65–68.

- *Bread is multiplied* sufficient to feed a multitude (6:1–15).
— *Outcome*: Jesus interprets the sign as revealing that he is life-giving bread from heaven (bread-of-life discourse) and provokes a negative crowd response as well as disciple defection.
- *Sight is restored* for a man born blind (9:1–7; complication of Sabbath timing)
— *Outcome*: The man formerly blind progresses toward authentic faith in Jesus, the "light of the world," in dialogue with Jesus and confrontation with Pharisees; Jesus spars with Pharisee detractors, whom he indicts for their culpable failure to see (truth).
- *Life is restored* to a dead man beloved to Jesus, Lazarus (11:1–45).
— *Outcome*: Many believe (11:45), but a hastily convened council of elite priests and Pharisees decides to put him to death (vv. 46–53).

The signs related in John 5, 6, 9, and 11 are embedded in lengthy narratives that develop the meaning of the event, either through discourse by Jesus or through dialogue (or debate) between him and observers, and also report the response to the sign, ranging from belief to controversy and hostility. The Sabbath-day timing of the signs in John 5 and 9 is problematic but soon yields to christological claims as the bone of contention. All four of these signs produce, at best, mixed response. In John 5, observers want to put Jesus to death when he claims to be doing the work of his Father 24/7 (5:18). In chapter 6, the response to the sign as interpreted by Jesus is less ferocious but nevertheless negative: the people's request to "give us this [life-nourishing] bread [from heaven] always" (6:34) becomes oppositional when Jesus claims to be that "bread from heaven."[87] In chapter 9, the episode ends on a note of vigorous debate between Jesus and Pharisees; his indictment of their incapacity to see the truth concludes the scene (9:39–41; his speech continues, without evident change of scene or listeners, through 10:18). Even in John 11, where the raising of Lazarus produces (sign-based) faith in many who hear of the remarkable sign (which epitomizes Jesus' power to give life), the outcome is antagonism, this time taking concrete shape in a formal decision to have Jesus killed. The signs Jesus performs, it turns out, reveal much not only about Jesus' identity and mission but also about the hearts and minds of the people who see and hear.

Revelation through Discourse and Debate

In John's narrative the works (or signs) Jesus performs, especially as he interprets them in the accompanying discourses or dialogues/debates, reveal his identity and the character of his mission: giving life and witnessing to truth. The dialogues are typically cast as debates and interrogation sessions, as

---

87. The crowd's initial reaction to the feeding itself is to regard Jesus as a prophet and press him to accept royal status (6:14–15).

though part of a sustained trial in which Jesus is the defendant. Therefore they also reveal the stance that Jesus' partners in dialogue and controversy are taking toward his mission and claims. I list below several of the major discourse and dialogue sessions and characterize their thematic emphases and story audience response:

- *Dialogue* with Pharisee-teacher Nicodemus (3:1–21)[88]
- — *Theme:* Participation in God's new world (reign) requires spiritual (re)birth "from above" (= by the Spirit); God has sent the Son with this saving mission in the world, but many will not embrace it.
- — *Response:* Nicodemus is bewildered.
- *Dialogue* with a Samaritan woman at Jacob's well (4:5–42)
- — *Theme:* Border-transgressing witness to Jesus as world Savior.
- — *Response:* The Samaritan woman witnesses to Jesus, and the whole village comes to believe in him.
- *Controversy-debate* sparked by a Sabbath-day healing (5:10–47)[89]
- — *Theme:* Jesus shares fully in the work of God his Father, both in giving life and in declaring judgment.
- — *Response:* Rage and pursuit of Jesus to kill him.
- *Discourse:* Bread of life / from heaven (6:25–71)
- — *Theme:* Jesus is the source of enduring life that can come only from God.
- — *Response:* Resistance and disciple defection.
- *Controversy-debate* centering on competing "paternity tests" (8:12–59)
- — *Theme:* Jesus claims Scripture as witness on his behalf and engages in reciprocal polemic centering on status as children of Abraham, God, and the devil.
- — *Response:* Rage and the desire to kill Jesus.
- *Controversy-debate* sparked by Sabbath-day provision of sight (9:8–41)[90]
- — *Theme:* Jesus is the "light of the world" through whose witness genuine (in)sight is possible.
- — *Response:* The man formerly blind comes to believe despite intense

88. The end point of Jesus' speech in this episode is ambiguous: the voice of the character Jesus blends seamlessly into the narrator's voice-over. Certainly by 3:16 the voice of the narrator seems to have taken over. In this case, it does not make much difference to John's audience, which has already been primed by the narrative to align closely the viewpoints of Jesus and the narrator, through whose storytelling the speech and action of Jesus are delivered to the reader.

89. The debate following the healing of the man in 5:1–9 concludes with Jesus' discourse and does not report the response of listeners after the enraged reaction in 5:16, 18 (though Jesus describes what he perceives to be their response in vv. 37–47). John 7 resumes this unfinished debate: e.g., Jesus explicitly engages the critique of his Sabbath-day conduct in this "one work" in 7:21–24.

90. This episode is unusual in John's Gospel: most of the dialogue debate features the increasingly assertive testimony of the man who received sight through Jesus' intervention. The voice of Jesus emerges only in 9:35, but he does get the last word in dialogues with the now-sighted man (vv. 35–38) and observing Pharisees (vv. 39–41).

opposition; Pharisees receive stinging indictment from Jesus for their refusal to see (truth) through his witness.

- *Discourse* on the true shepherd's leadership (10:1–21; no shift in audience from ch. 9)
— *Theme:* Jesus, the good shepherd, freely surrenders his life to protect his sheep; they know his voice and follow (only) him.
— *Response:* The audience reaction is divided, with some calling Jesus demon-possessed and others rejecting that view.
- *Dialogue* centering on Jesus as source of resurrection (and eternal) life (11:17–45)
— *Theme:* Jesus is the life-giver, and this gift of eternal life does not wait for a future resurrection but opens up even now for those who believe—with Lazarus as the sign/proof.
— *Response:* Many Jews who accompanied Lazarus's sister Mary believe, but then a council is convened by the high priest and Pharisees, and it determines to have Jesus killed (vv. 46–53).
- *Farewell discourse* and dialogue with intimate disciples (13:1–17:26)
— *Theme:* Jesus prepares the disciples for his departure, reassuring them that they will not be orphaned, for the Spirit/Paraclete (Advocate and Encourager) will come to teach and support them. (The prayer in ch. 17 petitions God for the safety and unity of his followers.)
— *Response:* Recurring confusion and distress; the positive effect of these chapters on the disciples' understanding and conduct is delayed until after the arrest and crucifixion of Jesus.

Central Motifs and Concerns

In this section I briefly discuss several of the most significant thematic emphases in John's narrative, all of which have surfaced in the course of the literary analysis above: (1) christological claims, focusing on Jesus as the revealer of God and the Son sent from the Father; (2) the link between believing and eternal life; (3) Jesus' collision with the world; (4) Jesus' death as victory and glory; and (5) continuing revelation through the witness of the beloved disciple and the work of the Spirit/Paraclete.

Central Motifs and Concerns in John's Gospel
• Christological claims: Jesus as revealer of God and Son sent from the Father
• Welcome to eternity—believing and eternal life
• Jesus' collision with the world
• "The hour has [finally] come": Jesus' death as victory and glory
• Revelation continues:
— the witness of the beloved disciple
— the work of the Spirit/Paraclete

*Christological Claims:
Jesus as Revealer of
God, the Son Sent
from the Father*

John presents Jesus as the revealer of God—the one who does the work of God and speaks the word of God (as himself the Word [*Logos*], as 1:1–18 calls him). It is as the Son "whom the Father has sent" that he carries out this mission of word and work with full divine authorization: he represents God in the world.[91] As to the work of God, Jesus' "defense" of a criticized Sabbath-day healing (specifically, his instruction "Take up [a] mat and walk," 5:8, 11) illustrates: "My Father is working still, and I am working. . . . The Son can do nothing on his own, but only what he sees the Father doing" (5:17, 19). What is that work? Above all, it is the power to render true judgment (5:22, 27) and to give resurrection life (5:25–26). In a later controversy, Jesus says, "If I am not doing the works of my Father, then do not believe me; but if I do them, even though you do not believe me, believe the works, so that you may know and understand that the Father is in me and I am in the Father" (10:37–38). What Jesus does is God's work, because Jesus is one with God—as the Son who represents the Father's character, purpose, and commitments. God's sending the Son has the purpose of making God known, of calling the world to believe, and thus of giving authentic, enduring life (e.g., 3:16–17, 36; 5:23–24; 6:40; 17:1–3).

It is the same with Jesus' word. The repeated "I am" (*egō eimi*) statements echo God's self-disclosure to Moses at the burning bush (Exod 3:14; cf. Isa 43:10, 13, 25) and thus closely identify Jesus with the name and character of God. This is clearest in the Johannine "I am" sayings that have no predicate (NRSV mg.: John 8:24, 28, 58; 13:19; 18:5, 6, 8; cf. 4:26). But the sayings that include a predicate also express Jesus' full participation in the divine gift giving of life and the things necessary for life and well-being. He says, "I am"

- *bread* to nourish and preserve life (without end, 6:35, 48–51)
- the *sheep gate* providing both access to pasture and protection and also the *shepherd* who self-sacrifices for the sake of the flock—in mixed shepherding metaphors (10:7–9, 11–18)
- the source of *resurrection life* (11:25–26)
- the *path* and the *truth* by which one may wisely navigate life and the world (14:6)
- the *vine* apart from which the disciple/branches die (15:1–6)

John's Jesus reveals God, and as God's fully authorized agent in the world, the Son sent from the Father, he bears the gift of authentic, enduring life. That gift comes to all who believe, who accept Jesus' work and word as from God.

---

91. This is an agency Christology, as Paul N. Anderson emphasizes; see, e.g., *Christology of the Fourth Gospel*, 260–61.

Welcome to Eternity!
Believing and
Eternal Life

In John's Gospel, the Synoptics' dominant image in Jesus' teaching—the reign or realm of God—morphs into "eternal life" or "life of the age" (*zōē aiōnios*).[92] In John's radical reconfiguring of space and time, and especially of eschatology, this is not only or even primarily a future reality associated with an end-time resurrection of the dead, although on occasion Jesus does claim sovereign authority over this event of future transformation (5:28–29; 6:39–40, 44). Rather, this is a quality of existence to which people have access in the present when they respond in faith to Jesus' word and work.[93] Jesus can make this claim unambiguously: "Anyone who hears my word and believes him who sent me *has eternal life*, and does not come under judgment, but *has passed from death to life*" (5:24, emphasis added).

Yet the relation of present and future life—always bound up with believing response to Jesus' revelation of the Father—is a bit more complex. In the very next verse, Jesus declares that "the hour *is coming, and is now here*, when the dead will hear the voice of the Son of God, and those who hear will live" (5:25, emphasis added). God as Father has already shared the possession of life with the Son and conveyed to him the authority to give it to those who have faith: "For just as the Father has life in himself, so he has granted the Son also to have life in himself" (v. 26). In the bread-of-life discourse, Jesus juxtaposes present and future without any evident tension between the two temporal planes: "This is indeed the will of my Father, that all who see the Son and believe in him may have eternal life; and I will raise them up on the last day" (6:40).

John's Jesus offers his climactic statement on this theme in the dialogues that precede his raising of Lazarus. When Jesus reassures Martha, "Your brother will rise again" (11:23), she acknowledges the hope of resurrection life at the end time (v. 24), but Jesus proceeds to revise her temporal assumptions: "*I am* the resurrection and the life. Those who believe in me, even though they die, will live, and everyone who lives and believes in me will never die" (vv. 25–26, emphasis added). The ensuing narrative, with mention of a death plot against Lazarus after his restoration to life (12:10–11) and Jesus' own death, makes clear that with the expression "will never die" Jesus is speaking not of the physical reality of death but of a quality of existence available even now to those with faith—an enduring life that the experience of death cannot touch and that will therefore persist beyond it. In John's presentation of Jesus' message, eternity has entered human space and forever transformed it for all with capacity to see and accept the gift. By virtue of

92. The phrase "reign [kingdom] of God" appears in John only twice (3:3, 5); cf. the reference to Jesus' kingship in 18:36. The phrase "eternal life" occurs 17x (by contrast: 4x in Matthew, 2x in Mark, 3x in Luke), nearly always in speech by Jesus; in John 6:68 Peter is parroting Jesus' message, and in 3:36 the narrator echoes Jesus' characteristic idiom.

93. Although the noun *pistis* (faith) never appears in the Fourth Gospel, the verb "believe" or "have faith" (*pisteuein*) occurs 98x (cf. Thompson, *John*, 303 n. 55). Faith is a verb in John: it means accepting and assenting to the claims of Jesus as revealer of God and giver of life.

enduring connection to Jesus (the "vine"), who is the source of life, disciples ("branches," 15:1–6) continue to enjoy this quality of life resulting from the infinite breaking into—disrupting—our finite spatial-temporal reality.

Jesus' Collision with the World

The world (*kosmos*) of God's creation (through the Word, John 1:1–3) is also the arena of God's loving, saving initiative in the sending of the Son. Eternal life comes to all who believe (e.g., 3:15–16). However, as John's narrative unfolds, humans to a great extent are unreceptive to God's self-disclosure in the mission of the Son. The prologue to the Gospel signals what lies ahead: "He was in the world, and the world came into being through him; yet the world did not know him. He came to what was his own, and his own people did not accept him" (1:10–11). Yet the Gospel's opening lines also affirm that the darkness into which the Son who reveals God shines light will not grasp that light—will neither "comprehend" (KJV) nor "overcome it" (1:5).

Opposition centers on *hoi Ioudaioi* (the Jews), typically the Pharisees and other Judean elite (especially the temple-based chief priests). In the prayer by Jesus in John 17, however, this field of opponents is broadened to simply "the world" (17:14, 16, 25; cf. v. 9).[94] Jesus' preference for the more general term "world," in contrast to the more restricted term "Jews" favored by the narrator in 1:18–12:50 and 18:1–19:42, picks up the universal, cosmic perspective of the Johannine prologue (summary of the data in n. 94). The specific conflicts that surface in the narrative concern Jewish legal practice and interpretation (e.g., Sabbath keeping), festivals, and norms of theological conviction (particularly monotheism). Yet the character Jesus appears to regard those conflicts as instances of a universal problem, the (human) world's rejection of the Creator's self-revelation (esp. through the agency

---

94. The word *kosmos* (world) occurs 18x in John 17—11x in a neutral sense, of the world as the arena in which the Son and now in prospect the disciples carry out their mission, and 7x with negative valence. The "world" also appears in this negative sense earlier in the farewell discourse (15:18–19; cf. 16:8, 20, 33). Lars Kierspel has drawn attention to the striking pattern of distribution of the terms *hoi Ioudaioi* ("the Jews," sg. *Ioudaios*) and *kosmos* (world) in John's Gospel (*The Jews and the World in the Fourth Gospel*, WUNT 2/220 [Tübingen: Mohr Siebeck, 2006], with charts tabulating the data on 77, 93). A more universal viewpoint associated with use of the word *kosmos* appears in the prologue (4x in 1:1–18, with none of *Ioudaios*) and in the farewell discourses (40x in chs. 13–17, with *Ioudaios* only once). Elsewhere, in the narrative of Jesus' ministry and in the passion narrative, *Ioudaios* significantly outpaces *kosmos* (70x vs. 33x). Interestingly, in the voice of Jesus, *Ioudaios* is rare (4x), while *kosmos* is common (64x); however, the pattern of usage by the narrator is the reverse (59x vs. 7x). Jesus, that is, favors the term "world," the narrator favors the term "Jew(s)." In general, Kierspel suggests, "the narrator describes the 'Jewishness' of the arising conflict (festivals, Sabbath, law, Moses, etc.) while Jesus points out the 'universally applicable characteristics' of the mostly negative response to his message" (ibid., 148). Jesus' speech "translates particulars into universals" (pointing readers beyond temporal limits within the narrated story). *Kosmos* is the more important term in John: "The Jews" are "only a part of an opposition that is universal in scope" (ibid., 153).

and mission of the Son). In this respect Jesus aligns his own viewpoint with that of the prologue narrator's voice-over for the whole story.[95]

That world is the object of divine love and the arena of God's saving initiative through the mission of the Son, but it is also the place (and the people) where (and among whom) that mission is opposed and rejected, and will continue to be opposed when Jesus hands the baton to his Paraclete-guided followers. Emblematic of the cosmic scale of the conflict are the allied roles of Rome (personified in Governor Pilate), the temple-based Jerusalem elite, and Satan. The identity of the chief antagonist, the "ruler of this world," is ambiguous, prompting readers to understand the powerful, menacing opposition to Jesus and his followers as both the Roman Empire and, on a cosmic plane and orchestrating affairs behind the scenes, the Evil One. But if John (and John's Jesus) is to be believed, the apparent world ruler has already been vanquished. Jesus assures the disciples, "In the world you face persecution. But take courage; I have conquered the world!" (16:33). In John's sociopolitical context, "the ruler of this world" must mean Rome, even if on a metahuman plane it also refers to Satan, which has been judged, defanged, and will be proved powerless (12:31; 14:30; 16:11).[96] Hard-pressed, discouraged members of the Johannine audience will receive these counterimperial claims as reason for hope, even if the claims are counterintuitive.

"The Hour Has (Finally) Come": Jesus' Death as Victory and Glory

If this is victory, then power and conquest have undergone radical redefinition (as is true of the Gospels as a whole, not to mention Paul's Letters and the book of Revelation!). The character of God's dominion (3:3, 5)—of Jesus' kingdom (18:36)—is worlds removed (pun intended) from that of the Roman Empire. So the long-delayed "hour" of Jesus (see 2:4; 7:6, 8, 30; 8:20; 13:1; 17:1) finally arrives as he approaches the passion. It is in his death that he accomplishes the purpose of his coming into the world, surrendering his life for the sake of the world and its life (10:10–11, 17–18). This is his moment of supreme honor, of glory (12:23, 27–28)—this most humiliating and dignity-depriving ritual of torture and execution. A more counterimperial image than the "King of the Jews" crucified, his pretension to royal status placarded in three languages from his cross, could scarcely be imagined. Yet

---

95. John 1:10–11 frames the fundamental conflict between God/Word and world in the widest terms: "He was in the world, and the world came into being through him; yet the world did not know him. He came to what was his own, and his own people did not accept him." In v. 11, "his own" (*hoi idioi*) may narrow the field to Jesus' Jewish contemporaries, thus placing the more universal and more particular rejections in parallel, or it may be synonymous with "world" in the previous verse—Jesus' own, that is, would be all humankind, not fellow Jews alone.

96. Kierspel thus suggests that in the sociopolitical context of the Fourth Gospel, "the term *kosmos* is part of a theodicy which aims to encourage readers who suffer under *Roman* persecution" (*Jews and the World in the Fourth Gospel*, 213; emphasis orig.).

his final words, "It is finished/accomplished," underscore the deep irony of it all.

Jesus' death, in John, is not his defeat but, instead, his victory. Though a Roman prisoner facing a capital charge, he controls his destiny. His death is also his departure and return to the Father who sent him: mission accomplished!

Revelation Continues: The Witness of the Beloved Disciple and the Work of the Paraclete

In the Fourth Gospel, Jesus is the one whom God has sent as the revealer, to make God known and to offer life to all who receive him. John uses two additional characters, the beloved disciple and especially the Spirit/Paraclete (*paraklētos*), to continue the work of revelation begun by Jesus. The narrative portrays the "disciple whom Jesus loved" as a model follower, and particularly as the reliable witness who has told the story from which the author has drawn in crafting the Gospel narrative (21:24; cf. 19:35). Unlike the other disciples, this "disciple whom Jesus loved" does not fail Jesus or misunderstand him. Spatial imagery is suggestive: at his very first mention in the narrative, he reclines next to the bosom of Jesus at the Last Supper (13:23), and he stands by him at the cross (19:26–27, 35). A glimpse of the empty tomb is enough to bring him to "believe" (20:8). The narrative gains authority when it can claim such an impressive and reliable source.[97]

If the beloved disciple has an especially important role in anchoring the tradition of witness on which the Fourth Gospel is secured, he is not the only one with good news to convey. His anonymity in the narrative allows him to have a representative function. All Jesus' followers are charged to testify to the truth they know. They will not do so untutored and unaided, for Jesus' promise of a Spirit/Paraclete to accompany them after his departure bridges from the bewildered disciples within the story to their mission between Easter and the time of the Johannine audience.[98]

In the time after Jesus' departure, the Spirit calls to memory all that Jesus had done and said, indeed guiding the community of the disciples into all truth (14:26; 16:13–15). In tandem with the beloved disciple, the Paraclete connects John's church to Jesus, the *Logos*. The Spirit bears several names in the Fourth Gospel: Spirit (1:32–33; 3:5–6, 34; 4:23–24; 6:63; 7:39), Holy Spirit (1:33; 14:26; 20:22); Spirit of truth (14:17; 15:26; 16:13); and Paraclete (*paraklētos*), a distinctively Johannine label for the Spirit and one confined to the farewell discourse (14:16, 26; 15:26; 16:7; cf. 1 John 2:1, where the word refers to Jesus).

97. See further Lincoln, *Gospel according to Saint John*, 24–25.
98. On the Holy Spirit in John, see Thompson, *John*, 318–22; Cornelis Bennema, *The Power of Saving Wisdom*, WUNT 2/148 (Tübingen: Mohr Siebeck, 2002); John R. Levison, *Filled with the Spirit* (Grand Rapids: Wm. B. Eerdmans Publishing Co., 2009), 366–406; Craig R. Koester, *The Word of Life: A Theology of John's Gospel* (Grand Rapids: Wm. B. Eerdmans Publishing Co., 2008), 133–60.

Aptly, in a narrative that has presented virtually Jesus' entire ministry as one long trial, the image of Paraclete suggests just such a public setting. The Spirit will continue to bear witness to truth, on Jesus' behalf, after his departure (15:26). Thus the world, in its persistent sin (rejection of divine revelation), will encounter in the Spirit a prosecutorial voice (16:8–11). It is in the bold prophetic speech of the community of Jesus' followers that the witness of the Paraclete will be heard (15:26–27).

Also important is the role of the Spirit as advocate for the disciples, standing with them and encouraging them, especially in their experience of distress and adversity. The Spirit as advocate/encourager assures the disciples that with Jesus' death and departure, they are not orphans; divine presence with them will not cease (14:16–18). Jesus' promise that he will return to be with them and the role of the Spirit merge. This is vividly enacted in the upper room scene on Easter: as Jesus commissions the disciples to continue his mission (20:21), he breathes his own breath/spirit on them and says, "Receive the Holy Spirit" (20:22; the imperative "receive" here is gift rather than command).

The narrative character of the Spirit assumes two distinct names and roles in the Fourth Gospel.[99] Especially in the first half of the narrative, the designation of Spirit or Holy Spirit dominates, and Spirit language images divine activity and power—to bring about new birth and give life (3:3–8, imagery of wind and water; 6:63, bound to Jesus' words; 7:37–39, associated with the metaphor of flowing water). Water and Spirit are linked also in the image of baptism; John says that Jesus will baptize with the Holy Spirit (1:33; cf. 3:5–6), though he does so at story's end not by water immersion but by imparting his breath (20:22).

In the farewell discourse, Spirit language adds the image of Paraclete, and the Spirit seems to assume a personal identity as successor to Jesus (14:16–17, 26; 15:26; 16:7, 13). This shift makes sense in the narrative setting; after all, in these chapters Jesus is preparing his closest followers for life after he has left them. Though distinct from Jesus and continuing his work of witness, revelation, and divine presence, the Spirit/Paraclete is no lone ranger but instead recalls to memory what Jesus has said and done, bears compelling witness to him, and honors him. The Spirit/Paraclete is "sent" or "comes" from both God the Father and Jesus (14:26; 15:26; 16:7); the mission he empowers in the community of disciples is thus an extension of Jesus' own mission as the one sent from the Father. As Marianne Meye Thompson puts it, "The Spirit carries on the work of both the Son and of the Father. In John, not only is it true that 'what the Father does, the Son does'; it is also true that 'what the Father does, the Spirit does.'"[100]

---

99. In the following discussion, I am drawing from the helpful analysis by Marianne Meye Thompson (*John*, 318–22).

100. Ibid., 320.

Concluding Reflection: The Aims and Impact of John's Narrative

In the shadow of Wayne Meeks's remarkable 1972 essay "The Man from Heaven in Johannine Sectarianism," many interpreters have regarded the Fourth Gospel and its author and first audience as *sectarian* in worldview.[101] The sharp dualism of the Gospel and its conflict-permeated narrative position Jesus and his followers *against* the world, not "of the world," and depict them as hated by the world (17:14, 16). This language betrays a sectarian orientation, the symbolic universe (worldview) of a group on the social margins that perceives itself against a potent, hostile society from which it has chosen to disengage. John's Gospel does have an "insider/outsider" or "us-against-the-world" character. The Gospel may well come, as Martyn and others have argued, from a Christian Jewish group whose experience of opposition or even persecution has hardened it and left it disillusioned, pessimistic about the world of human beings. Not to be overlooked, however, is that the Johannine group's sense of alienation and marginalization, whether imposed from outside or a matter of the group's own choosing, is also from imperial Roman society, not just Jewish social institutions. After all, Rome, the current world ruler, has been judged, and by a man tortured and executed on a Roman cross!

But there is more to say. This Gospel, despite its us-against-the-world rhetoric, does not finally permit the audience to remain in permanent retreat from the world. Rather, it sends them out as witness bearers in the world, after the example of characters like the Samaritan woman in chapter 4. They are not "of the world," to be sure; but they are still "in the world" (17:11), and now they are sent out as Paraclete-tutored witnesses to the truth they know, just as the Father sent the Son into the world.

Yet the prayer of Jesus in John 17 also points ahead to a tragic split that will bring even more turmoil and pain to John's first readers. The fervent petition "that they may all be one" (17:20–26) takes on tragic poignancy when heard in the light of the Letters of John. It turned out that they would *not* all be one. The letter 1 John, likely from a later chapter in the history of John's group, indicates that it was a house divided; one group within the Johannine church split off from it (see, e.g., 1 John 2:18–19). Coursing through the artful narrative spun by this "spiritual gospel" is the raw material for communal experience that will eventually bring shattered dreams and bitter estrangement. Forged out of much painful experience—in synagogues, in Roman society, and within the Johannine groups themselves—this Gospel offers its

---

101. Wayne A. Meeks, "The Man from Heaven in Johannine Sectarianism," in *The Interpretation of John*, ed. John Ashton, 2nd ed. (Edinburgh: T&T Clark, 1997), 169–206; orig. in *JBL* 91 (1972): 44–72. Among other proponents of the view that John and its first reading communities were sectarian in approach to the world, see, e.g., Fernando Segovia, "The Love and Hatred of Jesus and Johannine Sectarianism," *CBQ* 43 (1981): 258–72; Rensberger, *Johannine Faith and Liberating Community*, 25–29. Rensberger perceives the "Johannine community" as "a sectarian group of Jewish Christian origin, one that has distinctly introversionist features but . . . has not necessarily turned its back entirely on the possibility of mission to the world" (ibid., 28). Neyrey suggests that the more active stance of revolt is a more accurate descriptor than sectarian withdrawal (*Ideology of Revolt*, 204–6).

profound meditation on the meaning and significance of Jesus. Beautiful art often comes out of deep pain. And in the case of John, perhaps it causes deep pain as well.

John and Anti-Judaism

Before concluding our reflections on the aims and impact of John's narrative, we must acknowledge, though too briefly, the potential of this Gospel to generate readings that foster anti-Judaism. Recognizing that "both anti-Judaism and indebtedness to Judaism pervade the entire Gospel,"[102] what does responsible ethical interpretation of the Fourth Gospel look like? Does "the Fourth Gospel's declaration of God's boundless love for the world [undermine] its polemic against the Jews"?[103] Or does "the Fourth Gospel's polemic against the Jews" undermine "its declaration of God's boundless love for the world"?[104] Here the tension between (1) John's strident language of polarity and us-them boundary setting and (2) its vision of God's creative, saving purpose for the world and of the Word's capacity to illuminate all, even in and against the darkness—this tension requires the interpreter's response and decision. Does a decision for Jesus necessarily entail repudiation of all things Jewish or of a larger and largely antagonistic world?

It is crucial to observe that John's rhetoric of opposition and boundary construction arose in a particular historical moment, in a situation of sharp conflict in which the identity of God's people was contested—and specifically as a result of claims being made for Jesus as the definitive revealer of the ways and character of God. Polemic heated in the fires of such human experience must be identified with care and not repeated unreflectively. Culpepper urges recognition of the influence on John's theology of both the Jewish heritage and anti-Jewish polemic, and advocates "reasserting elements of John's theology that are discordant with its anti-Judaism."[105] I agree. And I add that John, even in the setting of bitter conflict, affords occasional glimpses of God's love for the whole world that transcends that historical moment and the often-dualistic narrative that resulted. God's love for the world, and the expansiveness of the community welcomed into that love, may be much greater than John or its first audiences—or, for that matter, its twenty-first-century readers—have dared to imagine. In Johannine terms, perhaps this is an image of a community of readers struggling to discern the Paraclete at work, leading the disciples into all—or at least needful pieces of—the truth for their own place and time.

102. R. Alan Culpepper, "Anti-Judaism in the Fourth Gospel as a Theological Problem for Christian Interpreters," in Bieringer, Polleyfeyt, and Vandecasteele-Vanneuville, eds., *Anti-Judaism and the Fourth Gospel*, 61–82, esp. 69.

103. R. Alan Culpepper, "The Gospel of John as a Document of Faith in a Pluralistic Culture," in "*What Is John?*": *Readers and Readings of the Fourth Gospel*, ed. Fernando F. Segovia, SBLSymS 3 (Atlanta: Scholars Press, 1996), 107–27, esp. 127.

104. Adele Reinhartz, "'Jews' and Jews in the Fourth Gospel," in Bieringer, Polleyfeyt, and Vandecasteele-Vanneuville, eds., *Anti-Judaism and the Fourth Gospel*, 213–27, esp. 227.

105. R. Alan Culpepper, "Anti-Judaism in the Fourth Gospel as a Theological Problem," 82. This approach is similar to that proposed in ch. 4 above on Matthew.

PART III

Coherence and Connections

Thematic Probes for
Twenty-First-Century Readers

7. From Ancient Gospels to the Twenty-First Century

As I have been writing this book, the world news has shown injustice, brutality, and suffering coming in relentless, ferocious waves. The litany of concerns is deeply troubling to people of faith and people of conscience. In years to come and in various places, the details will vary, but these sorts of things will continue to plague the global human family. Here are a few of the concerns presently on my mind:

- In a series of disturbing incidents, police have used deadly force against unarmed black persons in many cities in the United States.
- Nine faithful African American church people were gunned down amid a Bible study in Charleston, South Carolina, by a white supremacist young male.
- In the aftermath of that outrageous act of terrorizing violence, rather than arousing the conscience of a nation, what has followed is continuing polarization as some object to the slogan "Black Lives Matter" and resort to defense of the Confederate flag—symbol of the legacy of the slavery that has assaulted the dignity of so many African Americans.
- Despite recurring incidents of mass killings in schools, no substantive changes in law, policy, or law-enforcement practice result; indeed, any possibility of meaningful dialogue is virtually ruled out because of a strong and vocal lobby for the right to bear arms.
- In the Middle East, in repeated acts of brutality, the self-proclaimed Islamic State has been terrorizing Syria, among other things destroying or selling for profit archaeological treasures from antiquity. Nearly half the population of Syria has been dislocated as a result of a protracted civil war, with millions desperately seeking asylum in other countries.
- A presidential campaign in the United States gives headlines—and votes—to candidates who spout angry rhetoric of exclusion and xenophobic contempt.
- The social media are teeming with expressions of Islamophobic intolerance in the United States and in Europe.
- We are witnessing global climate change on a scale that poses a serious threat to the ecological viability of our planet, yet many people (among them, elected national leaders) simply refuse to consider relevant, available scientific evidence. (Since when did the human role as

stewards of creation include permission to destroy the ecosystems that enable life to flourish on this planet?)

The list, and the headlines, could go on and on. What do the Gospels have to say to us in the midst of all this human ugliness? Borrowing a phrase from popular (U.S.) American religious culture, WWJD ("What would Jesus do?"), we can reframe this as WWJS: "What would Jesus say?" Perhaps more to the point of this chapter, "What would the Gospels' Jesus have *us* do?"

A further, haunting question for me has been whether the New Testament Gospels have, in any significant measure, contributed to this ugliness, particularly through the harsh, other-assaulting rhetoric that many of their passages contain. But also this: how might these same Gospel narratives speak a healing, restorative word?

Probing for Connections, Listening for Harmonies

A primary interest of this book has been to foster appreciation for the distinctive presentation, literary shaping, and thematic emphases of each of the New Testament Gospels. The Gospels Portrait Gallery exhibits four quite different portraits of Jesus.

Four Gospels, Not One: (Select) Profiles of Distinctive Features

In *Mark's narrative*, Jesus' teaching and activity as the Messiah who discloses the coming-and-present reign of God has a decidedly apocalyptic texture, which accents the hiddenness of the transformative work of God's reign and the precarious, unstable place of insiders (the disciples). The fragility and vulnerability of the way of the kingdom are evident throughout: Jesus' vocation as Messiah is cruciform, taking its shape from the cross, and so is the vocation of his followers.

Matthew's Gospel embeds the life of Jesus and his mission as the Messiah deeply in the long history of Israel. His ministry centers on his role as teacher, as the definitive interpreter of the Torah (and Prophets) within the world as defined by the reign of God (heaven). He is forming a community of disciples who will embody that teaching in their shared life and in their engagement with the world. Yet the Matthean narrative knows that the community of disciples, no less than the surrounding world, is a mixed and ambiguous company. Action matters, and life faithfully lived—above all, enacting the twofold command of love for God and neighbor—fits one for participation in the eternal reign of heaven. Judgment, a prerogative of God, not the human community, will disentangle the faithful and the unfaithful, the good and the wicked, that life in the world seems inexorably to entangle. The Matthean Jesus' radical amplification of the Torah's (and thus God's) claim on human obedience points the audience toward the transformative power of vulnerable, nonretaliatory love. In Matthew's age or any age, this is a truly radical (and risky) alternative to the unending vicious cycles of retaliation and escalating violence that otherwise appear to offer no prospect for remedy or escape.

Luke's Gospel, like Matthew, embeds the story of Jesus in the history and promise-laden Scriptures of Israel, yet even more emphatically than Matthew signals the expansion of community boundaries to include persons on the social margins of the Jewish community and also outsiders to Israel. Luke's narrative sequel, Acts, will carry the baton much further, indeed to the "ends of the earth" (1:8), to the attentive *ethnē* (Gentiles or nations, 28:28; cf. the mission charge of Matt 28:19–20). Luke's Gospel challenges its audience to perceive the powerful, life-and-community-destroying lure of wealth and status seeking, and to create communities that extend mercy to the sinful, give welcoming hospitality to the outsider, and provide sustaining resources for those who lack them. This inclusive, prophetic impulse of Jesus' ministry in the Lukan narrative—with its shattering of familiar, socially constructed boundaries—is threatening to social convention, especially to the powerful and privileged, and therefore inevitably provokes fierce resistance.

John's Gospel, from its start, pictures the cosmic scope of God's concern, encompassing all of space-time within the creating, revealing, life-restoring mission that God (the Father) has given to the Son. Yet this world-encompassing vision is conveyed through a narrative that also highlights the world's stubborn refusal to embrace Jesus' witness and anticipates more of the same for his followers. So the community of disciples finds its place and its identity in the world as an alternative, countercultural reality (whether in opposition to synagogue or, in forms of nonviolent resistance, to imperial Rome). In the case of John, a beautifully artful narrative tapestry has been woven out of communal experience that is deeply conflicted and painful (a reality that continues in the post-Gospel life of the Johannine communities, as shown by the Letters of 1–3 John). In such a setting, John offers Jesus as the one through whom God confronts the world with truth and gives "eternal life" to all who accept the revealer (Jesus) as truly sent from God to make God known. But it is crucial, on John's terms, to say yes to that divine self-disclosure in and through the Son. Does such a singular focus on Jesus as the one who reveals God and gives life for those who believe pose unresolvable theological problems for persons of faith navigating an irreducibly multireligious world (the challenge, e.g., of John 14:6: "No one comes to the Father except through me")? Does the intense focus of concern on the disciples' love for *one another*—rather than for those beyond the community's borders—put ethics of the kind encountered in the Synoptics (e.g., the summons to love enemies) at risk in this Gospel?

Four Voices, One Chorus

While acknowledging the variations in context, form, and message that distinguish the Gospels from one another (only a sliver of these captured in the sketches in the previous section), it is important also to probe for areas of common concern and commitment, shared witness—particularly as we face the challenges of twenty-first-century planet earth.

In life-giving ways, Jesus' ministry embraces persons on the underside and outside of society. This is evident both in actions such as healings and shared meals and also in his spoken message. All four Gospels include scenes that highlight this feature of his mission, although it is most prominent in the Synoptics. In those three Gospels, the reign of God, as Jesus both speaks and practices it, entails reversals of status and place. Not the people who command power at the center but those who lack it on the fringes are the ones whom Jesus particularly embraces.

Contemporary disability studies would point interpretation of the healing stories in the Gospels toward their social and communal dimension.[1] In such stories as the healing of a woman with a chronic bleeding disorder (Mark 5:25–34 and parr.), the restoration of a Samaritan and nine others afflicted with leprosy (Luke 17:11–19), and the giving of sight to Bartimaeus (Mark 10:46–52), Jesus removes barriers to full participation in the community. Where healing or removal of a disability is not possible (or perhaps even desired), the concern to remove barriers to participation in the community remains as charge for the followers of Jesus.

Acts of hospitality and welcome, even toward persons branded as sinners, highlight the radical mercy and forgiveness of God, which Jesus summons his followers to enact in their relations with others. When those relations involve hostility and enmity, Jesus challenges followers to eschew the ordinary, self-defending posture for which retaliation is the first choice. Rather, far from avenging themselves, believers should seek the flourishing of others, even the enemy.

Nevertheless, the holy justice (or judgment) of God, while patient, does not—often despite appearances—simply tolerate and ignore the destructive, death-dealing forces humans so persistently unleash. In Mark and Matthew, and with some modulation of temporal horizons in Luke and especially John, the Gospels offer an apocalyptically tuned hope, both making sense of the evil in play within and around communities of faith and also empowering faithful witness and just action in the meantime. There is more to the world than the community-rending, life-destroying forces so much in evidence. Of this hope, tenacious even amid hurt, loss, and despair, the cross stands as potent symbol. For all of the mystery and multiple meanings of the diverse Easter stories, they converge in securing this hope: the life snuffed out by the empire's brutal military violence stands vindicated by God, taken up fully into the divine life,[2] and authoring—authorizing—the life-nourishing

---

1. See, e.g., Candida R. Moss and Jeremy Schipper, eds., *Disability Studies and Biblical Literature* (New York: Palgrave Macmillan, 2011); Jaime Clark-Soles, "Mark and Disability," *Int* 70 (April 2016): 159–71.

2. Cf. John Macquarrie, *Jesus Christ in Modern Thought* (London: SCM, 1990), 410: "His life has been taken up into the life of God, from whom it had drawn its power."

moves of a community that now takes its cues not from empire but from Jesus' cruciform way of challenging and transforming its ways.

<hr>

From First to Twenty-First Century: Interpretive Challenges and Ethical Resources

The Gospels were not written to us, but they may offer much to guide and instruct us. The cultural distance that stands between twenty-first-century readers and the earliest audiences of the Gospels is considerable and complicates the task of moving from first-century (or early second-century) narratives to the contemporary context. So readers today sometimes confront disconnects between what they believe, know, and experience and what they encounter in the pages of the Gospels—dissonances between certain Gospel themes and other sources of wisdom, including other biblical texts as well as experience and a deep fund of knowledge, ever growing and changing, from the sciences.

The following discussion identifies only a few of the interpretive challenges that the Gospels raise for thoughtful readers today. It suggests ways in which the Gospels may chart helpful, though not easy, paths through the elaborate, often bewildering mazes of contemporary social and ethical challenges set before us.

Reading the Gospels with Ethical Awareness: Interpretive Challenges

- Imagery of judgment and dualism
- Anti-Judaism
- Gender, sexuality, and marriage
- Mimicking empire?
- Other-regard beyond family, kin, and in-group
- Economies for the realm of God *and* for our world, too: poverty and wealth

---

Judgment and Dualism

At a number of points, the Gospels borrow the language and imagery of empire, including the central symbol of Jesus' message in the Synoptics, the *basileia* (reign or realm) of God, and such titles for Jesus as Lord (*kyrios*) and king (*basileus*). Moreover, especially in the Gospels of Matthew and John yet to a lesser degree also in Mark and Luke, readers encounter the theme of retributive or punitive judgment, sometimes presented with a harsh rhetoric that is problematic for many readers today, though such punitive violence was among the tactics by which the empire controlled its subject peoples. What are thoughtful readers—who are all too aware of the pervasiveness of violence and of excluding, other-annihilating rhetoric in their own setting—to do with this aspect of the Gospels? This is a particularly pressing concern precisely because biblical themes and images so often seem to fuel the other-harming speech and actions of twenty-first-century hate groups such as the Westboro Baptist Church (based in Topeka, Kansas) in my United States context.

It would be unhelpful to pretend that such elements are not present in the Gospel narratives. It *is* helpful to locate such features within the social-historical-political context from which and to which they speak. As postcolonial critics have emphasized, the response by groups subject to colonial domination characteristically expresses an ambivalence that includes partial adoption or mimicking of values and practices of the dominant group.[3] It would not be surprising, therefore, to see some mimicry of empire at play in the Gospels. At the same time, though, the influence of Jewish apocalyptic traditions and ideas in the articulation of the theme of (eschatological) judgment—most obvious in the discourses of Mark 13, Matthew 24–25, and Luke 17:22–37; 21:5–36—supports an anti-imperial function for this theme in the Gospels as a form of resistance literature.[4]

Moreover, and even more potently, the ways of empire, including coercive exertion of military power and retributive "justice" (all too often in the form of judicially sponsored terror and torture), come under severe critique in the Gospels. At the heart and climax of these narratives stands the cross, converted from badge of degrading dishonor and humiliation into the Messiah's (the authentic sovereign's) identity-defining image. Communities that derive their character and constitutive practices from this model participate in the formation of an alternative pattern of rule, social order, and community: a counterempire.

This community with a difference is called to follow the pattern of nonviolent, nonretaliatory—but courageous, insistent, and vigorous—resistance that is both commended and practiced by its Lord. The pattern of his ministry points them toward expansive other-regard and hospitality that includes rather than excludes diverse others across deeply entrenched, socially constructed boundaries, whether based on ethnicity, wealth, gender, or status (or other culturally constructed markers of identity and value). Jesus and his followers chart a sometimes perilous course of boundary-crossing activity. Here Jesus stands in Israel's robust prophetic tradition, which calls out the powerful for their exploitative abuse of the poor and for economic practices that oppress. So the nonretaliatory resistance that Jesus practices and urges his followers to pursue is not quietism in the face of injustice and cruelty, not

---

3. See the discussion of Mark 13 in ch. 3 above (the section "Collision of the Powers: The Reign of God and the Empire of Rome"), and of Luke and empire in ch. 5 ("Luke and Empire: Capitulation, Cooperation, Subversion, or Ambivalence?"); also, further discussion below.

4. On apocalypse as a critical response to empire, see the perceptive study by Anathea E. Portier-Young, *Apocalypse against Empire: Theologies of Resistance in Early Judaism* (Grand Rapids: Wm. B. Eerdmans Publishing Co., 2011).

silence and inaction, but solidarity with the hard-pressed and oppressed and persistent acts of justice seeking. This is the kind of life commitment that brought Jesus to a Roman cross and, according to the Gospels, may mean a similar outcome for disciples who follow his example. The healing stories so prominent in the Gospels also make clear that this pattern of life engaging the powers is liberative, healing, and life-giving in its aims: it is about human flourishing, not annihilation. The Easter accounts with which the Gospels picture the divine response to the crushing blow of crucifixion all emphasize, in their various ways, that it is not injustice, suffering, and death but instead justice, flourishing, and life that have the last say.

Thus Jesus' mission, and the task left to his followers to carry on after him, engages the powers—empire, enemies, and all the rest—in a way that finally resists the polarity of good and evil, the binary opposition of subject people and dominant occupying force (though esp. Matthew and John do contain numerous instances of dualistic language like this). In Jesus' discernment and practice of the sovereign rule of God in the world presently ruled by Rome, it is in keeping with the purposes of God to name and mightily oppose exploitative, oppressive injustice (as Israel's prophets repeatedly discerned and proclaimed). Yet there is also a summons to live by a radical other-regard that transcends the deep polarization fueling strife, distrust, and endless cycles of harm and retribution.

Anti-Judaism

As we have seen in the analysis of the Gospels in chapters 3–6 (above), most vividly in the case of Matthew and John, these New Testament narratives potentially contribute to anti-Judaism, a toxic element in the history of Christianity from at least the second century onward. We need to acknowledge this feature of the Gospels, to understand the social-historical realities that shaped such renditions of the mission of Jesus the Jew and, in the multireligious world of the twenty-first century, to chart a way forward that is ethically responsible. Conflict between Jesus and some of his Jewish contemporaries, as narrated in the Gospels, is sometimes intense, but it occurs within the family; stinging words Jesus can address to Pharisees, for example, have the character of intra-Jewish prophetic speech. Neither Jesus nor his first followers engage in conflict with Jewish people from outside the community. The debates can be heated, especially as Jesus' mission is refracted through the lens of later community conflict (esp. clear in Matthew and John), for after all, the identity, composition, and boundaries of the Jewish people are under discussion.

In the course of a discussion of anti-Judaism in connection with the Johannine passion narrative, Raymond Brown writes, "Sooner or later Christian believers must wrestle with the limitations imposed on the Scriptures by the circumstances in which they were written. They must be brought to see that some attitudes found in the Scriptures, however explicable in the times in which they originated, may be wrong attitudes if repeated today."[5] What I hope to have shown in my discussion of the Gospels in this book is that the Gospels also offer resources that may inform "right" attitudes today. Not least among them, whatever the harsh rhetoric of the Gospels' Jesus toward contemporaneous Jewish teachers, is the call that he issues to love others beyond conventional "us-them" borders, to love the *different* other, even the enemy, and to seek their flourishing, too.

Gender, Sexuality, and Marriage

Among the areas of ethical concern and social practice that have undergone the most rapid change in the United States in the last few decades are the ones having to do with human sexuality and marriage. These cultural shifts have also driven a wedge between Christian groups in the United States and Western Europe, on the one hand, and partner groups in other parts of the world. Polarizing debates over the ordination of LGBQT persons have weakened many church groups, especially in the United States, and changing legal codes regarding same-gender marriages (marriage equality) have forced churches to reconsider basic policies and practices regarding marriage. Do first-century Gospels have anything to contribute to this contemporary issue?

As with other areas of social practice and ethical concern discussed in this chapter, it is crucial to gain clarity about the cultural and historical influences that have shaped the Gospels' approach(es) to matters of human sexuality and marriage.[6] This is particularly important in connection with matters of sexuality and marriage because, especially in Europe and North America, dramatic cultural shifts in the structure and function of the family and in gender roles have opened up a substantial gap between the first century and the twenty-first.

Treatments of human sexuality, gender roles, and household and family relations in the Gospels generally assume a patriarchal social system, lower social status for women and children, heteronormativity (i.e., heterosexual

5. Raymond E. Brown, "The Passion according to John: Chapters 18 and 19," in *Worship* 49 (1975): 126–34, esp. 131.

6. For a sampling of approaches to this cluster of issues, see L. William Countryman, *Dirt, Greed, and Sex: Sexual Ethics in the New Testament and Their Implications for Today*, rev. ed. (Philadelphia: Fortress Press, 2007; orig., 1988); Raymond F. Collins, *Divorce in the New Testament* (Collegeville, MN: Liturgical Press, 1992); Richard B. Hays, *The Moral Vision of the New Testament: Community, Cross, New Creation; A Contemporary Introduction to New Testament Ethics* (San Francisco: HarperSanFrancisco, 1996), 347–78; Allen Verhey, *Remembering Jesus: Christian Community, Scripture, and the Moral Life* (Grand Rapids: Wm. B. Eerdmans Publishing Co., 2002), 157–240; Dale B. Martin, *Sex and the Single Savior: Gender and Sexuality in Biblical Interpretation* (Louisville, KY: Westminster John Knox Press, 2006); Russell Pregeant, *Knowing Truth, Doing Good: Engaging New Testament Ethics* (Minneapolis: Fortress Press, 2008), 336–46; A. K. M. Adam and Margaret B. Adam, "Sexuality," in *The Oxford Encyclopedia of the Bible and Ethics*, ed. Robert L. Brawley et al., 2 vols. (Oxford: Oxford University Press, 2014), 2:271–79.

unions, and distinct gender roles for male and female, regarded as normative), and a primary household concern with production rather than consumption—hence the central importance of property concerns in identifying a suitable marriage partner and completing arrangements for the marriage. As managers of domestic life within the household, women could and did play a crucial and productive economic role, so the subordinate position of women in Jesus' social world should not be overstated.

Divorce initiated by the husband was permitted, subject to certain constraints (Deut 24:1–4)—a topic of vigorous debate among the rabbis.[7] As Mark 10:12 indicates, in Roman society a wife could also initiate divorce, although legislation the emperor Augustus successfully promulgated in 19–18 BCE aimed to increase stability in marriage and family relations and encourage the bearing of children.[8] Jesus evidently weighed in on debates regarding the permissibility and scope of divorce, taking a stringent stance opposing the practice (Mark 10:1–12 and parr.). He lays down no legislation and issues no commands, but he brands marriage after divorce as the equivalent of adultery, apparently assuming the inviolability of the marriage relationship (an interpretation of the Gen 2:24 image of the two becoming "one flesh").

Whatever the motivations and rationale for this rigorous view,[9] it has challenged readers of the Gospels ever since—indeed, other New Testament authors such as the apostle Paul already applied this received teaching tradition with a measure of pastoral flexibility (e.g., 1 Cor 7:10–16). Given the prevalence of divorce and remarriage today, should other Gospel values and thematic emphases inform contemporary reflection on these issues? I would emphatically say yes. These concerns would surely include the importance of protecting the needy and vulnerable (e.g., women suffering domestic violence, children); the call to Jesus followers to love others and seek their flourishing; and, in the event of harm inflicted, to seek reconciliation and forgiveness but also to hold accountable those who are agents of harm to others.

---

7. The Mishnah tractate Giṭṭin discusses acceptable grounds for divorce and a host of procedural issues relating to the practice of divorce. The differing views of the rabbinic circles associated with Shammai and Hillel find compact summary in m. Giṭ. 9:10; the Shammai tradition recognized only sexual impropriety as grounds for a man's divorce of his wife, while the Hillel tradition gave wide latitude ("indecency in anything"), citing Deut 24:1.

8. There is evidence that Jewish communities located in Egypt and later elsewhere, in the period leading up to the Mishnah's consolidation of early rabbinic legal interpretations, provided for a woman's initiation of divorce proceedings. For Egyptian practices, see, e.g., marriage contracts in the Elephantine papyri; and for early rabbinic teaching, m. Ketub. 7:5–10; note the helpful discussion by Samuel L. Adams, *Social and Economic Life in Second Temple Judea* (Louisville, KY: Westminster John Knox Press, 2014), 34–39.

9. E.g., does Jesus reject divorce because of its asymmetry of choice, with only the husband able to initiate it (cf. Josephus, *Ant.* 15.7.10), and impact (the divorced wife's economic vulnerability)? The Dead Sea Scrolls also give evidence of radical critique of divorce within Judaism roughly contemporaneous with Jesus (e.g., CD IV, 14–V, 1).

In the first century, the economic viability of most households required marriage (assumed in the culture to be between a man and a woman), with procreation a primary concern. In contrast to conventions in the modern West (though not necessarily in other cultures), romantic interests and sexual attraction did not drive the search for a marriage partner. Rather, marriage relations "were negotiated by families for partnership, economic sustainability, kinship survival, and political or social power."[10] Much has changed, however, in the United States, Europe, and some other parts of the world. There has been a pronounced shift away from extended families and toward nuclear families that no longer reside near the extended family. Life expectancy has been dramatically increased, and the mortality rate of the young has decreased. Moreover, the principal economic function of the household is no longer production but consumption. The age of first marriage and childbearing is typically much later. Also, alternative family patterns have become more and more common and have received growing societal acceptance and legal protection, including single-parent households and same-gender marriages and parenting. In the light of such dramatic social-cultural shifts, it is unhelpful simply to impose first-century patterns of household and gender relations onto family systems today.

As already mentioned, in Jesus' culture, as well as those of the Gospel authors and their earliest audiences, marriage was assumed to unite heterosexual couples. However, no saying or action of Jesus reported in the Gospels explicitly addresses the question of homoerotic relations.[11] The contemporary reality of committed, enduring same-gender partnerships and marriages—now legally recognized in the United States and some other countries and also affirmed by many church bodies, though a source of painful contention between them and other communions globally—was not a relationship pattern with which Jesus or the Gospel writers would have been familiar. Again here, other values and thematic concerns highlighted in the Gospels' accounts of Jesus' mission should be drawn into the picture. Jesus does affirm marriage (assumed to be of husband and wife) as a sacred gift to be publicly celebrated (e.g., Mark 10:6–9; John 2:1–11). Yet much more prominent in his teaching is a countercultural message that relativizes household and family relations (even of spouses!) in light of the priority of Jesus' call to discipleship and to mission in advancing the cause of the divine reign (e.g., Mark 3:31–35; 10:28–30; Luke 14:25–27).[12]

10. Erin Dufault-Hunter, "Sexual Ethics," in *Dictionary of Scripture and Ethics*, ed. Joel B. Green et al. (Grand Rapids: Baker Academic, 2011), 723–28.

11. The biblical passages that do explicitly address homoerotic activity are Gen 19:1–10 (though sexual violence and failure to extend hospitality are the central concerns); Lev 18:22; 20:13; Rom 1:26–27; 1 Cor 6:9; 1 Tim 1:10. For a helpful, concise discussion and select bibliography, see Jeffrey S. Siker, "Homosexuality," in Green et al., *Dictionary of Scripture and Ethics*, 371–74.

12. In an intriguing dialogue with the disciples that elaborates on Jesus' affirmation of marriage and rejection of divorce (Matt 19:3–9), vv. 10–12 concede the viability of an alternative

To the extent that the Gospels reflect "apocalyptic family values," shaped by the conviction that the crises of present life point to the imminent arrival of the new age and call for an overriding, family-demoting commitment to the ways and work of God's reign, twenty-first-century readers will need to draw from other resources to craft a constructive ethical vision relating to marriage and family.[13] Critical in that work of ethical construction will be the image of Genesis 2:18: if it is good for the human creature to enjoy the partnership of intimacy and care rather than to be perpetually "alone," then religious, social, political, and economic structures that nurture those loving partnerships, as well as the family systems they create, are imperative. They are also congruent with Jesus' mission in its embrace and empowering of the socially marginalized and vulnerable.

Mimicking Empire? Postcolonial analysis has prompted some scholars to claim that the Gospel authors have appropriated language and ideology of empire even in opposing the reign of God to the realm of Caesar.[14] To be sure, as we have seen, the Gospels portray Jesus as "king" (*basileus*) of the Jews, and the Synoptics place the image of God's reign (or realm, empire, *basileia*) at the center of Jesus' message and activity. Jesus, as *kyrios* (Lord), supplants the sovereignty of the emperor. So there is a sense in which the Gospel accounts of Jesus' mission do mimic the ideology of (Rome's) empire. Yet as Jesus conceives and enacts it, the content and character of this counterempire, the divine realm, is worlds removed from the Roman exemplar of power. The focal image of Jesus' rule is the cross, where his reign is on display as parody of Rome's dominion, which was secured and reinforced through actions of coercive violence such as this. The model of leadership that Jesus sets before

approach that permanently refrains from marriage and sexual relations as a matter of voluntary choice: "His disciples said to him, 'If such is the case of a man with his wife, it is better not to marry.' But he said to them, 'Not everyone can accept this teaching, but only those to whom it is given. For there are eunuchs who have been so from birth, and there are eunuchs who have been made eunuchs by others, and *there are eunuchs who have made themselves eunuchs for the sake of the kingdom of heaven*. Let anyone accept this who can'" (emphasis added). Whether the image of the eunuch is to be read here as literal or metaphorical, the declaration recognizes that some persons—whether by biology, the forced actions of others, or deliberate decision—do not and will not participate in the social systems defined by heteronormativity.

13. I borrow the apt phrase "apocalyptic family values" from E. Elizabeth Johnson, "Apocalyptic Family Values," *Int* 56 (2002): 34–44.

14. See, e.g., on Mark: Benny Tat-siong Liew, *Politics of Parousia: Reading Mark Inter(con)textually*, BibIntS 42 (Leiden: Brill, 1999). On John: Stephen D. Moore, *Empire and Apocalypse: Postcolonialism and the New Testament*, The Bible in the Modern World (Sheffield: Sheffield Phoenix, 2006); notice the critique of Moore's view of John as the "charter document of Constantinian Christianity" by Tom Thatcher, *Greater than Caesar: Christology and Empire in the Fourth Gospel* (Minneapolis: Fortress Press, 2009), 139. Warren Carter suggests that John's Gospel mixes imitation and contesting of imperial claims (*John and Empire: Initial Explorations* [New York: T&T Clark, 2008], 250); John urges "less accommodation and more distance from Rome's empire" (ibid., 16).

his followers is other-honoring, self-renouncing service, in stark contrast to the economic exploitation and military domination that undergird Rome's empire. The Gospels give twenty-first-century readers who live within a powerful nation that aspires to global, imperial-like influence—or who experience that power from other places in the world—plenty to contemplate. In other respects, too, the Gospels provide readers today a rich fund from which to draw when analyzing and responding to challenges of our time.

Other-Regard beyond Family, Kin, and In-Group

Especially in the Synoptic Gospels, both spoken words and interpersonal interactions challenge customary social boundaries that typically restrict other-regard and altruism to one's own family, kin, and in-group. Beyond benefaction calculated to enhance status and honor, Jesus commends generosity that is not motivated by self-interest or advantage. Beyond love that seeks the well-being only of one's kin and in-group, Jesus urges acts of effective, compassionate care toward any in need, even enemies.

In my context (as I write in the United States late in 2015), what passes for public discourse far too often takes the form of polarizing language, even demonizing and maligning the motives of those with whom one disagrees. Capacity to listen, to engage in dialogue so as to learn from the different other rather than win arguments, is all too rare. Failure in empathy abounds. Xenophobia is evident in political campaign rhetoric, anti-immigration tirades, and totalizing equations of Islam and terrorism. In such a context, the Gospels' witness to the mission of Jesus provides an alternative model.

The community that Jesus' activity begins to form is one defined radically by grace, by trust in a gracious God who provides what is needed (e.g., Matt 6:25–34; Luke 11:1–13). It is therefore able to live in a way that is open to others, seeing them not as rivals and competitors for limited resources in a zero-sum game but instead as different others who are also recipients of God's benevolent care.[15] So this grace-defined community is able to emulate Jesus' own practice of including persons whose fortunes in life (whether arising because of gender, ethnicity, disability, or occupation) have assigned them a place on or beyond the social and religious margins (e.g., Luke 5:27–32; 7:36–50; 17:11–19, among many other passages).

To be sure, the Gospels contain passages that reflect and appear to perpetuate culturally constructed boundaries that exclude some persons (e.g.,

---

15. Robert Wright makes a case for nonzero-sum economics: see his books *Nonzero: The Logic of Human Destiny* (New York: Random House, 2000) and *The Evolution of God: The Origins of Our Beliefs* (New York: Little, Brown & Co., 2009). As Nadella puts it, summarizing Wright's approach, "It is a scenario wherein one gains not at the expense of, but in addition to and by cooperating with, the other. Wright believes that in the history of human evolution, greed, mistrust, and intolerance have been gradually making way for cooperation and inclusiveness"; see Raj Nadella, "The Two Banquets: Mark's Vision of Anti-Imperial Economics," *Int* 70 (April 2016): 172–83, esp. 177–78.

the Gentile "dogs" of Mark 7:24–30; Matt 15:21–28; cf. Matt 10:5–6; Luke 9:49–56). However, the accent of the Gospel presentations of Jesus' activity falls sharply on boundary-challenging, boundary-transgressing acts of hospitality, acceptance, and justice seeking.[16] Other-regard, Jesus-style, must extend beyond one's family, kin, or in-group, even to all. Moreover, in a time when the fragility of Earth's ecosystem is increasingly evident—much of it the result of human activity (e.g., destruction of rain forests, species extinctions, and global climate change), the extension of other-regard to encompass also persons not yet born, as well as the natural world, is an ethically responsible extrapolation from the Gospel presentations of Jesus' commitments and practices.[17]

Among the global challenges that have nearly paralyzed constructive diplomacy and international cooperation in the last decades of the twentieth century and first fifteen years of the twenty-first century are recurrent acts of terrorism, which both result from and intensify the distrust and hostility between people groups (whether or not identified with nation-states). Within the United States, too-frequently repeating episodes of mass violence carried out with guns coincide with an obsession to hold sacred the second constitutional amendment (the right to bear arms) fomented by the politically influential lobby of the National Rifle Association (NRA). For people of faith or conscience who look past the second amendment to the second commandment (Mark 12:31; Matt 22:39), the mandate to love neighbor—indeed, to love one's enemy (Matt 5:43–44; Luke 6:27, 35)—grounds expansive love for others in the even more expansive, generous love of God.

Economics for the Realm of God and for Our World, Too? Poverty and Disparities of Wealth

Wide and growing disparities in access to the resources needed to sustain life continue to plague the international community, including the United States. Just as in the first-century Roman Empire (the setting of Jesus' activity and of the Gospel authors and audiences), wealth today is concentrated in a very few hands, and poverty is the lot of many.[18] Core values of the Gospels' presentations of Jesus' message call this persistent wealth inequity

---

16. See the discussion by Brian K. Blount, "Jesus as Teacher: Boundary Breaking in Mark's Gospel and Today's Church," *Int* 70 (April 2016): 184–93.

17. See Holmes Rolston III, "Loving Nature: Past, Present, and Future," *Int* 70 (January 2016): 34–47. This is an uphill struggle. As Rolston observes, "Distant peoples and far-off descendants do not have much 'biological hold' on us. . . . Now that we live in a 'global village,' global threats require us to act in massive concert of which we evidently are incapable" (ibid., 43). Here Rolston draws on the work of Sober and Wilson, who claim that "there is no 'universal benevolence' among human beings: 'Group selection favors within-group niceness and between-group nastiness'" (Elliott Sober and David Sloan Wilson, *Unto Others: The Evolution and Psychology of Unselfish Behavior* [Cambridge, MA: Harvard University Press, 1998], 9). Support for this view is in ample supply in world events today.

18. Thus, e.g., OXFAM research indicates that by 2016, approximately 1 percent of the world's population will control half of the wealth. See http://www.nytimes.com/2015/01/19/business/richest-1-percent-likely-to-control-half-of-global-wealth-by-2016-study-finds.html.

into question. Jesus imagines God's reign taking concrete shape in the world in an *upside-down community* in which status and advantage do not belong to the wealthy. Rather, it is the poor who are specially honored by God, and Jesus summons community members with access to economic resources to a generosity that addresses the needs of persons who suffer from poverty (e.g., Luke 1:51–53; 4:18–19; 6:20–26; 16:19–31; 20:45–21:4). This prophetic emphasis of Jesus' mission continues a prominent theme in the Torah and Prophets, which were sacred writings for him (e.g., Exod 23:11; Deut 15:7–11; 24:14–15; Prov 19:17; Job 31:16–22; Isa 3:14–15; 58:7, 10; Jer 2:34; Ezek 18:12–13; 22:29; Amos 2:6–7; 4:1; 5:11–12; 8:4–6). The radical generosity to which the community of Jesus followers is called places the flourishing of the community and effective care for its most vulnerable and marginalized members ahead of personal self-interest and gain (e.g., Luke 14:7–24, 25–33; 18:18–30; 19:1–10). Jesus' vision and praxis of the reign of God bear little resemblance to the consumer capitalism and preoccupation with wealth acquisition and wealth maintenance that dominate so much of modern life and define its social and political structures. Ethically responsible readings of the Gospels must grapple seriously with this dissonance.

Postscript: Reading the Gospels and Ethical Challenges Today

In both Mark and Matthew, Jesus launches his ministry with the announcement that "the kingdom of God/heaven has come near" (Mark 1:15; Matt 4:17). In a similar way, Luke has Jesus open his mission by claiming that the era of divine favor (and Jubilee liberation) has arrived (Luke 4:18–19), and he sets about announcing the joyful news of God's reign (4:43). In the preferred idiom of John's Gospel, Jesus is the bearer of authentic, enduring ("eternal") life. Despite the inbreaking of God's life-giving reign in Jesus' activity of healing and teaching, however, the course of each Gospel narrative, like the course of human history ever since, brings complication: opposition, adversity, defeat, and death. So it turns out that the Gospels are not all that far removed from the wisdom of Martin Luther King Jr., whose realism about the civil rights struggle was wedded to confident hope: "The arc of the moral universe is long, but it bends toward justice."[19] This is finally a matter of hope, often against nearly all the empirical evidence, but precisely here the Gospels' affirmation of God's power and of the life that God bestows—even in the face of tenacious, life-crushing injustice, oppression,

---

19. Dr. King returned to this assertion frequently (e.g., in a sermon at Hollywood's Temple Israel on February 26, 1965; in a speech on the steps of the Alabama State Capitol in Montgomery on March 24, 1965; and again in Ebenezer Baptist Church, Atlanta, on April 30, 1967). He was quoting a much-cited phrase that appears to go back to a sermon by Theodore Parker, "Of Justice and the Conscience," first published in 1853 in *Ten Sermons of Religion* (Boston: Crosby, Nichols & Co., 1853), 66–101, esp. 84–85.

and evil—invigorates sustained commitment to work toward reconciliation and justice amid seemingly intractable challenges near and far: racism, poverty, xenophobia, gun violence, homophobia and violence toward sexual minorities, international conflicts and terrorism, global climate change, and damage to the ecosystem and natural habitats. The message and mission of Jesus inspire hope that the world is in process of becoming the world God rules, but the work of making it so, now entrusted to Jesus' followers, will never be easy and will often provoke intense opposition. Nothing new there, to judge from the four Gospel narratives.

Addressing the religious and ethical challenge of reading John's Gospel in a world of many religions, Alan Culpepper urges readers to accept responsibility for the way they read, in connection with the way they live: "Accountability requires us to seek interpretations that are both faithful to the text and ethically responsible. Only by asking whether our interpretation of the Gospel serves to put an end to violence against Jews and other ethnic minorities, to empower the marginalized and oppressed, and to bring understanding between persons of different religious traditions can we expect that our interpretations will stand the test of accountability when they themselves are read with a 'hermeneutics of suspicion.'"[20] The criteria for faithful and responsible interpretation that Culpepper proposes fit well the interpretive challenges we have been probing in this chapter, and many more besides.

Gospel readings that seek alignment with the message and activity of Jesus will spring to life in concrete ways in the world, evident in acts of solidarity with the poor, the vulnerable, the wounded, the neglected; in practices that foster ecological sustainability; and in courageous acts of justice seeking on behalf of the oppressed and hard-pressed. Richard Burridge proposes as the test of the adequacy of a New Testament ethic how well it works in connection with the issues raised by apartheid in South Africa.[21] In the context of the United States today, I submit that a critical test of the adequacy of an ethically responsible interpretation of the Gospels is how it positions readers to respond to the persistent racism and the fear of others who are different that plague U.S. American society. I have much more I would like to write about this, but it is time to leave my comfortable study and computer and venture out to confront some of those intractable challenges in the world. Perhaps I will meet you out there.

20. R. Alan Culpepper, "The Gospel of John as a Document of Faith in a Pluralistic Culture," in *"What Is John?": Readers and Readings of the Fourth Gospel*, ed. Fernando F. Segovia, SBLSymS 3 (Atlanta: Scholars Press, 1996), 107–27, esp. 127.

21. See Richard A. Burridge, *Imitating Jesus: An Inclusive Approach to New Testament Ethics* (Grand Rapids: Wm. B. Eerdmans Publishing Co., 2007), 1–4, 347–409.

Selected Bibliography

Works on the Gospels and Jesus (chs. 1–2)

Allison, Dale C, Jr. *Constructing Jesus: Memory, Imagination, and History.* Grand Rapids: Baker Academic, 2010.

Brown, Raymond E. *The Death of the Messiah: From Gethsemane to the Grave; A Commentary on the Passion Narratives in the Four Gospels.* 2 vols. New York: Doubleday, 1994.

Burridge, Richard A. *What Are the Gospels? A Comparison with Graeco-Roman Biography.* SNTSMS 70. Cambridge: Cambridge University Press, 1992.

Carey, Greg. *Sinners: Jesus and His Earliest Followers.* Waco, TX: Baylor University Press, 2009.

Carroll, John T., and Joel B. Green. *The Death of Jesus in Early Christianity.* Peabody, MA: Hendrickson Publishers, 1995.

Conway, Collen. *Behold the Man: Jesus and Greco-Roman Masculinity.* Oxford: Oxford University Press, 2008.

Henderson, Suzanne Watts. *Christ and Community: The Gospel Witness to Jesus.* Nashville: Abingdon Press, 2015.

Hultgren, Arland J. *The Parables of Jesus: A Commentary.* Grand Rapids: Wm. B. Eerdmans Publishing Co., 2000.

Levine, Amy-Jill. *The Misunderstood Jew: The Church and the Scandal of the Jewish Jesus.* San Francisco: HarperSanFrancisco, 2007.

Meier, John. *A Marginal Jew: Rethinking the Historical Jesus.* 5 vols. ABRL. New Haven, CT: Yale University Press, 1991–2016.

Moore, Stephen D. *Empire and Apocalypse: Postcolonialism and the New Testament.* The Bible in the Modern World. Sheffield: Sheffield Phoenix, 2006.

Powell, Mark Allan. *Jesus as a Figure in History: How Modern Historians View the Man from Galilee.* 2nd ed. Louisville, KY: Westminster John Knox Press, 2013.

Schottroff, Luise. *The Parables of Jesus.* Translated by Linda M. Maloney. Minneapolis: Augsburg Fortress, 2006.

Scott, Bernard Brandon. *Hear Then the Parable: A Commentary on the Parables of Jesus.* Minneapolis: Augsburg Fortress, 1989.

Scott, James C. *Domination and the Arts of Resistance: Hidden Transcripts.* New Haven, CT: Yale University Press, 1990.

Talbert, Charles H. *What Is a Gospel? The Genre of the Canonical Gospels.* Philadelphia: Fortress Press, 1977.

Tannehill, Robert C. *The Shape of the Gospel: New Testament Essays.* Eugene, OR: Cascade Books, 2007.

Wilson, Brittany. *Unmanly Men: Refigurations of Masculinity in Luke-Acts.* Oxford: Oxford University Press, 2015.

The Gospel according to Mark (ch. 3)

Beavis, Mary Ann. *Mark*. Paideia. Grand Rapids: Baker Academic, 2011.

Black, C. Clifton. *The Disciples according to Mark: Markan Redaction in Current Debate*. 2nd ed. Grand Rapids: Wm. B. Eerdmans Publishing Co., 2012.

———. *Mark*. ANTC. Nashville: Abingdon Press, 2011.

Blount, Brian K. *Go Preach! Mark's Kingdom Message and the Black Church Today*. Maryknoll, NY: Orbis Books, 1998.

Boring, M. Eugene. *Mark: A Commentary*. NTL. Louisville, KY: Westminster John Knox Press, 2006.

Collins, Adela Yarbro. *Mark: A Commentary*. Hermeneia. Minneapolis: Fortress Press, 2007.

Culpepper, R. Alan. *Mark*. SHBC. Macon, GA: Smyth & Helwys, 2007.

Driggers, Ira Brent. *Following God through Mark: Theological Tension in the Second Gospel*. Louisville, KY: Westminster John Knox Press, 2007.

Fowler, Robert M. *Let the Reader Understand: Reader-Response Criticism and the Gospel of Mark*. Minneapolis: Fortress Press, 1991.

Garland, David E. *A Theology of Mark's Gospel: Good News about Jesus the Messiah, Son of God*. Biblical Theology of the New Testament. Grand Rapids: Zondervan Publishing House, 2015.

Henderson, Suzanne Watts. *Christology and Discipleship in the Gospel of Mark*. SNTSMS 135. Cambridge: Cambridge University Press, 2006.

Iverson, Kelly R., and Christopher W. Skinner, eds. *Mark as Story: Retrospect and Prospect*. SBLRBS 65. Atlanta: SBL Press, 2011.

Kingsbury, Jack Dean. *The Christology of Mark*. Philadelphia: Fortress Press, 1983.

Leander, Hans. *Discourses of Empire: The Gospel of Mark from a Postcolonial Perspective*. SemeiaSt 71. Atlanta: SBL Press, 2013.

Levine, Amy-Jill, and Marianne Blickenstaff, eds. *A Feminist Companion to Mark*. Sheffield: Sheffield Academic, 2001.

Liew, Tat-siong Benny. *Politics of Parousia: Reading Mark Inter(con)textually*. BibIntS 42. Leiden: Brill, 1999.

Malbon, Elizabeth Struthers. *Mark's Jesus: Characterization as Narrative Christology*. Waco, TX: Baylor University Press, 2009.

Marcus, Joel. *Mark: A New Translation with Introduction and Commentary*. AB 27–27A. New Haven, CT: Yale University Press, 2000–2009.

Moloney, Francis J., SDB. *The Gospel of Mark: A Commentary*. Peabody, MA: Hendrickson Publishers, 2002.

Moore, Stephen D., and Janice Capel Anderson, eds. *Mark and Method: New Approaches in Biblical Studies*. 2nd ed. Minneapolis: Fortress Press, 2008.

Myers, Ched. *Binding the Strong Man: A Political Reading of Mark's Story of Jesus*. 20th anniversary ed. Maryknoll, NY: Orbis Books, 2008. Orig., 1988.

Rhoads, David, Joanna Dewey, and Donald Michie. *Mark as Story: An Introduction to the Narrative of a Gospel*. 3rd ed. Minneapolis: Fortress Press, 2012.

Shiner, Whitney. *Proclaiming the Gospel: First-Century Performance of Mark*. Harrisburg, PA: Trinity Press International, 2003.

Tannehill, Robert C. "The Disciples in Mark: The Function of a Narrative Role." *JR* 57 (1977): 386–405. Repr. in *The Interpretation of Mark*, edited by William R. Telford, 169–95. 2nd ed. Edinburgh: T&T Clark, 1995.

———. "The Gospel of Mark as Narrative Christology." *Semeia* 16 (1979): 57–95.

Telford, William R., ed. *The Interpretation of Mark*. 2nd ed. Studies in New Testament Interpretation. Edinburgh: T&T Clark, 1995.

———. *The Theology of the Gospel of Mark*. NTT. Cambridge: Cambridge University Press, 1999.

Tolbert, Mary Ann. *Sowing the Gospel: Mark's World in Literary-Historical Perspective*. Minneapolis: Fortress Press, 1989.

The Gospel according to Matthew (ch. 4)

Aune, David E., ed. *The Gospel of Matthew in Current Study*. Grand Rapids: Wm. B. Eerdmans Publishing Co., 2001.

Balch, David L., ed. *Social History of the Matthean Community: Cross-Disciplinary Approaches*. Minneapolis: Fortress Press, 1991.

Bauer, David R., and Mark Allan Powell, eds. *Treasures New and Old: Contributions to Matthean Studies*. Symposium Series. Atlanta: Scholars Press, 1996.

Carter, Warren. *Matthew and Empire: Initial Explorations*. Harrisburg, PA: Trinity Press International, 2001.

———. *Matthew and the Margins: A Sociopolitical and Religious Reading*. Maryknoll, NY: Orbis Books, 2000.

Davies, W. D., and Dale C. Allison. *Matthew*. ICC. 3 vols. Edinburgh: T&T Clark, 1988–97.

France, R. T. *The Gospel of Matthew*. NICNT. Grand Rapids: Wm. B. Eerdmans Publishing Co., 2007.

Guelich, Robert A. "Interpreting the Sermon on the Mount." *Int* 41 (1987): 117–30.

Gundry, Robert H. *Matthew: A Commentary on His Handbook for a Mixed Church under Persecution*. 2nd ed. Grand Rapids: Wm. B. Eerdmans Publishing Co., 1994.

Harrington, Daniel, SJ. *The Gospel of Matthew*. SP 1. Collegeville, MN: Liturgical Press, 1991.

Keener, Craig S. *The Gospel of Matthew: A Socio-Rhetorical Commentary*. Grand Rapids: Wm. B. Eerdmans Publishing Co., 2009.

Kingsbury, Jack Dean. *Matthew as Story*. 2nd ed. Philadelphia: Fortress Press, 1988.

Luz, Ulrich. *Matthew*. Translated by James E. Crouch. Edited by Helmut Koester. Hermeneia. 3 vols. Minneapolis: Fortress Press, 1992–2005.

———. *Studies in Matthew*. Translated by Rosemary Selle. Grand Rapids: Wm. B. Eerdmans Publishing Co., 2005.

———. *The Theology of the Gospel of Matthew*. Translated by J. Bradford Robinson. NTT. Cambridge: Cambridge University Press, 1995.

Neyrey, Jerome H. *Honor and Shame in the Gospel of Matthew*. Louisville, KY: Westminster John Knox Press, 1998.

Overman, J. Andrew. *Matthew's Gospel and Formative Judaism: The Social World of the Matthean Community*. Minneapolis: Augsburg Fortress, 1990.

Saldarini, Anthony J. *Matthew's Christian-Jewish Community*. Chicago Studies in the History of Judaism. Chicago: University of Chicago Press, 1994.

Senior, Donald. *The Gospel of Matthew*. IBT. Nashville: Abingdon Press, 1997.

———. *Matthew*. ANTC. Nashville: Abingdon Press, 1998.

Stanton, Graham. *Studies in Matthew and Early Christianity*. Edited by Markus Bockmuehl and David Lincicum. WUNT 2/309. Tübingen: Mohr Siebeck, 2013.

Talbert, Charles H. *Matthew*. Paideia. Grand Rapids: Baker Academic, 2010.

The Gospel according to Luke (ch. 5)

Ahn, Yong-Sung. *The Reign of God and Rome in Luke's Passion Narrative: An East Asian Global Perspective*. BibIntS 80. Leiden: Brill, 2006.

Alexander, Loveday. *The Preface to Luke's Gospel: Literary Convention and Social Context in Luke 1.1–4 and Acts 1.1*. SNTSMS 78. Cambridge: Cambridge University Press, 1993.

Bovon, François. *Luke: A Commentary on the Gospel of Luke*. 3 vols. Edited by Helmut Koester. Translated by Christine M. Thomas (vol. 1), Donald S. Deer (vol. 2), and James E. Crouch (vol. 3). Hermeneia. Minneapolis: Augsburg Fortress, 2002–13.

Braun, Willi. *Feasting and Social Rhetoric in Luke 14*. SNTSMS 85. Cambridge: Cambridge University Press, 1995.

Brawley, Robert L. *Luke-Acts and the Jews: Conflict, Apology, and Conciliation*. SBLMS 33. Atlanta: Scholars Press, 1987.

——. *Text to Text Pours Forth Speech: Voices of Scripture in Luke-Acts*. ISBL. Bloomington: Indiana University Press, 1995.

Byrne, Brendan. *The Hospitality of God: A Reading of Luke's Gospel*. Collegeville, MN: Liturgical Press, 2000.

Cadbury, Henry Joel. *The Making of Luke-Acts*. 2nd ed. London: SPCK, 1958. Repr., Peabody, MA: Hendrickson Publishers, 1999. Orig., New York: Macmillan, 1927.

Carroll, John T. "The Gospel of Luke: A Contemporary Cartography." *Int* 68 (2014): 366–75.

——. *Luke: A Commentary*. NTL. Louisville, KY: Westminster John Knox Press, 2012.

——. "Welcoming Grace, Costly Commitment: An Approach to the Gospel of Luke." *Int* 57 (2002): 16–23.

Carter, Warren. "Getting Martha out of the Kitchen: Luke 10:38–42 Again." *CBQ* 58 (1996): 264–80.

——. "Singing in the Reign: Performing Luke's Songs and Negotiating the Roman Empire (Luke 1–2)." Pages 23–43 in *Luke-Acts and Empire: Essays in Honor of Robert L. Brawley*. Edited by David Rhoads, David Esterline, and Jae Won Lee. PTMS 151. Eugene, OR: Wipf & Stock, 2011.

Coleridge, Mark. *The Birth of the Lukan Narrative: Narrative as Christology in Luke 1–2*. JSNTSup 88. Sheffield: JSOT Press, 1993.

Conzelmann, Hans. *The Theology of St. Luke*. Translated by Geoffrey Buswell. New York: Harper & Row, 1961. Orig., *Die Mitte der Zeit*. Tübingen: Mohr Siebeck, 1953.

Culpepper, R. Alan. "The Gospel of Luke." In *New Interpreter's Bible*, edited by Leander E. Keck, 9:1–490. Nashville: Abingdon Press, 1995.

Darr, John A. *On Character Building: The Reader and the Rhetoric of Characterization in Luke-Acts*. LCBI. Louisville, KY: Westminster John Knox Press, 1992.

Dillon, Richard J. *From Eye-Witnesses to Ministers of the Word: Tradition and Composition in Luke 24*. AnBib 82. Rome: Biblical Institute Press, 1978.

Dinkler, Michal Beth. *Silent Statements: Narrative Representations of Speech and Silence in the Gospel of Luke*. BZNW 191. Berlin: de Gruyter, 2013.

Esler, Philip Francis. *Community and Gospel in Luke-Acts: The Social and Political Motivations of Lucan Theology*. SNTSMS 57. Cambridge: Cambridge University Press, 1987.

Farris, Stephen. *The Hymns of Luke's Infancy Narratives: Their Origin, Meaning and Significance*. JSNTSup 9. Sheffield: JSOT Press, 1985.

Fitzmyer, Joseph A. *The Gospel according to Luke: Introduction, Translation, and Notes*. 2 vols. AB 28–28A. Garden City, NY: Doubleday, 1981–85.

Forbes, Greg W. *God of Old: The Role of the Lukan Parables in the Purpose of Luke's Gospel*. JSNTSup 198. Sheffield: Sheffield Academic, 2000.

Garrett, Susan R. *The Demise of the Devil: Magic and the Demonic in Luke's Writings*. Minneapolis: Augsburg Fortress, 1989.

Gaventa, Beverly Roberts. *Mary: Glimpses of the Mother of Jesus*. PNTS. Columbia: University of South Carolina Press, 1995.

Gonzalez, Justo L. *Luke*. Belief: A Theological Commentary on the Bible. Louisville, KY: Westminster John Knox Press, 2010.

Gowler, David B. *Host, Guest, Enemy, and Friend: Portraits of the Pharisees in Luke and Acts*. ESEC 2. New York: Peter Lang, 1991.

Green, Joel B. *Conversion in Luke-Acts: Divine Action, Human Cognition, and the People of God*. Grand Rapids: Baker Academic, 2015.

———. *The Gospel of Luke*. NICNT. Grand Rapids: Wm. B. Eerdmans Publishing Co., 1997.

———. *The Theology of the Gospel of Luke*. NTT. Cambridge: Cambridge University Press, 1995.

Hartsock, Chad. *Sight and Blindness in Luke-Acts: The Use of Physical Features in Characterization*. BibIntS 94. Leiden: Brill, 2008.

Heil, John Paul. *The Meal Scenes in Luke-Acts: An Audience-Oriented Approach*. SBLMS 52. Atlanta: SBL Press, 1999.

Jervell, Jacob. *Luke and the People of God: A New Look at Luke-Acts*. Minneapolis: Augsburg, 1972.

Johnson, Luke Timothy. *The Gospel of Luke*. SP 3. Collegeville, MN: Liturgical Press, 1991.

———. *The Literary Function of Possessions in Luke-Acts*. SBLDS 39. Missoula, MT: Scholars Press, 1977.

Karris, Robert J. *Luke, Artist and Theologian: Luke's Passion Account as Literature*. New York: Paulist Press, 1985.

Keck, Leander E., and J. Louis Martyn, eds. *Studies in Luke-Acts: Essays Presented in Honor of Paul Schubert*. Nashville: Abingdon Press, 1966.

Kim, Kyoung-Jin. *Stewardship and Almsgiving in Luke's Theology*. JSNTSup 155. Sheffield: Sheffield Academic, 1998.

Klutz, Todd. *The Exorcism Stories in Luke-Acts: A Sociostylistic Reading*. SNTSMS 129. Cambridge: Cambridge University Press, 2004.

Kuhn, Karl Allen. *The Kingdom according to Luke and Acts: A Social, Literary, and Theological Introduction*. Grand Rapids: Baker Academic, 2015.

Lehtipuu, Outi. *The Afterlife Imagery in Luke's Story of the Rich Man and Lazarus*. NovTSup 123. Leiden: Brill, 2007.

Levine, Amy-Jill, ed., with Marianne Blickenstaff. *A Feminist Companion to Luke*. London: Sheffield Academic, 2002.

Litwak, Kenneth D. *Echoes of Scripture in Luke-Acts: Telling the History of God's People Intertextually*. JSNTSup 282. London: T&T Clark, 2005.

Longenecker, Bruce W. *Hearing the Silence: Jesus on the Edge and God in the Gap; Luke 4 in Narrative Perspective*. Eugene, OR: Cascade Books, 2012.

Maddox, Robert. *The Purpose of Luke-Acts*. Edinburgh: T&T Clark, 1982.

Marshall, I. Howard. *The Gospel of Luke: A Commentary on the Greek Text*. NIGTC. Grand Rapids: Wm. B. Eerdmans Publishing Co., 1978.

Miller, Amanda C. *Rumors of Resistance: Status Reversals and Hidden Transcripts in the Gospel of Luke*. Emerging Scholars. Minneapolis: Fortress Press, 2014.

Moxnes, Halvor. *The Economy of the Kingdom: Social Conflict and Economic Relations in Luke's Gospel*. OBT. Philadelphia: Fortress Press, 1988.

Nadella, Raj. *Dialogue Not Dogma: Many Voices in the Gospel of Luke*. London: T&T Clark, 2011.

Nave, Guy D., Jr. *The Role and Function of Repentance in Luke-Acts*. AcBib 4. Atlanta: SBL Press, 2002.

Neirynck, Frans, ed. *L'Évangile de Luc—The Gospel of Luke*. Rev., enl. 2nd ed. of *L'Évangile de Luc: Problèmes littéraires et théologiques*. BETL 32. Leuven: Leuven University Press and Peeters, 1989.

Neyrey, Jerome H. *The Passion according to Luke: A Redaction Study of Luke's Soteriology*. TI. New York: Paulist Press, 1985. Repr., Eugene, OR: Wipf & Stock, 2007.

———, ed. *The Social World of Luke-Acts: Models for Interpretation*. Peabody, MA: Hendrickson Publishers, 1991.

Nolland, John. *Luke*. 3 vols. WBC 35A–C. Dallas: Word, 1989–93.

Parsons, Mikeal C. *Body and Character in Luke and Acts: The Subversion of Physiognomy in Early Christianity*. Grand Rapids: Baker Academic, 2006.

———. *Luke*. Paideia. Grand Rapids: Baker Academic, 2015.

Reid, Barbara E. *Choosing the Better Part? Women in the Gospel of Luke*. Collegeville, MN: Liturgical Press, 1996.

Rhoads, David, David Esterline, and Jae Won Lee, eds. *Luke-Acts and Empire: Essays in Honor of Robert L. Brawley*. PTMS 151. Eugene, OR: Wipf & Stock, 2011.

Rindge, Matthew S. "Luke's Artistic Parables: Narratives of Subversion, Imagination, and Transformation." *Int* 68 (2014): 403–15.

Ringe, Sharon H. *Jesus, Liberation, and the Biblical Jubilee: Images for Ethics and Christology*. OBT 19. Philadelphia: Fortress Press, 1985.

———. *Luke*. Westminster Bible Companion. Louisville, KY: Westminster John Knox Press, 1995.

Rowe, C. Kavin. *Early Narrative Christology: The Lord in the Gospel of Luke*. Grand Rapids: Baker Academic, 2009. Orig., Berlin: Walter de Gruyter, 2006.

———. *World Upside Down: Reading Acts in the Graeco-Roman Age*. New York: Oxford University Press, 2009.

Seim, Turid Karlsen. *The Double Message: Patterns of Gender in Luke-Acts*. Nashville: Abingdon Press, 1994.

Senior, Donald. *The Passion of Jesus in the Gospel of Luke*. Collegeville, MN: Liturgical Press, 1989.

Smith, Daniel Lynwood. *The Rhetoric of Interruption: Speech-Making, Turn-Taking, and Rule-Breaking in Luke-Acts and Ancient Greek Narrative*. BZNW 193. Berlin: de Gruyter, 2012.

Spencer, F. Scott. *Salty Wives, Spirited Mothers, and Savvy Widows: Capable Women of Purpose and Persistence in Luke's Gospel*. Grand Rapids: Wm. B. Eerdmans Publishing Co., 2012.

Squires, John T. *The Plan of God in Luke-Acts*. SNTSMS 76. Cambridge: Cambridge University Press, 1993.

Sterling, Gregory E. *Historiography and Self-Definition: Josephos, Luke-Acts and Apologetic Historiography*. NovTSup 64. Leiden: Brill, 1992.

Talbert, Charles H. *Literary Patterns, Theological Themes, and the Genre of Luke-Acts*. SBLMS 20. Missoula, MT: Scholars Press, 1974.

———. *Reading Luke: A Literary and Theological Commentary on the Third Gospel*. New York: Crossroad, 1982.

———. *Reading Luke-Acts in Its Mediterranean Milieu*. Boston: Brill, 2003.

Tannehill, Robert C. "Israel in Luke-Acts: A Tragic Story." *JBL* 104 (1985): 69–85.

———. *Luke*. ANTC. Nashville: Abingdon Press, 1996.

———. *The Narrative Unity of Luke-Acts: A Literary Interpretation*. 2 vols. Philadelphia: Fortress Press, 1986.

Tiede, David L. *Luke*. Augsburg Commentary on the New Testament. Minneapolis: Augsburg, 1988.

Tyson, Joseph B. *The Death of Jesus in Luke-Acts*. Columbia: University of South Carolina Press, 1986.

———. *Images of Judaism in Luke-Acts*. Columbia: University of South Carolina Press, 1992.

———. *Luke, Judaism, and the Scholars: Critical Approaches to Luke-Acts*. Columbia: University of South Carolina Press, 1999.

Verheyden, Joseph, ed. *The Unity of Luke-Acts*. BETL 142. Leuven: Leuven University Press, 1999.

———. "The Unity of Luke-Acts: What Are We Up To?" Pages 3–56 in *The Unity of Luke-Acts*. Edited by Joseph Verheyden. BETL 142. Leuven: Leuven University Press, 1999.

Vinson, Richard B. *Luke*. SHBC. Macon, GA: Smyth & Helwys, 2008.

Walton, Steve. "The State They Were In: Luke's View of the Roman Empire." Pages 1–41 in *Rome in the Bible and the Early Church*. Edited by Peter Oakes. Carlisle: Paternoster, 2002.

Weissenrieder, Annette. *Images of Illness in the Gospel of Luke: Insights of Ancient Medical Texts*. WUNT 2/164. Tübingen: Mohr Siebeck, 2003.

Wolter, Michael. *Das Lukasevangelium*. HNT 5. Tübingen: Mohr Siebeck, 2008.

Yamazaki-Ransom, Kazuhiko. *The Roman Empire in Luke's Narrative*. LNTS 404. London: T&T Clark, 2010.

York, John O. *The Last Shall Be First: The Rhetoric of Reversal in Luke*. JSNTSup 46. Sheffield: Sheffield Academic, 1991.

The Gospel according to John (ch. 6)

Anderson, Paul N. *The Christology of the Fourth Gospel: Its Unity and Disunity in the Light of John 6*. Valley Forge, PA: Trinity Press International, 1996.

———. *The Riddles of the Fourth Gospel: An Introduction to John*. Minneapolis: Fortress Press, 2011.

Ashton, John, ed. *The Interpretation of John*. 2nd ed. Edinburgh: T&T Clark, 1997.

———. *Understanding the Fourth Gospel*. 2nd ed. Oxford: Oxford University Press, 2007.

Attridge, Harry. "Genre Bending in the Fourth Gospel." *JBL* 121 (2002): 3–21.

Barrett, C. K. *The Gospel according to St. John: An Introduction with Commentary and Notes on the Greek Text*. 2nd rev. ed. Philadelphia: Westminster Press, 1978.

Bauckham, Richard. *The Testimony of the Beloved Disciple: Narrative, History, and Theology in the Gospel of John*. Grand Rapids: Baker Academic, 2007.

Bennema, Cornelis. *Encountering Jesus: Character Studies in the Gospel of John*. 2nd ed. Minneapolis: Fortress Press, 2014.

———. *The Power of Saving Wisdom: An Investigation of Spirit and Wisdom in Relation to the Soteriology of the Fourth Gospel*. WUNT 2/148. Tübingen: Mohr Siebeck, 2002.

Bernier, Jonathan. Aposynagōgos *and the Historical Jesus in John: Rethinking the Historicity of the Johannine Expulsion Passages*. BibIntS 122. Boston: Brill: 2013.

Bieringer, Reimund, Didier Polleyfeyt, and Frederique Vandecasteele-Vanneuville, eds. *Anti-Judaism and the Fourth Gospel*. Louisville, KY: Westminster John Knox Press, 2001.

Brant, Jo-Ann A. *John*. Paideia. Grand Rapids: Baker Academic, 2011.

Brown, Raymond E. *The Gospel according to John*. 2 vols. AB29–29A. Garden City, NY: Doubleday, 1966–70.

———. *An Introduction to the Gospel of John*. Edited by Francis J. Moloney. New York: Doubleday, 2003.

Bruner, Frederick Dale. *The Gospel of John: A Commentary*. Grand Rapids: Wm. B. Eerdmans Publishing Co., 2012.

Bultmann, Rudolf. *The Gospel of John*. Philadelphia: Westminster Press, 1971.

Carter, Warren. *John and Empire: Initial Explorations*. New York: T&T Clark, 2008.

———. *John: Storyteller, Interpreter, Evangelist*. Peabody, MA: Hendrickson Publishers, 2006.

Cassidy, Richard. *John's Gospel in New Perspective*. Maryknoll, NY: Orbis Books, 1992.

Coloe, Mary L. *God Dwells with Us: Temple Symbolism in the Fourth Gospel*. Collegeville, MN: Liturgical Press, 2001.

Conway, Colleen. *Men and Women in the Fourth Gospel: Gender and Johannine Characterization*. SBLDS 167. Atlanta: SBL Press, 1999.

Culpepper, R. Alan. *Anatomy of the Fourth Gospel: A Study in Literary Design*. Philadelphia: Fortress Press, 1983.

———. *The Gospel and Letters of John*. IBT. Nashville: Abingdon Press, 1998.

Culpepper, R. Alan, and C. Clifton Black, eds. *Exploring the Gospel of John: In Honor of D. Moody Smith*. Louisville, KY: Westminster John Knox Press, 1996.

Dube, Musa W., and Jeffrey L. Staley, eds. *John and Postcolonialism: Travel, Space, and Power*. London: Continuum, 2002.

Fehribach, Adeline. *The Women in the Life of the Bridegroom: A Feminist Historical-Literary Analysis of the Female Characters in the Fourth Gospel*. Collegeville, MN: Liturgical Press, 1998.

Fortna, Robert, and Tom Thatcher, eds. *Jesus in Johannine Tradition*. Louisville, KY: Westminster John Knox Press, 2001.

Gench, Frances Taylor. *Encounters with Jesus: Studies in the Gospel of John*. Louisville, KY: Westminster John Knox Press, 2007.

Haenchen, Ernst. *John 1: A Commentary on the Gospel of John, Chapters 1–6*. Philadelphia: Fortress Press, 1984.

———. *John 2: A Commentary on the Gospel of John, Chapters 7–21*. Philadelphia: Fortress Press, 1984.

Hakola, Raimo. *Identity Matters: John, the Jews, and Jewishness*. NovTSup 118. Boston: Brill, 2005.

Hengel, Martin. *The Johannine Question*. London: SCM; Philadelphia: Trinity Press International, 1989.

Hera, Marianus Pale. *Christology and Discipleship in John 17*. WUNT 2/342. Tübingen: Mohr Siebeck, 2013.

Hunt, Steven A., D. Francois Tolmie, and Ruben Zimmermann, eds. *Character Studies in the Fourth Gospel: Narrative Approaches to Seventy Figures in John*. WUNT 2/314. Tübingen: Mohr Siebeck, 2013.

Hylen, Susan E. *Imperfect Believers*. Louisville, KY: Westminster John Knox Press, 2009.

Keener, Craig S. *The Gospel of John: A Commentary*. 2 vols. Peabody, MA: Hendrickson Publishers, 2003.

Kierspel, Lars. *The Jews and the World in the Fourth Gospel: Parallelism, Function, and Context*. WUNT 2/220. Tübingen: Mohr Siebeck, 2006.

Koester, Craig R. *Symbolism in the Fourth Gospel: Meaning, Mystery, Community*. 2nd ed. Minneapolis: Fortress Press, 2003.

———. *The Word of Life: A Theology of John's Gospel*. Grand Rapids: Wm. B. Eerdmans Publishing Co., 2008.

Koester, Craig R., and Reimund Bieringer, eds. *The Resurrection of Jesus in the Gospel of John*. WUNT 2/222. Tübingen: Mohr Siebeck, 2008.

Köstenberger, Andreas J. *A Theology of John's Gospel and Letters.* Biblical Theology of the New Testament. Grand Rapids: Zondervan Publishing House, 2009.

Langer, Ruth. *Cursing the Christians? A History of the Birkat HaMinim*. New York: Oxford University Press, 2011.

Larsen, Kasper Bro. *Recognizing the Stranger: Recognition Scenes in the Gospel of John*. BibIntS 93. Leiden: Brill, 2008.

Lincoln, Andrew T. *The Gospel according to Saint John*. BNTC 4. Peabody, MA: Hendrickson Publishers, 2005.

———. *Truth on Trial: The Lawsuit Motif in the Fourth Gospel*. Peabody, MA: Hendrickson Publishers, 2000.

Lozada, Francisco, and Tom Thatcher, eds. *New Currents through John: A Global Perspective*. SBLRBS 54. Atlanta: SBL Press, 2006.

Malina, Bruce J., and Richard Rohrbaugh. *Social-Science Commentary on the Gospel of John*. Minneapolis: Fortress Press, 1998.

Martyn, J. Louis. *History and Theology in the Fourth Gospel*. 3rd ed. Louisville, KY: Westminster John Knox Press, 2003.

Mason, Steve. "Jews, Judaeans, Judaizing, Judaism: Problems of Categorization in Ancient History." *JSJ* 38 (2007): 457–512.

McHugh, John. *A Critical and Exegetical Commentary on John 1–4*. ICC. Edinburgh: T&T Clark, 2009.

Meeks, Wayne. "The Man from Heaven in Johannine Sectarianism." Pages 169–206 in *The Interpretation of John*. 2nd ed. Edited by John Ashton. Edinburgh: T&T Clark, 1997.

———. *The Prophet-King: Moses Traditions and the Johannine Christology*. NovTSup 14. Leiden: Brill, 1967.

Meyer, Paul. "'The Father': The Presentation of God in the Fourth Gospel." Pages 255–73 in *Exploring the Gospel of John: In Honor of D. Moody Smith*. Edited by R. Alan Culpepper and C. Clifton Black. Philadelphia: Westminster Press, 1996.

Michaels, J. Ramsey. *The Gospel of John*. NICNT. Grand Rapids: Wm. B. Eerdmans Publishing Co., 2010.

Minear, Paul S. "The Audience of the Fourth Gospel." *Int* 31 (1977): 339–54.

Moloney, F. J. *Belief in the Word: Reading John 1–4*. Minneapolis: Fortress Press, 1993.

———. *Glory, Not Dishonor: Reading John 13–21*. Minneapolis: Fortress Press, 1998.

———. *The Gospel of John*. SP 4. Collegeville, MN: Liturgical Press, 1998.

———. *Signs and Shadows: Reading John 5–12*. Minneapolis: Fortress Press, 1996.

Neyrey, Jerome H., SJ. *The Gospel of John*. New Cambridge Bible Commentary. Cambridge: Cambridge University Press, 2007.

O'Day, Gail. "The Gospel of John." In *The New Interpreters Bible*, edited by Leander E. Keck, 9:493–865. Nashville: Abingdon Press, 1995.

Parsenios, George L. *Departure and Consolation: The Johannine Farewell Discourses in Light of Greco-Roman Literature*. Boston: Brill, 2005.

———. *Rhetoric and Drama in the Johannine Lawsuit Motif*. WUNT 2/258. Tübingen: Mohr Siebeck, 2010.

Reinhartz, Adele. *Befriending the Beloved Disciple: A Jewish Reading of the Gospel of John*. New York: Continuum, 2001.

Schnackenburg, Rudolf. *The Gospel according to St. John*. 3 vols. New York: Crossroad, 1982.

Schneiders, Sandra. *Written That You May Believe: Encountering Jesus in the Fourth Gospel*. Rev. ed. New York: Crossroad, 2003.

Schnelle, Udo. *Das Evangelium nach Johannes*. THKNT 4. Leipzig: Evangelische Verlagsanstalt, 1998.

Segovia, Fernando. *The Farewell of the Word: The Johannine Call to Abide*. Minneapolis: Fortress Press, 1991.

Skinner, Christopher W., ed. *Characters and Characterization in John's Gospel*. LNTS 461. London: Bloomsbury, 2013.

Smith, D. Moody. *The Fourth Gospel in Four Dimensions: Judaism and Jesus, the Gospels, and Scripture*. Columbia: University of South Carolina, 2008.

———. *John*. ANTC. Nashville: Abingdon Press, 1999.

———. *John among the Gospels*. 2nd ed. Columbia: University of South Carolina Press, 2001.

Stibbe, Mark G. *John as Storyteller: Narrative Criticism and the Fourth Gospel*. SNTSMS 73. Cambridge: Cambridge University Press, 1992.

Talbert, Charles H. *Reading John: A Literary and Theological Commentary on the Fourth Gospel and the Johannine Epistles*. New York: Crossroad, 1992.

Thatcher, Tom. *Greater than Caesar: Christology and Empire in the Fourth Gospel*. Minneapolis: Fortress Press, 2009.

———, ed. *What We Have Heard from the Beginning: The Past, Present, and Future of Johannine Studies*. Waco, TX: Baylor University Press, 2007.

Thatcher, Tom, and Stephen D. Moore, eds. *Anatomies of Narrative Criticism: The Past, Present, and Futures of the Fourth Gospel as Literature*. SBLRBS 55. Atlanta: SBL Press, 2008.

Thompson, Marianne Meye. *The God of the Gospel of John*. Grand Rapids: Wm. B. Eerdmans Publishing Co., 2001.

———. *John: A Commentary*. NTL. Louisville, KY: Westminster John Knox Press, 2015.

Van der Watt, Jan, and Ruben Zimmerman, eds. *Rethinking the Ethics of John. "Implicit Ethics" in the Johannine Writings*. Kontexte und Normen neutestamentlicher Ethik/Contexts and Norms of New Testament Ethics. Vol. 3. WUNT 2/291. Tübingen: Mohr Siebeck, 2012.

From Ancient Gospels to the Twenty-First Century (ch. 7)

Blount, Brian K. *Then the Whisper Put on Flesh: New Testament Ethics in an African American Context*. Nashville: Abingdon Press, 2001.

Burridge, Richard A. *Imitating Jesus: An Inclusive Approach to New Testament Ethics*. Grand Rapids: Wm. B. Eerdmans Publishing Co., 2007.

Hays, Richard B. *The Moral Vision of the New Testament: Community, Cross, New Creation: A Contemporary Introduction to New Testament Ethics*. San Francisco: HarperSanFrancisco, 1996.

Matera, Frank J. *New Testament Ethics: The Legacies of Jesus and Paul*. Louisville, KY: Westminster John Knox Press, 1996.

Pregeant, Russell. *Knowing Truth, Doing Good: Engaging New Testament Ethics*. Minneapolis: Fortress Press, 2008.

Verhey, Allen. *Remembering Jesus: Christian Community, Scripture, and the Moral Life*. Grand Rapids: Wm. B. Eerdmans Publishing Co., 2002.

Index of Ancient Sources

Index of Subjects and Modern Authors